Defying Male Civilization

Women and Modern Revolution Series

Series Editors

Jane Slaughter
University of New Mexico

Richard Stites
Georgetown University

DEFYING MALE CIVILIZATION:
WOMEN IN THE SPANISH CIVIL WAR

by

Mary Nash
Professor of Contemporary History
University of Barcelona

WOMEN **&**

MODERN
REVOLUTION
SERIES

ARDEN PRESS, INC.
Denver, Colorado

Library of Congress Cataloging–in–Publication Data

Nash, Mary.
   Defying male civilization : women in the Spanish Civil War / by
Mary Nash.
         p.   cm. -- (Women & modern revolution series)
   Includes bibliographical references (p.   ) and index.
   ISBN 0-912869-15-1 (hard cover) . --ISBN 0-912869-16-x (pbk.)
   1. Spain--History--Civil War, 1936-1939--Women.   2. Feminism-
-Spain--History--20th century.   3. Women--Spain--History--20th
century.   I. Title.   II. Series : Women and modern revolution
series.
DP269.8.W7N38   1995
946. 081--dc20   95-18301
                                                              CIP

*Cover photo, "Unknown Miliciana," reprinted by permission of the Instituto
Histórico Municipal de Barcelona*

Published in the United States of America

Arden Press, Inc.
P. O. Box 418
Denver, Colorado 80201

"Two things have begun to collapse because they are unjust, class privilege based on the parasitical civilization which gave birth to the monster of war; and male privilege, which turned half of mankind into autonomous beings and the other half into slaves; a male civilization based on power which has produced moral chaos throughout the centuries."

Suceso Portales
Mujeres Libres, Num. 10

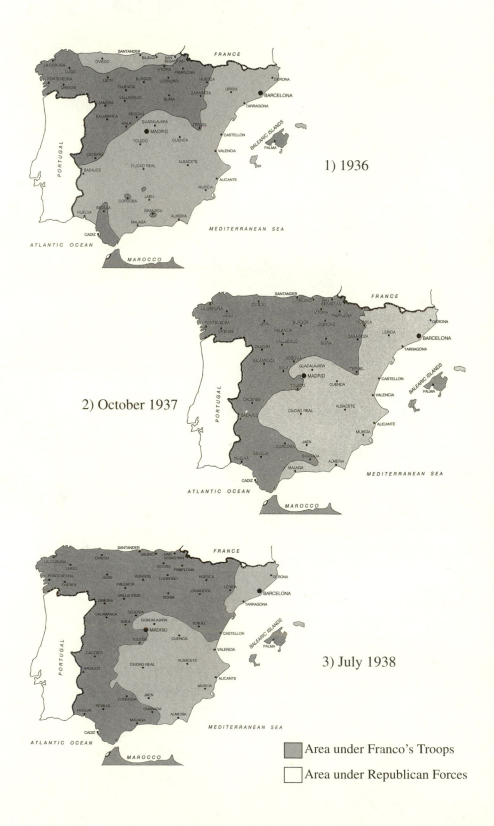

1) 1936

2) October 1937

3) July 1938

Area under Franco's Troops

Area under Republican Forces

TABLE OF CONTENTS

Acronyms

AMA – Agrupación de Mujeres Antifascistas

ANDJ – Aliança Nacional de la Dona Jove

ANME – Asociación Nacional de Mujeres Españolas

BOC – Bloc Obrer i Camperol

CNT – Confederación Nacional del Trabajo

ERC – Esquerra Republicana de Catalunya

FAI – Federación Anarquista Ibérica

FETE – Federación Española de Trabajadores de la Enseñanza

FIJL – Federación Ibérica de Juventudes Libertarias

FSPOUM – Female Secretariat of the POUM

IAPD – Institut d' Adaptació Professional de la Dona

IWA – International Workingmen's Association

JSU – Juventudes Socialists Unificadas

MLE – Movimiento Libertario Español

PCE – Partido Comunista de España

POUM – Partido Obrero de Unificación Marxista

PSOE – Partido Socialista Obrero Español

PSUC – Partido Socialista Unificado de Cataluña

UDC – Unió de Dones de Catalunya

Editors' Introduction to the Series

The history of the twentieth century has been marked by frequent revolutions and mass popular resistance to oppressive, dictatorial regimes. Few segments of the globe have remained untouched by these conflicts, which have sparked the interest of historians, political scientists, sociologists, and others who seek to understand the unique character of each conflict as well as the themes common to all. An ever–growing body of literature explains the causes or pre–conditions for these mass mobilizations and collective rebellions, examines the role of ideology in the revolutionary process, analyzes leaders and insurgent organizations, and assesses the results of social conflict. The scope of the scholarship on the topic is impressive, but with rare exceptions, until quite recently the actors considered in each drama have been almost exclusively male.

Marie Mullaney, in her work *Revolutionary Women*, begins with a review of existing analyses and notes that "the biggest problem with the available literature...is neither its unscientific quality nor its reductionist nature, but rather its unstated assumptions regarding the gender of revolutionary participants."[1] The gender bias in revolutionary studies is illustrated in a work by Ted Gurr entitled, appropriately, *Why Men Rebel*, which seeks to determine the specific values that serve as motivation for rebellion. The author points out that among classes of values which drive groups to act, welfare values (material conditions and economic hopes) and power values take precedence over interpersonal values, communality (desire to be useful to others), or an improved sense of social and political responsibility in the community.[2] If women's motivations had been assessed along with those of men, Gurr's conclusions might have been quite different.

Leaders of Revolution, published in 1979, offered a revisionist approach to the subject, criticizing earlier psychoanalytic, psychohistorical, and sociological approaches as speculative, non–empirical, and intuitive. The authors proposed a new model defined as the "Situational Approach," which combines a set of personal characteristics with a "particular socio–historical context" to produce a profile of the revolutionary leader. The study statistically analyzed the lives of thirty–two such leaders from around the globe, all of them male.[3] The absence of women from such scholarly endeavors is, of course, not a problem confined to the study of revolution.

In recent years, women's history, the "new" social history, and women's studies in general have recognized and sought to redress imbalances in our historical perspective. We had to begin by naming and locating the women in the past. We now know that there have been female revolutionary leaders and soldiers and women's organizations integrally involved in revolutionary actions. Having discovered this historical material, we are now in a position to move beyond simple description by focusing on gender itself as a category of historical analysis. The implications of this approach were clearly stated by Natalie Zemon Davis in her 1975 address to the Berkshire Conference on Women's History. "Our goal is to understand the significance of the sexes, of gender groups, in the historical past. Our goal is to discover the range in sex role and sexual symbolism in different societies and periods, to find out what meaning they had and how they functioned to maintain the social order or to promote its change."[4]

Though the focus of history in this series is on women and the female experience, the authors recognize that one gender does not stand alone, but is embedded in relationships with the opposite sex and conditioned by class, ethnicity, and age, among other factors. The sex–gender system as defined by Gayle Rubin is "a set of arrangements by which a society transforms biological sexuality into products of human activity."[5] All societies have such a set of arrangements, but their particular function in social organization and their relative importance in determining the course of human history vary. The multiple and complex set of relationships arising from gender and the connections among these relationships and other fundamental forces in history provide the framework for our studies.

Our purpose in this series is twofold. On the one hand we are examining the function of sex/gender systems in the revolutionary process. Our authors will ask the usual questions about revolutions: what are their causes, social components, ideologies, organizations, goals, and results? But in each case they are also asking what is gender–specific about these; do revolutions perhaps mean different things to men and women, and if so, why? We need to know, therefore, what motivates women to become involved in collective rebellions, what women contribute, what their expectations are, and ultimately what happens to women objectively and subjectively as a result of this involvement. Such an analysis of revolutions will add to our more general understanding of the place of sex/gender systems in human history.

The study of revolutions can be informed and improved by asking questions and testing conclusions raised in other works in women's history. The histories of nineteenth–century American female networks and early female volunteer associations, and the development of turn–of–the–century women's suffrage and moral reform organizations, can be used to understand women's motives, mobilization, and goals. Analyses of the more recent entry of women into public politics and the growth of contemporary feminism can shed light on questions of women's perspective, the growth of feminist consciousness, and the ability to effect broader social change.

The volumes in this series are linked by a variety of common themes; among them are the connections between women's culture and women's politics, the ways in which specific gender experience motivates individuals to act and in turn shapes expectations and goals, and, finally, how gender interacts with other historic forces to determine the outcome of a revolutionary movement. It is essential to understand how individual actions and reactions coalesce in movements and organizations with specified goals, but equally important is the analysis of "the political institutions and state structures through which [they] must operate if their agenda is to be realized."[6] On this latter point it is important to understand the relationship of women and their organizations to what Jane Jenson has described as the "universe of political discourse," which

> defines politics, or establishes the parameters of political action, by limiting the following: first, the range of actors who are accorded the status of legitimate participant; second, the range of issues considered to be within the realm of meaningful political debate; third, the policy alternatives considered feasible for implementation; and fourth, the alliance strategies available for achieving change.[7]

Whether women are able to enter this world and challenge its limitations is crucial to assessing the results of any activism.

These common themes are set within the diverse conditions of discrete national histories, and here it is important to emphasize the significance of comparative studies. General questions are addressed in all the volumes of the series, but specific processes and outcomes vary. Comparative studies must consider particular events of national history, different levels of economic development, and characteristic political traditions.[8] Ultimately, by making sense of these differences, we can begin to understand the possibilities and the limitations for women's participation in the world of politics and how such participation may be changing the gender structures of society. Today, as women and men grapple with the complex meanings and values of sameness and difference, we are well advised to seek enlightenment through the study of our common history.

1. Marie Marmo Mullaney, *Revolutionary Women: Gender and the Socialist Revolutionary Role* (New York: Praeger, 1983), p. 3.

2. Ted Robert Gurr, *Why Men Rebel* (Princeton, NJ: Princeton University Press, 1970), pp. 70–71.

3. Mostafa Rejai and Kay Phillips, *Leaders of Revolution* (Beverly Hills, CA: Sage Publications, 1979), pp. 19, 31, 55.

4. Cited in Joan Kelly–Gadol, "The Social Relations of the Sexes," *Signs* 1:4 (Summer 1976), p. 817.

5. Gayle Rubin, "The Traffic in Women," in Rayna R. Reiter (ed.), *Toward an Anthropology of Women* (New York: Monthly Review Press, 1975), p. 159.

6. For these two approaches, see, respectively, Janet Saltzman Chafetz and Anthony Gary Dworkin, *Female Revolt: Women's Movements in World and Historical Perspective* (Totowa, NJ: Rowman and Allanheld, 1986); and Mary F. Katzenstein and Carol M. Mueller (eds.), *The Women's Movements of the U.S. and Western Europe* (Philadelphia, PA: Temple University Press, 1987).

7. Jane Jenson, "Struggling for Identity: The Women's Movement and the State in Western Europe," in Sylvia Bashevkin (ed.), *Women and Politics in Western Europe* (London: Frank Cass and Co., 1985), p. 7.

8. Sharon Wolchik, "Introduction," to Sharon Wolchik and Alfred G. Meyers (eds.), *Women, State and Party in Eastern Europe* (Durham, NC: Duke University Press, 1985), p. 1.

Acknowledgments

I would like to thank a number of people who made the creation of this book possible. First of all, I wish to acknowledge my debt to Professor Emili Giralt of the University of Barcelona, who, in 1971 under the Franco regime, accepted the, then, quite outrageous proposal to do research on women in the Spanish working–class movement. His initial support allowed me to undertake pioneer research on women's history in contemporary Spain and, later, to pursue an academic career based on women's history. My special debt is to the many women of the Civil War who since the early 1970's have given generously of their time and shared their story and experiences with me in many hours of interviews.

I am appreciative of the ongoing support of my colleagues at the Department of Contemporary History at the University of Barcelona, Gabriel Cardona for his assistance with the maps, Pelai Pagès for providing documentation, and, particularly, Susanna Tavera for her intellectual support and friendship throughout the years. I would also like to thank Maria Carmen García–Nieto, Giuliana di Febo, Hilari Raquer, Joaquim Puigvert, Jon Arrizabalaga, my fellow historians of the Spanish Association of Women's History, archivists Rudolf de Jong and Kies Rosenberg, and the library staff of the archives and libraries I have consulted throughout the years for the resources and assistance they have provided. I would like to thank Llorenç Martínez for his technical assistance with the maps. I am also indebted to Antonio González, then Director of the Archivo Histórico Nacional – Sección Guerra Civil, Salamanca, for having provided me with the occasion to direct the Symposium and Exhibition on Women in the Civil War held under the auspices of the Archivo Nacional in October 1989, which was a decisive impulse to the further development of historical research in this area.

I am particularly indebted to Richard Herr and Emilie Bergmann for the opportunity to hold a postgraduate seminar on Iberian Women between the Wars at the Iberian Studies Program and Department of History at the University of California, Berkeley in the spring of 1992. I also wish to thank Milton Azevedo of the Institute of International Studies and the Gaspar de Portolà Catalan Studies Program, University of California, Berkeley for supporting this initiative. The stimulating discussion and the opportunity to explore material from this book with a non–Spanish audience gave me many useful insights for writing the book. I am very appreciative, too, of the support of Temma Kaplan, Ellen Friedman, Michel Froidevaux, and Karen Offen and also wish to thank Susan Conley of Arden Press for editing the manuscript.

My greatest debt is to colleagues and friends Geraldine Nichols and Enric Ucelay daCal for their careful reading, stimulating comments, and development of ideas on the initial manuscript and, especially, to Marcy Rudo, whose enthusiasm, suggestions, and decisive editing were essential to complete this book. Finally, Richard Bristow provided a sense of humor and unhesitating support.

Introduction

This book addresses the nature of women's experience and their role in war and revolution in Spain during the Civil War (1936-1939). Was Suceso Portales, a dressmaker, anarchist activist, and member of the women's anarchist organization Mujeres Libres, correct when she made the following claim in a 1937 article?

> Two things have begun to collapse because they are unjust, class privilege based on the parasitical civilization which gave birth to the monster of war; and male privilege, which turned half of mankind into autonomous beings and the other half into slaves; a male civilization based on power which has produced moral chaos throughout the centuries.[1]

Was it indeed the collapse of the social bases of male supremacy, of "male civilization" as she optimistically claimed, or only a case of blurring gender-specific goals during the generalized struggle against fascism? To what extent did the revolutionary drive of anarchists and dissident communists result in a loss of specific female identity and the subordination of women's issues to the overall revolutionary cause? Were women involved in revolutionary activism and antifascist resistance on their own terms? Or were they politicized but channelled into supportive roles that did not challenge prevailing forms of gender subordination? To what extent was there a commonality of interests among women on a gender basis, or were class and political polarization more relevant? Did the mobilization of women into female groups exhibit a distinct pattern of specific gender consciousness? These are some of the issues that will be discussed through the exploration of women's agency and collective experience during the period of the Spanish Civil War.

1

Any attempt to answer these questions must draw on a theoretical framework. One of the significant tasks of women's history has been to identify and lend a voice to women from the past. In the last twenty-five years, studies in women's history propelled by new methodologies have favored the recuperation of women's collective memory and a greater visibility of their path through history.[2] Women's historical experience has been claimed as a decisive component in the dynamics of history. Moreover, women's history has made major contributions to the critical revision of all historical scholarship.

In the developmental stages of women's history during the seventies, many of the historical approaches were conceived from rigid methodological categories that polarized women's collective historical experience. Thus, opposing, binary categories such as public/private, victim/heroine, power/submission, confrontation/consent were often employed in the interpretation of women in history. One of the predominant interpretative schemes in this first stage of women's history focused on the historical victimization of women. Confrontation with patriarchal oppression was its key focus. Priority was given to those women who had challenged the restrictions of gender subordination and undertaken a heroic struggle for their emancipation.

Current trends in women's history have developed analytical tools that go beyond these oppositional categories that perceive women as either victims or heroines. The challenge to rigid binary interpretations has helped formulate alternative interpretative proposals. These look to the articulation of women's historical experience through the intersections of public and private spaces and examine the ongoing interaction in the dynamics of gender power relations. In this way, women's past is understood as a complex process that also relates the gender-specific experience of women to their social, cultural, political, and economic environment.

In the 1980's, the historiographical debate on the notion of female historical victimization and women's heroic struggle to overcome oppression made it clear that such an approach was too restrictive. In the ensuing debate, historian Ellen DuBois defended the fundamental need for women's history to address women's resistance to their oppression, and, more specifically, to focus on the study of political feminism.[3]

Historian Carol Smith Rosenberg proposed an alternative view that addressed the study of women's history through the exploration of women's culture. She contended that historical feminism can be explained through a process of consciousness and that a global study of women's culture and female relations can lead to a deeper understanding of the structures of hierarchical gender power relations.

From a different analytical perspective, French historians Michelle Perrot, Cécile Dauphin, and Arlette Farge, among others, have raised the issue of the relation between power and women's culture.[4] Their line of argument stresses the need to contemplate women's power, or powers, as well as the real compensations women receive within the unequal dynamics of gender power relations.

Other historians have insisted, furthermore, on the idea of women's consensus and complicity in their social subordination. Historian Gerda Lerner has highlighted one of the major paradoxes in the gender system: the role of women in the perpetuation of their subordination.[5] Current debate in women's history suggests the necessity of combining the study of patriarchal oppression through the detection of change or continuity in the historical experience of women and the global contextualization of their historical itinerary.[6]

This present book has a different theoretical framework than other studies the author wrote in the 1970's on women in the Spanish Civil War.[7] Writing a doctoral dissertation and doing research in the early 1970's on left-wing Spanish women during the Second Republic and the Civil War (1931-1939) was an inspiring experience, despite the daunting circumstances of living in Spain under the Franco dictatorship, doing research in archives still under military control, and interviewing women activists from the Civil War who continued to be in exile in France. In a country where the Franco dictatorship enforced collective historical amnesia concerning the Second Republic and the Civil War, and in an international historiographical environment just discovering women in history, encountering the extraordinarily active presence of women leaders, women's organizations, and mass female mobilization during the Civil War was not only inspiring but crucial to the discovery of revolutionary foremothers and democratic activists who had participated in the fight for freedom.

In the initial phase of its struggle for political legitimacy in the early 1970's, the Spanish women's movement was held back by the lack of a historical model. The overall collective historical amnesia that so characterized the postwar period in Spain, together with the distortion and exclusion of historical social movements and political processes by Francoist historiography, had led to a misrepresentation of Spanish social reality prior to the outcome of the Spanish Civil War.

Contemporary Spanish historiography thus set about to redress this imbalance and, in so doing, tended toward developing a more politicized history of the prewar period.[8] Logically, the historical amnesia about women was even more acute, and there was a general lack of knowledge regarding Spanish women's collective historical experience.[9] Thus, the first studies on women's historical experience had a political focus and a heroic approach. The exciting discovery of women's intrepid past was an encouraging lesson for women in the opposition movement against Franco and a key feature in the consolidation of a new democratic society. The identification of feminist and activist foremothers was also decisive in the development of the merging feminist movement.

However, there is a continuing need to rewrite history in the light of new concerns and understandings. The development of women's history as well as cultural and social history during recent decades has permitted current scholarship to deepen our understanding of women's historical experience. This rewriting of women's history in the Civil War may appear to be less heroic, but it undoubtedly gives us a greater understanding of the complexities of women's past in war and revolution. Its purpose is to highlight the contradictions and tensions of change, contestation, and collective action, and to explore the forces of continuity and gender constraints in the volatile environment of war and revolution in Spain. It focuses not only on extraordinary heroic achievements, but also on the limitations of change, despite those achievements. It attempts to confront revolutionary rhetoric with social reality and to differentiate between gender-specific and overall social transformation.

Women's role in antifascist resistance and revolutionary change developed from experience, and women's historical itinerary was an apprenticeship in collective action and social responses. Experience incorporated socio-economic reality and diverse cultural and ideological perceptions; it structured collective mentality that inspired resistance strategies, choices, and ways of conceiving survival. The diverse expressions of gender reality, social class, cultural identity, and political culture were crucial in the formulation of the numerous manifestations of women's experience of war and revolution and accounted for the pluralistic strategies of resistance and survival by women and the decisions they made throughout the war. But the historical study of gender interaction cannot be limited to a dichotomy between forms of consensus and conflict, but rather must address ongoing female agency for social transformation in constant interaction with the historical mechanisms of social control and pressures of conventional gender roles and values.

This book is not a political history of women in the Spanish Civil War. Its main focus is on the history of women's social and cultural collective experience and agency in the war. Questions regarding women's antifascist and revolutionary organizations, exceptional political leaders, and the novel experience of women in arms, the revolutionary *milicianas*, are addressed. However, other issues are explored that are also crucial to a study of women in war and revolution: women's role in everyday survival on the homefront and their capacity to provide strategies for civil resistance and social welfare. The definition of a feminist or women's agenda by historical women's movements is addressed, and accounted for are the choices Spanish women made during the time of upheaval, changes, and revolution. This definition must be seen in its own context and in the light of women's collective experience.

The transposition of current concerns of feminism to historical contexts represents a distortion of historical reality. It is the task of historians to pinpoint the priorities of a women's agenda in its own terms and explore the factors that led to its establishment. Preconceived suppositions regarding the definition of feminism and women's agency can indeed distort interpretations of women's collective experience, choices, and concerns. Collective historical experience shapes collective response. The issues that concern women in times of radical change may often signify that other issues associated with women's rights, such as abortion, are not included in the agenda of women and feminist organizations, while other important questions such as education and prostitution can be identified as priorities for change. This book explains these choices and decisions.

Women's social mobilization for survival in daily life and civil antifascist resistance led to the identification of collective social priorities that did not necessarily always respond to a gender or feminist definition of goals. Nonetheless, it more sharply defined other specific goals for women that ultimately led to a redefinition of gender role models and women's expectations in society.

The cultural domain of women is also explored in this book, which contends that images and cultural representations are decisive in the construction and maintenance of gender roles and cultural notions of femininity and masculinity. Gender discourse, cultural rhetoric, and imagery are significant mechanisms of social control that enforce gender models. The recourse of symbolic violence through cultural representations explains the uses of consent and maintenance of gender conduct in society.[10] This study examines changes in the cultural representation of women throughout the war and accounts for the utilization of revolutionary images and its significance in the redefinition of the social relations between the sexes.

Over the past two decades, historians have sought to overcome the invisibility of women. Their voices are being heard in historical texts and studies. This book focuses on women's greater visibility in a time of war and revolution and considers the relationship of visibility, image, and the social reality of women. The greater visibility of women, and particularly the wider projection of women's image in the scenario of the Spanish Civil War, was not necessarily a mirror of the social reality of Spanish women but rather an example of the complex ways even trailblazing heroic images of women such as the *miliciana* could convey a message that did not deeply alter more conventional views of women and gender roles. For despite appearances and women's expectations, society has often continued to define norms of activity and gender-appropriate behavior even during processes of revolutionary change.

The purpose of this book is to account for change and continuity in women's experience during the war. This rereading of women in the Spanish Civil War describes not only the innovative figure of the *miliciana* defending the antifascist cause at the war fronts or the activist antifascist women leaders, but also explores the significance of women's role at the homefront and the collective experience of anonymous Spanish women. The importance of women's collective role in the civil antifascist resistance against Franco must be assessed, and the implications of women's involvement in antifascist mobilization must be explored.

Given the lack of available publications in the English language on women in contemporary Spanish history, this book also includes an introductory overview on the general situation of women in late nineteenth- and early twentieth-century Spain. The purpose is to provide background on the previous collective experience of Spanish women that illustrates their capacity to generate change and develop initiatives despite the restraints of their historical experience. This book was written to fill a gap in the English language on the Spanish Civil War, to introduce readers to the complex reality of war and revolution from a gender perspective, and to provide a deeper understanding of women's collective experience at a time of social and political upheaval. The masses of Spanish women fighting against Franco were neither heroines nor victims. The terms of their collective endeavor can be measured only against the background of their courage and heroic dedication to the antifascist cause, the constraints of historic gender restrictions, and their specific agency and experience as women.

■ 1 ■

The Construction of Gender Roles: Women in Contemporary Spain

The early twentieth century opened onto a disheartening panorama regarding the social position of women in Spain. The dismal lot of Spanish women was clearly based on openly practiced gender and occupational segregation, political and educational inequality, and legal and labor discrimination. The severe constraints placed on the female population in cultural, economic, and social arenas were due in large part to the predominant ideology of domesticity which reinforced male supremacy, the sexual division of labor, and the restriction of female activities to the private sphere but also must be understood in the wider context of the slow development of social and economic structures in Spain in the nineteenth century.[1]

The disintegration of the Ancien Regime, with its absolutist monarchy based on divine right, and the consolidation of the new liberal constitutional system in the 1830's arose from an intricate combination of economic problems, internal dissensions in the absolutist ranks, and a compromise between the weak liberal political class and the privileged ruling estates of the Ancien Regime. This problematic model of transition to a liberal state was to mark Spain's future development, underline its conservative tendencies, and weaken the impulse of the forces of change in political and economic areas. Economic and industrial advancement was thwarted as it confronted the political and economic interests of the former nobility against the weak commercial and industrial bourgeoisie.[2] The fragility of the liberal state and the deep conservatism of the Spanish ruling class throughout the nineteenth century strengthened the conservative nature of existing social structures and, where women were concerned, reinforced traditional mores and values. Furthermore, the Catholic church, a pervasive social institution and political instrument, also played a decisive role in maintaining the status quo and a conservative stance with regard to women.

Moreover, the social and political landscape was far from homogeneous, as profound regional differences accounted for varying social and economic paths. The uneven economic growth in the different regions explains the sharp contrast in women's social condition among, for instance, highly industrialized Catalonia, the *latifundios* (great estates) in southern Spain, and the agrarian small holdings in Galicia. Because the development of women's consciousness was inextricably linked with the political and social development of the different regions, cultural and national differences also must be taken into consideration. It is significant that one of the first movements to promote improvement in women's cultural and educational status, which attained a considerable degree of cohesion in the early twenties, was instigated by the Catalan bourgeois nationalists, an ongoing political and cultural movement that defended Catalonia's political, economic, and cultural interests. In a scenario where politics was the privilege of a minority oligarchy (until the change in the political regime in 1868, the existing property tax-based suffrage shifted between 1 and 4 percent of the population), it is not surprising to find women absent from the political domain. The intensity of the power struggle between conservatives and progressive liberals throughout the nineteenth century left no room to consider redressing the political inequality of women. The historical process in nineteenth-century Spain is characterized by sharp discontinuities in the liberal revolution and by the ongoing struggle to modernize the State and consolidate progressive liberalism.

The Sexenio Democrático (1868-1874), the outcome of political unrest and the exile of Queen Isabelle II, followed the lines of liberal bourgeois revolutions and represented just such an attempt to establish not only a liberal system but a democratic one.[3] This brief, frail, democratic experience, which also included the first switch from a monarchy to a republic in Spain, heralded important advances in such areas of liberal democracy as freedom of speech, religion, and education; and universal male suffrage.

It is significant, however, that any improvement in the social condition of women at that time was not due to a specific policy to redress grievances but was rather a side effect of the general revision of existing legislation. Thus, the introduction of civil as opposed to religious marriage resulted from dominant anticlerical feelings and the desire to separate church and state rather than a reconsideration of married women's subordinate status. The articles of the new law on civil matrimony retained the clauses related to women's dependency, wives' obedience to husbands, and their obligation to obtain their husband's permission to involve themselves in such crucial activities as administering their own personal belongings, legal activities, and the publication of scientific or literary works. The liberal democratic governments were unsympathetic to female demands, as can be seen from their refusal to adhere to a petition to allow women to be employed in the postal, telegraph, and railway services and also by the fact that these defenders of universal male suffrage failed to contemplate the issue of female political rights.[4]

Undoubtedly the major benefits for women in this period derived from the progress made in the field of education. This was due to the extraordinary influence and dedication of the progressive Krausistas, who proposed a rationalist, secular education that renovated educational patterns and encompassed female education in their overall movement. This reform represented a step toward modernization and was a decided advance with respect to the general field of female education, which, at the time, was primarily devoted to needlework, piety, deportment, and social behavior. Nonetheless, as Giuliana di Febo has rightly pointed out, it failed to present an overall critique of women's situation in Spanish society. The Krausistas' conception of women's education was based on the traditional ideology of domesticity, oriented toward the improvement of women and a certain widening of their cultural horizons with a view to their achieving a better performance in their traditionally assigned roles of nurturance as wives and mothers.[5] This situation was, of course, no different from that of other progressive educational trends in Europe at the time.[6]

Political instability, social conflict, and civil war during the six years of the Sexenio Democrático eventually led to the restoration of the monarchy and the Bourbon dynasty in 1875 when Alfonso XII, Queen Isabelle's son, was proclaimed king of Spain. The restoration of the Bourbons represented a new stage in Spain's political development that was eventually to restrict progress in the field of women's rights. Historian Jose María Jover Zamora has characterized the fictional constitutional system of the Restoration as one that resembles the southern European submodels of parliamentary regimes in the epoch of imperialism. This model is based fundamentally on a dualism: the existence of a formal liberal constitution combined, in practice, with the real functioning of the political system based on patronage, the detraction of the parliamentary system, fraudulent elections, royal government appointments, the maintenance of a minority elite power group, and the political exclusion of vast proportions of the population.[7]

This complex political system operated to guarantee the existing social structures and impede access to power by any political forces that questioned the foundations of the regime. So, in fact, the actual political structure in Spain toward the end of the nineteenth century resisted the development of liberal political feminism such as had arisen in Great Britain and the United States, countries whose political and social climates were undoubtedly more favorable to the development of political feminism based on the demand for political rights than was the case in Spain. This was partly due to the development in these countries of liberal democracy and the quest for coherence within a liberal policy based on equality and non-discrimination on the grounds of sex at least among the white community.[8] This is not to suggest that the development of nineteenth-century Western feminism was a lineal process or exclusively political. Nor was it the automatic outcome of the degree of political development in those countries.

An analysis of the political system in Spain in the late nineteenth century points to the inadequacy of the interpretation of individual equality and political enfranchisement as the basis for the construction of Spanish feminism. Anglo-American or northern European models of interpretation for the development of feminism in Spain are not necessarily valid for the Mediterranean. In Spanish society, even in the early twentieth century, individual rights tended to be ignored in practice, and the actual elitist political structure was extremely unfavorable for the development of liberal political feminism based on suffrage and political rights. The social legitimization of individual rights was not even the key factor in the Spanish liberal and democratic tradition until the 1930's.

In late nineteenth-century Spain, the fragility of the liberal political system and the popular association of its malfunctioning with the actual system itself led to a political culture that did not necessarily identify political progress with political rights, leading to the growth of the anarchist movement and the distancing of many social forces from political participation. Moreover, acute polarization of social tensions led the labor movements to focus on strategies that were, on the whole, indifferent to the legal and political injustices perpetrated on women. At the most, anarchists and socialists paid but sporadic attention to issues such as women's work and education but did not subscribe to feminist requests. In these circumstances, the absence of women in the political domain and the lack of a specific political agenda are not surprising.

Conservative ideology related to women, reinforced under the Restoration, was perpetuated through a series of legal restrictions that clearly delimited women's social role. These were to have long-lasting consequences, as the core of this legislation was maintained practically intact until the reopening of the new democratic and republican liberal period in 1931 with the Second Republic. But the structural and political changes inaugurated in the thirties signified a pointed quickening in the pace of social change in the country as a whole and also in the specific situation of women.

The Perfect Married Lady: The Constraints of the Female State

The predominant discourse on women in the late nineteenth and early twentieth century was based on the ideology of domesticity, evoking a female prototype of the *perfecta casada* (perfect married lady), whose primordial gender role was that of caring for home and family.[9] Women were depicted as *angeles del hogar* (angels of the hearth), angelical nurturers who sustained the family. According to this model, women were to be self-effacing and submissive with total loving dedication to their children and husbands or parents, but they were also to be functional in their efficient management of the home. Women's social duty as the family caretaker was far from being considered trivial. On the contrary, the vital importance of the woman's homemaking role in the upkeep and development of the family was constantly stressed in the numerous pamphlets and books published precisely to counsel women on this decisive task.[10] Thus, mothers, wives, and daughters were paradoxically attributed the dual role of ethereal "angels" and vital agents in the correct functioning of the family. A treatise published in 1886 in the collection "Library for Young Ladies" described the complex array of duties ascribed to women, which ranged from the running of the domestic economy to elevating the moral tone of the family:

> The well being of the family depends on the woman....She, just like a protecting fairy, looks after at the same time...her children's health, her husband's happiness and the prosperity of the family which is a consequence of a reasonable economy.
>
> The woman is the primordial element in the government of the house, under her influence losses and grief are repaired, the acquired fortune is conserved, ideas of morality are inculcated, each individual is shown his duties and all this is attained not through the expression of force but with the beautiful prestige of love, as the lady of the hearth masters all souls.[11]

Women were thus epitomized as being sweet, fairy-like, and angelical but also hard-headed administrators of the home, guardians of the family fortunes, and arbiters of moral progress. There is, then, in this ideological stance on motherhood a positive conception of women's social worth and women's contribution to the family. An example of the value attributed to maternalism is the demand made in 1916, by primary school inspector Leonor Serrano de Xandri, that housework be duly remunerated and recognized as a profession and that motherhood be considered social work and so receive state protection.[12] Despite such insights on the social worth of women's role in society, most approaches to the "Perfect Married Lady" were ambivalent, to say the least, as they placed women in an overtly inferior position to men in a clear hierarchical gender order. Society was presented as a male-defined social order where social stratification, male supremacy, and female subordination were the key features.

Many late nineteenth and early twentieth century texts still openly affirmed female inferiority. An article in *La Vanguardia*, one of the principal Spanish newspapers, stated in 1889:

> From her intelligence to her stature, everything in her is inferior and
> contrary to men. Everything in her goes from outside to inside. All is
> concentrative, receptive and transient; just as in a man all is active and
> expansive....In herself, a woman, unlike a man, is not a complete
> being; she is only the instrument of reproduction, the one designed to
> perpetuate the species while man is the one charged with making her
> progress, the generator of intelligence, at the same time creator and
> *demiurge* of the social world. So it is that everything tends towards
> non-equality between the sexes and non-equivalency; thus women,
> inferior to men, should be their complement in social functions.[13]

Although by the early twentieth century such overt claims regarding the
inferiority of women tended to be displaced by more subtle affirmations
advocating equal but complementary status, many women still continued to
internalize this gender discourse and the cultural values it transmitted. Articulate
women interested in improving their lot often remained deeply conservative in
their view of women's status and social role and at times explicitly condoned male
supremacy in an overtly patriarchal system.

Such was the case of Dolors Monserdà (1845-1919), a writer and one of the
most significant figures of Catalan conservative nationalism and the Catholic
reform movement dedicated to the promotion of women at the beginning of the
twentieth century. Monserdà was a highly cultured woman, committed not only to
writing but to actively promoting women in education, work, and culture.
However, she combined these activities with public statements endorsing the
notion of male moral supremacy and female submission to men. Monserdà's
position is indicative of the overwhelming pervasiveness of Roman Catholic
doctrine with regard to women in early twentieth century Spain. Although she was
a self-proclaimed feminist and constructed her own version of conservative
Catalan Catholic feminism, Monserdà also acknowledged women's subordination,
which she attributed to both natural and divine laws:

> It is not in my mind to speak or detract in the slightest way the
> submission which women, by natural law, by the mandate of Jesus
> Christ and by her willing acceptance on contracting matrimony, have
> to have for men, as this submission is altogether necessary for the
> correct running of the family and society: submission, which in women
> is an impulse of the heart, which she always obeys, whenever the
> supremacy recognized by divine and human laws is combined with the
> moral superiority of the man who imposes it.[14]

In other European countries that had undergone a more profound process of
secularization during the nineteenth century, the arguments used to justify female
subordination were gradually formulated on secular pseudo-scientific reasoning. In

Spain, gender discourse on women, although eventually influenced by that line of argument, was still, in the early twentieth century, deeply influenced by Roman Catholic doctrine.[15]

There was more debate on the question of women's intellectual capacity in other European countries and in the United States than in Spain, where the belief in women's intellectual inferiority persisted among the various classes and practically all social groups. Even radical and working-class sectors occasionally manifested serious doubts about women's intellectual capacity despite their theoretical declarations to the contrary. As late as the 1930's we find straightforward declarations to the effect that women were innately inferior to men on an intellectual level. In 1931 the conservative Francesc Tusquets was still arguing forcibly that

> women have shone a lot less than men in the cultivation of the sciences, letters and arts. This fact is due primarily to talent and natural activities, which differ a lot from one sex to the other: differences in aptitudes which are innate and therefore fundamental and permanent.[16]

Earlier on, other writers had attributed woman's supposed intellectual inferiority to the fact that the "principal motive of all her acts, the foundation of her psychology, conscious or unconscious, is the reproduction of the species."[17]

A more subtle argument developed over the years and attained a notable degree of consensus in Spanish society. The theory of the differentiation and complementary nature of the sexes was formulated and propagated by the eminent endocrinologist Gregorio Marañón, who argued that women were not inferior but simply different. Their primary function was to be mothers and wives; therefore, any other activity undertaken was to be conditioned by this. Marañón proclaimed that only under very exceptional circumstances, such as in the case of single or widowed women, could women undertake activities similar to those normally engaged in by men.[18] The theory of differentiation, then, just as that of women's supposed intellectual inferiority, sustained a strict division of the spheres and the sexual division of labor. Both conservative and progressive writers proclaimed this theory, attributing it to the different psychological and temperamental characteristics of women.

The prevalent model of gender prototypes in the early decades of the twentieth century still presented an acute differentiation between the sexes. Thus, reason, logic, reflection, analytical and intellectual capacity, and creativity were said to be the prerogatives of men, while sentimentality, affectivity, sensitivity, sweetness, intuition, passivity, and abnegation were exclusive characteristics of women. This proposed gender model was, of course, extremely effective in reinforcing the view that women were naturally apt for complete dedication to the home and family. Men were assigned the fields of work, politics, and culture: "Men make laws, govern nations, dedicate themselves to industry, the arts, the sciences and even study you [women]," wrote Dr. Polo Peyrolon in 1882, "while women form customs, as they indirectly control the heart of men as wives and mothers."[19] Some fifty years later women were still being reassured that their "natural state" was that of matrimony and their destiny to preside over the home and raise and educate their children.[20]

In the late nineteenth and early twentieth century, gender discourse was based on the cult of domesticity and the model of the *perfecta casada* initially described by Fray Luis de León in the sixteenth century. Nonetheless, it is also quite clear that not all Spanish women ascribed to this model. Indeed, many aspired to and engaged in activities that went beyond the strict confines of the home and traditional gender roles. Such was the case not only of the women workers who formed the core of the labor force in the Catalan textile industry in the nineteenth century, but also of a minority of middle- and upper-class women who demanded women's rights and the option to open up their horizons well beyond the home.

Lawyer and prison reformer Concepción Arenal (1820-1893) advocated both in her writings and in her everyday life that women had to aim to be more than wives and mothers. "It is a grave error and one of the most harmful," she argued in her report presented at the Pedagogical Congress in 1892, "to inculcate women with the idea that their sole mission is that of being a wife and mother: it is the equivalent of telling them that by themselves they cannot be anything, and of annihilating their moral and intellectual *self* by training them with depressing absurdities for the great struggle of life...." Arenal urged that women "must first affirm their personality, independent of their state, and persuade themselves that, single, married, or widowed, they have duties to carry out, rights to vindicate, a job to do.... Life is something serious, and if they take it as a game they will be unremittingly treated as a toy."[21] Arenal was one of the few nineteenth-century Spanish women who achieved public recognition. She had no formal education, and, at a time when women were not allowed to attend the university, she attended law lectures disguised as a man. She became an internationally known figure in the field of criminality and penitentiary reform and one of the leading figures in nineteenth-century feminism.

Over the years other women developed Arenal's arguments, but they were few. What is more disquieting is the acquiescence surrounding Marañón's theory of sexual differentiation. Lucia Sánchez Saornil was a singularly outstanding exception who publicly challenged Marañón's theories. Sánchez Saornil was a radical anarcho-feminist, a telephone operator, poet, and anarchist activist whose feminist concerns led her to become a founding member of the female anarchist organization Mujeres Libres (Free Women) in 1936. Aware of the pervasive influence of Marañón's theory, Sánchez Saornil argued that it was just a subtle, pseudo-scientific method to justify the social relegation of women. The conception of women as primarily wives and mothers signified their subjection to a biological process, to procreation, converting woman into a "tyrannical matrix which exercises obscure influences to the furthest folds of her brain."[22] Sánchez Saornil felt motherhood and maternity could never annul a woman as an individual. Women had the same capacity and potential as men, and therefore women's horizons were to extend far beyond the confines of her reproductive function. Maternity was just one of the many options open to women.

This subversive line of argument was highly exceptional, even among radical and left-wing sectors, and it was supported by very few of the women who defended what could be called a working-class feminism.[23] Indeed, from an anarchist or socialist perspective, the dominant ideology of domesticity was so pervasive that gender values continued to be internalized by women. But Spanish women cannot be considered as mere passive victims; they were active agents in promoting social transformations that questioned existing gender relations. Nevertheless, the overwhelmingly powerful, coercive mechanisms of gender control in an already conservative society made it extremely difficult for Spanish women to attain a collective social and feminist consciousness and to struggle to improve their lot.

Informal social control through conservative ideological tenets was not the only mechanism implemented to enforce women's subordination. Legal discrimination, work segregation, and unequal educational opportunities all reinforced gender norms. Here the State played a decisive role in the articulation of power relations between the sexes; so, together with an ideological discourse that perpetuated the gender power system, economic, legal, and political norms also guaranteed the asymmetry between the sexes. Complex mechanisms of informal and formal social control regulated gender roles and appropriate behavior.[24] Galician writer and feminist Emilia Pardo Bazán indignantly pointed out in 1890 that many of the cultural and political advances achieved throughout the nineteenth century had increased the distances between the sexes: "Freedom to teach, freedom to worship, the right to hold meetings, suffrage, and parliamentarism have been used [by men] so that half of society gains in strength and activities at the expense of the female half."[25]

Despite some political advances, until the democratic constitution of the Second Republic introduced the principle of political equality between the sexes in 1931, women's subordination was guaranteed by law. Over the decades, Spanish legislation had implemented formal social control to guarantee the gender system. The Civil and Penal Code clearly established women's subordination. Married women were particularly constrained by the existing legislation. For instance, Article 57 of the Civil Code (1889) established that "the husband must protect his wife and she must obey her husband." Women were obliged to establish their residence wherever the husband decided (Article 58). The husband was the administrator of the goods and chattels of the couple as well as the representative of his wife, who needed his permission to participate in any public act such as lawsuits, purchases, and sales (except those for normal family consumption) or any kind of contract (Articles 58-62). Women needed the authorization of their husbands to carry out any type of business. Even a recently married woman who had been running a business as a single woman was required to get her husband's permission to continue working. Women dedicated to business, shopkeeping, or commerce were totally dependent on the goodwill of their husbands, as their permission could be arbitrarily revoked at any time.

Furthermore, women did not control their wages, which by law were administered by their husbands. Indeed, despite the numerous reforms in the legal treatment of women during the Second Republic, the new Law on Work Contracts (November 1931) still maintained the husband's control of his wife's salary, although it did foresee the possibility of allowing women to administer their wages if given prior permission by their husbands or in the case of legal or *de facto* separation.[26]

According to the law, marital authority was to be obeyed automatically, and any transgression was to be severely punished. Disobedience and verbal insults were sufficient motive to have a woman imprisoned, whereas a man was punished only if he ill-treated his wife (Penal Code, Article 603).

The double moral standard was legally entrenched, as can be seen by the treatment of crimes of passion and adultery. According to the Penal Code, the punishment of a husband who caught his wife in adultery and killed either her or the adulterer or caused them serious injury was banishment to a minimum radius of 25 kilometers from his legal address for a period that could vary from six months and a day to six years. If minor injuries were caused, the husband was exempt from punishment. For women who committed such crimes, the punishment was significantly different. Crimes of passion that resulted in the death of the husband were considered parricides and punishable by life imprisonment (Penal Code, Article 238).

Adultery also had different gender connotations. Any married woman who lay with a man not her husband was subject to a prison sentence of two to six years, while a husband's infidelity was not even considered adultery unless he "had a concubine in the conjugal house or elsewhere" and furthermore had caused "public scandal" (Penal Code, Article 448.452). According to gender norms of conduct reinforced by law, the double sexual standard was considered legitimate; only when the social institution of the family or public decorum was threatened by male behavior was it deemed necessary to restrain and punish the man. On the contrary, any woman, however discreet, who transgressed the gender sexual code was guilty of questioning male supremacy and a husband's right to control his wife's body and therefore was considered a profound threat to the maintenance of the family. Such deviant behavior was considered too threatening to be acknowledged on any level by the dominant conservative gender ideology and thus had to be explicitly punished by law.

Of course, within the family, men had a sharply defined hierarchical authority over wives and children. Paternal control was such that married mothers had no authority over their children, and even in the case of widows, this authority was lost if they remarried, unless the previous husband had explicitly stipulated the contrary. Legal endorsement of such discriminatory treatment of women continued until the legislative democratic reforms of the thirties, and even then only Catalonia introduced complete juridical equity between spouses.[27]

Provident and Industrious: Education and Woman's Mission

The slow advancement in the area of women's scholastic and cultural education also constitutes a crucial factor of gender discrimination. The spread of liberal states in Western Europe in the nineteenth century had signified the expansion of public instruction as a means to extend bourgeois culture and to consolidate the liberal regimes. Although women were considered a social group that required a different education than that provided men, little by little, the initial opinion that education could be physically or mentally harmful to women was discredited. In the late nineteenth century, providing women with an adequate education had become a common topic of debate in educational circles. However, such a change in attitude did not cause a questioning of gender hierarchy: female access to education was designed to consolidate the sexual division of labor and provide women with an adequate training in their traditional roles as wives and mothers. Nonetheless, it did represent considerable progress, as the increasing demand for education led to the realization that ignorance did not guarantee greater domesticity, obedience, or compliance with housewifely duties.

In Spain the overall quality of education was appalling, and female education was notably worse. Concepción Arenal, writing at the close of the nineteenth century, pointed out that "in the girls' schools (that is when there are any) most of the time is spent on needlework, and only exceptionally the schoolmistress knows how to read with some sense, write correctly and to do the most elementary arithmetic."[28] The major deficiencies in the education of lower-class girls were also present in the education of the upper and middle classes. Carmen Karr, a journalist, director of the women's journal *Feminal*, and leading Catalan feminist in the early twentieth century, constantly complained about the poor standard of education available to women of the upper classes, who usually received their lessons from unprepared, ignorant nuns. Karr actually developed a detailed project for an Institute for Female Culture whose aim was to provide upper-class girls with a quality education. Her educational program provided not only the usual secondary school curriculum but also training in physical education, fine arts, hygiene, domestic economy, and religion, together with the development of the sentiments and a "cultural spirit."[29] At the beginning of the twentieth century, Karr's position, and that of many other upper- and middle-class women, although conservative, was indicative of the change in opinion regarding female education, as the conversion from the ideal *perfecta casada* to an educated woman gradually came to be accepted and, more significantly still, claimed by the women themselves.

This change of attitude did not produce a substantial increase in the demand for an egalitarian educational model for boys and girls.[30] Gender differentiation in education was deeply embedded in cultural norms. An influential work first published in the 1850's that had several editions in later decades—*El libro de oro de la educación de las niñas*—made the distinction quite diaphanous: "Far be it from me the idea to give women the scholastic education that men receive: on the contrary, they must be taught to be women, provident as an ant, industrious as a bee."[31] Over generations women internalized gendered educational norms. To a large degree women continued to aspire to an education that failed to respond to their own personal development and to the widening of their cultural and educational horizons but provided specific training within the confines of their traditionally ascribed gender role. By the early twentieth century, the important advances in the cultural expectations of middle-class women underlined by Carmen Karr were also illustrative of their very limitations:

> Women want to understand the problems that form the spiritual life of a man, so that they will not be only the servant, the dispenser, the prolific mother, or the frame for jewels or precious clothes that serve only to proclaim the wealth of the head of the family....
>
> While not aspiring to being scholars they have managed to understand that the veritable science of a modern woman is to elevate her spirit and her taste in such a way that men will find in her something eminently necessary for his spiritual life and his improvement.[32]

Women's interest in expanding their educational opportunities should not be viewed as an overt challenge to women's traditional family role but as a symptom of change that shows a revision of more traditional viewpoints on education and women's relation to men. The aspiration to become educated represented a certain degree of upgrading in the status of the wife and also wider female cultural expectations. No doubt the emergence of this concern for female education can also be attributed to the modernization of the family and a growing awareness of the need for better educated mothers to carry out their task of socialization and education of their offspring. Furthermore, not all women encouraged or accepted a gender-designed education aimed to foment male prerogatives. Some were most outspoken in their attack of such initiatives. As early as 1892, Emilia Pardo Bazán, with exceptional clearsightedness, had already vigorously denounced the utilization of women and the gender focus of female education: "The present-day education of women, in truth, cannot be called *education* as such," she caustically proclaimed. "Rather must it be called *taming*, as its proposed objective is obedience, passivity and submission."[33]

In the course of the nineteenth century the advances in public instruction in other European countries such as France and Great Britain had led to the gradual levelling of differences in illiteracy between the sexes.[34] In Spain, the deficiencies in the school system and the failure of innovative educational initiatives and educational reform resulted in high illiteracy rates among the whole population. Nonetheless, female illiteracy rates were substantially and consistently higher than those of males.

Toward the mid-nineteenth century there was an extraordinarily high level of female illiteracy. In 1860, 86 percent of the female population was illiterate, and by the beginning of the twentieth century, this rate had been reduced to 71 percent in contrast to 55.57 percent male illiteracy. By then, only 25.1 percent of females knew how to read and write. During the course of the first decades of the twentieth century, there was a slow decrease in overall illiteracy. By 1930, illiteracy figures had dropped to 47.5 percent female and 36.9 percent male. This extremely high level of illiteracy, affecting almost half the female population of Spain, was a significant factor in reinforcing traditional constraints on female cultural and employment opportunities. Despite the reduction in overall illiteracy rates, gender differences in the level of instruction increased.[35]

During the thirties, however, under the reforms of the Second Republic, the situation improved considerably as educational reform policies focused on the creation of elementary schools and the elimination of illiteracy among children. By 1936, illiteracy rates had dropped to 39.4 percent among females and 24.8 percent among males. Not surprisingly, the period of social change inaugurated by the Civil War and revolution in 1936 also mobilized women in an offensive against female illiteracy in which women's organizations focused on educational drives designed for adult women.

The obstacles limiting female access to primary, secondary, and professional education were even more acute when it came to higher education. A few exceptional women had attended university lectures by the end of the nineteenth century, and it was no longer necessary to disguise themselves as men, as Concepción Arenal had been obliged to do. Nonetheless, at the turn of the century, men still totally monopolized higher education. Only one female was registered officially as a university student in 1900.

Until 1910, legal restrictions on female higher education continued. By the late twenties, the situation had improved somewhat, but the female university population was still very low and women students were concentrated in the fields of pharmacy, medicine, and humanities. More significant still was the fact that few women pursued careers after attaining their degree.[36] Women doctors and lawyers who actually practiced were highly exceptional figures, and the few who did so gained renown as political figures in the thirties. In fact, lawyers such as Clara Campoamor and Victoria Kent became parliamentary deputies and played a decisive role in the discussion on female suffrage, albeit from opposing political views.

Parallel with the progress of public education, alternative strategies of pedagogical renovation and popular education were developed by the Spanish labor movement. Without any doubt, the *ateneos* (cultural forums) and other popular cultural centers, sponsored by anarchists and socialists, responded to a real social demand for culture and education. The diffusion of knowledge through these centers was, of course, aimed toward transmitting a cultural message in consonance with the sponsors' political and social ideals. The long established tradition of popular education encompassed elementary and technical training as well as a wide range of cultural activities. This educational and cultural drive was, however, clearly gender-defined and scarcely responded to the very real needs of working-class women. It is true that some activities dealt sporadically with issues specifically relevant to women, with lectures on topics such as the family, sexuality, birth control, and hygiene, but there was no systematic effort to develop popular education specifically designed for women.[37] The greater number of female illiterates, their lower level of instruction, and their lack of technical and professional training constituted a situation that required specific attention and policies to redress such discrimination. But even in left-wing radical sectors, male cultural hegemony and the profound prejudices toward women's access to culture made it very difficult for working-class women to accede to an education, even when available in the context of popular initiative.

Together with the lack of gender-specific educational priorities, the obstacles to the education of adult women were further incremented by the existing sexual division of labor, which made women solely responsible for housework and the care of children. Women had to carry out both wage and domestic work; this double burden allowed them little free time to attend centers of popular education. Furthermore, the time schedule of these cultural activities, the need to commute, the lack of specific attention to encourage her presence, together with the absence of a concrete educational agenda designed to fulfill her needs and expectations, all made it very difficult to overcome the numerous obstacles and prevalent prejudices toward adult female education. Thus while a levelling of literacy rates among boys and girls increased, the needs of the most deprived sector in the field of adult education— women workers—were to remain practically unattended.

Both anarchists and socialists, the two main sectors in the Spanish working-class movement, claimed that education was the key to the emancipation of the working class and also a fundamental means toward achieving female emancipation. Despite such declarations and the open recognition that women lacked educational facilities, neither group conceived a systematic strategy to provide women with a compensatory education on equivalent terms with male workers. Although the Spanish socialist party, the Partido Socialista Obrero Español (PSOE), included the demand for an integral education for both sexes in its political program as early as 1879, the socialists developed few initiatives geared to facilitate such education for women.

Not even the women's socialist groups incorporated specific educational programs for women in their agenda, although they usually paid lip service to the importance of educating women. The case of the Madrid Women's Socialist Group illustrates this lack of systematic attention. Created in 1906 and dissolved in 1927, this group expressed some interest in furthering female education. In fact, the first point of its program stated that its purpose was to "educate women in order to exercise their social duties, in accordance with socialist principles."[38] However, the records of the group show that they dedicated most of their energies to creating political propaganda for the benefit of the socialist party. The literary evenings to celebrate the group's anniversaries, the sporadic talks given to laundry women and dressmakers, and the campaigns to gain support for socialist leaders cannot be considered a systematic effort to facilitate an education for women.[39]

The integral education of both sexes, together with the demand for the emancipation of women, had figured in the program of Spanish anarchists ever since its formation. Anarchists had always placed particular emphasis on the development of alternative popular education, as they felt that education and pedagogy were the key to the integral development of the individual.[40] A circular addressed to workers by the Spanish Regional Federation of the International Workingmen's Association in 1871 had declared: "We want integral teaching for all individuals of both sexes in all grades of science, industry, and the arts, so that those intellectual inequalities which are almost totally fictitious may disappear."[41]

There are some indications of educational activities oriented specifically toward women and girls in the late nineteenth century, such as the school for girls organized by the Catalan Ateneo of the Working Class established in 1872, which proposed a program of reading, writing, arithmetic, grammar, domestic economy, needlework, darning, and dressmaking in the elementary courses, as well as drawing, geometry, geography, and embroidery for the more advanced. A rational method was followed so that "the teaching gave the desired fruit and united the conditions of real utility for the present and the future of the working-class."[42] Such initiatives were not widespread, and although dedication to female education was greater in the libertarian movement than in other sectors of the working class, specific initiatives favoring female education tended to be sporadic. While anarchist *ateneos* did include in their programs topics relevant to women, their educational agenda did not contemplate female education as such. In fact, in none of the working-class cultural environments was the presence of women really assimilated or promoted.

By the late 1920's and early 1930's, female participation in working-class cultural centers had increased somewhat, although suspicion and misunderstanding about their presence still persisted. At the same time, there was an increasing feeling of discontent among women about the sexist treatment they were getting. Women had become more assertive in their rejection of male prejudices about female education and accused men of treating them as sexual objects. They attacked the code of norms that belittled female aspirations for culture and education and particularly men's insistence that women remain in a state of ignorance.[43]

Such attitudes were widespread not only in conservative traditional circles but also among radical men, as male opposition to female education was blatant even among political revolutionaries. An article by Lucía Sánchez Saornil in the anarchist newspaper *Solidaridad Obrera* denounced the sexist attitudes and behavior of anarchist companions. This example of open male rejection of female education and culture is highly illustrative of a generalized state of opinion most women had to confront even in a radical left environment:

> On several occasions I had occasion to speak with a compañero who seemed quite sensible and I had always heard him insist on the need for women to integrate more into our movement. One day when a lecture was being held in the Centre I asked him:
>
> "And your companion? Why did she not come to the lecture?" His answer left me frozen.
>
> "My companion has more than enough to do looking after me and my children."
>
> Another day I was in the corridors of the Court. I was in the company of a compañero who held a leadership position. A woman lawyer came out of one of the court rooms. Perhaps she had been defending the cause of a proletariat. My compañero looked at her askance and murmured while giving her a spiteful smile, "I would send women like her home to scrub."[44]

The question of a specific education for women was not seriously addressed until women began organizing themselves. The awareness that most women who wanted access to culture and education would be put off by the obstacles of male antagonism and sexist prejudices was, in fact, what originally led to the creation of the women's anarchist organization Mujeres Libres in April 1936. The first group was formed by a number of women who resented the male hostility at the classes held at the Local Federation of the anarchosyndicalist union, the Confederación Nacional del Trabajo (CNT). One of the founding members of Mujeres Libres, the writer and journalist Mercedes Comaposada, explained that the initial objectives of the group were cultural and educative, designed to train women, give them self-esteem, and broaden their work and social horizons. According to Comaposada, women were to be reconverted into "proprietors of...a feminine personality...,to be able to hold down any post in the organization and so take away the label it seemed to show...,for men only;...or simply to help them deal with the slavery of ignorance, slavery as a female, and slavery as a worker."[45]

Thus, before the outbreak of the Civil War there had already been considerable development in female consciousness of the need to further women's education in both the public and the popular arena. In 1936, the socio-political context of the war was crucial to women's attempts to establish a specific agenda for female adult education.

Invisible but Crucial: Women and Work

Work was another area in which powerful coercive mechanisms articulated unequal gender power relations and enforced work segregation and female discrimination. The prevailing hostile attitudes toward female wage work exerted an important influence on the distribution and working conditions of the female labor force. They also reinforced the idea of the social unacceptability of women's involvement in the economic process. These factors, together with the slow, unequal development of Spanish industrialization, curtailed women's options in the labor market. Women workers had fewer job outlets, they were concentrated in unskilled jobs in poorly paid sectors, and they were always paid much lower wages than those of male workers.

The debate on women's access to wage work underwent few decisive changes over the decades. The ideological foundations of the conservative stance and also of one of its most important exponents, the Catholic Church, were based on the cult of domesticity and the rigid separation between public and private spheres. A woman was taught from childhood that her purpose in life was to fulfill her duties as wife and mother in the context of the home. Thus, any incursion into the public sphere of work was considered unnatural and a discredit to her "sublime" mission as mother and "angel of the hearth." The rejection of female wage work centered primarily on the argument that it represented a threat to the security and well-being of the family.

Shortly before the military uprising in 1936, an article by Joan Gaya in the conservative journal *Catalunya Social* openly rejected women's integration into the labor market. The author's argument is indicative of the continuous assimilation of traditional gender discourse on domesticity, as female wage work was rejected primarily because it led to a questioning of male authority, one of the basic tenets of the traditional institution of the family. The article argued that the

economic independence of the wife undermined the husband's authority and
dignity as well as his psychological self-esteem. Thus, men felt that any change in
women's economic role threatened male power and status both within the family
and in society at large. Only in the case of dire economic straits, provoked mainly
by male unemployment, was female wage work to be allowed, and then only in
paid jobs considered more appropriate to the female sex, even if that meant earning
lower wages. The conclusion of the article is almost apocalyptic:

> On throwing him out of Paradise, it was on man that God imposed
> the obligation to earn his living by the sweat of his brow. He did not
> order woman to do the same, rather with the necessary suffering..., she
> was to look after her children....While women elude what they have
> been ordered to do and insist on occupying men's place, there is no
> point in being worried: the world will follow along the horrible paths
> of death and misery along which it has been walking now for some
> centuries.[46]

What is significant is that by the mid-1930's the rejection of female wage labor
by conservative ideologues gained momentum precisely because of their
awareness of the trend toward female participation in the labor market. What
worried men like the conservative Joan Gaya was that, by the 1930's, middle-class
girls no longer accepted marriage as their only mission in life, or at least they were
more selective in their choice of a husband.[47] What he feared was a breakdown in
the gender code of norms surrounding male supremacy and female subordination
and even more so, an opening up of women's demands that could lead to a
questioning of their traditional gender role as submissive "angels of the hearth"
and docile spouses.

The rejection of women's wage work centered on the belief that women's
continuing economic dependence was crucial for safeguarding a gender hierarchy
within the family. The wage-earning wife came to constitute a symbol of male
degradation. The rejection of female wage work was not exclusive to any particular
social sector. Conservative ideologues were more vociferous in their expression of
such rejection. However, hostility toward female extra-domestic labor came from
all classes and was practiced, although not necessarily formulated in their theory or
political agenda, by those on the left.[48] The position taken by anarchists and
socialists was highly ambivalent, as their theoretical acceptance of women's right
to work was combined with rejection in practice. This occurred despite early
stances accepting women's right to paid work.

The anarchist movement, practically since its creation, linked women's right to
paid work to their right to autonomy and independence. The radical declaration
approved in 1872 at the Second Congress of the Spanish Regional Federation of
the International Workingmen's Association held in Saragossa illustrates the early

sympathy within the Spanish anarchist movement toward the question of women's paid work:

> A woman is a free and intelligent being, and as such, responsible for her acts, just like a man; then, if that is so, what is necessary is to facilitate the conditions of freedom so that she will develop according to her faculties. However, if we relegate women exclusively to housework, that signifies submitting her, as has been done up to now, to dependence on men, and therefore, taking away her freedom. What means exist that will facilitate the conditions of freedom for women? The only one is work.[49]

Despite such a decided defense of women's right to wage work and the advances made on behalf of women by the Spanish labor movement in the late nineteenth and early twentieth centuries, workers' reticence and open hostility toward female wage work was both explicit and constant.[50] Most trade unions and working-class organizations assumed that female workers were a threat to existing working conditions and decent wages as well as an obstacle to the advance of the labor struggle.[51] Most hostility was verbal, and, at times, enormous pressure was exerted on women to desist from aspiring to jobs.

Male strategies to prevent women from holding jobs were many, but few reached the degree of provoking a strike, as happened in Barcelona in the summer of 1915.[52] The workers in a number of soup factories initiated a four-month strike with the explicit goal of driving out women who occupied "men's jobs" and enforcing work regulations that would prevent women from holding manual labor jobs in those factories.[53] The workers' explicit hostility with regard to female wage work, together with the pressure of the predominant discourse on domesticity, created significant obstacles for women. The workers also favored channelling women into specific jobs, thus consolidating occupational segregation.

In reality, discourse on women's wage work did not reflect women's constant life-time labor experience but rather rendered women's work invisible. Most women had worked, be it in textile industries, home work, domestic services, street commerce, housework, or in agriculture. Although most historians of economic development have ignored a gender perspective on the development of Spanish industrialization, and women's role in economic growth in the diverse regions of Spain has yet to be fully documented, women's involvement appears to have been considerable.

Catalonia, the first region to undergo industrialization, had a long tradition of female labor in the textile industry, and, toward the mid-nineteenth century, female and child labor made up 60 percent of the textile workers.[54] In fact, women textile workers represented 40 percent of the total Catalan work force. During the first stages of industrialization, much of the production in the cotton sector of the Catalan textile industry was carried out by women.

In less developed economic areas such as Galicia, Andalusia, and Central Spain, women's work in agrarian holdings was absolutely crucial. In the mining area of the Basque country, income generated through catering for lodgers, laundry services, and cooking was vital to the survival of the working classes.[55] Moreover, in all major cities, services provided by women in laundry, cooking, ironing, and sewing were yet another invisible feature of women's work.[56]

Numerous historians have pointed out the importance of women's contribution to the family economy during this period and have emphasized that the family's economic survival often depended on the contributions of all its members.[57] This would also appear to have been the case in Spain. Although there are few studies dedicated to such an analysis, fragmentary evidence does exist. For example, children's nurseries were included in the series of demands presented by the Catalan working class to the Central Government in the course of social conflict during the change to a more progressive government in the two-year period of the Bienio Progresista (1854-1856).[58] This demand apparently indicates that a significant number of married women were working for wages and that women were involved in the Catalan working-class movement during this period.[59] A survey carried out by the Commission for Social Reform in 1883 appears to confirm this hypothesis, as it shows that women's economic contribution was indispensable to the survival of the family. However, women's integration into the labor force was still considered admissible by male workers only in cases of dire economic necessity. Working-class men unquestionably accepted the traditional gender stance on women's wage work. They, too, rejected it out of hand and considered it shameful if women in their family had to work. As one witness to the Commission put it: "The worker tends to fulfill his obligations to maintain his family, so that only in the case of the material impossibility to fulfill his duty does he resign himself to his wife and daughters working, especially outside the home."[60] Gender discourse defined male identity through work and evoked the male worker as the family's sole economic provider, the family breadwinner, thus reinforcing male opposition to women's right to wage work.

Eventually, the economic reality could no longer be denied—most families were in dire need of women's wages. Consequently, wage work within the confines of the home became a more viable proposition, acceptable both to working-class and middle-class ideologues. In the early twentieth century, home work came to be proposed as the best work option for women, as it allowed them to combine their duties as a housewife with wage work.[61]

Spanish women's contribution to the family wage economy was exemplified by their massive participation in home work during the First World War. In this period of expanding production due to Spanish neutrality, home work was intensified as a mechanism that allowed the economy to meet the increase in demand without being obliged to undertake technological renovation or increases in costs. This decentralized production system, based on subcontracting, labor-intensive work, worker control, and low wages, was founded on an informal job market composed primarily of women.[62] From 1914 to 1918, rising inflation led to an enormous deterioration in the standard of living of the Spanish working class. In this context, the vital need to contribute to the family wage economy explains the constant offer of female labor in home work and women's acceptance of starvation wages as their only strategy for survival at a time when job alternatives for women were severely limited.

Throughout the late nineteenth and early twentieth centuries, a number of factors dictated the configuration of the female labor market. The consistent lack of professional training limited women's options to only unskilled jobs, thus reinforcing discriminatory occupational segregation. Moreover, the existing prejudices concerning women's incorporation into wage work and the general assumption that female work was temporary and merely a substitute or complement to male wages helped to legitimize wage discrimination. Toward the end of the nineteenth century, women earned less than half of what men earned even in similar job categories. This tendency continued throughout the twentieth century, and, despite attempts to redress wage discrimination during the years of the Second Republic and the Civil War, the disparity remained, although to a lesser degree.

Because of the traditional lack of professional training, women had few opportunities to acquire skills and thus had limited access to better paid jobs. The employment they did obtain was considered harmonious with the supposedly "natural" female talents: the garment industry and domestic service. By 1930, women represented only 12.65 percent of the total labor force. Women workers at that time were distributed in agriculture (26.67 percent), in industry (31.82 percent), and in services (41.51 percent). Women's integration into white-collar jobs was very slow, as women were not allowed to enter public administration until 1918, and, of course, there were few women in the liberal professions, so the high number of women in services mainly represented women in traditional jobs in domestic service (75 percent). Of course, figures from official sources did not consider the rull range of female work, since official statistics did not take into account the underground labor market. Moreover, a significant number of women worked in agriculture and were not represented in official data.[63]

Freedom, Bread, and "Bad" Women: Gender and Social Change

In the late nineteenth and early twentieth centuries, coercive mechanisms of gender control were overwhelmingly pervasive. Discriminatory measures enforced by the State ensured female subordination through legal discrimination, educational and political inequality, and labor restrictions. The predominant conservative ideology also enforced gender mechanisms of domination and subordination. Women were, however, far from being mere victims of a patriarchal society. They were protagonists of social dynamics, potential agents of change in a complex historical process in which they, as a social group, were actors with a significant role to play.

By the twenties and thirties, the collective historical experience of women surpassed the boundaries of the home and gave rise to a complex articulation between private and public domains. Despite numerous obstacles, at times timorously, at others forcibly, women demanded a redressal of grievances and achieved cultural and educational advances. They did not always consider themselves as victims in their traditional roles as wives and mothers, and mobilization in defense of the interests of their families occasionally led to violent agitation and even incursions into the political arena. A few exceptional, articulate women broke the chains of conformity by openly voicing their discontent and demanding wider educational and political options for women. In addition, a number of the women's associations formed during this period demanded political franchise for women.

The fragmentary state of our historical knowledge makes it difficult to gauge to what extent female mobilization in Spain was gender-specific or part of more general overall social conflicts. The collective historical experience of Spanish women has yet to be fully documented, and so it is difficult to discern what resistance strategies were used and why or how women mobilized and with what objective. The silence surrounding the collective memory of women is just being penetrated, so the glimpses of their participation in collective action are impressionistic and necessarily incomplete. Nevertheless, the evidence does tend to support the view that female protagonism in the domain of social action in the nineteenth century was more extensive than existing historiography has led us to believe.

The role women played in the struggle between the liberal forces and the repressive absolutist Ancien Regime has yet to be studied. However, a number of events indicate some degree of female involvement in the ongoing liberal struggle of the early nineteenth century—such as the existence of a female liberal battalion that supported General Lacy in the early struggles of Spanish liberalism, the execution of Mariana Pineda for aiding the clandestine liberal movement, and the eloquent image of Barcelona working women who in the 1820's aided the liberal cause by pulling "cannons in order to get them up on the walls" and forming "several squadrons of female militias, armed with pikes, whose task was to aid the injured."[64]

There is also evidence of women's significant participation in the complex socio-political economic conflict that took place in Barcelona in the summer of 1835. While the conflict lasted, six convents were burned down, the highest-level representative of the Madrid government was killed, and official documents were publicly destroyed to the slogan "Long live the Fatherland! Long live Freedom!"[65] Finally, the newly inaugurated modern textile factory, commonly known as El Vapor (the steam factory), a symbol of Catalan's burgeoning industrial capitalism, was burned down. The chain of events are closely linked with the crisis of Spanish absolutism and the inception of the liberal revolution in Spain.

The ingredients of this popular revolt are to be found in the complex traditional and modern reaction to the economic crisis—a classic food riot due to rising food costs and a struggle by workers against the introduction of new technology in the textile industry. Increasing proletarianization due to developing industrialization also affected women's situation as workers. The revolt also had political connotations, as it implied a political struggle for power among rival forces in the decisive transition to a new liberal state in Spain.[66]

Women appear to have played a significant role in these conflicts. In the summer of 1835, the authorities published a ban expressly forbidding women to meet in the streets and to participate in the protests. Women were subjected to specific gender differentiation, as the ban proclaimed that women who were activists in the disturbances were to be considered "public women," that is, prostitutes, and punished as such:

> Women who follow the tumult, on contravening the Bans, show that they have a very indelicate soul and that they are of very indecorous origin; therefore they will be considered as public women and they will be applied the punishment which the laws have established....[67]

Writers commenting on these conflicts at a later date underlined the important role of these "bad women," who apparently had to be discredited for penetrating the public arena and transgressing the accepted codes of gender behavior.[68] Their motivation for participating in protests appears partly derived from their roles as mothers, nurturers, and providers of their families' primary needs. It seems probable that they aimed to impede an encroachment on their standard of living. Their support for political change and their involvement in this social conflict may have represented a strategy for family survival, as their slogan "*Vinga Cristina y vinga farina!*" ("Up with Cristina [the Royal Regent] and let flour flow") seems to indicate.[69]

Even as early as 1835, women were involved in social conflict and mobilized around issues concerning them as workers, citizens, and mothers. As their slogan addressing the figure of the Regent Queen shows, these women were as aware of the political environment as they were of their gendered social roles.

On this occasion, women acted as members of a household, their interests being family-oriented rather than gender-specific. One of the key factors to an understanding of Spanish social relations in this period is the crucial predominance of the family. The unequal process of industrialization throughout Spain meant that even in areas of greater industrial development and a growing working class, such as in Catalonia or the Basque country, the family acted as the stepping stone between individuals and the changing society. Although women tended to act on the basis of the sexual division of labor and the acceptance of their gender role as nurturers and custodians of the home and family interests, they had a crucial role to play in contributing to family strategies for survival and the improvement of their standard of living. In fact, it was women's willingness to assume this role that projected them beyond the confines of the private sphere into the public world of production, politics, and social change. Moreover, women periodically assumed this strategy even though it meant being branded as prostitutes, harpies, furies, or "raging" women.[70]

Women played an important role as instigators and participants in social protests during the Bienio Progresista (1854-1856).[71] Numerous riots took place in Castille to the cry of "Freedom" and "Bread." Steep increases in food prices and unemployment led to the burning of shops, factories, and houses in central Spain. The documentation of the trials shows that women were involved and that their punishment was not any less severe because of their sex.[72] In this case, the motive behind their mobilization was their acceptance of the gender division of labor. Their nurturing role as safeguard of family interests appears to have led to the women's involvement in a struggle centering on issues such as food supplies and fair prices, but these also became more politicized as the movement developed.[73]

The paucity of evidence makes it difficult to trace female participation in labor conflicts and women's mobilization within class organizations in this period. One of the first known incidences of the massive mobilization of working women occurred in Madrid in 1830 when over 3,000 women cigarette makers lay down their tools and attacked the director of the State Tobacco Factory.[74] Although the conflict presents some of the social characteristics of the classic urban riots of the eighteenth century, the documentation seems to indicate that it was also a modern labor conflict linked to the work place. Apparently, women workers mobilized in a defensive movement to protect their working conditions and wage level at a time when the working class's standard of living was deteriorating. In later periods, female cigarette workers were involved in numerous labor conflicts, but these appear to have been related to specific labor issues rather than larger social or gender-specific issues.[75]

During the formation and initial growth of the Spanish labor movement, we find some degree of female integration into class associations. Such was the case of the approximately 8,000 women affiliated with the Manufacturing Union in 1873. Of these, some 5,000 were members of the Spanish Regional Federation of the International Workingmen's Association (IWA), through which they were purported to be entering "the fecund universal working-class movement in order to cooperate in the advent of the Social Revolution, in order to establish Anarchy and

Collectivism, equality of duties and rights."[76] By then there were two female sectors of the Spanish IWA, and there is evidence that strikes were held by seamstresses in Palma, Majorca and by female spinners in Valencia. There is also evidence of female participation in the activities of the anarchist movement, particularly in Andalusia.[77]

By the late nineteenth century, we also find fragmentary evidence of a spontaneous effort by working women to set up their own representative organizations to protect their interests. In 1891, Catalan working women attempted to establish one of the first autonomous female associations. During a series of mass meetings organized by women workers to celebrate the First of May (International Workers' Day), it was proposed that an association be set up for women workers of all trades and occupations with the aim of defending their interests, improving their working conditions, and "counter-arresting the greed of the bosses who condemn us to shameful poverty and continuous suffering."[78] Women of many different trades were present at the initial meeting. The speakers, all women, included a shirtmaker, a book-binder, a shoemaker, a textile worker, a domestic servant, and a tailor.

Forty-seven different female workers groups were represented at the meeting on April 26, 1891, where the grievances of the women workers were aired. Although the meeting appeared to have been set up by the spontaneous initiative of the women workers, women anarchists played a decisive role in its organization. The main speaker was the well-known anarchist activist and textile worker Teresa Claramunt, who urged the women to articulate their grievances and to work together to redress them. The general conclusions that resulted from the meeting pointed to the absolute need to get women to associate with each other in order to resist the exploitation of female labor. Soon after the formation of the women's association, new sections were established by seamstresses, shoemakers, and garment workers, and a general section was formed for a variety of trades.

Among these women workers, there was a surprising degree of consciousness of gender identity. In fact, one of their resolutions stated that a segregated, autonomous women workers' association would be established excluding men from its direction, administration, and representation in order to avoid "male impositions based on a supposedly female inferiority." This clear stance on separatism and female autonomy can no doubt be attributed to the influence of anarchist Teresa Claramunt, who some years later was to publish one of the first tracts by a woman worker on the social condition of women in Spain.[79] In the tract Claramunt stressed that one of the major obstacles to women's advancement was men's sense of superiority. She was also one of the first social activists to advocate the self-emancipation of women workers. This would be achieved, she claimed, only through a specific struggle as women.[80] However, many women workers were far from having achieved Teresa Claramunt's degree of feminist consciousness, and the demand for total equity between the sexes in all spheres was not to figure in their agenda. In fact, they did not even demand equity with their male peers. Gender division of labor and occupational segregation were accepted by many of these women, and it is significant that some of the women speakers actually pointed out that female working-class organizations were particularly desirable because they would prevent women workers from occupying jobs that traditionally were held by men.

Evidence of the attempt to create an autonomous working women's association is fragmentary, but the lack of information about its development suggests that it failed to flourish. The association's heterogeneity of objectives and tactics, along with a very patriarchal and hostile male working-class movement, appears to have been responsible for its inability to mobilize Catalan women workers in these segregated autonomous organizations.

Increasing female integration in the work force was to give rise to women's more extensive participation in labor conflicts, especially in industrial Catalonia, the Basque country, and Valencia.[81] Participation was particularly significant in the textile industry, which not only was the most mechanized and modernized sector but the one with the greatest concentration of women workers. According to official data, women workers did not hesitate to participate in mainstream working-class struggles. From 1905 to 1921, more women workers than men workers went on strike.[82] Recent research has revised the usual image of Spanish women workers as lacking in labor and social consciousness and acting as an impediment to the development of labor and social struggles. Spanish women can no longer be portrayed as apathetic, docile workers instrumentalized by right-wing ideologues, for they, too, showed a high level of combativity and resistance.

It remains to be established how gender influenced the motives and patterns of female mobilization in labor and class struggles. In most labor conflicts that involved women, a number of different demands surfaced. Approximately 60 percent of all labor conflicts centered on demands for higher wages, hardly surprising considering that women suffered acute wage discrimination, earning less than 50 percent of male workers' wages. Other common issues were related to discipline, firing, work schedules, relations with superiors, and the right to unionize. More gender-specific issues were related to women's frequent mobilization for the purpose of striking to defend their physical integrity and to put an end to sexual harassment.

An example of massive mobilization by women workers was the Constancy Strike, which mobilized over 13,000 women workers in Barcelona in the summer of 1913.[83] Strikers demanded a nine-hour working day, an eight-hour night shift, and wage hikes. Initially, women were mobilized around a basic labor issue, the implementation of legislation on women's night work. However, the collective action instigated by women actually went far beyond mere trade union goals and created new channels of organization and struggle that encompassed the organized labor movement and the working class. Women mobilized decisively around such issues as food scarcity, increased prices of basic goods, and their distribution.

During the First World War, female mobilization was triggered by food shortages and high prices in a context of overall social agitation and deterioration in standards of living of the working class.[84] Resorting to direct action, women attacked stores and food distribution centers in Barcelona, Málaga, Córdoba, Vigo, Madrid, and Alicante, among other towns. In the better documented cases of Barcelona and Málaga, female networks were established, and these permeated both the local community and the workplace, with women playing a significant role in the leadership and development of the conflicts and demands.[85]

Toward a Feminist Consciousness: Women's Organizations and the Construction of Feminism

In their roles as workers, workers' wives, mothers, and custodians of the working-class family, women took part, on numerous occasions, in mobilizations and collective struggles dealing with social and labor issues. However, the group interest in these conflicts was not gender-specific. Women's specific interests appear, on the whole, to have been incidental. Women's involvement, motivated by gender consciousness and defense of the sexual division of labor, sometimes resulted in confrontations with the authorities about food prices and the standard of living. Women's defense of traditional rights gave rise to incidences of direct popular action that were disciplined and had clear objectives. By adhering to their traditional gender roles as mothers and nurturers, they legitimized, to some degree, their transgression of gender norms confining women to the private arena and their open confrontation with established authority.

Working women took part in labor conflicts and strikes, and, in some cases, they were integrated into the organized structures of the working-class movement. Here their interests as a specific collective were also incidental because their identification with social struggle appears to have derived mainly from their position as wage workers. However, at times, there was some degree of specific gender consciousness in their struggles when demands not only responded to their labor interests but also touched on issues that differentiated them as women, such as wage inequality and inaccessibility to better paying jobs. This association between class and feminist consciousness was slow to develop. Nonetheless, some degree of this dual consciousness was formulated by Teresa Claramunt in the context of the anarchist movement in the late nineteenth century, although several decades were to pass before it was articulated into a collective strategy for feminist and social change under the auspices of the female anarchist organization Mujeres Libres (Free Women) in 1936.

The development of feminist consciousness and collective action based on issues intrinsic to women was a gradual process. Carmen de Burgos (1879-1932), the schoolteacher, writer, feminist, and member of the Radical Socialist Party, claimed that the first public act of Spanish feminists took place in 1921, when a manifesto demanding civil and political rights for women was handed out in the streets and presented at Parliament and the Senate.[86] Feminist politics in these early years seldom led women to collective mobilization and action or to any degree of influence on public policy.[87]

Early evidence of feminist consciousness can be found among the social utopians, particularly followers of French social utopian Charles Fourier in Cádiz, where a small number of women poets and writers collaborated in the publishing of the journal *El Pensil de Iberia* (The Garden of Iberia) in the 1850's.[88] This journal, which included lyrical poetry, philosophical essays, and social criticism from a democratic perspective, spread Fourier's thought throughout Spain and paid considerable attention to women. It examined women's situation with respect to both the home and the workplace. Although they viewed the world through the filter of Christian thought and romantic idealism, the Cádiz Fourierists advocated equality between the sexes, an end to male supremacy, and the development of new foundations for the relations between the sexes based on Fourier's idea of "attractive passion." They also denounced the social injustice of the exploitation of working women and advocated social harmony. Censorship and political repression impeded the continuing publication of the journal, which, despite the fury it aroused among the established authorities, appears to have remained isolated from a larger audience of women.[89] The women involved with the Fourierists were later closely associated with spiritist, freethinking groups and Freemasonry, which, toward the end of the nineteenth century, became a significant forum for the development of feminist thought.[90] Despite some isolated incidences of vindications of women's rights, at the end of the nineteenth century, not a single social movement in Spain had attempted to mobilize women to redress grievances and attain political franchise.[91]

The debate on the historical construction and definition of feminism in recent years has underscored the complexity of feminism as a movement and a generator of an ideological discourse on women.[92] Conventional interpretative frameworks for Northern European and North American feminism are not always valid for an analysis of feminism in Spain. Recent Spanish scholarship, influenced by such interpretative schemes, has stressed the weakness of feminism in Spain.[93] It has also tended to portray feminism from the perspective of equality, and preferential attention has been given to political feminism, the redressment of political grievances, and the attainment of individual political rights. This interpretative scheme has portrayed Spanish feminism as a liberal development based on the application of the principles of equality of the French Revolution and political rights to women. In this sense, feminism has come to be somewhat narrowly defined as suffragism. In other words, the focus of this literature has constricted the definition of feminism to individual political rights and equality with men, thus limiting the conceptualization of feminism as a social movement. As a result, feminism as a historical movement appears to have been of little incidence in Spain.

As has been underscored in this chapter, existing political structures in Spain in the nineteenth and early twentieth centuries were not conducive to the development of a popular political culture based on the unquestioning acceptance of the liberal or democratic systems. The corrupt and inefficient political system led to a general mistrust and questioning of politics as a viable means for social progress. Thus, in line with the population at large, women, as a social collective, were not inclined to direct their energy toward a political struggle based on the demand for equality and political rights. In this context, limiting the goal of feminism to securing political rights fails to account for other manifestations of collective aspirations of women. But rather, Spanish feminism in both the late nineteenth and early twentieth century can be characterized more by its social than its political orientation. As a movement, it was not singularly suffragist in focus, and the core of Spanish feminist arguments for women's rights was not individual rights based on the idea of gender equality.

The few eminent nineteenth-century feminists—such as Concepción Arenal and Emilia Pardo Bazán—did not overtly defend women's political rights, although they came to demand the recognition of women as individuals who are not exclusively defined by their gender function as mothers and wives. Spanish feminism tended to fundament its justification for women's rights on the idea of gender difference and maternalism and focused on civic and social rights for women rather than equality with men. This insistence on civic and social rights rather than political prerogatives must be attributed not only to the weakness of the liberal and democratic political systems in Spain but also to the predominance of the ideology of domesticity and the social construction of gender roles.

Mainstream feminist thought was based on gender difference and the projection of women's social role as wife and mother to the public arena. Although it did not come to question women's gender definition as a mother, it represented, to some extent, a questioning of one of the basic parameters of the ideology of domesticity, that is, women's restriction to the private sphere. This questioning of the separation of public and private and the redefinition of women's spaces within the confines of both were eventually to facilitate the legitimacy of a more public, individual, and egalitarian discourse in the formulation of Spanish feminism. Significantly, the Catalan promoter of women's rights, Dolors Monserdà, understood feminism as a struggle both to attain women's rights and to perfect women's mission in the family and society. Feminism's aim was to "work for the improvement of women, for the defense of her rights, to protest against the vexations and injustices perpetrated against her, and, finally, for the perfection of her mission in the family and society."[94]

Although the discourse of gender difference prevailed and feminist claims were articulated from a socio-familial context, the components of Spanish feminism were quite complex. Although it was not based on equality with men, through its diverse channels feminism's growth encompassed collective political rights through its reclamation of collective social rights vis à vis its link with the Catholic social reform movement, and nationalist demands in the case of the Basque country and Catalonia.[95] These varied formulations, at times, achieved a redefinition of the terms of equality and difference, political and social, public and private. The historical construction of feminism in Spain is characterized through its diverse women's groups by its specific redefinition in contrast with other, foreign definitions of feminism.

Many of the women's movements in early twentieth-century Spain were actively involved in the Catholic reform movement and thus redefined a version of feminism more in consonance with their ideological convictions. Dolors Monserdà, in line with the political and ideological parameters of the Catalan nationalist movement and the Catholic reform in which she was active, redefined the term "feminist" in her 1907 study, *Estudi feminista*. She explicitly rejected the lay, secular, and alien cultural basis of British and American feminism and redefined her version of feminism in keeping with traditional Catalan values.[96] As she proclaimed, the specific goal in writing her book on feminism was to counteract the effect of an alien feminism that "flourishes in lay centers where, under the promise to improve women's lives, subversive, tremendously demoralizing doctrines are expressed; because they change the principles and fundamental truths of Religion, Family and Society."[97]

Anticlericalism and a severe critique of religion, were, in contrast, the basis of another current of feminism that flourished in republican and freethinking circles. Angeles López Ayala was the major promoter of this view of feminism in the late nineteenth century and, in numerous publications, such as *El Libertador, Periódico defensor de la mujer y órgano nacional del Librepensamiento*, and *El Gladiador del Librepensamiento*, favored the emancipation of women through their release from the restrictions imposed on them by the Church and religion.[98] Republican women were quite active in Catalonia, Andalusia, and Madrid in the early twentieth century but remained within the framework of social feminism. They understood that women's franchise was not an immediate demand of feminism due, among other reasons, to the conservative influence of the Catholic Church on women's vote.[99]

The harmonious union of working and middle-class women within a highly stratified social hierarchy was the aim of the fairly widely extended Catholic women's movement in Spain, promoted by the Catholic reformist María de Echarri, a work inspector and member of the Institute for Social Reform. According to her view of women's emancipation, women were to work in interclassist harmony, in a "great social family" described by Echarri as a stratified society "where there are no animosities, where no vengeance exists, but rather those above protect those below and those below respect and love their superiors."

The stated goal of the Catholic women's movement was to combat the growth of a "socialism without God, with no respect for the divine or the human" and to promote social harmony within a socially stratified society.[100] Although conservative in outlook and openly defensive of traditional gender values, these women, at the same time, readjusted their aspirations toward "regeneration" and modernization of Spanish women by providing them with facilities for an adequate education and professional training that would allow them better preparation for their role in society. Their rejection of static, traditional attitudes toward women led them to call for greater educational facilities for women and an upgrading of women's status, but always within the confines of gender roles. Such an attitude did not, however, lead them to question male supremacy or women's fundamental role in society, although it did influence them to seek more educational and job options for women as well as greater acceptance of women's right to paid work. No doubt, too, the articulate, educated, upper-class women involved in the educational endeavors and social reform activities during those years were forging new terrain in the public arena. These women had little room to develop their talents in the public sphere, and the causes of education and Catholic social reform were admissible in their social circles because they conformed to the mores and values of Spanish society.

The mobilization of women within the canons of conservative nationalist discourse and the socio-political projection of women activists offer considerable insights into the actual development of Catalan and Basque nationalism in the early twentieth century as well as the underlying gender construction of national identity.[101] The trajectory of the women's movement in Catalonia shows quite clearly that the classical interpretation of the development of first-wave feminism in areas of greater economic and industrial growth and of a wider middle class is not necessarily valid because, precisely in the two main areas of industrial growth, the Basque country and Catalonia, the movement to promote women was less suffragist and had a conservative nationalist and Catholic reformist grounding. Undoubtedly, the growth of both the Emakume Abertzale Batza, the Basque women's organization modeled on the Irish women's nationalist organization Cumann na mBan, and the Catalan nationalist women's movement[102] must be placed in the wider context of the development of nationalist movements in both regions.[103] The Catalan movement generated collective interest in the promotion of women and acted as a forum for the construction of a type of feminism based on Catalan cultural identity, a decisive component in this regional form of feminism.

Furthermore, in Catalonia, the development of the women's movement is also linked to the struggle for the modernization of the State, including its socio-economic structures. This struggle in turn led to a growing interest in the creation of a national Catalan version of the "new modern woman" not only in consonance with the parameters of European modernity but also as the guardian of traditional Catalan cultural values.[104] The modernization of Catalonia was undertaken under the aegis of an ideological framework founded on political conservatism, Catalan nationalism, and Catholic reformism geared to implement and guarantee the political hegemony of the Catalan bourgeoisie, reduce class tensions in the highly conflictive Barcelona, and mobilize all the population in an interclassist Catalan nationalist movement. Women of the Catalan bourgeoisie, such as Dolors Monserdà and Francesca Bonnemaison, had a specific interest in promoting a line of "feminism" that corresponded to their political interests. In their agenda, priority was given to mobilizing women to the cause of conservative Catalan nationalism and the establishment of working-class women's organizations in conjunction with the Catholic reformists.

From 1910 on, the cultural vision of women changed in accordance with modifications in cultural models and the ideological discourse on women, while the development of a new national identity had significant gender connotations. Major Catalan political leaders like Enric Prat de la Riba clearly expressed the importance of women's involvement in the formulation of Catalan national identity through their socialization of children and as guardians of the family. Catalan women were quite aware of the importance of that role and the need for specific preparation and cultural training in that regard.

Significantly, one of the major Catalan women's journals, *Or y Grana*, published in 1906 under the auspices of the Catalan movement, Solidaritat Catalana, was subtitled "An Autonomist Weekly for Women, Promoter of a Patriotic League for Ladies." *Or y Grana* ("Gold and Red," the colors of the Catalan flag) claimed that it was the "female incarnation of patriotic sentiments," while the "Patriotic League for Ladies" linked the development of the fatherland to the family and thus to women as the basic nurturers of both family and fatherland. Its manifesto declared: "The foundation of the Fatherland is the Family; the foundation of the Family is woman. Catalan women: by upholding the Fatherland we uphold the Family. By upholding the home we uphold love."[105]

Although conservative from a political perspective, the Catalan movement for the promotion of women came to question some gender norms and behavior and demanded women's access to the public arena and public recognition of women's social position. Catalan women argued for social rights for women. They demanded a reconceptualization of women's work, while at the same time claiming women's rights to professional training and adequate wages.

This movement also played a crucial role in the improvement of educational opportunities for women in Catalonia. As we have already seen, their educational drive was partly oriented toward upper middle class girls; however, priority was given to professional training for girls in the new female white-collar professions in the fields of commerce and office work. The Institut de Cultura i Biblioteca Popular de la Dona, initiated by Catalan women, was undoubtedly the major educational establishment in Spain providing modern professional training for girls of lower middle class and working-class origin. The feminization of office work and the inevitable fact that many women were obliged to earn a living led the Institut (1910-1936) to offer a general cultural, domestic, and professional education to girls that prepared them for jobs and an active role in civil society. It did not, however, question the gender role of domesticity and accepted differentiated gender roles.[106]

Catalan and other Spanish women sought out new grounds on which to base their activities that were compatible with their overall conservative Catholic background. Thus, charitable and social works were also a focal point on their agenda. At a number of newly created female working-class associations, such as the Federation of Needle Workers and the Syndical Federation of Female Workers, paternalistic efforts to improve the working conditions of women were mingled with an ideological message based on class harmony, political conservatism, and Catholic ethics. These women also promoted the celebration of the First Congress on Home Work held in Barcelona in 1917, among other activities.[107] This movement, then, was not characteristically suffragist, as it did not present a broad commitment to the principle of sexual equality or political enfranchisement for women. Yet, from a gender perspective, many activist Catalan women were openly critical of predominant norms that limited women's horizons and obliged them to assume a subordinate role in society. They held an active role in Catalan society, in cultural, educational, and social forums. They clearly resisted women's confinement to prescribed roles within the home and family and actually developed an acute feminist critique of gender restrictions by occupying the public arena. Although *Or y Grana* supported a more traditional gender role for women, one of its title pages showed a powerful caricature by Junoy of a giant lady leading a tiny man by a lead.[108] Imagery at times depicted fear of greater feminist demands.

Female cultural identity was based on clear-cut gender differentiations of masculinity and femininity. Although, on the whole, claims for feminist rights continued to be articulated on the basis of gender difference, their development in the context of a political struggle for nationalist rights and the modernization of Catalonia eventually led to a public platform and, to some extent, to their being acknowledged as "political rights."

Although women's role in the nationalist movement was based on differential gender roles to claim women's emancipation, the formulation of feminist demands through the filter of nationalism gave a more political content to women's rights and led to a more egalitarian discourse in the late 1920's. Feminism and an awareness of cultural identity thus forged a new definition of the parameters of gender relations.

Other organizations such as the Asociación Nacional de Mujeres Españolas (National Association of Spanish Women) and the more radical Liga Internacional de Mujeres Ibéricas e Hispanoamericanas (International League of Iberian and Hispanoamerican Women) and Cruzada de Mujeres Españolas (Spanish Women's Crusade) were more convincingly suffragist and feminist in their approach.[109] The Asociación Nacional demanded an end to legal discrimination of married women, access to posts in accordance with the "moral and material interests of her sex," and equal rights to promotion and wage parity. This organization, which defended female political franchise, was founded in 1918 and survived until 1936. Although a minority organization, it purported innovative feminist policies over the years. In 1934, it attempted to create a feminist political party and then to sponsor its own female candidate in the Popular Front elections of 1936. By then, however, the more radical feminist positions of some of the organization's members were no longer supported by the majority.

Carmen de Burgos, a schoolteacher and prolific writer, was the principal leader of the Cruzada and the Liga, organizations that were similar in political orientation to the Anglo-American suffragist movement.[110] Writing in 1927, de Burgos classified Spanish feminism in three groups: Christian feminism; revolutionary feminism, which looked to socialism as the means to achieving women's emancipation; and independent feminism, with which she herself identified. De Burgos had been a member of the Women's Socialist Madrid Group on two occasions but felt that socialist dedication to women was insufficient. She did not agree with the conventional opinion in socialist circles that socialism automatically implied the liberation of women.[111] De Burgos advocated sexual equality, egalitarian relations between the sexes based on political franchise, an end to the legal discrimination of women, equity in jobs and wages, and the establishment of a divorce law. She did not foresee separatist working organizations for women but rather advocated women's participation in the existing structures of the socialist trade unions. Her rejection of paternalistic policies toward women workers is in sharp contrast to the protective legislation defended by reformers of all political colors and by socialist Margarita Nelken.[112]

By the 1920's, an organized feminist movement was beginning to develop in Spain. However, as a collective endeavor, it was not at all comparable to the vast mobilizations of the first wave of feminism in other countries. This incipient phase of an organized collective movement was promoted by a small elite of women who were not all overtly suffragist in their demands. The feminist movement covered a wide spectrum in its objectives, policies, and strategies, which ranged from demands for education and work facilities to the right to vote to a redressal of discriminatory laws.

In Spain, as in some other European countries, feminism was a social rather than a political issue, and for a long time, women tended to internalize traditional norms and so considered politics and the public arena as alien to them.[113] Although, by the late 1920's, political feminism based on the principle of equality and franchise had become more clearly formulated, the feminist movement constituted a clear minority with very little capacity to undertake collective mobilizations on issues such as the vote. Thus, when political franchise was granted to women in 1931 by the new democratic republican regime of the Second Republic, its concession cannot be attributed to the pressure of suffrage groups, although they did achieve some resonance, but rather to the overall revision of legislation undertaken with the establishment of the new democratic regime.

Although there had been some prior political initiatives to introduce a restrictive female franchise, women were not conceded the vote until 1931.[114] Even then, there were enormous discrepancies among women about the immediate political validity of women's suffrage. Despite the theoretical commitment to equality and women's political rights, significantly, two of the three women deputies then in Parliament (Victoria Kent of the Radical Socialist Party and Margarita Nelken of the Socialist Party) disagreed with the enfranchisement of women at that particular moment on the grounds of political expediency, as they feared women would make a conservative use of their political rights. However, the parliamentary deputy of the Radical Party, Clara Campoamor, made a brilliant defense of women's suffrage in the Parliament, illustrating the growing adherence to the principle of equality and the concession of political rights to women. Female voting patterns in the 1930's have yet to be systematically studied. However, it is quite clear that the female vote was not consistently conservative, as women's vote was decisive in the victory of the Popular Front in the February 1936 elections.[115]

In the course of the Second Republic, women benefitted from the passage of substantial reform legislation. Maternity insurance plans, labor legislation, education reform, civil marriage laws, and the establishment of divorce, together with the abolition of regulated prostitution, constituted undoubted advances in the overall situation of women.[116] Although gender structures were not overtly questioned, the modernization of the State, the development of political democracy, the secularization of education, and the growing participation of women in the organized working-class movement were all conducive to the development of women's consciousness and a reevaluation of their social status. For the first time, a small elite of women had access to important political and administrative positions, while others benefitted somewhat from the new cultural trends and modernization of Spanish society.

Women's position in Spanish society was undoubtedly less disheartening than it had been at the opening of the century. Nonetheless, even under this democratic regime, discriminatory procedures still prevailed and the patriarchal mentality was even slower to change. The social upheaval of the Civil War would present a new, invigorating context which, as we shall see, in some fields acted as a catalyst to accelerate social and gender changes, while providing a different environment favorable to women's mass mobilization.

▪ **2** ▪

Revolution and Antifascist Resistance: Women in Revolutionary Imagery and Rhetoric

Until recently, the abundant historiography on the Civil War had a macro-historical perspective, with politics and economics, military strategy, and international diplomacy providing the key to its comprehension.[1] Historiographical advancements in recent years have led to a revision of interpretative schemes once considered valid for all of Spain; recent studies have tended to elaborate a more regional approach in their focus, thereby generating a wider understanding of the complexity of the phenomena of war and revolution in the different regions of Spain.

In spite of these changes with respect to geographical terrain that have resulted in the adoption of a micro-historical approach, traditional perspectives continue to predominate. With the exception of the specific conference focusing on women in the Civil War held at Salamanca in 1989, few papers presented at the numerous conferences on the fiftieth anniversary of the Civil War introduced gender issues, which have been practically ignored by mainstream historiography.[2] Thus, if we wish to focus our analysis on the terrain of everyday life, such as the changes in value systems and the norms of conduct related to women, we find that our knowledge is extremely fragmentary and it is difficult to articulate a comparative discussion from a gender perspective. One cannot be surprised by this situation, given the fact that Spanish historiography has only recently incorporated a social history approach to its studies and has practically overlooked the contribution of women's history.[3]

There are considerable intrinsic obstacles involved, as it is extremely difficult to gain access to documentary material that illustrates the social dimension. The outcome of the Civil War and the ensuing years of repression led to the destruction and disappearance of great quantities of documentation from ministerial archives, from archives of union and political parties, and from private and personal records. Moreover, the political nature of the conflict induced both participants and later historians to focus on the public sphere and to ignore aspects of everyday life and survival.

The development of Spanish historiography in the past decades accounts for several specific characteristics in the treatment of the Civil War period. Historians opposed to the Franco regime tended to concentrate their research on the 1930's as a demonstration of opposition to the dictatorship; this allowed them to highlight former models of democracy or working-class resistance as legitimate political goals. The need to overcome the collective amnesia regarding the democratic Second Republic and the Civil War due to repression and historical studies under the Franco dictatorship fostered many studies on these subjects. Present-day historians have become increasingly aware of the politicization of the historians and writers who have written about the Spanish Civil War, a factor that had undoubtedly led to a certain mythification of the people, events, and changes undertaken.[4] Current historical studies reviewing this period suggest the need to revise the predominant interpretative scheme, which viewed the Civil War as an absolute breaking point with the democratic regime of the 1930's and the beginning of a social revolution.[5] As one historian has observed, "The CNT-FAI (the anarchist movement, Confederación Nacional del Trabajo/Federación Anarquista Ibérica) confused the social collapse that accompanied the revolution with the revolution itself."[6] In the same way, historians have become more aware of the need to differentiate between appearances and social reality and to establish the boundaries between the dynamics of revolution and social transformation.

The extent of the changes that came about in this period must be appraised with an understanding of women's position at the time and explored within an analytical framework that accounts for factors of continuity as well as constituents of change. If shifts of mentality, cultural values, or gender relations are to be addressed, historical analysis must go beyond a presentation of political policies and discourses or legislative changes, while together with well-known women, ordinary women's lives and experience must be explored. Without denying the importance of political and ideological discourse as indicators of innovative change, notwithstanding methodological and documentary difficulties, women's experience in both public and private spheres must be addressed and political and ideological statements contrasted with social reality. Rereading gender discourse and the cultural representations of women can illuminate the global dimensions of women's collective experience while at the same time accounting for its achievements and limitations.

Focusing on factors of change and continuity does not imply a lack of acknowledgement of female agency and women's accomplishments. Rather, it allows us to reflect more accurately on the degree and limitations of change in women's lives and the extent to which current perception of a feminist agenda can cause initiatives such as the ongoing drive for adult women's education to appear insignificant when, in fact, it represents a gigantic change in the context of the time, or, on the contrary, distort the reality of measures that actually were of little consequence to women, such as revolutionary rhetoric or the regulation of voluntary abortion (December 1936). Social transformation constitutes a dynamic process that is not necessarily lineal; if feminism is perceived as a social movement and an ongoing process, then patterns of change must be pursued in the specific context of its historical background, in this case, in the background of war and potential revolution.

The Nature of the Conflict

In April 1931, the outcome of the elections led to an overwhelming victory for republican forces in the major cities of Spain. Given these results, King Alfonso XIII abdicated, thus ending the traditional monarchy in Spain. The newly established political regime was proclaimed a republic, the Second Republic. Furthermore, it was groundbreaking politically, as it established a democratic system. The new democratic constitution (1931) proclaimed the principles of equality and human rights. Its democratic laws contrasted sharply with the former dictatorship of Miguel Primo de Rivera (1923-1929), which had restricted political and social rights.

The first two years of the Second Republic under the leadership of republican Manuel Azaña, a progressive reformist republican and socialist coalition government ruled. Decisive reforms in many crucial areas were introduced in this period, although they were later to be considered insufficient by those who had heralded the coming of the Second Republic as the beginning of a social revolution.[7] What has been described as the Republic of the "New Deal" undertook an overall reformist policy geared to the modernization of Spanish society.[8] Major socio-political problems inherited from former regimes were confronted with mixed results. In the midst of economic difficulties, social conflict, and political polarization, the government tackled agrarian and military reform, the separation of Church and State, a solution to the autonomy claims of historical nationalist regions such as Catalonia and the Basque country, labor legislation, and educational reform.[9] In the 1933 elections, a swing to the right restored political hegemony to the conservatives and the process of reform slowed considerably.[10]

The offensive against the progressive reforms undertaken by the former government, mounted by the newly elected Right, led to a growing radicalization of the labor movement. At the same time, anarchist opposition, together with the more radical sectors of the socialist movement, adopted a less conciliatory strategy of resistance and collective bargaining in labor conflicts compared to the former two-year period of social reform.[11] However, the social and political polarization that led to an increase in social conflicts culminating in the Asturian Revolt in 1934, when the coal-mining community attempted to promote a social revolution, may be attributed not only to the tense political situation but also to numerous social and economic factors, such as increased unemployment and the contention of welfare and social reforms.[12] Political polarization and the accentuation of social and political conflicts can also be attributed to the breakdown in traditional political representation of class interests among different social sectors due to the deterioration of the economic situation in some regions and to the fact that economic development was constrained by the international economic crisis of the early thirties.[13]

Again, regional differences must be taken into consideration.[14] In Catalonia, the months before the military rebellion were fairly tranquil. The victory of the Popular Front in the February election of 1936 signified a renewal of the reformist policies of former years; amnesty was granted to political prisoners, the Catalan Parliament reopened, and agrarian reform was renewed.[15]

Spain was governed by a republican government, this time without a socialist coalition. In the spring of 1936, social tension increased and there were numerous strikes and lockouts. Many conflicts were resolved by reciprocal violence between owners and workers rather than through legal channels. Military and right-wing interests conspired to oust the democratic regime while at the same time developing contacts with international fascism. Conflictive situations were used by Rightist propaganda to destabilize and discredit the government and provoke political changes, although the degree of conflict and social tension undoubtedly has been exaggerated in many accounts of this period.[16]

Present-day historiography has proved the falsity of the allegation made by the Right at the time and later propagated by Francoist historians that the military uprising was undertaken in order to counteract communist conspiracy and revolutionary change by the government of the Second Republic. Indeed, although there was a degree of social tension during the years of the Republic, the republican governments never attempted to introduce anything but typical democratic reforms. The claim that there was a revolutionary process underway before the military rebellion is totally unfounded, and, as a recent study has pointed out, even the Popular Front government did not develop radical social or economic policies.[17] The strikes and conflicts encouraged by the two major wings of the Spanish labor movement, the anarcho-syndicalist union Confederación Nacional del Trabajo (CNT) and the socialist trade union Unión General de Trabajadores (UGT), did not at all converge in a concerted strategy to achieve revolutionary change in Spanish society. Rather, these were disconnected incidences stemming mainly from the social situation and determined only incidentally by factors such as political confrontation between Right and Left, although Spanish society was undoubtedly riven by a plurality of conflicts related to work, labor conditions, education, and agrarian reform.

On July 18, 1936, the military uprising initiated by General Francisco Franco against the democratic Republic began in North Africa and immediately spread to the peninsula. This coup d'etat was instigated by a group of conspirators who were mostly military, but it was also backed by a variety of right-wing political contenders such as Bourbon monarchists, Carlist supporters of the Pretender to the Throne, Don Carlos, Catholic traditionalists, and *falange*, fascist followers. Their objective was to eliminate the democratic regime and restore political power to the hands of the traditionally hegemonic Right. However, the military coup failed, due to popular resistance, and brought about a civil war.

While the war lasted, the construction of the "New State" under the authoritarian formula prescribed by Franco unified the Right. The republican side undertook the complex task of antifascist resistance, while in some regions anarchists, dissident Marxists, and some sectors of the socialist Left promoted revolutionary change.[18] In contrast to republican, centrist socialist, and communist policy, these more radical forces sought to combine the antifascist war with significant changes to the political, social, and economic structures of Spanish society. In fact, the actual military rebellion and its short-term failure created the historical conditions that led to the undertaking of a revolutionary process within the context of antifascist resistance and in defense of the democratic republican regime. The mobilization of the people in arms led some more radical sectors of the population to combine antifascist resistance with revolutionary struggle. Moreover, the Civil War acted as a catalyst by mobilizing Spanish people into a political involvement far beyond the usual bounds of indifference regarding everyday political life. However, it is also true that for many, mere geographical circumstances of being in a region under republican or Franco control compelled them to an involvement in one or another of the opposing forces. Under these circumstances, women found themselves catapulted into new agency in the social and political arena.

Just as any historical explanation of the Civil War must be placed in the context of a conflict with roots in former periods, so, too, an analysis of female protagonism in the war must also take into account former historical conditioning, since women's socio-political consciousness was time- and culture-bound. It is true that the social condition of women had improved significantly during the Second Republic. The reform policies undertaken at that time had led to the elimination of a considerable part of the discriminatory legislation that had maintained female subordination in politics, labor, and the family. The concession of rights in these three areas, together with educational reform, was an important step toward securing the social and political advancement of Spanish women.

Initially, however, the social reality of women changed only slightly. Occupational segregation, wage discrimination, and the traditional opposition to female wage labor continued while, due to the weight of cultural gender norms, only a small number of women took advantage of their political rights to challenge the male monopoly in politics. In fact, despite ongoing reforms and the modernization of the country, attitudes regarding women were slow to change. Women's cultural and work options and personal and social horizons were still clearly influenced by the weight of a gender discourse of domesticity that reinforced the separation of the public and private spheres and confined women to the domestic world of housework and family. The cult of motherhood and domesticity and the survival of an ideology that saw women primarily as mothers and "angels of the hearth" hindered the effectiveness of the republican reforms and made it enormously difficult for women to penetrate the public sphere and consolidate a visible place in the domain of politics, culture, and work.

Heroines, Combative Mothers, and Mythmakers: The Changing Images of Women

Gender identities are to a large extent consolidated and propagated through the image of women. The cultural representation of women is highly functional in the creation of gender roles and the dissemination of social norms through popular collective imagery. Models of femininity transmitted through the symbolic representation of women in gender discourse can become a decisive manifestation of informal social control in the channeling and maintenance of women in gendered roles. It is quite clear that images and representations do not mirror the complex world of women. Gender discourse and symbolic representations do not necessarily reflect reality. In fact, their normative framework may blur contestation or dissonance in the historical experience of women, obscure their renegotiation of gender contracts and relationships, or distort the reality of women's experience. Nonetheless, cultural representations can give us a clue to the system of ideas against which women had to measure their behavior and to the meanings of their challenges or compliance.[19]

It can be argued that the greater visibility of women, and particularly the wider projection of their image in the scenario of the Spanish Civil War, was not necessarily a mirror of the social reality of Spanish women but rather an example of the complex ways even groundbreaking new images of women or renovative adaptations of more traditional ones could convey a message that did not deeply alter more conventional views of women and gender roles. Nonetheless, the swift modification of images of women in this period plays a significant role in the social construction of gender in times of upheaval and social disruption caused by war and/or revolution.

Although revolutionary/war imagery cannot be viewed as a direct reflection of reality, it may point to readjustments in patterns of social behavior and the representation of gender roles. While a discussion of the cultural representation of the *miliciana* or the forms of women's dress during the war may, at first glance, appear to be frivolous or irrelevant, the construction of gendered cultural and symbolic imagery is crucial to the exploration of women's experience in the war. The Civil War acted as a catalyst for female mobilization and gave rise to a readjustment in attitudes toward women and their social role. The initial stages of the war seemed to promise an immediate change in the treatment of women, as the war generated a new discourse and a different image of them. In contrast to the indifference and inhibition of former years, all the political parties and unions launched a general appeal for female mobilization. Women were no longer told to remain in their homes but rather were urged to get involved in the multiple activities the war effort required in the public arena. Hitherto unappreciated female endeavors in volunteer social work, education, and housework were called to the fore and were conceded new importance as part of the task of reorganizing a society at war. Female virtues of deference and self-effacement were to fall into the background, and women's social involvement was openly demanded for the war effort. In fact, the massive mobilization of the population signified, to varying degrees, a breakdown in the traditional confinement of women to the home and gave them public visibility.

Of course, such a breakdown did not occur throughout all of republican Spain, and there were sharp differences in the patterns of female mobilization and protagonism among the different regions. Changes came about more quickly in urban environments such as Barcelona, Madrid, and Valencia, where the tempo of change was faster due to a higher incidence of progressive social forces. Although there was an extraordinary degree of antifascist activity by women in the Basque country, the war did not precipitate an immediate questioning of the traditional limitations of women's social role, as in some urban areas. In rural Spain, surviving the adverse circumstances of the war, while accentuating the need for women's labor and economic commitment to family subsistence, did not necessarily imply a questioning of traditional modes of behavior or gender structures.

Within republican Spain, the Civil War signified a degree of discontinuity regarding views on the social role of women, although a redefinition of social relations between the sexes and a real questioning of women's gender role was not forthcoming. Nevertheless, the situation had changed. The war against fascism and the revolutionary dynamics brought into play constituted an exciting ambience and a context for potential change for women. Despite traditional constrictions, many women adapted swiftly to a changing scenario and eagerly participated in the struggle against fascism.

During the first months of the war, women were featured frequently in revolutionary and war imagery and rhetoric. There was a significant shift in anarchist, socialist, and republican propaganda, as women were featured in war posters, in war slogans, and in war imagery. Women acquired new dimensions through the emergence of a new social imagery, that is, a symbolic representation through which traditional collective cultural representations of women were modified and renovated.

One of the symbols of the revolution and antifascist resistance in the early fervor of the war was the figure of the *miliciana*, the militia woman. Revolutionary art, seen primarily in war posters, portrayed attractive young girls, with rather masculinized silhouettes, clothed in blue overalls, a style of dress with revolutionary connotations George Orwell so aptly described—guns slung over their shoulders heading off to the front with a determined step and an air of self-confidence.[20] This representation of women was a radical change, projecting the image of an active, purposeful, enterprising woman dedicated to the war effort. The message was crystal clear. Women were to play a crucial role both in organizing the homefront and in fostering male involvement in the military resistance.

In the summer of 1936, the heroic figure of the *miliciana* rapidly became the symbol of the mobilization of the Spanish people against fascism. Women like the young communist activist Lina Odena came to personify antifascist resistance in the war legends. Odena was an outstanding leader of the Juventudes Socialistas Unificadas (JSU), the communist youth movement, and secretary general of the National Committee of Antifascist Women. She fought in the south of Spain in the early weeks of the war and, in September 1936, killed herself when on the point of being captured by Franco's fearsome North African corps of Moorish troops at the Granada front.[21] Her dramatic suicide was usually presented as death in action, and she was constantly evoked as the archetype of female heroism.

Lina Odena had a battalion named after her, while Rosario *La Dinamitera* (the Dynamiter) became part of popular culture through a poem dedicated to her by poet Miguel Hernández.[22] Heroines such as Caridad Mercader, who later died in prison, and other lesser known or anonymous women killed or wounded in the war formed part of the popular legends of courage, resistance, and hope. They exemplified the capacity of the Spanish people to confront the brutal aggression of the fascist rebels. Their heroic deaths were evoked in terms of the "glorious" fight against fascism.[23] War rhetoric in the early period stressed the courage and bravery of those who formed the popular resistance as exemplified by these young heroines.

The belligerent image of the woman combatant in her blue overalls was predominant in the war posters and was presented as more protagonistic than the male images. The posters aggressively urged men to enlist in the popular militias. For example, one well-known poster by artist Arteche shows a militia woman dressed in a blue *mono* (overalls), a gun in her uplifted hand with revolutionary militians marching with their flags in the background. The *miliciana* in the poster persuasively asserts: "The militia needs you."[24] Other posters show *mono*-clad militia women calling on people to fight, to join the revolutionary struggle, or posing among male militians in combat positions.[25] Such images were of undoubted impact precisely because they broke with tradition. They portrayed women in a militaristic, revolutionary, and aggressive light. Furthermore, they were not directed toward a female audience but rather to men, exhorting them to undertake their duty and participate in the antifascist military resistance.

Many foreign observers depicted the experience of the Spanish people in arms.[26] For our purposes, Orwell's description of Barcelona is highly illustrative, for he described not only the political scene but also the signs of change in everyday life and customs, and most important, the tempo of change and of continuity, and the social chronology of the war. Orwell's writings have a representative quality, absent in many other foreign chroniclers of the war, as he was an outsider who strove to be an insider. Despite his lack of knowledge of the language and of Spanish customs, his involvement with the rank and file and his talent for observation allowed him to draw a significant outsider's portrait of the Catalan political scene, as reflected in his masterful chronicle on the Spanish Civil War, *Homage to Catalonia.*

Orwell's sense of detail allowed him to perceive at least outward manifestations of change. In his first visits to Barcelona, he described what he saw as revolutionary fervor and a clear hegemony of the working class. For Orwell, one of the salient elements configuring the proletarian physiognomy of the city was the change in clothing and dress style. His initial impressions of Barcelona in December 1936 were enthusiastic and gave rise to his description of revolutionary Catalonia as the "worker's state" where "practically everyone wore rough working-class clothes, or blue overalls or some variant of the militia uniform."[27] It was a city where "well-dressed" people had disappeared and external appearances indicated a clear predominance of the working class.

In *Homage to Catalonia,* Orwell emphasized clothing as one of the exterior signs indicating the degree of proletarianization of Catalan society and the political dominion of the working class. At that time he thought the revolution was achieved, as evidenced by the visible details of everyday life, social behavior, and clothing. He accepted appearances as real and did not realize, until later, that some people disguised themselves as proletarians and that blue overalls might even be converted into a passing fashion.[28] Orwell himself later pointed out the precariousness of the social changes carried out in the revolutionary restructuring of Catalan society, and by May 1937 he noted that blue overalls had once again given way to bourgeois suits.[29]

How representative were the *milicianas* depicted in revolutionary attire? If for men the change to blue working overalls represented a symbol of political identification, for women the wearing of trousers or *monos* acquired an even deeper significance, as women had never before adopted such masculine attire. So for women, donning the militian/revolutionary uniform not only meant an exterior identification with the process of social change but also a challenge to traditional female attire and appearance. The adoption of male clothing undoubtedly minimized sex differences and could be read as a claim for equal status. However, the women who wore blue overalls were few. They were usually identified with the militia and did not represent a significant sector of the female population. Quite the contrary, the majority of working-class women quickly rejected the *miliciana* in her *mono* and opted for a more traditional style of clothing perceived as being more feminine and respectable.

In Barcelona, overall-clad women were a small minority. The mainstream of active women rejected militian attire. Traditional fashion magazines of the time, such as *El Hogar y la Moda*, made no decisive shift to revolutionary fashions, and, in fact, female clothing differed very little from former years. Women's antifascist magazines, such as *Noies Muchachas*, had sections dedicated to fashions that retained easy-to-make traditional clothing, although in simpler forms.[30] In her memoirs, the young communist leader Teresa Pàmies enthusiastically evoked the freedom the pantaloons-skirt represented for many young women:

> The important, momentous change for us was the pantaloons-skirt, which allowed us to jump on trucks, ride a bicycle, climb up lamp-posts, leave with a "Brigade to Aid the Peasants" or help uncover the ruins...after an air raid.[31]

Small changes in clothing thus reflected extraordinary modifications in women's life experience. Freedom of body movement represented by the pantaloons-skirt was a new experience outside the confines of traditional gender roles.

Few women's organizations condoned the adoption of revolutionary attire by women. Moreover, as early as October 1936, women wearing *monos* were even viewed with distrust and accused of frivolity and coquetry and of following a fashion that had little to do with antifascist or revolutionary commitment: "Women who show off with blue overalls in the city center have confused the war with a carnival. More seriousness is needed. And an end to those magazines which publish photos of women armed with a gun who have never fired a shot in their lives."[32] Later evidence has shown that some bourgeois girls adopted working-class women's clothes as a fashionable trend.[33]

Although Spanish society was, by this time, somewhat more receptive to a changing image of women, the *miliciana* definitely did not constitute the new model of woman associated with antifascist resistance. The sharply aggressive, militant image of the *miliciana* with a Mauser represented only a tiny minority, and for a very brief period of time. The image is associated only with the initial phase of the war and the early enthusiasm created by antifascist and revolutionary fervor. In many ways, the imagery formed part of the spirit of summer vacation and adventure associated with the front line in the months of August and early September 1936. By December 1936, posters and propaganda depicting *milicianas* had disappeared. This, no doubt, had to do with the actual tempo of revolutionary change and the political developments over those months. By then, too, as we will see in another chapter, militia women were no longer evoked as heroines but as disreputable figures who impeded the correct development of the war effort. Furthermore, the image of the *miliciana* publicized in international photo reports had a deleterious effect on European opinion and, indeed, proved a god-send to Franco's propaganda aimed at misrepresenting and distorting women's role in the antifascist resistance.

"Gender-appropriate" behavior, which subscribes to expected social norms of respectable femininity, embodies patterns of beliefs, customs, values, and rules of conduct. Male-defined social conventions are embedded in social structures and cultural norms. Moments of social upheaval and unsettlement facilitate a breakdown of such norms and legitimize changes in behavior. Although in such circumstances women may not be limited to narrowly defined domestic roles, the change might be temporary. It's important, then, that the depth and consistency of changes in social roles and behavior be ascertained. For despite appearances and female expectations, Spanish society was yet to redefine norms of activity and gender-appropriate behavior.

In the initial stages of the Civil War, the innovative imagery of the *miliciana* appeared to be a break with former models of norms and social roles for women. Nonetheless, a further analysis, taking into account both imagery and social reality, indicates that the militia woman was not a genuine new female prototype but simply a symbol of war and revolution. The model projected is not that of a "new woman" who arises from the socio-political context but one created to fill the needs of the war. Indeed, in many ways, Spanish Civil War posters resemble those of World War I both in their representation of women and the message they transmit. Despite the strong female protagonism depicted, they are not necessarily mirrors of reality or a sign of female incorporation into the war effort at the front.

Moreover, the figure of the militia woman was directed toward a male rather than a female audience. She represented a woman who had impact, who provoked because she took on what was considered to be a male role and thus obliged men to fulfill what was at times described as their "virile" role as soldiers. Such an image was effective for propaganda purposes, as it fostered male identification with the antifascist cause. It seduced, enticed, or shocked men into carrying out their military duties. Rather than representing an elaboration of an innovative image of women consonant with a new reality, it appears to have been produced as an instrumentalization of women solely for war purposes. The image inspired the masses to mobilize while challenging male cultural identity and arousing men to assume their traditional patriotic duties to the fatherland.

Few women would have identified with this seductive model. In fact, the aforementioned poster by Arteche offers an insight into the fragility of this attempt to construct a new prototype and image of women combatants. The model who portrayed the militia woman in this poster projected a physical prototype more associated with the facial features of Marlene Dietrich than with Spanish working-class women and was the same model who, in 1934 in the magazine *Crónica*, had illustrated a series of articles as a sex symbol.[34] In contrast to war posters, photos of the time show how most *milicianas* more closely resembled working-class Spanish women, even if they were youthful or attractive. Furthermore, the message of the *miliciana* does not appear to have been addressed to women to urge them to enlist in the *milicias*. The predominant slogan of the time was "Men to the Front. Women to the Homefront," while both war rhetoric and war imagery through the cultural representation of the "Homefront Heroine" insisted on a clearly differentiated gender dedication to the war effort.[35] That is not to say that there was not a new image or consciousness among women or a certain degree of identification, among young women particularly, with this new model of a woman who broke with traditional constraints. However, it is revealing that the posters directed toward women produced by political and union organizations had a more persistent military tone, while those produced by women's organizations focused not on the war but on the rehabilitation and dignity of women.[36]

This militaristic image of the *miliciana* contrasted with the predominant classical image of woman the mother, the nurturer—the authentic homefront heroine. Most images were of mature women portrayed as mothers and wives who worked at the homefront to support the war. The new art form of socialist realism that characterized war posters came to represent a return to the previous traditional images of women. Mother and child images, contrasted with the brutal devastation of war, encouraged people to collaborate in the fight against fascism. War posters evoked more often the traditional image of women as nurturers, healers, auxiliary relief workers, and hospital workers, staying at home looking after the material and moral interests of their loved ones engaged in war on the battlefields. Pathetic portrayals of mothers with savagely injured or dead children were meant to stir other mothers to show solidarity with republican Spain.

Homefront heroines such as wives and mothers dedicated to the antifascist cause constituted the prevailing model for women to imitate. Of course the republican appropriation of the symbol of motherhood was not new. Reverence for and the exaltation of motherhood were omnipresent in Spanish society. It was traditional for women to be addressed as mothers by political organizations. Since the granting of female suffrage in 1931, electoral propaganda of both Right and Left had always made use of the symbol of motherhood and women's identification with their maternal role to draw women to their parties.[37] An appeal to motherhood and the mother's right to defend her children from fascist brutality was a forceful, effective method of mobilizing women. The image of motherhood, and particularly the rights and duties derived from that role, projected onto a social scale became a significant factor in the strategies to mobilize women to the antifascist and revolutionary causes.

Motherhood was a powerful image with which Spanish women identified. The women's organizations of different political tendencies incorporated the symbol of motherhood into their diverse strategies. Women were constantly addressed as mothers and, as such, exhorted to participate in the war effort. They were to fight against fascism in order to protect their children. Both male political propaganda and women's organizations, such as the Agrupación de Mujeres Antifascistas (AMA), portrayed women not as individuals with separate identities but as persons whose cultural identity derived from their biological role as childbearers. Significantly, the membership card of the AMA shows how embedded this concept was, as it linked war and fascism only indirectly to women through their children:

> The characteristic of woman is her constructive spirit and her maternal love; and war and fascism imply destruction and hate. War destroys the home which she created with such tenderness; it murders her husband and her son. And fascism takes away something worth more than life, which is freedom and the desire for improvement which every mother has for her children.[38]

Motherhood evoked not only courage and bravery but also sacrifice. It protected the rights of children. While motherhood was initially used as a symbol of the defensive side of the conflict, it significantly acquired belligerent and combative connotations. Maternity not only implied protection but also sacrificing one's sons for a greater cause. The vital role of mothers was to urge their children to participate in the collective war effort.

> Spanish women want to play a primary role in the struggle against fascism. They played such a role in those first moments when many went with our comrades to the Sierra to face the enemy, imbuing them with their bravery and fortitude....They have done so later in their role as mothers who not only do not hold back their sons but tell them: "Go and die if it is necessary in the trenches, because the people call you, the Fatherland which will be yours, which you are forging with your own blood."[39]

In 1937 and 1938, as the republican side faced increasing difficulties, war rhetoric insisted that mothers provide soldiers for the defense of the Republic. Paradoxically, then, while mothers were urged to reinforce their maternal role, they were also told to risk the lives of their sons. Mothers were inherently proud of their sons, but they were to be even prouder when the moment came for them to fight "in defense of a just cause." According to a popular communist view, victory depended on the attitudes of mothers:

> Victory...will be forged by the sacrifice of those sons whom you had such difficulty bearing, and for whom you have so much hope. This blood which flows so generously is yours; it is the blood of the most generous of our women....To you, then, to your blood, to your flesh, we will owe victory.[40]

This generously borne sacrifice by mothers also purported far-reaching effects in the future. Mothers bore sons who in turn would determine the fate of future generations. As a slogan in the Catalan antifascist women's journal *Companya* put it: "Our sons defend life and the happiness of our grandchildren."[41]

Mothers were to feel involved in the war. They were to promote commitment among the undecided and get them involved in the antifascist resistance. Combative motherhood not only implied the active involvement of mothers in the war effort but gave them moral authority and even compulsion to oblige their sons to fight.[42] It also comprised a universal dimension. The sacrifice, pain, and courage of Spanish women were to be projected to embrace all of suffering humankind, particularly those under other fascist regimes. The defense of the Republic against fascist aggression was conceived as a commitment that would benefit not only Spanish offspring but the children of all the mothers of the world: "Mothers and Women of the World! Our children have to be saved from this strife, our children who do not belong to us mothers, but who are also the hope of mankind."[43]

Combative motherhood was also to forge a collective identity for Spanish women and a common effort for the future. Women identified with this social projection of motherhood on both national and international levels. An article in *Mujeres*, the antifascist women's newspaper, gives an insight into the degree of consolidation of this collective identity with combative motherhood, where women were seen as forming a "vanguard of mothers":

> Women in the Basque Country today form part of a vanguard. It is the vanguard of mothers—mothers who are that for having given to life the generous tribute of other lives, others for their feeling of motherhood.

This vanguard is invincible. Neither life nor death will detain us....We are under a commitment to defeat fascism, to crush it like a harmful animal caught in a snare. And we will carry it out.[44]

Women did not have to be biological mothers to achieve the rank of motherhood; maternal feelings were sufficient. Thus, all women potentially could be defined as mothers. However, biological mothers presented some problems that derived from their protective role, as they were not always willing to induce their sons to enlist and take part in warfare. They were constantly reminded that their sons were not really theirs but belonged to the larger community—to humankind. Such a noble endeavor was considered just compensation for possible loss and bereavement. Many mothers considered the sacrifice of their sons an acceptable, though difficult, duty. As one mother put it:

> With my youngest going away...,I have given to the Fatherland everything that was possible to give. Four sons I had; now three are left defending antifascist Spain and I am left on my own and have to work in order to eat. That's all right. Yes, it is. The blood spilled by one of my sons, whom I will never again see, at the Andalusian front, and the fight of the others to annihilate the invading foreigner are well worth it.[45]

Many of the poignant speeches by the internationally renowned communist leader "Pasionaria" Dolores Ibárruri, the epitome of the brave, courageous, but exacting Spanish mother who enfolded all Spanish men in her maternal embrace, hammered home this message of international solidarity and international expectations and hope from the sacrifice of Spanish sons. Women's antifascist organizations constantly appealed to the mothers of the world to support their cause:

> Mothers and women of the world! Sisters of the countries of the Spanish tongue! Women, all! Do not allow our children to perish with hunger and cold. Respond to our call. Respond with generosity, as the heart of a woman knows how to.[46]

There is a decidedly male tone in war imagery and the representation of motherhood. Mothers' concerns are directed toward their sons and not their daughters. Daughters remain quite invisible in this imagery of motherhood. Daughters were not to be drafted into the military ranks, and thus their contribution to the war effort does not figure visibly and is not outlined. Sons constituted the main concern and were the main thrust within the symbolization of motherhood dedicated to the war effort.

Imagery detailed the pain of war and expressed the outrage and anguish of mothers. However, the "pain" of motherhood was used to urge people to support the republican cause. In a speech to the women of the world, Pasionaria insisted:

"Hear the painful cry of our mothers and our women who walk their mourning through the bloody paths of Spain, which is fighting for peace and the freedom of the world."[47] Women "who know the pain of being a mother" were urged by anarchists to avail themselves of their sacrifice not only to win the war but to change the social structures of society.[48]

Curiously enough, motherhood was also prominent even in discourses that questioned to some degree its fundamental underpinnings. Women were addressed primarily as mothers, even when asked to break with motherhood's proprietary expectations. According to the anarchist women's organization Mujeres Libres, the triumph of the revolution entailed mothers not only fulfilling their task as childbearers but also breaking with the links motherhood implied. Mothers were urged to overcome the limitations of their feeling for their children and home in order to embrace the needs of the community, even of civilization, as part of their dedication to revolutionary change.[49] War and revolutionary endeavor sanctioned a reduction in maternal dedication. As one of the slogans claimed: "The mother who hugs her child to her breast is not a better mother than she who helps to forge a new world!"[50]

This new social image of combative motherhood and homefront heroine was more in keeping with a traditional approximation to Spanish women than was the militia woman. The social projection of motherhood and maternalism constituted an important characteristic of women's historical experience during the war. However, this cultural model also constituted a renovation of the conventional female archetype: the "angel of the hearth." Despite the predominance of apparently traditional models of women engaged in antifascist war efforts, both these cultural representations and the gender role of women were gradually to acquire new connotations over the months as they became politicized and acquired new social relevance within the wider process of popular mobilization. Motherhood became politically charged, while women's traditional roles and skills were attributed a new content, higher status, and firmer purpose. The model of the typical responsible adult woman as mother and nurturer knitting sweaters for soldiers, healing the wounded, and looking after refugees came to symbolize the new social value of women and quickly replaced the more innovative image of the militia woman. This new image was to last for the duration of the war.

Despite the continuity of a more traditional depiction of women, the effect of the war was to transform women's lives and change their expectations and self-image in significant ways. For in the first weeks of the war, women became spontaneously involved in the war effort, breaking with the usual constraints that had kept them isolated from political and social life. The war broadened female agency and opened up new fields of activity to them. Women appeared, unchaperoned, in the streets by the thousands with greater freedom of movement. They engaged in multiple war activities—building barricades, nursing the wounded, organizing relief work, sewing uniforms or knitting sweaters, carrying out auxiliary services, developing educational courses and professional training, and working in transport or in munitions factories.

The war brought new roles to women and expectations for a wider range of activities. Although these were limited and did not break with the gender division of labor, work segregation, or traditional portrayals of women, there was, nonetheless, an opening up of political, cultural, and social horizons. A remarkable plenitude of works and ideas took shape, and, in a break with the stultifying constraints of the past, women were stirred to an immediate participation in antifascist resistance and, for some, revolutionary endeavors.

Thousands of women became decidedly combative in their outlook and activities. Many spokeswomen, particularly of the women's organizations, spoke in terms of the birth of a brilliant dawn full of hope for women. While the participation of women in political activity and the war effort was undoubtedly part of and fomented by a wider process of social change, the dramatic circumstances provoked optimism, even euphoria, and a sense that the tempo of change had accelerated, together with the conviction that change was to affect women specifically. There was a new-found sense of purpose and initiative among women.

The following account of the first moments of the war gives some sense of the naivete, the intense activity, the expectation of change, and the commitment to a social cause:

> Schoolmistresses peeled potatoes, nurses scrubbed floors, maids went in droves to the preparatory classes which had been improvised, the hundred per cent feminists looked after children and hospitals, dressmakers took up the gun; many hurried with their sewing machines to sew uniforms; others made sandwiches and refreshments and established posts at the barricades to offer to the platoons of militians who were off to reconquer towns....The word Revolution had rung and the maid ran to free herself from her ignorance and the dressmaker left the tyranny of the needle to carry out her dream of adventure...,leaving aside the ancestral apathy which the class struggle and social phenomena had always caused her....She did not vacillate and ran decidedly to the streets beside the workers....And she offered her young life, full of youthful hopes, in the first days of the heroic struggle, in which each man was a hero and each woman was the equivalent of a man.[51]

Others, in a more modest tone, praised women's courage and dedication:

> Without lamentations, without running away from danger, without even trying to avoid it, women have helped, have supported their comrades. They have given it all: life, men, sons, brothers and fiancés.[52]

Of course, women's role in the war effort, even in the early months of the war as the above citation shows, was mostly seen as a contribution, a help, or a dedication on a very different level from that of men. And yet again, women's major contribution was seen as that of having contributed their men—husbands, brothers, sons, or fiancés—to the war effort. The point of reference was always the man. As the above citations clearly show, women became heroines when they became the equivalent of men. But women themselves refer to the need to be useful, to play a positive role, and to overcome prejudices and conventional behavior in order to play a decisive part in the war effort.[53] For those who viewed the war as the beginning of a revolutionary process, optimism and the prospect of immediate changes were clearly present. For women, the decisive moment had arrived when

all women were to leave their independence, their home, their life. When all women were to feel the responsibility and creativity of the moment. When all women were to form female unity of triumph and progress.[54]

Indeed, anarchist women were highly optimistic about the possibility of converting anarchist utopian ideals of an egalitarian, non-hierarchical, anti-authoritarian world into a reality, where a non-patriarchal mode of life would challenge gender power relations.[55]

No doubt, a limited number of women identified with the revolutionary struggle. Many, undoubtedly, remained isolated from the war effort and antifascist struggle and devoted themselves to individual survival. However, what is important is the commitment of thousands of Spanish women in the collective endeavor to eliminate fascism. Female popular mobilization took place on a vast scale, as will be seen in the following chapters, and there was an intense burgeoning of activities among ordinary women.

Obviously, more is known about the women who were to gain renown and recognition in politics than about average women. Dolores Ibárruri and Federica Montseny were important figures and mythmakers. The outstanding oratorical talents of communist leader Ibárruri, popularly known as Pasionaria, led not only to her acclamation within communist ranks, but to national and international popularity.[56] Some of the slogans popularized by Ibárruri—"*no pasarán*" ("they will not pass")—became pillars of antifascist propaganda. Indeed, the rather maternal figure of Ibárruri, the miner's daughter from Asturias, came to symbolize working-class mothers in the tragedy of the Civil War. In an analogy, the poet Miguel Hernández saw her as the infinite mother, the voice of working-class Spain:

Through your voice, Spain speaks, the voice of the mountain ranges, of the poor and the exploited, heroes full of palm tree grow and pilots and soldiers die, saluting you.[57]

Ibárruri's vehement stance, charisma, and prodigious humanity captured international attention, while in Spain she became a familiar figure at the front, uplifting the morale of the soldiers, consoling the wounded, and encouraging the resistance to fascism. Ibárruri became an honorary commandant of the Fifth Regiment, and, as a deputy and vice president of the Parliament, she was one of the best known and renowned female politicians. She became one of the great legends of Spanish resistance to fascism, and, on an international level, she symbolized the popular struggle against international fascism and oppression.

The anarchist Federica Montseny was undoubtedly an outstanding counterpart to Ibárruri.[58] Already a prominent leader of the anarchist movement, a prolific writer, and a revolutionary activist, Montseny played a decisive role in the mobilization against fascism and in the revolutionary struggle. Both she and Pasionaria were to symbolize the fight against fascism, but Montseny also was to become the symbol of the revolutionary struggle. Her extraordinary oratorical prowess, her charisma, and her capacity to move the masses made her a decisive figure in the political scenario of the time. Indeed, she was the first woman in Spain to become a minister of the government. In November 1936, she was appointed Minister of Health and Social Assistance by radical socialist Francisco Largo Caballero.

Both Montseny and Pasionaria are remarkable symbols of Spanish women's extraordinary role in the resistance to fascism. Other women of somewhat lesser fame would play significant, visible roles in the war effort. They included the former socialist, then pro-communist Margarita Nelken, who had a women's social trade union group named after her;[59] socialist Matilde Huici; republican Victoria Kent; Catalan Left republican Dolors Bargalló; and anarchist Lucía Sánchez Saornil.[60] Others were to be incorporated into public administration, local councils, and political offices.

The popular mobilization of women involved not only a minority elite of formerly politicized women but, more significantly still, thousands of ordinary Spanish women who committed themselves to the collective endeavor to eliminate fascism. This mass mobilization of women was conducted mainly through gender-specific organizations whose numbers increased dramatically over the war years. Female activism was undertaken on a collective level, and women's organizations designed policies to capture and channel women's energy and potential toward the war effort.

▪ 3 ▪

Women's Organizations During the War

During the Civil War, women's mobilization was channelled through a series of female organizations that reflected the political panorama of republican Spain at that time. These organizations embodied the class polarization and increasing political divisions of society and were characterized by their heterogeneity and tight links to existing political forces. But no universal goals emerged on a gender basis, and the ever-widening rift among political contenders was reflected in the factions among the women's organizations.

Anarchist and dissident Marxist proposals for a combined antifascist and revolutionary fight were sharply contested by communists and socialists who rejected any revolutionary changes and defined war politics exclusively in terms of antifascism. The open confrontation between these political adversaries led to the civil war within the civil war in Barcelona in May 1937 and to the eventual disappearance of anarchists and dissident Marxists from the political arena. Women's organizations felt these disputes acutely, and, despite some attempts at transpolitical collaboration, hostility and contention characterized the relations among communists and socialists vis à vis anarchist and dissident Marxists.

Superficially, there was an apparent harmony of interests and policy among different women's organizations on certain basic issues, such as access to education, work, and involvement in the war effort. However, there was neither a sense of transclass unity among women of different social levels nor an interclass identification with a common social or gender agenda among those who espoused left-wing causes and identified with the working class. Since the plurality marking the political and social scenario was reflected in the women's organizations, overall female concurrence cannot be assumed on either gender or social issues.

There was no cohesive identification based on a common agenda among the women who mobilized in the antifascist cause.

The heterogeneity of women's interests and issues during the Civil War must be recognized. Female associations and mobilization in this period are characterized by their diversity. Although political pragmatism and, even more important, the pressure generated by war needs may have blurred these distinctions and resulted in an apparent commonality of policy, the theory, goals, and resistance strategies on both social and gender issues differed enormously among the major women's organizations. The diversity of interests and proposed strategies coincided to a large degree with the patterns of political confrontation during those years, and, indeed, the adhesion to one or another of the women's organizations can be attributed, in part, to an individual's prior identification with existing political tendencies rather than to gender-specific factors.

Of course, women mobilized from a different social position than men, and this difference was to shape goals, programs, and strategies and imbue them with a distinctive gender content. Nevertheless, gender issues and content were not primary or crucial to the programs and strategies of all the women's organizations at all times. Thus, the chronology and changing tempo of war and revolution must be taken into account, and their effects can be observed in the fading of specific gender issues in moments of increasing pressure during the war. Some organizations expressed a firm and cohesive feminist policy right from the start, while, for others, gender issues were merely accessory to the overall goal of antifascist struggle.

Men were not mobilized through male antifascist organizations but through the usual channels of political affiliation, the work force, and military recruitment. Men were already involved in the public domain and therefore were not marginalized from political affairs as women were. Thus, it was unnecessary to promote male organizations in order to recruit men for the war effort, as cultural norms of the time defined the army and even the militia as male organizations. In contrast, in order to mobilize women, new organizational channels had to be developed, mostly by women themselves, attempting women's integration into the antifascist struggle and establishing their role in the conflict. In fact, one of the salient features of the war was this new-found militancy and combativeness among women who refused to be kept apart from the antifascist resistance movement. Women's allegiance to antifascism provided the impulse to coordinate and harness female energy to the antifascist cause, while commitment for some went beyond those bounds to embrace revolutionary change and women's emancipation.

Women's Popular Front: Women's Allied Antifascist Organizations

During the war, a cluster of the most important women's organizations formed a united front: Agrupación de Mujeres Antifascistas (AMA); its Catalan equivalent, Unió de Dones de Catalunya (UDC); and the youth organizations Unión de Muchachas (UM) and the Catalan Aliança Naçional de la Dona Jove (ANDJ). The communist-inspired Antifascist Women's Organization (AMA) existed before the military uprising but was revitalized and further developed during the war years. Created in 1933 under the auspices of the Spanish Communist Party (PCE), by 1934, within the general change of strategy of the Third International, the communist-oriented International Workingmen's Association, to favor Popular Front policy, the initial Spanish organization of antifascist women, Women against War and Fascism, had developed links with the international organization. In August 1934, the AMA participated in the International Congress of Women against War and Fascism in Paris. By this time, the Spanish organization had held activities and demonstrations against war and military policy. Members of the AMA took an active part in support of the miners' families involved in the Asturian revolt in October 1934,[1] when the mining community attempted to establish a social revolution. Repressed immediately, the organization kept up its relief work under the cover of another organization, Pro Infancia Obrera (Pro Working-Class Children).

During the 1936 elections, the organization actively supported the Popular Front candidates and increased its membership. With the military uprising and the onset of war, the organization, by then known as the Agrupación de Mujeres Antifascistas, extended throughout republican Spain. By the summer it had more than 50,000 affiliates,[2] and in February 1937 a second national committee was set up in Bilbao for the area of the Basque country.[3] During the three years of the war, provincial committees were founded in Asturias, Toledo, Cuenca, Valencia, Madrid, Guadalajara, Castellón, Almería, Murcia, and Córdoba, and more than 255 local associations were established.[4]

The immediate purpose of the AMA was to integrate Spanish women to the antifascist cause and to promote the predominance of the Spanish Communist Party (PCE) among women.[5] The AMA's strategy to defeat fascism was based on the creation of a national alliance of women under the common objective of the total elimination of fascism.[6] In accordance with PCE strategies on the political scenario and with a strong resemblance to the policies of the PCE youth movement, from the outbreak of the war the AMA purported to become a women's Popular Front and, thus, the only legitimate transpolitical umbrella organization of antifascist women.[7] It claimed to be open to women of all political tendencies as well as to non-politicized women. According to a report by the AMA's secretary general, Encarnación Fuyola, antifascist unity constituted the top priority of the organization:

> The movement of antifascist women was born under the sign of unity, of all the antifascist organisms and for women without parties too. No political tendency should predominate in it. No partisan policy is carried out in our committees. The union of all working for a common objective guarantees a firm antifascist policy.[8]

Although Fuyola acknowledged that the union of all women was a guarantee that the non-politicized women would not be imposed on by partisan policies and programs, she did admit that the core of the organization was constituted by the women who belonged to political parties.[9] In fact, although Fuyola herself categorically denied it, the AMA constituted a female Popular Front under communist control.[10]

The AMA's constituency encompassed communist, socialist, and republican women as well as the Catholic Basque republicans. Women involved in the political parties who were identified with the Popular Front formed the core of the organization. The AMA particularly cultivated the presence of Catholic republicans in the antifascist organization in the Basque country as an indication of the plurality and transpolitical nature of its organization. At a local level, the AMA does show that, at times, women of diverse political affiliations were members. Thus, in reply to a query from a group of women in a small town who wanted to call their group the "Libertarian Antifascist Committee," the Provincial Committee of the AMA instructed them that any specific political orientation was inadmissible in their organization and thus could not be reflected in the name of a local group.[11] Moreover, the AMA was a national organization that applied a strict uniformity of policy, organization, and discipline to which local groups were required to comply.

Many of the local groups had members of diverse political affiliation, such as was the case of the small town of Godella in the Valencia region. It had a total of 102 members, of whom 43 were non-party, 35 were affiliated with the Unión General de Trabajadores (UGT), 12 were communist members of the PCE, 7 were affiliated with the anarcho-syndicalist union Confederación Nacional del Trabajo (CNT), 2 belonged to the communist youth organization Juventudes Socialistas Unificadas (JSU), while there was 1 member each of the Catalan republican Left and the Federal Party.[12] Nonetheless, the fragmentary documentation available also points to a more general pattern of local groups composed almost exclusively of UGT and UGT-PCE members.[13]

The AMA's claim to be a multi-partisan organization encompassing both politicized and non-politicized women was valid, to some degree, as many of its members were also affiliated with communist, socialist, and republican parties. Still, the core of the organization was composed of women involved in Popular Front parties. The AMA's claim to be a representative organization also requires further review. For although the rank and file was indeed composed of women of diverse political orientation, the AMA was the vehicle for orthodox communist mobilization of Spanish women, and the direction, programs, and policies of the organization show a definite communist focus.

At a local level, the composition of the committees reflects political plurality, but with a much greater incidence of socialists and communists. For example, in the Levante region in southeastern Spain, there were more socialists than communists among the rank and file members in UGT.[14] But at a local leadership level, an analysis of a series of committees in this same region shows a clear hegemony of members of the PCE and the communist youth organization, JSU, in positions of authority.[15] More significant, however, is the high incidence of communist women in the provincial and national committees, which, given the hierarchical nature of the organization and the strict control exercised by the national and provincial committees, were highly influential organs of power.[16] Local groups did not have autonomy. They followed policy directions and guidelines from above and were also obliged to send regular detailed reports on their activities, members, and agenda to their superior committees.[17]

Dolores Ibárruri, the prominent communist leader known as La Pasionaria, presided over the National Committee. Although there was significant representation on the committee of communist, pro-communist socialist, and socialist members, along with a few republican delegates, the direction of the AMA was quite clearly in the hands of the Communist Party. A further indication of Ibárruri's powerful influence and of her charisma, so useful for propaganda purposes, is that one of the antifascist women's newspapers, published in Valencia, was called *Pasionaria*. The three general secretaries were also prominent communists: Lina Odena, leader of the communist youth organization JSU; Encarnación Fuyola, member of the PCE; and Emilia Elías, member of the Women's Commission of the Communist Party Central Committee. The two propaganda booklets published on the AMA were written by Elías and Fuyola.[18]

During the Civil War, on an internal level, the Communist Party centered its main activities related to women on developing the antifascist women's organizations. In contrast to its lack of interest in and dismissal of women's issues in the early thirties, the PCE paid considerable attention to women during the war years.[19] However, the Communist Party was unsuccessful in attracting a mass female membership. According to official sources, it had a membership of 4,203 women in 1938.[20] Nevertheless, the party penetrated the mass women's antifascist organization and channelled its activities to fulfill its own goals for female antifascist mobilization. The internal documentation of the AMA shows its close link with the PCE, while communist reports openly acknowledge the party's overt manipulation of the antifascist women's organization.[21] A report to the Provincial Committee of the Communist Party in Madrid explained that the agitation and propaganda section of the Women's Committee of the PCE Provincial Committee had published more than 420,000 propaganda items (such as posters and leaflets) inciting women to work in factories and on farms. It concluded by saying: "Six assemblies were celebrated, drawing over 30,000 women. This job, although done by the party, was carried out *under the name of* Mujeres Antifascistas."[22]

Together with the Unió de Dones de Catalunya (UDC) and the youth organizations, the AMA did in fact become the major women's organization of the time. It is impossible to ascertain the exact number of women affiliated, although it was probably in the region of 60,000 to 65,000. According to an approximation by Dolors Piera, the Catalan communist leader closely associated with its development, the Catalan antifascist organization (UDC) had between 30,000 and 40,000 members in 1938.[23]

What is significant is the fact that the antifascist women's organizations also mobilized many thousands of women who did not necessarily become affiliated with the AMA but did participate in temporary antifascist activism under its auspices. Despite some initial success in attracting apolitical women, particularly housewives, to the local branches, it appears that the organization was not very successful at attracting such women for permanent involvement in its activities.[24] As late as December 1938, the AMA Executive Committee admitted that the organization consisted primarily of women associated with political parties, while non-party women such as workers, housewives, and intellectuals had been neglected in its propaganda efforts.[25]

The heterogeneous membership of the antifascist women's organization at times led to discrepancies in policy and priorities. Particularly vociferous was a group of prominent socialist women that included Matilde Huici, Matilde Cantos, and Matilde de la Torre.[26] However, the weakness of the socialist women's caucus, along with the disintegration of a cohesive women's socialist policy during these years, undoubtedly debilitated the socialists' position within the AMA and prevented their influencing the movement's direction to any ostensible degree.[27] Of course, socialist women's organizations did not disappear during the Civil War. Female socialist groups, such as the Star of Civilization in the small town of Navas de San Juan, in Jaen, Andalusia, created in 1931 to educate women in their social duties as well as to organize women workers,[28] continued to be active during the Civil War, although the available documentation shows few innovative activities undertaken during this period that were specific to women.[29]

Evidence also seems to indicate that some specific socialist women's groups disbanded and fused into local socialist organizations, but it is impossible to determine whether this became a general pattern.[30] Although the socialist press did give sporadic coverage to the activities of women's groups, and in the spring of 1937 the socialist paper *Claridad* inaugurated its first weekly page dedicated to women, there was no concerted drive by socialist women to design new strategies and programs to respond to this new period of war and revolution and potential change for women.[31] So at a time when women in the orthodox Spanish Communist Party (PCE), in the dissident communist party, the Partido Obrero de Unificación Marxista (POUM), and in the anarchist movement were striving to form specific female organizations, the development patterns of the socialist women's groups were quite distinct.

As their main forum of active expression was the AMA, the socialist women were undoubtedly in a subordinate position within the direction of the antifascist women's movement. The weakness of the socialist women's movement was due in part to increasing political polarization within the socialist movement; the pro-communist leaning of many socialists, particularly in the socialist union (UGT); and the overall political developments of the time.[32] Moreover, the lack of a collective feminist definition in previous decades made it difficult for the caucus of socialist women to formulate an alternative political and gender option for Spanish women.[33]

In Catalonia, the Unió de Dones de Catalunya (UDC), created in November 1937, was the antifascist women's umbrella organization. The pattern of development of the earlier Catalan Women Against War and Fascism was similar to that of the national women's antifascist movement. However, the initial political configuration of the antifascist women's organization in Catalonia differed somewhat from its counterpart in the rest of Spain because the Esquerra Republicana de Catalunya (ERC), the republican populist Catalan nationalist party, had maintained a decisive role in its creation and evolution in the early years. Maria Dolors Bargalló of ERC was one of the most significant figures at that stage. Although with the outbreak of the Civil War the Catalan antifascist women's organization disintegrated, by early 1937 the stated policy of the Catalan communist party, Partit Socialista Unificat de Catalunya (PSUC), was to promote a national alliance of antifascist women in Catalonia; this objective was accomplished with the creation of UDC in November 1937. Nonetheless, despite the active initiative of the communists in establishing the Unió de Dones de Catalunya, the organization developed a greater degree of autonomy with respect to communist intervention.

In its initial stages, UDC was conceived as a transpolitical united front. The manifesto of its founding congress was signed by women from a wide range of political tendencies. Delegates from communist, republican, nationalist, socialist, federal, syndicalist, anarchist, peasant, and antifascist associations, parties, and organizations were present at the First National Congress in November 1937.[34] There appears, then, to have been a great degree of political plurality within the Catalan organization in the first months of its existence. The presidency was held by Maria Dolors Bargalló, who chaired the First National Congress.

Nevertheless, as the political hegemony of the PSUC became increasingly consolidated in Catalonia after 1937, so too did communist hegemony in the UDC, which identified more and more with PSUC programs and policies. In fact, there was a clear influence of the Catalan communist party right from its creation, as can be seen by the fact that, despite the presidency of the republican Bargalló at the First National Congress in November 1937 and the presence of two other delegates from ERC and the radical nationalist party Estat Català, the communists held the majority with the remaining six delegates of the Presidential Committee.[35] Moreover, the publication of the UDC journal *Companya* was financed by the PSUC and was used as a vehicle to transmit communist goals and policies.[36] According to a prominent communist leader, it was the Catalan communist party that gave the journal its "wide perspective and political content."[37] The fact that the Catalan communist party was defined as a united socialist party that adhered to the Third International meant that as a "coalition" party it was easier to organize united fronts.

The program of the Catalan antifascist organization was very similar to that of the AMA. The UDC's agenda centered on the incorporation of women into the war effort; women's wage work and work parity; the defense of the homefront; the protection of the health of mothers and children; the development of education, culture, professional training, and social assistance; and the elimination of prostitution. Initially, the Catalan organization tended to show more empathy toward gender-specific objectives than its Spanish counterpart. This, perhaps, can be attributed to the greater dynamism of the Catalan communist party, to the fact that until 1937 Catalonia was not on the immediate war front, and, even more significantly, to the vigorous presence of the anarchist women's movement in Catalonia. This movement represented a powerful rival to communists and socialists in the political terrain.

The influence of communist parties on the youth movements was more obvious, as prominent leaders of the communist youth organization were among the leaders and members of the Unión de Muchachas (UM) and the Aliança Naçional de la Dona Jove (ANDJ) and were instrumental in the creation and development of the antifascist female youth organizations.[38] In fact, the female youth organizations were more radical than their adult equivalents in their demands for access to work, training, education, jobs, and equal treatment with men. They were also more articulate in expressing the need for overall changes in cultural models and norms of behavior. The conclusions of the Conference of the Young Women of Madrid held in May 1937 under the auspices of the UM stated as one of its primary problems the need "to finish once and for all with the spiritual inheritance of the old capitalist regime, which has subjected us to its prejudices, archaic customs and terrible lack of culture."[39] In addition, the Catalan ANDJ demanded that "new families" formed during the war be recognized as legal entities even though the partners had not been legally married.[40]

The available evidence shows that the overall social constituency of the antifascist organizations was working class and lower middle class. Many members were housewives, seamstresses, factory workers, shop assistants, servants, and office workers, with a smaller number of civil servants, schoolteachers, lawyers, pharmacists, and other professionals.[41] The 800 delegates who attended the National Congress of the UDC in Barcelona in November 1937 had the following occupational provenance:[42]

Workers in factories and workshops	62.8%
Housewives:	21.8%
Commerce	8.8%
Intellectuals	6.0%
Peasants	0.6%

The leaders of the antifascist organizations were quite well known, and generally either they or their families had previously been involved in politics. A report on the composition of the National Committee established at the Second National Conference of the AMA in October 1937 illustrates this. Nineteen of the twenty-three members of the National Committee identified by name were fairly well known and active in politics or related to people who were. The unidentified members were all delegates from factories.[43]

The importance of the AMA was derived from its ability to attract and channel the activities of women on the homefront. Another factor in the organization's success and strength is that it constituted the only women's organization officially backed by the government. In August 1936, a decree from the prime minister's office charged the AMA to create a Commission of Women's Aid to help the ministries of war, industry, and commerce with the task of organizing supplies for the war fronts and relief work for combatants.[44] According to this decree, the ministries were to delegate to the commission the production "of articles for the use of combatants and whose manufacture was suitable to the female element." By 1938, the failure of this initiative was acknowledged even in official circles. However, a new commission was formed that summer to intensify women's role in auxiliary support work dedicated to the wounded and the families of the soldiers.[45] The new commission was required to present proposals to the government in the following areas: 1) intensification of direct female aid in workshops of all organizations associated with the War Ministry and the creation of new workshops directed and serviced by female personnel; 2) contact with the Military Supplies Headquarters for the distribution of articles that were not part of the usual combatant equipment; 3) nomination of female delegations to visit hospitals in order to aid the wounded; 4) creation of orphanages for the children of combatants; and 5) organization of official aid for women workers in war industries and for their children.[46]

The antifascist women's organization did not achieve full integration into the hygienic, sanitation, medical, and supply services of the ministries. Despite its official status and state sponsorship, the project failed once again. Lack of strong leadership, the low political status of the women's organization, and internal divisions weakened the capacity of the AMA to implement its official policy. More significantly, however, this failure came from the official resistance to the presence of women in war and military activities. Traditional mistrust of female competence together with ingrained hostility, particularly at the War Ministry, toward the presence of women in a traditionally male domain, militated against the evolution of female collaboration, despite the official designation of a women's commission. State sponsorship was insufficient to dissuade traditional gender values and norms of conduct, despite the severe needs generated by the war. Underutilization of the women's antifascist organizations indicates considerable distrust and inhibition regarding the enormous potential of female mobilization on the homefront and particuarly in relation to military needs. Moreover, the official conception of women's role in the antifascist struggle as that of auxiliary relief work is a salient indication of government views on the function of women. The official view also set the pattern for non-official attitudes on women's antifascist activism.

The failure to consolidate its position meant that the influence of the AMA in official circles was of little significance. The AMA was reduced to sporadic auxiliary support activities. The fact that it was unable to reenforce its presence and fulfill its maximum potential within official organizations also indicates the weakness of the organization in the political scene. The antifascist women were not powerful enough to oblige official institutions to overcome their reticence and accept women's collaboration. The limitations of the AMA's perception of women's social role in the antifascist struggle are obvious here; it appears the AMA never questioned its assignment to an auxiliary support role. Quite the contrary, a support role fit perfectly into the organization's overall resistance strategy, which conceived women's role precisely in this light.

The primary goal of the antifascist women's organizations was to struggle against fascism and defend the democratic republic under the auspices of the Popular Front. As the Basque Committee of Antifascist Women stated, "...women have risen up to offer their open arms to the Popular Front,"[47] while the Second Conference of Antifascist Women held in Valencia in October 1937 declared unconditional commitment to the Popular Front:

> The antifascist women will fight with all their energy to strengthen the Popular Front and they have agreed to invite...parties and organizations to channel their aspirations and efforts toward a common goal: to win the war, supporting with discipline and enthusiasm the orders of the Government.[48]

In accordance with communist policies, the AMA did not perceive the Civil War as a moment for revolutionary change. Quite the contrary, it rejected any such pretensions and insisted that its primary goal was antifascism and the defense of the democratic republic. The AMA had no dilemma in choosing between antifascist war and revolution, as radical social change was not on its political agenda. Women of the AMA understood antifascist activism exclusively as a defense of the democratic republic:

> We fight against fascism in defense of the democratic freedom which the people gave itself....We women defend this freedom because it is the only one which guarantees our rights as women, our right to intervene in the political and social life of the country, and which the reactionaries have always denied us knowing that we can only use it in defense of our interests and of our children's interests.[49]

Antifascism, then, was the key to their existence, the *raison d'être* that it identified with the general interests of humankind and was seen as a means to liberate oppressed peoples. In fact, as was common among other political groups, the antifascist women also identified the war as a war of independence. Here popular collective memory and historical mythology made a direct association between the 1808-1814 Spanish War of Independence against Napoleon and the war against national and international fascism taking place in Spain.[50]

Peace was also proclaimed to be one of the goals. However, according to the secretary general of the AMA, Emilia Elías, permanent peace could be guaranteed only by carrying out a successful war to annihilate international fascism.[51] Defending the right to freedom and self-determination, to justice, to culture and education, together with the vindication of political democracy, constituted the core of the AMA's program throughout the years of the Civil War.

Again, the primary goal common to the diverse antifascist women's organizations was undoubtedly the mobilization of Spanish women to the antifascist cause. Although some gender-specific issues were also included in their agendas and some lip service was given to the effect that the antifascist struggle implied the defense of "their own specific rights as women,"[52] such issues were peripheral and became even more ancillary as the pressures of the war grew. AMA propaganda insisted on the significance of fascism to women in its attempt to attract large masses of women to the organization. However, the discourse was traditional and rooted in the gender-specific ideology of "separate spheres" and a commitment to women's primary role as mother and nurturer. Women were rarely addressed in their own right as rational beings who could reject fascism as individuals but rather as mothers and spouses to whom fascism was presented as a threat to home and family.

The AMA discourse followed the lines of political propaganda aimed at women from all political sectors prior to the Civil War. This could be explained as a temporary propaganda tactic to attract the maximum number of women to the antifascist cause with a message that appealed to their maternal feelings and to the primary role society had assigned to them and to which they were accustomed. As gender identification was established to a large degree through motherhood, it is, perhaps, not surprising that the women's organizations also exploited maternalism and articulated their own discourse on this basis. It is also true that there was no public sanction for articulating feminist ideas and gender-specific demands. Nevertheless, this insistence on conventional gender roles and values cannot be attributed to a mere temporary strategic attempt to make women more receptive to ideological causes, for the mainstream of antifascist women did not question gender values and cultural models. Rather, the strategies reveal the lack of any systematic reflection or awareness of gender-specific issues within the organizations. Thus, deference to the traditional vision of women predominated, and there was a decided lack of questioning of patriarchal gender values.

The programs of the antifascist women's organizations occasionally addressed specific women's issues, such as the "right of all women to the benefits of scholarship" in order to free them from the slavery of ignorance, the liberation of women from "oppressive maternity," and their incorporation into public and social life.[53] In contrast to these sporadic references to specific gender issues, however, these organizations espoused a much more consistent and cohesive policy on antifascism. Even the defense of women's rights tended to be couched in terms of maternal rights, while feminism came to be identified with the antifascist struggle. As the Basque antifascist Astrea Barrios wrote, the "real feminism" proposed by the AMA was one that stimulated a girl to sew clothes for militiamen, raise the morale of the wounded, or replace her male comrades at work so that they could go to the front line.[54] The AMA defined feminism not as a struggle for women's rights, equality, or emancipation but as a fight against fascism. Gender-specific issues were lost in this designation of feminism. Specific feminist issues such as access to birth control, political parity, and social rights received little coverage in the agendas of these organizations. Only an extremely small number of committed antifascist women gave highest priority to gender-specific issues. Such was the case of socialist lawyer Matilde Huici, a vehement critic of women's social situation in Spain. According to Huici, with the exception of the right to vote, the situation of women had remained practically unchanged since 1931, during the years of the Second Republic. Women, and most particularly married women, were still openly discriminated against. Huici bitterly denounced the discrimination against women by all political parties and unions in their blatant perpetuation of male privilege:

> Public offices, especially the most important, with extremely rare exceptions...continued to be held by men; and married women, although they might allege constitutional injunctions, were ignored, hindered, if they wished to do something without the consent of their husbands.[55]

As Huici pointed out, even legislative measures to ensure equality, such as the Decree on Civil Parity of Women promulgated in February 1937, had yet to be effectively put into practice. In addition to her denunciation of the political inequality of women, Huici was unique in her attempt to address the questions of sexual education, birth control, and abortion within the AMA. Despite the fact that the need to relieve women of "oppressive maternity" figured in the AMA's program, only Huici included such issues in her report on the situation of women, and even then she did not manage to have the issue discussed at the Second Conference of the AMA in October 1937. Such a public avowal of feminist consciousness was clearly unusual; few women bothered to insist that specific women's issues be addressed, particularly if they were not immediately related to the war effort.

It is not, in fact, surprising that little attention was actually paid to specific female issues by the antifascist women's organizations. The AMA was developed under the aegis of the Spanish communist party, which, of all the left-wing parties in Spain prior to the Civil War, had paid the least attention to specific gender issues.[56] The party's interest in women was limited to work-related issues, such as wage discrimination and maternity leave, and it paid little attention to the classical Marxist thesis that the incorporation of women into wage work represented the basis for their future emancipation.[57] The specificity of female emancipation was not dealt with; on the contrary, such an emancipation was expected to occur automatically with the overthrow of capitalism. Given this reductionist view, women were urged not to take up any specific struggle for their emancipation but rather to partake in the overall struggle for social change. Despite sporadic warnings by Pasionaria, the most articulate of Spanish communist women on such matters, orthodox Spanish communists clearly neglected women's issues and advocated total subordination of any specific female issue to the ongoing class and party struggle.

During the Civil War, in accordance with the political directives of the Soviet Union and the Third International since 1935, the political stance of the Spanish Communist Party (PCE) was very clear: defense of the democratic republic, concentration on the war effort, and opposition to any attempt to introduce a process of revolutionary change. Increased interest in women focused on the need to incorporate them en masse into the party–the Catalan communist party (PSUC) was especially active in this area–and to increase female antifascist mobilization through their integration into one of the allied women's antifascist organizations.

The female sectors of the communist parties concentrated on relief work, education and professional training, mobilization against the Fifth Column (saboteurs, fascist supporters, and spies), and the political instruction of women to prepare them to replace men as cadres in the party whenever the circumstances of war might require it.[58]

In contrast to the Communist Party, the AMA had a wider and less politically oriented approach. Its program was presented in terms of justice, peace, and the defense of culture and freedom. It focused on antifascism while accepting, to a large degree, traditional assumptions about women's gender role. In fact, the conclusions of the important Conference of Antifascist Women, held in Valencia in October 1937, typified antifascist women's unresponsiveness to gender-specific issues and their identification with the antifascist struggle. The conclusions centered on a program for the improvement of women's status, especially in their demands for the immediate integration of women into the work force, wage parity for women "when they were as productive as men," and the setting up of an infrastructure of collective canteens, nurseries, and child care facilities for working mothers.[59] However, all of these programs were geared primarily toward the war effort and women's integration into war production. In other words, although such demands were obviously to benefit the overall situation of women, the reasoning behind the demands was not feminist but rather part of the general strategy to mobilize womanpower for antifascist resistance. Given increasing military recruitment, harnessing women to the work force appeared to be crucial to maintaining the pace of production necessary to the war economy. Once again, antifascist commitment had priority over any gender consciousness or demands.

To stand up for women or to canvas for improvement in their social condition, it is not necessary to possess a feminist consciousness. However, in a less obvious way, the making of such demands and the actual dynamics of integrating women into this mass social movement led them to develop an awareness not only on a political and social level, but also as women. Although specific gender demands were subordinated to the overall struggle to eliminate fascism, the difficulties encountered, the responsibilities undertaken by women, and women's growing perception of their own capacities led to a gradual heightening of consciousness not yet overtly expressed, but nonetheless present among a growing sector of women.

It is, of course, quite true that the experiences and perceptions of those in positions of leadership are not synonymous with those of the rank and file and that spokeswomen do not speak for all women or even represent women as a collective. Nevertheless, conclusions drawn by some of these female leaders may be indicative of a certain shift in awareness not yet generalized in society as a whole. One senses an increasing awareness during the years of the war by many women of the differential treatment afforded them by state and political organizations. This became particularly evident when women were marginalized in the antifascist resistance, which led to increased discontent among the leaders of the antifascist women's movement and, in turn, to further denunciations of discriminatory gender treatment. Some women began to vindicate their own ability to play an important role in the struggle. They did not intend to be brushed aside with false allegations of lack of training or aptitudes, as militant antifascist activist Astrea Barrios pointed out:

> Given the moment of danger...,the Government and the authorities must remember that women in Spain...are citizens with broad civil rights....
>
> Therefore women demand with more insistence than ever... their place in the struggle against barbarianism.
>
> The allegation that women lack preparation for certain tasks is inadmissible; women, just like antifascist men...cannot tolerate the existence of professional impediments, when those impediments serve to open the way for the common enemy: fascism.
>
> Did our comrades know how to use arms on the 19th of July?
>
> No; and yet, they went to the front line; time has given them the practice which today allowed them to undertake the Popular counteroffensive.
>
> Women will have the same experience in whatever posts they are assigned to.[60]

The war fostered female identification with the antifascist cause, thus breaking down traditional gender constraints on women's intervention outside the confines of the home. Female involvement in the multiple activities of the war effort and the intense push for education, culture, and professional training spurred women to develop their education and self-esteem. The above citation shows quite clearly their confidence in their own capabilities despite their lack of training. Women demonstrated that they could efficiently undertake many war-related tasks, which further enhanced their self-image and self-reliance.

At times, women's mobilization led to a collective process of political and social education on a very elementary level. For example, the local committee of the AMA in the small town of Ruzafa decided to "buy the daily newspaper in order to read and comment on it and in this way gradually educate their comrades politically."[61] The collective endeavor to organize also provided women with the opportunity to develop their potential. In fact, simple instructions on how to create local groups of the antifascist movement and to develop activities were propagated with the idea of getting hitherto uncommitted women involved in the war effort while also making them aware of their own capacity and potential. As the secretary general of the AMA put it:

> Very often our companions do not dare to accept work because they think they are not prepared. Many think they don't know anything. Each of us knows how to do something, is useful for something. Women who had only sewn clothes for their family, through a thousand trials and errors, learned in a very short time how to become outstanding workers.[62]

Dolors Piera, the Catalan communist leader, pointed out the need to overcome "the false sentiment of inferiority which practically all women have"[63] as an important step in developing women's potential in the war effort. Undoubtedly, as women overcame their sense of inferiority, their self-esteem and self-confidence grew, and with that development came greater expectations and social aspirations. The war made available new spaces and opportunities for women to meet and work together collectively, particularly in the cities and towns. Although many local groups were housed in buildings belonging to other political parties, they provided a physical meeting space, which women had lacked until then.[64]

For many of the thousands of women of all age groups involved in antifascist activism under the auspices of the AMA, the war provided the first opportunity for collective mobilization and the initiation of self-education and social consciousness.[65] Although not openly formulated in terms of feminist awareness or even gender consciousness, this collective experience did provide a solid base for a shift in this direction. However, the lack of gender specificity within the antifascist women's program undoubtedly discouraged the articulation of a coherent program for social change that included female emancipation among its priorities.

Anarchist Strategies To Free Women: Mujeres Libres

The other major mass women's movement during the Civil War was Mujeres Libres (Free Women), an anarchist organization with the clearly articulated feminist goal of female liberation from the "triple enslavement to which [women] have been subject: enslavement to ignorance, enslavement as women and enslavement as workers."[66] Founded shortly before the outbreak of the Civil War, in April 1936, the organization, which had just a few hundred members in the first months of its existence, expanded throughout republican Spain during the years of the war. It is impossible to ascertain the exact number of its membership, which ranged from 20,000 to 60,000 members, according to official sources. However, the most credible figure appears to be around 20,000 members, used most frequently in the internal documentation of the organization, where there is less need to inflate membership.[67] More than 168 local groups were established in towns and villages throughout republican Spain, with greater incidence in central

Spain and Catalonia (with 58 and 46 groups, respectively) followed by Aragon and Valencia, Andalusia (with 35 and 29 local groups).[68]

Although anarchism as a theory of revolutionary change focuses on the relationship of dominance, subjugation and power, and the establishment of a non-hierarchical, non-authoritarian society, as a social movement Spanish anarchism had shown glaring contradictions between theory and practice.[69] The contradiction between theoretical egalitarianism and male authoritarian sexist practice was still notorious some months before the outbreak of the war, when it was denounced by A. Morales Guzmán, a militant anarchist sensitive to women's issues:

> We cannot understand how a worker who is so vilely exploited can turn into a tyrant in his home....Where is the moral basis for these *compañeros*' protest?[70] Isn't their home a small violent authoritarian State? Are they not bosses exploiting their "wives," snatching away their freedom? Aren't they jailers turning their homes into prisons?[71]

Anarchism showed greater feminist sensitivity in contrast to other strands of the Spanish labor movement. It officially endorsed women's rights and gender equality in its programs. However, despite the active feminist position of some male anarchists, in practice, gender power relationships prevailed and women's relegation was common within the movement. In the 1930's, a growing consciousness of the sexism within the anarchist movement had led some women to challenge the contradictory stance of anarchist militants and their organizations. Activists such as María Luisa Cobos and Trinidad Urién had denounced how women were ridiculed, ignored, and, at worst, treated like sex objects when attending cultural activities. In fact, female marginalization from regular activism within the officially structured movement was common, as was recognized by a male militant in July 1935:

> When we go to a meeting or a lecture, we are enormously surprised at the presence of a dozen women; when our female *compañeras* ask a question about ideas we shrug our shoulders, and don't pay any attention to it; when a woman expresses her opinion at a talk, an assembly or at home, we ask with perplexity: Is she mad?[72]

Most male anarchists preferred to cultivate female "talents as cooks" to developing their intellectual capacities or opted for sexual relations rather than giving women "the cultural food which would revolutionize their mind,"[73] which women sought by attending *ateneos*, the cultural clubs of the libertarian movement.[74] In the autumn of 1935, telephone operator and self-taught poet and writer Lucía Sánchez Saornil, the major feminist thinker among Spanish women anarchists, began an open debate on the role of women in the male-dominated libertarian movement with a series of articles in the major anarcho-syndicalist newspaper, *Solidaridad Obrera*.[75] In these articles, she denounced the attitude of many ostensible revolutionaries who advocated a traditional domestic role for women, wanting their wives and *compañeras* to be kept away from any activity centered on women.[76] Sánchez Saornil, like other anarchist women, saw the marginalization of women within the anarchist movement as a male and not a female problem. Sexist attitudes, gender-specific ideology concerning separate spheres, the cult of domesticity and motherhood, and the maintenance of male hegemony in anarchist organizations were all factors that diminished female participation in these organizations.

María Luisa Cobos claimed that there were thousands of women ready to take part in the anarchist cause but that, in fact, they were discouraged from doing so. She accused male militants of "dissuading them from participation on the sole basis of their belonging to the opposite sex."[77] Sánchez Saornil suggested more aggressively that the propaganda to attract women should not be addressed to women but to male militants and concluded with a proposal to create an independent organ of expression exclusively for women.[78] Some months later, in April 1936, a group of anarchist women in Madrid and Barcelona initiated the creation of an exclusively female anarchist organization, Mujeres Libres, the first working-class women's movement to espouse both the revolutionary and the feminist causes on an equal basis.[79]

The initial caucus of Mujeres Libres was formed by Lucía Sánchez Saornil, Dr. Amparo Poch y Gascón, and journalist Mercedes Comaposada.[80] They decided to publish a journal called *Mujeres Libres* that would interest women in social issues and thus attract them to anarchist ideals. In a letter to the well-known U.S. anarchist leader, Emma Goldman, asking for her support, they explained that the purpose of the journal was to recruit women to anarchism: "We try to awaken female consciousness to libertarian ideas, which the immense majority of Spanish women–who are very backward socially and culturally–know nothing about."[81] Emma Goldman responded positively to the request with an extensive article on the situation of women in the Spanish Civil War.[82] Initially cautious about openly declaring their anarchist affiliation, and to avoid an offhand rejection, Mujeres Libres explained:

> We will try to maintain a moderate tone in the magazine, in line with our cultural goal; moreover, as our primary goal is to attract women, we will not identify it as anarchist, since that might be enough to frighten women away.[83]

Although prudent about being identified as anarchist, from the beginning Mujeres Libres was presented as a specifically female initiative addressed to and promoted by women. It was not, then, an official undertaking by the anarchist movement to create a female organization[84] but rather "a personal task carried out for love of ideas and of our sex."[85] One of the principal motives behind the creation of a female organization where women's specific interests could be addressed and attended to was dissatisfaction with male hostility and indifference to women within the anarchist movement. The initial agenda of Mujeres Libres was essentially cultural and educational. *Mujeres Libres*, its lively, well-illustrated journal, was an efficient instrument in the popular dissemination of the organization's policies and viewpoints and played a decisive educational role.[86]

The immediate goal was to provide women with basic education and some political instruction that would enable them to take part in anarchist activities, thus breaking male monopoly in the various branches of the organization. The organization also sought to furnish women with professional training that would enhance their employment opportunities.[87]

Of course, the development of Mujeres Libres as a movement has to be considered in the context of the awareness of women's issues within Spanish anarchism since its creation.[88] However, Mujeres Libres represented a breakthrough not only because of its sharpened feminist consciousness but also because it presented a collective, organized contestation to women's subordination. It was, in fact, the first mass women's organization to attempt to put anarcho-feminism into practice. Mujeres Libres' challenge to the male-dominated anarchist movement gained momentum and impetus during the war.

July 1936 inaugurated a revolutionary period for Spanish anarchists, whose simultaneous goals were the destruction of fascism and the revolutionary transformation of society. For some women, this context heightened the need to accelerate a breakdown in patriarchal structures. But they were also aware of the overt machismo in the behavior and mentality of Spanish men, including anarchists. At the height of the revolutionary period, Emma Goldman drew attention to this in an article published in *Mujeres Libres*:

> Men always ready to struggle heroically for their emancipation are far from thinking the same about the opposite sex....The triumph of the revolution shows the high revolutionary potential of Spanish workers. But...the majority of Spanish men do not seem to understand the real meaning of liberation or at least wish to keep their wives from discovering it.[89]

Or as Suceso Portales, a dressmaker and leader of Mujeres Libres, impatiently denounced:

> We hear too much every day about the freedom of the oppressed and the noble cause of social justice. But we never, except on a handful of occasions, hear these liberators refer to the need to declare women entirely free.[90]

Contrary to the antifascist women's organizations that rejected any agenda of revolutionary change and in line with anarchist political strategy that defended immediate social revolution, Mujeres Libres saw the Civil War both as an antifascist struggle and an opportunity for revolutionary transformation. Furthermore, these women felt that the time had come to assert their specific view on revolutionary change and to try to enforce a redefinition of gender relations in consonance with the theoretical egalitarian anarchist position. Mujeres Libres believed that women's emancipation was indispensable for the success of the overall revolutionary process; unable to accept that this would come about automatically as a result of the revolution, it endorsed the use of specific pressure and direct strategy to implement change in the terrain of personal relations and women's social and personal identity. It firmly advocated the ideas of self-determination and self-emancipation; women were to be promoted as a progressive force and as agents of change in the revolutionary process.

The nature of the revolutionary process sharpened the feminist consciousness of these anarchist women as they noted the disparity between the social transformations undertaken and women's essentially unchanged gender subordination. The more sensitive of their male companions pointed out the failure to break down traditional gender norms and modes of conduct. An editorial in the anarchist newspaper *Tierra y libertad* clearly illustrates the continuity of women's subordination:

> The example is clear all over; in most of the unions in towns, while the male *compañeros* discuss or resolve affairs, women still carry out "female" jobs of cooking, washing, etc....with the same servile spirit as before. Since the fight has begun, we have travelled through many towns of antifascist Spain, and except in some unions, where they have accepted little bourgeois girls who are more or less pretty, more or less typists, we have seen women humiliated in the same slavery as ever.[91]

The response to this blatant contradiction at a time of potential revolutionary change was a more defined gender consciousness and the development of a strategy for female emancipation within both the anarchist movement and Spanish society. Although on the one hand the war provided a sense of immediacy that encouraged the rapid development of gender and feminist consciousness, paradoxically, the pressure of the war impeded a clear-cut development of a gender-defined strategy for anarchist change. The requirements of the war effort blurred feminist demands and, in practice, forced all the women's organizations to conform their activities to focus on survival and winning the war against fascism. Mujeres Libres had to modify the long-term objective of emancipating women through a gradual program of cultural activities and education when the organization found itself in the midst of a revolutionary conflict that required the immediate participation of women both in the antifascist war effort and the social revolution they promoted as anarchists.

The immediate goals of the anarchist women's organization linked the creation of a "conscious and responsible women's force which would act as the vanguard of revolution" with emancipation from the different forms of subordination that maintained women in an inferior social position.[92] Gender subordination was identified with female enslavement to "ignorance" (lack of access to educational, cultural, and social activities), with the gender-specific condition as women in a male-dominated society, and with their social condition as workers.[93] Together with this initial definition of gender-specific goals, the statutes of the organization, formulated by a commission set up at the First National Conference held in Valencia in August 1937, established a clear political link with the anarchist movement and its different organizations, the anarcho-syndicalist union, CNT, the radical anarchist group, the Federación Anarquista Ibérica (FAI), and the anarchist youth organization, Federación Ibérica de Juventudes Libertarias (FIJL):

> In order to achieve these goals it will act as a political organization identified with the general objectives of the CNT and the FAI. Its primary goal for women's emancipation aspires to create female intervention and collaboration in humankind's emancipation by offering their acquired knowledge, enriched with their specific characteristics, in the task of structuring the new social order.[94]

Mujeres Libres had a decided class content in its approach to women and social issues. It had a clear political identification with the policies and goals of the Spanish anarchist movement, which attempted to establish an egalitarian revolutionary society. Although some of its leaders were of lower middle-class backgrounds, it was mainly run by working-class women, many of whom were self-taught.

Such was the case of dressmakers Suceso Portales and Lola Iturbe, who also wrote under the pseudonym Kiralina. They were self-taught and played a significant and articulate role both in the women's organization and in the libertarian movement.[95] Suceso Portales (Badajoz 1908) was an excellent organizer and orator. She played a decisive role in organizing Mujeres Libres in central Spain. She was secretary of the Provincial Committee for central Spain and secretary of the National Sub-Committee of Mujeres Libres in 1938. Later, in exile, she was one of the reorganizers of Mujeres Libres and maintained the publication of *Mujeres Libres* during the Franco regime. Lola Iturbe was an extraordinarily significant activist. She played an important role in the publication of the anarchist newspaper *Tierra y libertad* and introduced the women's page in it in December 1935. Later, in exile, she was one of the first to write on women's role in the Civil War.

The constituency of Mujeres Libres was basically of the working class, and the organization addressed itself specifically to working-class women. Indeed, Mujeres Libres was quick to point out that one of the main factors of female subordination was women's condition as workers. It felt that economic independence was a fundamental basis for female emancipation but also linked women's situation as workers to the overall class struggle and oppression of the working class under the existing capitalist system. Thus, the gender-specific goals of the anarchist women's organizations were intimately related to an ongoing social project based on an anarchist model of social transformation. Mujeres Libres argued that, while female emancipation could not be isolated from a broader class and social struggle, the emancipatory model of anarchism would be incomplete if it did not include the specific strategy and goal of women's emancipation.

The women of Mujeres Libres were, in fact, quite unique in their elaboration of both a theory and practice that could be qualified as a working-class anarcho-feminism. Indeed, Mujeres Libres posed the very contemporary problem of double militancy: feminist and political. Of course, such a novel stance was problematical, and it would be wrong to think that the 20,000 members of the anarchist organization had a clear perception of the implications of such militancy or even a sharp awareness of the need for a specific gender struggle. Nonetheless, we do find a surprising degree of gender-specific consciousness in the organization, which is quite exceptional among mainstream Spanish anarchists.

Mujeres Libres did not identify with the term *feminist*. In line with other women anarchists, it associated feminism with bourgeois middle-class political feminism and thus rejected it for its social limitations.[96] Still, the theory and practice of Mujeres Libres can undoubtedly be defined as anarcho-feminism, for the organization recognized the gender specificity of women's oppression and the need for an autonomous female struggle to overcome it. Mujeres Libres explicitly acknowledged the existence of a patriarchal system–the "male civilization" to which Suceso Portales referred[97]–in which women suffered subordination due to their sex. More significant still, Mujeres Libres developed a strategy of resistance based on the idea of the "double struggle" and the creation of a separate women's organization in order to carry it out.

The theory of the "double struggle" was built on a parallel gender and social discourse that linked the struggle for women's liberation to a theory of revolutionary social change based on an anarchist model of an alternative social system. Thus, women had to engage in double militancy in a parallel struggle: a revolutionary one founded on the elimination of social and economic exploitation and the destruction of the State, and a parallel feminist struggle that would challenge male supremacy and put an end to patriarchal structures. In fact, the theoretical stance espoused by Mujeres Libres actually defined specific gender issues and called for a review of gender power relations. Not only that, the organization also argued that a redressal of patriarchal relationships and asymmetry between the sexes would come about only if women, by themselves, took the initiative on both an individual and collective level. The solution to female subordination and the elimination of the sources of gender discrimination could be resolved only through female initiative and women's commitment in the social and feminist struggle. In her prewar writings, Lucía Sánchez Saornil had stressed that she viewed the struggle for female emancipation as a male problem. However, re-educating male *compañeros* was not on the agenda of anarchist women during the war years.

Mujeres Libres' approach to female emancipation is surprisingly similar to that of present-day feminists, for it did not confine itself to demanding political and social rights or even economic and work parity. Significantly, one of the crucial factors it contemplated in the elaboration of an emancipatory life project for women was the development of their psychological independence. Freedom for these women included psychological liberty, the development of female identity, personal autonomy, and self-esteem. This inner freedom that women were to acquire could be achieved only through individual initiative and struggle:

> Revolutionary men who are today struggling for their freedom fight alone against the world, against a world opposed to desires for freedom, equality and social justice. Revolutionary women, on the other hand, have to fight on two levels; first they must fight for their external freedom. In this struggle, men with the same ideals are their allies in an identical cause. But women also have to fight for their inner freedom, which men have enjoyed for centuries. And in this struggle, women are on their own.[98]

In fact, women were warned not to rely on male support to gain their autonomy. In an article on women's double struggle published in *Mujeres Libres*, one militant warned that the most considerate and well-intentioned of men were misogynous and impeded the development of female potential: "He has so much hidden vanity that, without realizing it, and under the appearances of love and friendship, he frequently works against women's liberation."[99] At worst, blatant sexism and defense of male interests prevented genuine commitment to promoting women's emancipation. In the debate on women held just a year earlier, the well-known activist Mariano Vázquez had admitted quite frankly that there was no hope that men, including anarchists, would easily give up their privileges and renounce their male hegemony. As he explained:

> You are not surprised, are you, that a bourgeois doesn't want to give up his position, not even to have parity with his workers? No, we consider it just. We know it is more pleasant to give orders than to obey....Between a woman and a man the same thing occurs. The male feels more satisfied having a servant to make his food, wash his clothes....That is reality. And, in the face of that, to ask that men cede [their privileges] is to dream.[100]

Mujeres Libres was quite aware of the need for a specific struggle to achieve women's liberation in the face of male opposition, although it was also made explicit that women were not to undertake a "war" against men, as male and female interests were not incompatible in the long run.[101] This unusual awareness of the need for an individual struggle to overcome obstacles to self-development and self-confidence can no doubt be attributed to the ongoing tradition of individualistic anarchism in Spain. What is interesting is how Mujeres Libres availed of the different tendencies of Spanish anarchism in its development of an overall strategy for female emancipation. For together with this more individualistic approach, espoused by such prominent anarchist thinkers as Federica Montseny, albeit not in a gender context, Mujeres Libres also advocated a parallel collective strategy to free women from the ties of subordination.[102]

Mainstream anarchism had traditionally rejected the specificity of female subordination--the position taken by Federica Montseny–and viewed the issue of human emancipation as being outside the context of gender differences. In fact, the subordination of women and women's liberation were peripheral concerns of the Spanish anarchist movement, although they did evoke a much wider degree of attention and sensitivity than any of the other trends of the Spanish labor movement.[103]

Federica Montseny dedicated numerous articles to the issue of women's emancipation, but she did not believe there was any specific woman question. For her, the crux of the question was "the problem of the sexes," the fact that men "were an enigma to women, and women were an enigma to men."[104] According to Montseny, the solution to the problem lay in establishing libertarian communism and, more specifically, in developing a new human personality for males and females. Through a process of self-transcendence, Montseny proposed the creation of a "new mentality, a new point of view, a new moral life, self-vivification, the self-creation of a balanced and redeeming personality."[105] The prototype of the new woman advocated by the anarchist leader was one full of confidence and awareness that the destiny of humankind depended on her. However, this model of superwoman proposed by Montseny, the product of individual consciousness and self-transcendence, would have been extremely difficult for the average Spanish woman–whom Montseny herself had qualified as ignorant and backward–to emulate.[106]

In contrast to Montseny's individualistic approach to the problems of female and human emancipation, Mujeres Libres proposed a double strategy based not only on individualism but also on a collective response that would offer women the fundamental support and training to enable them to achieve freedom as women. Mujeres Libres felt the need for women to respond as a group to female subordination and to engage women in a common endeavor to overcome it. Its strategy for emancipation was based on a collective approach to the problem. A mass organization was established that catered specifically to women's problems and needs. This enabled exceptional women to free themselves and attain their autonomy but also gave working-class women who were mostly illiterate access to guidance, educational, and professional facilities for the first time.

The strategy of an independent female anarchist organization broke with anarchist tradition and challenged the male hegemony of the organized anarchist movement. In the Spanish labor movement's other political organizations, women's groups and associations had been created, but Mujeres Libres was groundbreaking in its demand for institutional autonomy. These anarchist women envisioned the formation of an independent female organization within the overall anarchist movement. They constantly sought official recognition and asserted institutional independence with respect to the other anarchist organizations, such as the anarcho-syndicalist union CNT, the radical activist anarchist group FAI, and the youth organization FIJL, which constituted the conglomerate of the Spanish libertarian movement of the time. Mujeres Libres tried to have its status recognized on a par with these other branches of the anarchist movement.

This determination to achieve institutional autonomy represented an extraordinary breakthrough within the Spanish labor movement, as hitherto women's claims had been repeatedly subordinated and female organizations had been invariably reduced to ancillary sections dependent on party or union hierarchy. Women's organizations had been used basically as mechanisms to attract females to their respective parties or unions, and of course they were subjected to the dictates of the party or union to which they belonged.[107] Mujeres Libres considered itself independent and resisted encroachment by other anarchist organizations. It refused to be subjected to the dictates of the other branches of the anarchist movement and, in spite of blatant hostility, indifference, and lack of collaboration, strove to maintain an independent institutional status. However, it was unsuccessful in its efforts and never attained official recognition by the libertarian movement, which did not consider Mujeres Libres comparable to the other branches, CNT, FAI, and FIJL. In fact, Lucía Sánchez Saornil had warned earlier of the difficulties in store, due to male attempts to instrumentalize female mobilization:

> There are a lot of *compañeros* who sincerely desire women's collaboration in the struggle; but this desire does not spring from a modification in their concept of women; they want her collaboration as a constituent who can help achieve victory, as a strategic contribution we could say, but that does not imply for one minute that they think of female autonomy, or renounce considering themselves as the center of the earth.[108]

The arguments of those who opposed the recognition of Mujeres Libres as a branch of the anarchist movement were complex. Some had a sexist bias, while others were more related to issues of power and institutional interests within the movement. Of course, the existence of an independent women's movement was totally incompatible with the predominant concept that rejected the specificity of women's subordination. If women did not have a distinct gender problem, then there was no point in having a specific female organization. This was the line of argument defended by Federica Montseny after the creation of Mujeres Libres, whose existence she refused to acknowledge even after the organization had been functioning for several months. In an interview with the German reporter H. E. Kaminski, Montseny, by that time minister of Health and Social Assistance in the socialist government of the Republic, maintained that women could follow whatever mode of life they wanted if they were strong-willed enough to do so. She then reiterated her view on women: "The two sexes are oppressed, not just women. Therefore there is only one liberation for which both men and women have to fight. That is why we do not have any exclusively female organization."[109]

On a more pragmatic level, the main reason for rejecting the petition requesting official recognition of Mujeres Libres presented to the national and regional committees of the anarchist movement[110] in September 1938 was that an independent women's organization would undermine the overall strength of the libertarian movement and inject an element of disunity that would have negative consequences for the development of working-class interests and the libertarian movement on the whole.[111] The youth organization FIJL had more explicit reasons to reject the proposal, accusing the women's organization of recruiting girls who were potential members of FIJL.[112] Beyond this, most anarchist militants thought that women were neither competent enough to administer such a complex organization nor sufficiently prepared to carry out the requirements of active militancy.[113]

This rejection and lack of sensitivity toward Mujeres Libres' demands illustrates once again the major contradiction between egalitarian theory and sexist practice within the anarchist movement. The need for a gender-specific movement that would defend the distinctive needs of women was never acknowledged. However, this rejection cannot be attributed solely to an ideological stance or to sexist behavior, as other more pragmatic factors were also to determine this decision: power politics within the anarchist movement. The petition from the women's organization came in September 1938 at a crucial moment in the development of the anarchist movement, just when the CNT, FAI, and FIJL undertook the restructuring of the hitherto loosely organized conglomerate of anarchist groups into a more cohesive movement: the MLE, the Spanish Libertarian Movement (Movimiento Libertario Español).[114] In this context, the claim for recognition of Mujeres Libres on par with the other branches of the libertarian movement must also be explored from the political perspective of the potential to recruit followers to anarchism. Other umbrella organizations, such as the AMA, undoubtedly acted as a front to attract women who would otherwise have remained outside the orbit of the communist movement.

In the case of Mujeres Libres, its capacity to attract new members was not so clear from the point of view of the MLE components. In political terms, Mujeres Libres did not necessarily cover a terrain or guarantee a new constituency; the CNT and the FIJL also recruited women. In fact, these other organizations viewed Mujeres Libres as a rival force. Furthermore, Mujeres Libres was considered incapable of innovating a base from which to inject new life into the libertarian movement. Federica Montseny described it as a "likeable group of women who had created this organization with the intention to fight against men's prejudices towards women."[115] Despite the argument that Mujeres Libres would provide an effective platform for female recruitment, the MLE saw no reason to recognize it as a new branch of the libertarian movement. This decision was feasible also because the MLE did not anticipate any problems to result from its rejection of the organization.

On the whole, Mujeres Libres opted for a conciliatory tone in its relations with the MLE and even adopted an ambiguous position on its feminist identity in its petition for official status. Its requests definitely underplayed its gender-specific orientation and never mentioned its theory and program of the double struggle. Women's perspectives and specific needs were not argued, while, on the contrary, the political advantages of having a women's organization were underscored. Mujeres Libres emphasized its ability to recruit women for the anarchist movement and spoke of the 20,000 women "withdrawn from the Marxist orbit of influence."[116] Despite this tactic, its proposal that it be awarded official status was rejected. Without recognition as legitimate members on a par with the CNT, FAI, and FIJL, the women of Mujeres Libres were unable to present official delegations that could challenge the sexism of these organizations at an institutional level.

The rejection, indifference, and sexism of the male militants were sources of constant irritation. Male anarchists were warned to overcome their "archaic concepts of women"[117] and cautioned that their attitude was politically prejudicial, as other women's organizations, particulary those under communist influence, were aware of the lack of institutional support for the anarchist women and benefitted from the weakness of Mujeres Libres. In the face of anarchist hostility and indifference, Mujeres Libres succeeded in building up an important mass movement of women who identified in one degree or another with the organization's feminist and anarchist postulates. Despite its tense relationship with the movement, Mujeres Libres never proposed disassociating itself from the anarchists. Quite the contrary, as the months went by and political polarization increased throughout republican Spain, it identified more and more with the anarchist movement while its more radical gender-specific position became diffused. Moreover, the fine line between institutional autonomy and real autonomy is difficult to gauge when moving from a theoretical arena to practical politics. It would be unwarranted to consider the women's organization as totally independent. It identified with the anarchist cause and acted within the confines of the libertarian movement. During the war, it had a clearly defined anarchist political projection, and, significantly, it also depended on the support and sponsorship of the anarchist movement for its survival.[118]

In fact, one of the major problems of Mujeres Libres was finding ways to break down political barriers and reach beyond women already identified with anarchism.[119] Although some of the organization's most active members came from other political groups, such as Mercedes Comaposada and Pepita Carpeña,[120] on the whole, the majority had some contact, either through their families or friends, with the anarchist movement. Family environment was crucial to women's cultural and educational formation, not just in anarchist circles but in general among the Left in Spain. Prior to the war, the restriction of movement made it difficult for young girls to have direct access to political forums, hence the enormous importance of cultural forums, *ateneos*, and hiking and sports clubs in their political development.[121] The overt political message and revolutionary stance of Mujeres Libres made it difficult for the organization to attract non-politicized women. The predominant working-class characteristics may have also contributed to this failure. Despite the fact that a few non-anarchist women, such as writer Carmen Conde, collaborated with Mujeres Libres, it was not very successful at attracting prominent women, intellectuals, or, indeed, non-politicized women.

Unlike Mujeres Libres, the transpolitical, non-revolutionary nature of the allied antifascist women's organizations made it easier for them to recruit non-politicized women, and of course they had access to many more resources because they were backed by state institutions. Mujeres Libres lacked both governmental sponsorship and official recognition by the political organizations with which it identified and relied on for support. Consequently, it remained more isolated than the other women's organizations.

Internal documentation confirms that one of the explicit goals of Mujeres Libres was to attract women to the anarchist cause. From the perspective of other political groups, Mujeres Libres was seen as a female branch dependent on the anarchist movement. Indeed, a majority of anarchist militants also saw it this way. That is not to say that Mujeres Libres lost its gender specificity and feminist consciousness during the war, but certainly the feminist philosophy of the organization was not shared by all of its 20,000 members. The preoccupation with the "double struggle" and feminist issues was undoubtedly that of a minority of women within the organization, and it seems clear that the majority of the affiliates of Mujeres Libres paid little attention to the more feminist connotations of its program and theory.[122] Many of the members who participated in the organization's activities, particularly in its educational, literacy, and professional agenda, simply wanted to improve their knowledge and training.

The major mass response to all the women's organizations was precisely in the field of education and professional training, which corresponded to a basic social need of Spanish women. However, it cannot be assumed that the majority of women who attended these activities assimilated and identified with the theoretical position of the organization. In fact, not all of the leaders of Mujeres Libres adopted a decidedly feminist stance. One of the founders of the organization, Mercedes Comaposada, gave a very conventional view of the goals of the organization in August 1938:

> Our organization was created and exists with the goal of preparing women for the home and for public life. In short, for future society. Whoever imagines that it is a feminist organization is mistaken. No. It is simply a center for the training of women in all fields: cultural, economic, social....To my understanding, the authentic redemption of women in Spain and in the World resides in this preparation.[123]

Like the antifascist women's associations, Mujeres Libres was conditioned by the cultural confines of its time. As will be discussed in later chapters, with the development of the war there was a growing consensus of policy among the different women's organizations that geared their activities to literacy and educational drives and professional training. In many cases, a similar vocabulary was used by the various organizations. For example, the term *capacitación* was commonly used for training, education, and social preparation that would fully develop women's potential.[124]

The preceding discussion is not intended to diminish the extraordinary historical significance of Mujeres Libres, whose theoretical position was indeed groundbreaking, but rather to aid in evaluating the organization in the background of its historical context and practice. Although Mujeres Libres included a wider range of women's issues in its agenda than did the antifascist women's organizations, and despite its undoubtedly more coherent feminist stance, the anarchist women failed to consider such issues as the sexual division of labor and women bearing sole responsibility for child care. And despite the innovative theoretical position of its more articulate and radical leaders, most members still tended to exalt motherhood as the primary task of women. In fact, Lucía Sánchez Saornil's more radical position that motherhood is merely one of many options for women may perhaps be attributed to her own life experience as a lesbian, rather than to her anarchist challenge to the gender discourse of domesticity.[125] In addition, surprisingly, given the legalization of abortion in Catalonia in December 1936 under the initiative of the anarchists in the Ministry of Health and Social Assistance of the Generalitat,[126] Mujeres Libres never openly broached the subject of abortion or dealt with such issues as family planning and birth control. Its educational drives related to these subjects were limited to preparation for maternity, child care, and some elementary knowledge of anatomy.[127]

Oral history provides an important corpus of documentation for attaining insight into women's experience. However, it must be placed in context and considered in light of cultural conditioning of present-day society. The filter of time and cultural models often influence the memory of historical experience. This is certainly true of the views of Spanish women on Mujeres Libres. In the early 1970's, well before the development of a women's movement in post-Franco Spain, these women's memories emphasized the political definition of the organization rather than a gender-specific and feminist consciousness. However, in more recent interviews with Mujeres Libres militants, they view their historical experience and the development of their organization from a much more sharpened feminist perspective. In fact, it is quite significant that, in interviews in the early 1970's, members of Mujeres Libres insinuated, in a disapproving tone, that two of the founding members of the organization–Lucía Sánchez Saornil and Amparo Poch y Gascón–were lesbians, while in a recent video documentary this was stated quite openly.[128]

Despite the gap between the theoretical feminist position of Mujeres Libres and its everyday practice, the women's mobilization carried out under the auspices of the organization was a decisive step in the growth of feminist consciousness, self-identity, and self-esteem for the many thousands of working-class women who participated in its activities. At a very basic level, and for the first time, the literacy and educational drives provided working-class women with a collective opportunity to develop their own capacity and potential.[129] Mujeres Libres provided women's institutes and local groups with space where working women could congregate and collectively develop their self-confidence and knowledge.

The organization's aggressive confrontation with male anarchists enabled women to sharpen their self-expression and defend their collective interests while at the same time progressing in their awareness of their specific interests and struggle as women. The ongoing gender consciousness that explicitly underlay the theory of the double struggle provided women with a novel theoretical framework in which to reflect on their life experience as women. The dynamic feminist stance of some of the leaders of the organization, together with the explicit formulation of the need for a double militancy and parallel feminist and social struggle, represented an important stage in the process of development of a working-class feminist movement in Spain.

Although the pressure of the war and of political events over the months did produce a certain fading of its feminist definition, which can in fact be discerned in the tone and content of its journal, *Mujeres Libres*, the ultimate goal of social and female emancipation remained undeterred. The actual identification of a process of social transformation that required specific attention to women, an identification of women's collective interests, and a strategy to combine both social struggle and female liberation undoubtedly shaped anarchist women's perception of the antifascist struggle in a distinct way and allowed them to develop, at different levels of consciousness, a specific social and gender view of the Civil War.

Dissident Marxists: The Female Secretariat of the POUM

The Female Secretariat of the dissident Marxist party, the Partido Obrero de Unificación Marxista (POUM), had a defined political identity and developed its program on women in close relationship with the party. Despite the traditional attention paid to women by the worker and peasant block, Bloc Obrer i Camperol (BOC),[130] one of the cofounding parties of the POUM,[131] the Female Secretariat was not created until September 1936, one year after the POUM was established. According to María Teresa Andrade, secretary general of the Secretariado Femenino, the meeting to create the women's organization was convoked by Pilar Santiago, a member of the executive committee of the youth organization Juventudes Comunistas Ibéricas. The Committee of the Secretariat was formed by Andrade, Santiago, Olga Nin, Isabel Gironella, and two other unidentified members.[132] The issue of women's subordination was peripheral in the party; any attention paid to women's concerns focused on political work that could help to recruit more female members for the POUM. One of the few inclusions of women in their program was the panel on the political work of women in the agenda for the Second Congress of the POUM scheduled for February 1936 but which was never held. Even here a man (Narcis Molins i Fàbregas) was nominated on the panel to elaborate the proposal together with María Teresa Andrade, Josepa Albiol, and Pilar Santiago.[133]

Unlike Mujeres Libres, which claimed independent, institutional status, and the communist-influenced antifascist women's organizations, which were, at least, transpolitical in formal terms, the Female Secretariat of the POUM (FSPOUM) constituted an official organism of the party. Although it enjoyed some degree of autonomy and attempted to avoid male interference at its meetings,[134] the Female Secretariat remained a dependent section of the POUM. In fact, there was close party control of the women's organization, as local committee members of the Secretariat were nominated by the local committees of the party and the Central Committee was nominated by the Executive Committee of the POUM.[135]

Membership of POUM was quite small, with a few hundred affiliates;[136] POUM had local groups in twenty-six towns situated mainly in Catalonia. The short time between the creation of the POUM in September 1935 and its practical disappearance from the political scene after the events of May 1937 hindered the development of the party,[137] and the women's group suffered as a consequence. Furthermore, the First Conference of the Female Secretariat, held in March 1937, announced that the consequence of overall disorganization and inefficiency was the failure to recruit a significant number of women. The conference then proposed the restructuring of the Secrtariat. However, this was never accomplished, due to the repression and progressive elimination of the POUM in the weeks following what has been called the civil war within the war, in May 1937.[138]

There was a degree of gender-specific consciousness among some of the women of the POUM. In their newspaper, *Emancipación*, they denounced male supremacy and the sexism of communist militants in belligerent terms, comparing sexist behavior to nazism:

> In most cases, men, although they may call themselves communists, make possible in their homes what nazism has imposed in Germany-women disappear from social, cultural and political life and are relegated to the simple duty of a beast which produces human material for the war.[139]

Male party members were warned to be aware of their sexist, reactionary behavior, but despite such sporadic criticisms of male domination, these female Marxist dissidents failed to acknowledge the gender specificity of female subordination and saw no need to initiate a distinctive female struggle to achieve women's emancipation.[140] Their view on women was couched more in political than in gender-specific terms. Male and female interests were not held to be incompatible, and, in line with the traditional Marxist approach, male and female emancipation was linked to the implantation of an egalitarian communist regime. The pamphlet published by the Female Secretariat of the POUM in 1937, *La mujer ante la revolución*, clearly stated its party allegiance and the identification of the proletarian struggle with the defense of their interests as women:

> We must repeat it constantly: the problem of women is only part of the struggle of the working class. That is why we became members of the party which most firmly fights to defend the interests of the proletariat, and, therefore, to defend our specific interests [as women].[141]

The growing political persecution of the POUM after the victory of orthodox communists in May 1937 may have hindered any efforts of the dissident Marxist women to formulate a clearer gender definition in their program. However, some of the most prominent members of the women's organization, such as its secretary general, journalist María Teresa Andrade, had always rejected any specific feminist dimension in the design and strategy of the organization.[142]

Another factor that accounts for the secondary status of gender issues is that the FSPOUM was not created in response to a female initiative to establish an organization to defend women's specific interests. Rather, it was created by the party as a political vehicle to channel female initiative and recruit more women to its Marxist political program: "The Female Secretariat is the mass organization of women and from there numerous militants can be attracted to the Party."[143] Furthermore, many of the most prominent women in the Female Secretariat had become involved in party politics through their family and personal relationships and thus lacked the experience of an autonomous political and gender militancy. Women such as María Teresa Andrade, Olga Nin, Antonia Adroher, Teresa Rebull, Luisa Gorkin, and María Manonellas came from such a background, while the major expression of the Secretariat on its policy on women–*La mujer ante la revolución*–appears to have been written by Katia Landau, the partner of Kurt Landau, Trotsky's ex-secretary.[144] Male hegemony in the party and the pressure of male activists in their immediate family made it even more difficult for these women to develop a more gender-conscious, independent strategy.

The Female Secretariat lacked a specific gender identity because its basic conception was as a vehicle to transmit party politics to women and not as an organization that would develop a strategy for women's emancipation. Feminist consciousness became blurred under this political pressure, even more so once the POUM recommended that all female militants in the party belong to the Female Secretariat.[145] This undoubtedly hindered the development of a more collective gender approach to women's issues by those militants who had developed a more sharpened feminist consciousness.

The FSPOUM was originally created to attract more women to the party[146] and to educate women "in Marxist principles, the only ones which can lead to the victory of the proletariat."[147] Its program gave clear priority to the political and revolutionary preparation of women to engage in their role in the revolutionary struggle. The women's organization gave a clear class content to its program and, unlike orthodox communism, identified completely with the dissident Marxist viewpoint that saw the war as both an antifascist and a revolutionary struggle. Political propaganda, revolutionary preparation, and a theoretical Marxist training of women were the immediate goals. Both the party and the Female Secretariat held that the revolution was the long-term objective.

Undoubtedly, revolutionary commitment in the context of potential social change within the Civil War had priority over any gender consciousness and demands. In February 1937, the first issue of the organization's newspaper, *Emancipación*, launched the slogan: "The true emancipation of women is only possible in a communist society"[148] while the Female Secretariat's declared program underscored the political character of the organization:

> Recruit the maximum number of women for the POUM.
>
> Foster women's fight together with their class brothers for the total emancipation of the proletariat.
>
> Make women understand that without their firm collaboration the triumph of the revolution is not possible.[149]

Many of the leaders of the FSPOUM were middle class and had a good education, such as Secretary General María Teresa Andrade, who had a degree in philosophy and worked as a journalist, and Antonia Adroher, who was a schoolteacher. Nevertheless, the FSPOUM women saw themselves as a proletarian organization whose constituency was working class. Most of the articles in *Emancipación* were addressed specifically to working-class women. In fact, with the exception of some of its leaders, most of its members were of working-class origin, with a fairly large number of schoolteachers and office workers.[150]

Both the program and the activities of the women's organization had a decidedly political tone, while any non-revolutionary stance on the antifascist resistance was summarily rejected. Significantly, the very title of the organization's newspaper, *Emancipación*, was explained more in political than in gender terms, as it expressed the purpose of the Female Secretariat to be "the revolutionary emancipation of the proletariat in its struggle for the destruction of capitalism and the conquest of power." However, specific attention to women was not entirely obscured, as this goal also included the "emancipation of woman from antiquated prejudices which place her in a situation of frank inferiority in social and economic life."[151]

Programmatically, the FSPOUM focused most of its attention on political education and the incorporation of women into the work force, which the leaders believed would further the development of production and the revolutionary conquests of the war while at the same time contributing to women's emancipation. No attention was given to the sexual division of labor or the implications of the responsibility of child care and domestic activities on female subordination. The gender specificity of female oppression was never acknowledged. According to the commonly held reductionist view, women's liberation would emerge automatically from the construction of a new social order:

> The new society concedes to her (the working-class woman) not only economic and social parity with men, but also a definitive equality of rights to both sexes.[152]

Active engagement in the war and revolution by the FSPOUM followed a similar pattern to the other women's organizations, with the development of comprehensive literacy and training programs, relief work, and the political organization of women. However, no doubt influenced by the writings of Alexandra Kollontai, whose works were well known and published by the dissident Marxists, the FSPOUM's approach to the issues of sexuality, birth control, and abortion was much more open and direct than that of other female organizations.[153] The FSPOUM was also quite unique in providing military training for women, although it agreed with the general view that women were to contribute to the war effort at the homefront and not in the trenches.[154] Of course, the brief lifespan of the organization, together with its unquestioning assumption that its primary function was to transmit party politics to women, left little room for a confrontation with male hegemony or the development of a strategy for revolutionary change that would contemplate gender distinctions or a feminist agenda. The eight-month period of initial expansion came to an abrupt halt with the intense repression of dissident Marxist activities after May 1937. This also affected the impact of the FSPOUM. Despite its many activities and publications, it had very little resonance among the general population.

The Widening Rift Among the Women's Organizations

Intense political rivalry characterized the relations among the different women's organizations. Overt hostility was frequently demonstrated by outspoken attacks in the press and at public meetings, which reflected the acute divisions among the different women's organizations. Their politicization prevented the development of a transpolitical women's movement. Political affiliation rather than gender identity informed the programs and strategies of anarchist, antifascist, and dissident Marxist women and conveyed the clear impression that these women shared no common gender-based goals. The political polarization of women and their organizations discouraged collaboration on specific issues and weakened the impact of any struggle to break down patriarchal ideology or behavior. Women were circumscribed to specific areas of action defined by political affiliation, while gender consciousness was insufficiently developed to challenge closed political differences.

It is true that some initiatives were undertaken to overcome women's organizational disunity. These were fostered particularly by the hegemonical women's organization Agrupación de Mujeres Antifascistas (AMA), which attempted to apply its overall policy of transpolitical unity to the dissident Marxist and anarchist women. In an attempt to unify the women's organizations, it invited the anarchist women to participate in the National Alliance of Women:

> Antifascist women, convinced of the need to unite all forces in order to win the war, are ready to undertake an effort to ensure that from the great National Conference of Antifascist Women the conclusion will be reached that Mujeres Libres, Libertarian Youth, Unión de Muchachas, and Antifascist Women, united by the same desire, will form a National Alliance of Women which, under the glorious banner of the Popular Front, will be the firmest pillar to achieve our victory.[155]

The National Federation of Mujeres Libres declined the invitation on the grounds that it was not only a women's organization but also had a clearly defined anarchist identity. Thus, it felt that unity should be expressed on a political level among parties and unions integrated into the Popular Front.[156] Because of its anarchist affiliation, Mujeres Libres' political conception of the war was incompatible with the views of the AMA, which, following orthodox communist policy, rejected any revolutionary implications to the antifascist resistance.

Mujeres Libres had "a clear consciousness that its mission went far beyond limited antifascism" to espouse the cause of the revolutionary transformation of society.[157] In an open letter to the press in response to another invitation by Dolores Ibárruri to join the AMA, Lucía Sánchez Saornil denounced the political ambiguity of the AMA.[158] In fact, the rejection was not based solely on the supposed lack of political definition of the umbrella organization but also on the Communist Party's influence on its direction. As Mujeres Libres reported to the Libertarian Movement (MLE), the AMA wanted a "unity which would avoid party politics and the imposition of a unilateral criterion in the direction of the war and the government of the country."[159] The same arguments were repeated by Mujeres Libres in its rejection of further proposals by the AMA and the Unió de Dones de Catalunya when it claimed that the Communist Party had infiltrated and imposed its policies on the AMA.[160]

Mujeres Libres distrusted the AMA's initiatives and suspected that the organization had a hidden agenda, "the unconfessable goal" of absorbing the anarchist organization once it joined the AMA.[161] Mujeres Libres denounced the constant attempts to pressure the anarchist organization into joining the AMA as coercion to accept the antifascist women's program.[162] The communist and antifascist women were also accused of deriving political and economic fringe benefits from their membership in the AMA.[163]

Despite some sporadic joint initiatives, consisting mainly of public meetings by women from the rival unions of the CNT and the UGT,[164] relations between anarchist and antifascist women were always belligerent and characterized by continual mutual accusations. The account by communist militant Soledad Real of the tense relations between communist and anarchist women in Barcelona tells of a climate of physical tension and aggression between the rival organizations.[165] Rival newspapers constantly reported varying versions of the activities of the women's organizations.[166] The journal *Mujeres*, published by the AMA in Bilbao, was an exception, with its somewhat more open, general disposition toward other political women's groups.[167] On the whole, Mujeres Libres was more on the defensive, given the political hegemony of the AMA, which adopted a more conciliatory tone in order to achieve its goal of unifying the women's groups. Of course, the very existence of the anarchist and dissident communist women's organizations, which refused to join the antifascist organization and openly questioned its claimed unity and transpolitical character, represented a clear sign of the failure of the AMA to achieve consensus on a united women's antifascist movement.

Relations were more cordial between the dissident Marxists and Mujeres Libres. In fact, the mutual confrontation with antifascist women's organizations and the Communist Party led both organizations to support one another. Mujeres Libres publicly defended the dissident Marxists and initiated negotiations with the FSPOUM to engage in a coordinated action to benefit women.[168] There was also some internal rivalry among the different groups in the antifascist organizations. Tensions among some of the socialist, republican, and communist leaders were manifest at times, as were rival strategies among the orthodox communists with regard to the leadership of the young women's movement in Catalonia.[169] As communist Teresa Pàmies candidly relates in her memoirs, contention among members of different organizations often was based on personal rivalry and class jealousy rather than on political disputes.[170]

The acute political confrontation between the orthodox communists (PCE) and the dissident Marxists (POUM) quickly went beyond the bounds of verbal aggression to an open offensive by the communists against the POUM, which culminated in the repression and elimination of the POUM by June 1937. Logically, this political conflict was reflected in the rivalry among the women's organizations. Open hostility characterized the relations between the Female Secretariat of the POUM and the communist-dominated antifascist women's organizations. Dissident Marxists rejected the reformist political strategy of the orthodox communists and the antifascist women's organizations. Margarita Abril, an FSPOUM militant, was outspoken in her denunciation of the antifascist women's organizations, where she claimed all reactionary women had found shelter. She was particularly emphatic in accusing the AMA of political ambiguity.[171]

Revolutionary Marxist women were warned to be on the alert so as not to be taken in by such an ambiguous political stance, hence the POUM's insistence on the need for a solid political formation of working-class women that would allow them to discern the correct strategy for revolutionary change.[172] In fact, the women of the POUM proposed the creation of a class alliance of women—the Revolutionary Front of Proletarian Women—which was to have specific revolutionary content and unite women in the endeavor to eradicate capitalism and establish a revolutionary society.[173] Logically, given the extreme debility of the movement and its political isolation, this project remained merely a hypothetical proposal.

Just as political confrontations impeded collaboration among the different tendencies on the Left, so, too, only a negligible proportion of women overcame political rivalry in an attempt to establish unity on gender and social issues. Despite the symbolic presence of a few token women from the CNT in the antifascist women's organizations,[174] political differences impeded the development of a genuine allied women's organization. What is significant is that political barriers were broken down more easily at a local rank-and-file level, where we find some evidence of sporadic and more long-term collaboration among women of different political affiliations. For example, 4 percent of the members of five local branches of the AMA in Levante were of anarchist affiliation, while in Catalonia there was some sporadic anarchist collaboration with the UDC.[175] The more diffused political identity found among women of the rank and file made such blurring of political differences easier and facilitated the development of common projects.

However, on the whole, female cohesion and unity on gender and social issues did not exist. Political polarization prevented the development of transclass unity around a common gender cause, and alternative political models hindered the realization of a common social or gender project among the women on the Left. Gender consciousness was insufficiently developed to break down the political impermeability of the women's organizations, which acted within closed arenas. Undoubtedly, political consciousness was more significant than gender identity. It is true that, among the rank and file, political stances were less significant, allowing for some collaboration on gender-specific issues. Nonetheless, despite a commonality of policy and activities, political polarization and open discord discouraged collaboration around specific projects. These projects were dealt with individually by the different organizations, thus debilitating the overall contribution to the war effort and, more significantly, the drive to improve women's social condition and to achieve women's emancipation.

Frederica Montseny, anarchist leader, Minister of Health and Social Assistance 1936-1937. (Photo Centelles). Reprinted by permission of the Centre d'Estudis Històrics Internacionals, Barcelona University.

Communist leader Dolores Ibárruri, "Pasionaria." Reprinted by permission of the Centre d' Estudis Històrics Internacionals, Barcelona University.

Lina Odena, a miliciana who died during the
first days of the war. Reprinted by permission
of the Centre d'Estudis Històrics
Internacionals, Barcelona University.

Dolors Bargalló, leader of the
Catalan antifascist organization at a
meeting at the Olympia Theatre in
Barcelona, September 20, 1936.
Reprinted by permission of the
Instituto Histórico Municipal de
Barcelona.

While men enlisted at the fronts, women took on work in factories. Private Collection.

Women demonstrating during the war. The banner held by the women's organization of the dissident Marxist party, Partido Obrero de Unificación Marxista, says: "Better to be the widow of a hero than the wife of a wretch." Reprinted by permission of the Instituto Histórico Municipal de Barcelona.

Flight from Almudeva (Huesca), which was occupied by Franco's troops. Private Collection.

Crèche at a camp for children of milicianos. Private Collection.

As the war developed, thousands of refugees were relocated to other areas of Republican Spain. Private Collection.

Group of milicianas about to leave for the Huesca front, August 28, 1936. Reprinted by permission of the Centre d'Estudis Històrics Internacionals, Barcelona University.

War poster with the famous slogan "No pasarán!" Reprinted by permission of the Centre d'Estudis Històrics Internacionals, Barcelona University.

War poster. "The Militias Need You." The image of the miliciana was used to entice men to take up arms. Reprinted by permission of the Centre d'Estudis Històrics Internacionals, Barcelona University.

War poster aimed at international antifascist solidarity. Reprinted by permission of the Centre d'Estudis Històrics Internacionals, Barcelona University.

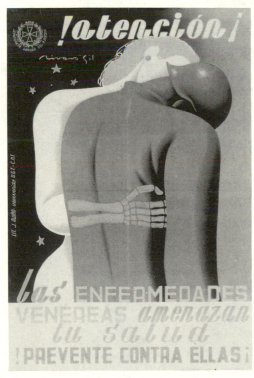

War poster warning against venereal diseases. Reprinted by permission of the Centre d'Estudis Histórics Contemporànis, Fundació Figueras, Barcelona.

War poster. Hiding from air raids. "Help Madrid." Reprinted by permission of the Centre d'Estudis Històrics Contemporànis, Fundació Figueras, Barcelona.

▪ 4 ▪

"Milicianas" or Homefront Heroines: Women's Place in the War

Some women's organizations refused to accept female inequality and drafted a more feminist–oriented agenda, but the overall activities of the different women's groups tended toward supportive and complementary antifascist activities. What is surprising is the clear consensus among all the groups that women were to be actors in the social arena only at the homefront.

At a time when there was greater social acceptance of women moving beyond the confines of the private domestic sphere into the public arena of work, politics, and culture, this strict delimitation of the bounds of women's activity to the homefront becomes particularly significant. Women were expected to dedicate themselves wholeheartedly to the war effort–but not at the war fronts. War rhetoric and imagery in slogans, propaganda, and war posters evoked the innovative figure of the *miliciana* clad in revolutionary blue overalls and armed with a rifle or a gun. The *miliciana*, as was discussed in chapter 2, projected a provocative image with multiple readings. She evoked the courage and bravery of the people in their fight against fascism and was also an enticement to take up arms in war. Nonetheless, although she was a woman in arms, she was not encouraged to take up arms as a soldier; indeed, the *miliciana* was not at all representative of women's resistance during the Civil War. Although constraints on female action were blurred slightly in the first weeks of the war, soon thereafter, women's organizations and political forces coincided in limiting women's war resistance to the homefront. The dominant mobilizing slogan–"Men to the War Front, Women to the Homefront"–evoked little opposition, even among militant women.

Gender, Militarism, and Antifascism

The fact that most women backed the policy to limit their role in the conflict to the homefront does not mean that they questioned militarism or felt disaffection with the war. Women participated enthusiastically in the war effort, and most of them supported military resistance to fascism.[1] Many were avowedly militarist, but gender differentiation channeled female mobilization into supportive, complementary roles in the antifascist resistance at the homefront. Despite the pacifist background of the Agrupación de Mujeres Antifascistas (AMA) and its earlier incorporation into the international peace movement to resist fascism, the organization unquestioningly supported the policy of military resistance to the fascist uprising.[2] All of the women's organizations identified with the war effort and took a militaristic position on this issue. They backed warfare, did not openly challenge the predominant militarist discourse, and rarely voiced a different gender perception of the war. Militarism, not pacifism, tended to inform their attitudes to the fascist uprising.[3]

As the war developed and the initial enthusiastic mobilization of the first months of 1936 wore off, women became more active in campaigns to arouse active military support for the war effort. The belligerent cry of communist leader Pasionaria in the early weeks of the war–"Better be the widows of heroes than the wives of cowards"–became a commonplace slogan taken up by women. At a meeting held in Catalonia in February 1937, a banner read, "We Catalan women have never bred cowards; our sons must not forsake their duty."[4] Militarist recruitment communiqués constantly urged women to comply with their duty to enlist their sons and husbands in trench warfare. Female heroism was equated with maternal sacrifice; women able to engage their sons in military resistance were considered heroic.[5] Vigilante committees were set up by women, particularly in the antifascist women's organizations and the communist groups, to detect draft dodgers and report them to the authorities.[6] Women were warned that if they helped Fifth Columnists (saboteurs and men who avoided recruitment), they were endangering their own sons and brothers.[7] Couched in a discourse that considered women primarily in relation to their family, militarist policies addressed toward women were also gender-defined and maintained traditional gender definitions of masculinity such as courage, honor, and virility:

> You cannot have a man by your side who has felt the shame of hiding, who has not had the virility to defend you, who has to blush when he stays while others who hear the cry of duty in the intimacy of their conscience leave for the front, proud to defend freedom, honor, the future and welfare of their family.[8]

When Pasionaria was named honorary commandant of the Fifth Regiment, she delivered a speech warning the soldiers that "if [the fascists] triumph, and [you are sent] to concentration camps, you can think about what your wives and mothers will tell you: 'Cry like women, since you did not know how to fight like men.'"[9] This echoes a traditional line in Spanish political discourse in which bravery was identified with virility and symbolic of manhood. By autumn 1937 and particularly in 1938, as the situation grew steadily worse for the republican army, women were often urged in public speeches to accuse able–bodied men seen on the streets out of uniform of being cowards and to encourage civilian men to enlist. Communist-influenced groups and organizations were particularly belligerent in attempting to persuade civilian men to accept their responsibilities and enlist. In an address to AMA women, Commandant Valentín González, the miner and well-known communist military leader popularly known as "El Campesino" (the peasant), urged women not only to adopt such policies but also to "become police and search out spies and Fifth Columnists."[10]

The belligerent tone and coaction implied in female recruitment of soldiers was denounced by the anarchist organization Mujeres Libres, which claimed, "It is too ridiculous to offer a prize of love to the husband, fiancé or son who decides to fight against fascism." The organization called instead for a general mobilization of the population and better arms.[11] The greater level of pacifist consciousness among Mujeres Libres can be attributed to the traditional formation of pacifist values in the anarchist movement which, unlike other political tendencies that fomented a military spirit, persisted during the war years in promoting pacifist educational values.[12] On the other hand, the constant propaganda inducing women to encourage male enlistment may have implied that women were loathe to provide soldiers for the war. Nonetheless, in the first eighteen months of the war, there does appear to have been a genuine identification by many thousands of women with furthering the military resistance to fascism. Reports from local AMA groups show that vigilante committees were formed to control slackers and "traitors," although it is difficult to assess whether these surveillance measures were effective in enforcing militarist policies during this period.[13]

It should also be noted that not all women were fervent republicans or promoted enlistment in the antifascist ranks. Some women were killed, fined, or imprisoned for their subversive support of fascists. Here again, traditional patriarchal structures were maintained, as in some cases the husband was obliged to pay a fine for his wife's subversive activities.[14] Toward the end of the war when defeat seemed inevitable, particularly in the spring of 1938 when seventeen-year-olds were conscripted in what was popularly called the Quinta del Biberón, the "Diaper Levy,"[15] many women resisted the enlistment of their sons.[16] By then, martial fervor was at odds with maternalism, and earlier claims of motherhood as a duty to the Fatherland ("We wish to deliver our sons to the Fatherland to defend it") were discarded.[17]

Although many women may have eventually practiced passive resistance to military recruitment by hiding their sons, they did not openly challenge the call to women to provide soldiers for the war. With the exception of the anarchists, most women's organizations collaborated enthusiastically in propagating a militaristic discourse to men and women. Women's pacifist disaffection with the war was not expressed at the time. However, in anarchist sources there are some attempts to give a more gender-specific perception of the war. In a speech given to Mujeres Libres in August 1938, the well-known anarchist leader Federica Montseny reviewed women's reaction to war and claimed that women were fundamentally pacifist: "Woman, by temperament, by her passion for her children, by her love of life, is a pacifist."[18] Montseny argued that the Spanish Civil War was unique in that it was a "pacifist war." This justified women's intervention in the war effort as the only path to freedom; fighting to end fascism could thus be considered pacifist. Montseny's discourse also repeated the common view of women's role as mothers, and she argued that, paradoxically, in order to guarantee a peaceful future and freedom for coming generations, women had to be militarist in this antifascist war:

> As women and mothers, we have to carry out our human, individual and collective duty by fighting against oppression, for freedom and justice, and [we have] to think that the sons we give to the war fronts and homefront today, tomorrow will have a more dignified life, peace and culture, school and well being which all great Spaniards dream of for the children of others and our own.[19]

In a less common approach, some women anarchists dealt with women directly as individuals who had to confront the reality of war unmediated by their relationship with their immediate family. Here one can detect a slight degree of gender disaffection with war, although a militarist line is defended in order, ultimately, to promote peace:

> We have to practice using arms...,in spite of the fact that doing so breaks our souls with pain, because women have always hated war, but for this very reason, we must now fight those who always promote it, and we must eliminate them so that Peace and Happiness may reign in Spain.[20]

Militia women who actually engaged in trench warfare at the fronts tended in their later testimonies to justify their decision by presenting this war in a different light, as a defensive fight for justice and freedom: "I participated because I felt I had the same duty to defend...the freedom which they [the enemy] wanted to take away; that is what we did. We women did not make war; we went to defend what they...were taking away from us."[21] The few who expressed gendered considerations on the war agreed that this war was not comparable to any other. Defensive and pacifist in aiming to eliminate fascism, women's participation in the war effort was thus justified.

"Milicianas" and Women's Experience at the War Fronts

In the first weeks of the war, all the women's organizations converged in channeling female energy to the war effort at the homefront. However, a small number of women joined their male comrades and enrolled in the militia. In the initial upsurge of antifascist fervor, some women spontaneously opted for active military combat and headed off for the war fronts in Aragón, in Guadalajara, in the mountains of the Basque country and the Sierra of Madrid, in Andalusia and Majorca, and in the Maestranza, among others.

In this early stage of popular mobilizations, many women simply took up arms as an immediate response to fascist aggression, just as the men did. Rosario Sánchez, "La Dinamitera" (the dynamiter), a member of the communist youth organization JSU, commented in a later testimony that she was not militarist but felt immediately responsible for what could happen after the fascist rebellion "because if the rebels were not stopped we would have a dictatorship and we workers would have a bad time." So she decided to enlist in the militia, knowing that it meant having to take up arms and engage in shooting.[22]

Catalan anarchist Conchita Pérez, who later fought in the defense of Belchite, did not regard her gender as an issue when she decided to embrace armed resistance: "The group that went, we went as a man. We went, not as soldiers, because we did not consider ourselves to be soldiers, but as a group. And I tell you, there were ten of us, as we considered that there were ten of us, nine men and a woman!"[23] The young communist Lena Imbert went off to the trenches because she felt that posts at the homefront were for the wounded or for children.[24] Basque anarchist Casilda Méndez, who during the Republic had actively accompanied her *compañeros* in the social struggle, which included sabotage, continued with them in military combat in the mountains of Peñas de Aya.[25] In a letter to her family, a young *miliciana* who would soon be killed at the Aragon front clearly showed that she did not believe women should be excluded from a military role:

> My heart cannot remain impassive seeing the struggle my brothers are carrying out....And if anyone says to you that fighting is not for women, tell them that discharging revolutionary duty is the obligation of all who are not cowards.[26]

There are countless tales of the heroism of the *milicianas* who took part in the fighting at the fronts, although one can detect a slight element of surprise in the reaction of the militiamen when they described acts of direct combat and bravery performed by women that they had witnessed. They appeared to expect different conduct by women and did not quite know how to deal with female bravery in combat. Their descriptions of such episodes tended to be couched in paternalistic terms. An account of an anarchist woman who took part in a skirmish with the enemy at the Aravaca front ended with the words of the militiaman Román:

> He lifts her up...and fraternally takes her right hand and deposits a kiss of respect on it....Román does not know what to do and his lips mumble these tender words full of emotion.
> "Comrade, you are a brave and valiant woman."[27]

For most women, as for men, the decision to participate in armed combat appears to have derived from their social and political consciousness. They were motivated to defend the political and social rights acquired during the Second Republic and to demonstrate their repudiation of fascism. For many, armed fighting was just a continuation of their earlier involvement in union and social movements. It is significant in this light that Casilda Méndez rejected the term *miliciana*, preferring to call herself a "revolutionary" or a "combatant."[28] In her case, as in many others, her political consciousness impelled her to take up arms in yet another battle. Lena Imbert's revolutionary zeal and desire for action attracted her immediately to armed combat,[29] while, by contrast, a less politicized, anonymous militia woman at the Majorca front whose testimony has been recorded by Josep Massot i Muntaner appears to have been inspired by more general ideals of equality, fraternity, and liberty.[30] Press reports differentiated between armed combat undertaken by women with a history of political commitment, such as Catalan communist Caridad Mercader, and that of others who were purported to have had less serious reasons for donning *miliciana* gear:

> Without paying it too much attention, our companion exchanged the typewriter for a mauser, just like so many other men and women had done.
> Therefore, Caridad Mercader is as far removed from the rowdy girl who wears "overalls", for reasons nobody can figure out, as she is from the girl who appears today in illustrated pages of a certain press which is always sensationalist and even at times yellow.[31]

Of course, not all women had the same motivations for joining up. Together with the evident attraction of an immediate physical response to fascist aggression, there was also the appeal of assuming a totally new role that broke with the constraints of traditional norms of gender behavior. Young, self-assertive women could opt spontaneously to fight just like their male counterparts, and this was actually accepted in the initial rhetoric of antifascist mobilizations.[32] Some wished to reject a secondary role at the homefront. Others, influenced by their own particular circumstances, accompanied their husbands or fiancés to the fronts.

The oral testimony of Concita Pérez Collado, who as a *miliciana* participated in warfare at the Belchite and Huesca fronts, tells how personal relations also influenced women's choices to join the militia. "There were couples, too. There was one..., a very united couple, who had a child then....Well, they were like a married couple but they were not married. The two of them were there...; they respected one another."[33]

Romanticism and high ideals also influenced the decision of some women to follow the example of other members of their family: "The sister of some militiamen was there....She had been about to become a novice, to be a nun, and, on the contrary, when she saw her brothers and her friends all going to the front, she came with us, to help us. I mean that it was pure romanticism."[34] For others, there was the appeal of adventure in the early summer months, even a certain holiday spirit and the possibility of developing new personal relations, as the anonymous *miliciana* recounts in her diary detailing the experiences of 30 *milicianas* in Majorca in the summer of 1936.[35] She, in fact, was highly critical of "those girls who think they have come on holidays" or those like her friend Teresa, who deserted the group because "she prefers better company and spends the day chatting, going for walks or bathing on the beach."[36]

From the scanty documentation available, a general trend appears to emerge of young women, already integrated into political parties or unions, who headed off with their comrades and friends to join the militia. Most of these young women appear to have come from politicized anarchist or communist youth backgrounds and were already integrated into political circles. Thus, they were on familiar terms with the men with whom they enlisted.[37] Another group was comprised of militia women who enlisted with friends, husbands, or *novios* (fiancés).[38] Such was the case with Casilda Méndez and with Mika Etchebéhère, who initially came from France to fight in Spain with her husband, a commander of the POUM militians. He was killed in the first weeks of the war, and she stayed on and was promoted to captain of the Second Company of the POUM.[39] While most of the *milicianas* were young, and thus free of the domestic responsibilities of older women who were mothers,[40] a few women volunteers were older, and there is documentation that some mothers accompanied their sons into battle.[41]

Women's entry into the militia seems to have been entirely spontaneous, as there was no official recruitment policy for women. In the early days of the war, Artur Cussó, the secretary of the women's organization of the Catalan Communist Party, PSUC, urged women to set up a female militia.[42] Even this call was ambivalent, however, as it appeared to depict women's role as supportive and spiritual, focused on aiding the families of the dead combatants rather than on direct combatant activity. Nonetheless, by early August, a women's battalion, which included women from Barcelona, Sabadell, and Mataró, had been formed in Catalonia. This battalion was incorporated into the republican forces that left Barcelona to defend Majorca against the fascist rebels in the summer of 1936,[43] but all evidence indicates that auxiliary support services were the basis of their everyday experience.[44]

The *Diario del Quinto Regimento de Milicias Populares* made several calls to arms for both male and female recruits in the summer of 1936 and established a nursery for the children of militians.[45] However, women generally did not join up through official channels, and, by the autumn of 1936, such sporadic calls for female military recruitment were abandoned. In fact, some women tried to join up through regular channels and were bitterly disappointed when they were turned away because of their gender. The women's disappointment occasionally led to attempts at mobilization to demand access to military warfare. Such was the case of the young Catalan Carme Manrubia, who, on being refused entrance to the School for War Commissaries, tried to gain support for female military mobilization.[46] However, by the winter of 1936, it was quite clear that the women's organizations concurred in limiting women's mobilization to the homefront.

It is impossible to ascertain the number of militia women who carried out military or auxiliary roles at the war fronts. However, all the existing testimonies suggest that there were relatively few. The Basque *miliciana* Casilda Méndez was the only woman in her unit in the Basque country, and, later, when she went to the Aragon front after the fall of the North, only one other woman was in her unit.[47] The Catalans at the Aragon front comprised a small elite of women, while the largest group appears to have been the contingent of 30 militia women who accompanied a male contingent of 400 to the Balearic Islands in August 1936.[48] Mika Etchebéhère's testimony also points to the small number of militia women at the fronts in Central Spain, although the Fifth Regiment did have a number of women present in the early months. Other accounts document a small number of Asturian militia women, one of whom was a captain in the machine gun company of the Second Asturias Battalion.[49] It is difficult to interpret these low numbers because not all women who wished to serve as militians were able to do so. Many women who tried to enlist were told that it was a man's job, while others were persuaded they would be more useful at the homefront.[50]

During the first months of the war, the *milicianas* executed a complex series of functions at the fronts, dedicating themselves mostly to ancillary supportive tasks. It is true that many women fought like male soldiers, frequently undertaking combat duties. Others performed significant work as political advisers, such as the communist leader Anita Carrillo, political coordinator of the Mexico Battalion.[51] However, there was a decided degree of sexual division of labor even at the fronts, for women usually undertook culinary, laundry, sanitary, postal, liaison, and administrative assignments. In the Fifth Regiment, women took care of most of these auxiliary tasks. Occupational segregation was quite prevalent at the fronts, and armed combat was reserved, with few exceptions, for male soldiers. The delegation of women to non-combat duties at the fronts was justified on the grounds of their lack of military training as well as their purportedly greater capacity to carry out such supportive responsibilities. Generally, this rationale was accepted by women, but there are some signs that not all *milicianas* agreed with being assigned culinary, laundry, cleaning, or nursing jobs. Conchita Pérez Collado explained:

> All the women I saw carried guns...and did guard duty, and when we were sent to an attack–we went. And we were not laundry women. If things had to be washed, well, we all washed them...and we did everything together with them [the militiamen].[52]

Two *milicianas* decided to abandon the Fifth Regiment and to transfer to the POUM column captained by Mika Etchebéhère, where they were not obliged to wash and cook. Their assignments were the same as the male members of the column. As Manuela, one of the militia women, explained to Etchebéhère's column:

> I have heard that in your column the *milicianas* have the same rights as the men, that they do not wash the clothes and the dishes. I have not come to the front in order to die for the revolution with a kitchen cloth in my hand.[53]

Although Manuela was applauded by the male militians,[54] Etchebéhère had experienced difficulties in the column she captained because the men had expected the women *milicianas* to launder and mend their clothes, wash up, and scrub. In fact, they had refused to take on "women's" jobs themselves because they alleged that, in the Fifth Regiment, women attended to those chores. Eventually, Etchebéhère managed to persuade the men to accept an egalitarian division of tasks in the column, but this was undoubtedly feasible only because the commanding officer was a woman with a highly exceptional feminist consciousness regarding women's equality. In fact, the major justification for the presence of women at the fronts was based on the fact that they carried out "womanly duties."[55] There was little questioning of traditional female roles even in such novel, exceptional circumstances as trench warfare. Although militia warfare had initially represented a breakdown in hierarchical structures, it, too, formulated its own gender rules and norms of conduct.

Changing Attitudes toward the "Milicianas"

In the early weeks of the war, the *miliciana* was represented in the press, in speeches, and in war rhetoric and imagery as the "heroine of the Fatherland."[56] Heroism, courage, and strength formed part of the legend of the woman soldier in arms against fascism. Women who opted for armed combat were initially praised as symbols of generosity, bravery, and popular antifascist resistance:

> She did not vacillate. And with a decided step she launched herself to the street beside the worker....And she offered her young life, bursting

with youthful illusions, in the first days of the heroic struggle, when each man was a hero and each woman the equivalent of a man.[57]

Foreign war reporters and members of the International Brigade spoke of the bravery that characterized many *milicianas* and described the "very business–like and attractive young partisan" girls mobilized at the fronts.[58] As the poet Miguel Hernández wrote, the *miliciana* could retain her female identity while undertaking masculine duties: "Rosario, the dynamiter, / you can be a man and you are / the cream of women, / the spume of the trenches."[59]

Very quickly, however, attitudes changed. As was discussed in chapter 2, propaganda shifted toward mobilizing women in their effort at the homefront. Women were quite clearly told that they should not consider themselves the equivalent of men and that the roles of men and women in the conflict were different. During the war, military vocabulary increasingly permeated antifascist discourse. "Mobilizations," "female militia," and "women's battalions" became commonplace terms to describe female antifascist resistance, but these terms carried a clearly defined distinction–women's role was strictly circumscribed to non–military activities at the homefront. As Dolors Piera, the leader of the Catalan antifascist group Unió de Dones, stated, "At the homefront each woman has to be a soldier."[60] A clear gender division of roles emerged. Men were appointed to military combat duties in trench warfare, while women were assigned to auxiliary, supportive service in the rear guard. As Orwell described, the attitude toward militia women changed dramatically in a short period of months. The women went from being eulogized to being ridiculed and discredited.[61] For once, there was consensus among severely divided political parties, unions, and even women's organizations on the need to oblige *milicianas* to withdraw from the war fronts, and, by September, a policy was being implemented to coerce them to leave the fronts. In late autumn, this policy was sanctioned by the socialist head of the government, Prime Minister Largo Caballero, who endorsed military ordinances ordering women to withdraw from the militia.[62] Not all women abandoned the war fronts immediately, but by the beginning of 1937 their numbers had been reduced drastically.[63]

It is true that a small number of *milicianas* like Casilda Méndez and Lena Imbert went from front to front even as late as 1937. However, these women were highly exceptional. By December 1936, foreign volunteers were being warned that women could not join the militia.[64] By early September, the Catalan Communist Party reversed its earlier call for militia women and asked women to organize at the homefront. The slogan "Men to the War Fronts, Women to the Homefront" became commonplace in most political circles. A communist spokesman, while acknowledging that the initial impulse of women to join the militia had been a noble one, emphasized that it had also been fundamentally an empty gesture. He argued this on the grounds that the lack of preparation by the *milicianas* had limited their usefulness at the fronts:

We must acknowledge the merit of those brave girls, who in the flower of youth offered their lives in defence of freedom; but we must not forget that one must have a certain degree of knowledge and preparation in order to assist an operator who is trying to save life in serious danger. Unfortunately, not all women have such knowledge. And that is the reason why, despite the enthusiasm of these beautiful *milicianas*, on many occasions they are of little use in the barracks or at the hospitals.[65]

Although they believed that women had played a positive role at the fronts, a number of *milicianas*, nonetheless, returned to the homefront because they themselves were convinced that their skills would be more useful there.[66]

A puzzling feature in this development and one that is difficult to assess is the fact that none of the women's organizations publicly challenged the campaign to make women give up armed combat. Indeed, one senses a degree of complicity and a certain unwillingness to discuss this matter openly, although sporadic references recount the bitter disappointment of many *milicianas* on being obliged to leave the fronts. We do not even find an open concerted defense of militia women in the women's journals of the time. Few texts criticized the disdain expressed toward women by men in power structures,[67] and none defended female competence or questioned the validity of the argument that women's lack of military or professional training limited their usefulness at the war fronts.[68]

This lack of a sustained challenge to official positions points to the persistence of traditional parameters of gender division of labor and norms of social conduct that appear to have prevented a reformation of gender roles. The implication was that *milicianas* were odd and atypical of the vast majority of women. Furthermore, the tone in the women's journals tended, on the whole, to be apologetic. Phrases like "true women did not bring dishonor to the front"[69] and "whenever we speak of women at the front, we associate [the experience] with certain disagreeable memories"[70] were quite common, while even the Female Secretariat of the POUM, the women's organization that had most actively defended women's need for military training, alleged that male and female duties in the war should be different and that women's proper place was not at the war fronts.[71]

Many reasons were given to justify the hidden agenda of women's confinement to the homefront. The principal contention was that women were more effective there, as they had the training to carry out the tasks necessary to support the war effort; concomitantly, their lack of military training and unfamiliarity with weapons made them unfit candidates for armed warfare. This argument was presented both by women's organizations and political groups. In fact, the militia women themselves acknowledged the validity of this line of reasoning and rationalized their dedication to supportive relief work and ancillary sanitation and hospital services on the grounds that they were better trained for such tasks. They did not attribute this gender-based division of labor to any innate qualities inherent to women but rather to their lack of military training and skill in handling guns. Moreover, their performance at the front failed to improve because men were reluctant to provide them with arms training.[72]

Many women also felt that a direct military role was inappropriate for them. Their supposedly "natural" preference for peace negated dedication to warfare. The women's organizations also denounced women's involvement in armed combat, considering it an inadmissible emulation of male peers and improper conduct for women. Gender differences were upheld to explain role differentiation and the distinct functions of men and women in the antifascist resistance. The women's organizations also argued that psychological and biological differences mandated the confinement of women to the homefront. Even anarchist Mujeres Libres espoused gender differences as an explanation for distinct gender roles in war in their assessment of women's role published in their journal *Mujeres Libres* in July 1937.

> Women...understood that street skirmishes did not at all resemble the desperate, regular, methodical struggle of trench warfare. Understanding this, and recognizing her own value as a woman, she preferred to exchange the gun for an industrial machine and war energy for the sweetness of her WOMANLY soul....She has known how to imprint the delicate sweetness of her female psychology on the vulgar ambience of the war. She has a mother's care for those who, tired of long days' fighting, return to their homes and she tries to keep optimism alive when morale is low.[73]

Another matter was at the heart of the debate. By autumn, the question of prostitution had become inextricably linked to women's presence at the war fronts. Thus, a new, more ambiguous allegation–that the *milicianas* were acting as prostitutes–was decisive in discrediting them and resulted in the popular demand that they be dismissed from the war fronts. Women were directed to return immediately from the fronts before venereal disease was spread further. This allegation received a good deal of coverage in both the republican and fascist press and was highly instrumental in restricting women to a support function in the war effort. *Milicianas* were often linked to prostitution, and it was even insinuated that they represented the Fifth Column and infiltrated antifascist supporters:

> At first prostitutes joined the Popular Militia, apparently with great decision and much enthusiasm; but when the heads of military divisions realized the ravages which certain well-dressed *milicianas* caused, they immediately put an end to their activity, which undoubtedly obeyed a preconceived plan of the fascists to initiate the counterrevolutionary movement.[74]

Former militia women have denounced what they considered a slanderous attack on their integrity orchestrated both by fascist propaganda and republican sources.[75] The identification of militia women with prostitutes is too simplistic to be tenable if applied generally to all *milicianas*. Some prostitutes did go to the front in the initial stages of the war as militians or nurses, as did some male criminals released from prisons.[76] The latter, however, were not felt to discredit all militians and soldiers. It is impossible to give an estimate of the numbers of prostitutes at the war fronts, but they appear to have been a very small minority and to have remained at the fronts only a short time. The famous anarchist leader Buenaventura Durruti, who was responsible for the collectivization of the land in Aragon and the creation of the Aragon Defense Council, is said to have had a number of prostitutes executed when they refused to leave the Aragon front.[77]

As was the case with militiamen and soldiers, female *milicianas* were a heterogeneous group. The anarchist sexologist, writer, and sex reformer Dr. Félix Martí Ibáñez established a triple profile of the women who went to the war fronts. Like many other writers, he differentiated among the genuine revolutionaries, politically experienced women, and other women whose motives were questionable. According to this classification, the genuine *milicianas* formed only a very small minority. The second and largest group was composed of what Martí Ibáñez called the "romantic" women who "on an impulse, left for the front as nurses, dreaming of being Joan Crawford, dressed in red and white uniform and attending invisible, lyrical wounds of blond photogenic heroes, and then fainted in front of the body of a militian or a soldier mutilated by shrapnel."[78] According to Martí Ibáñez, this romantic, false image of war had more to do with novels than with a realistic assessment of warfare and led many women to look for a compensation for their suffering in the arms of the militians. The gender bias of Martí Ibáñez prevented him from seeing the reverse side of his argument, that the boys might want to be heroes à la Gary Cooper and look for solace in the arms of war front heroines. Together with these two categories, Martí Ibáñez presented a third group of women mercenaries who went to the fronts to commercialize their bodies as prostitutes.

Equating the figure of the *miliciana* with a prostitute became more generalized by early 1937. Yet, despite lack of sources, a closer reading of the situation of the *milicianas* through their testimony at the fronts points in fact to quite a different reality, where prostitution was far from rife. Former *milicianas* reiterated the point that, while at the war fronts, they did not see or have contact with prostitutes. It is true that, in contrast to the rigid traditional norms of gender behavior, there was a certain relaxation in the development of personal relations between some men and women at the fronts.[79] New relationships occasionally were formed, but many of the women had already developed steady bonds with the men they had accompanied to the fronts. In fact, many of these men and women later got married. Other militia women commented that at the fronts there was no time to think of personal or sexual relations, as they were so busy struggling for survival and fighting the cold, hunger, lice, and the enemy.[80] Some women pointed out that even while sharing beds with militians they were never harassed.[81] The *miliciana* Casilda Méndez claimed that the development of sexual relations was a natural, conscious, and, therefore, admissible choice of men and women at the front:

> There was an end to [the sort of] woman who could only hope to please her husband through housework and the bed. What they say about women going to the front in order to go to bed with the militians...all that is a lie. Now, it is unavoidable for empathy and affinities to develop between women and men; some call it chemical or cellular attraction, and relationships develop, particularly in areas isolated from urban areas, like the Aragon Front. Physical, moral and spiritual contacts can exist between a man and a woman who are at the war fronts. The contrary would be an aberration.[82]

The argument that women should be retired from the fronts because of the danger of spreading venereal disease was often voiced and undoubtedly became one of the main factors in the growing discredit of the militia woman. It is true that one of the major sanitation problems of the war was the control of venereal diseases, which had become a grave health hazard by 1937. The records of the Department of Derma–syphology of the Hospital de la Santa Cruz and San Pablo (General Hospital of Catalonia) in Barcelona show a substantial increase in this problem during the war years, while a nurse recorded that "prostitutes caused more casualties among the men than the enemy's bullets."[83] The Central Government and the Catalan Government developed health policies in this area. Very little documentation exists on the issue of venereal disease, but it is interesting to note that the spread of venereal diseases may have owed more to the extraordinary development of prostitution at the homefront, where the industry grew to meet the demand of soldiers on leave, than to sexual activity at the war fronts.

Even radical defenders of female emancipation and equality took a sexist position on the issue of women's removal from the fronts. One particularly significant example is provided by sexologist Dr. Martí Ibáñez, one of the major proponents of the anarchist sex reform movement and instigator of the legislation legalizing abortion in Catalonia in December 1936.[84] In a tract called "Eugenical Message to Women," he introduced another dimension to the argument to justify women's dismissal from armed combat, contending that their removal from the fronts would help conserve biological energy for the war effort by avoiding sexual intercourse.

According to Martí Ibáñez, the war had created new biological and social duties for women. They were to inspire men to dedicate themselves to the war through the mobilization of their spiritual and physical energies. Thus, women's duty was to facilitate "continence, sexual discipline, and harmony in erotic relations."[85] Biological energy should not be wasted on erotic relationships but rather concentrated on the war effort. Human energy should be economized; as a result, chastity and sexual discipline had to be imposed temporarily in order to channel maximum human potential to the war effort. Thus, Martí Ibáñez argued that women should fulfil their duty to the cause by staying in the rearguard and giving up their claim to fight at the fronts. He depicted many *milicianas* as promiscuous mercenaries of love incapable of reform:

> And you, mercenaries or half virtuous women,... who in the midst of a Revolution tried to convert the sacred land of the war front, covered with proletarian blood, in a garden of pleasure, go back! If the militia man seeks you out, let it be in his free time, and under his own moral responsibility, helped by existing hygienic resources. But do not make him stray from his path nor put the softness of erotic fatigue in the steel of his muscles....You cannot give up your previous lifestyle by sowing the battle front with venereal diseases....Venereal diseases must be extirpated from the front, and in order to do so, women must first be removed.[86]

One can detect sexist undertones in the analysis of this issue among all political sectors. Communist and military sources were even more hostile to *milicianas* and openly discredited them. There is no attempt, not even by women, to redress the imbalance and to pose questions regarding male sexual harassment at the fronts. It is true that most testimonies of former *milicianas* confirm the honorable behavior of their comrades and the lack of sexual harassment. However, there is also some evidence of tension arising in personal relations among men and women at the front.

The diary of a *miliciana* at the Majorca front speaks of her fear of sexual overtures and harassment by male soldiers and the difficulties involved when women did not acquiesce to men's wishes.[87] During their sporadic contacts with soldiers at the fronts, women were often harassed by soldiers. Teresa Pàmies describes such an incident when, as a seventeen-year-old with almost missionary-like fervor to provide moral support and political indoctrination to the soldiers at the fronts, she was scorned and insulted because she declined the invitation of a young militian to join him behind the olive bushes. Pàmies's description illustrates the gap that must have existed between politicized, relatively liberal women such as herself and the majority of the young soldiers she accompanied. Facing this "serious and politically responsible" girl who "wished to fraternize with the combatants of the Republic" was the earnest young soldier who kept reiterating: "Yes. All right. But why don't you and I go for a tumble among the olive trees, love?"[88] When she refused to comply, he retorted bitterly: "What do you know about what combatants need? It's the only thing that excuses you, your ignorance. I bet you a leg of *serrano* ham that you are still a virgin, you brazen wench."[89]

Episodes of this sort were undoubtedly common at the time and point to the mutual lack of understanding and different expectations between young men and women. Men's attitudes toward women had not changed; women continued to be considered sexual objects. The frank bewilderment of the highly politicized but naive young Pàmies led her later to attempt to understand the young man's bitter reaction and to wonder whether she should have acquiesced in order to "take away the tender sadness from those adolescent eyes."[90] In oral testimony, Antonia García, a communist and antifascist activist, told of frequent incidences of sexual harassment at the homefront and claimed that the saying that "men are communist, socialist, or anarchist from the waist up" was very popular among women. According to her testimony, even politically conscious men "had no control and all women were the same for them. They acted just like an Andalusian *señorito* or a capitalist."[91]

Finally, the question of military discipline and the decision to militarize the popular militia played a decisive role in justifying the campaign to eliminate women from the war fronts. The popular militia had emerged as a response to the military fascist aggression in the first days of the war when the republican army had collapsed. The civil population of workers, intellectuals, and peasants–the "people in arms"–took on the fight against the fascist military rebellion. The popular militias were armed groups that did not respond to traditional army discipline or military hierarchy. They were organized mainly by anarchist, dissident Marxist and union organizations with military guidance by soldiers and officials loyal to the Republic. The popular militia provided a collective, non-hierarchical model of armed resistance that also tended to espouse the revolutionary cause. The initiative undertaken by the communists to regulate the military in 1937, when the initial revolutionary impulse was contained, led to the revival of the traditional military model of a regular, tightly disciplined, conventional army. The anarchist defeat in May 1937 meant the gradual elimination of the militia as a popular armed response to antifascist warfare.

So, in fact, women found themselves caught up in a larger political struggle between two models of military institutions: the non-hierarchical, voluntary militia service and the highly stratified regular armed forces. The militia woman did not fit within the disciplinary structure of the regular army. With the disappearance of the militia, the option of armed resistance for women became untenable. Militia women appear to have had little control over the terms in which their struggle was being enacted and were unable to maintain their credibility as heroic armed combatants against fascism. Neither they nor the women's organizations developed a concerted, collective front to challenge the definition of women's role in the conflict.

"War Godmothers," Volunteers, and Non–combatant Activities

Although the policy of armed mobilization was rejected by the women's organizations, women had frequent contact with the war fronts, not only as nurses but in support activities for the combatants. The different women's organizations participated in "winter campaigns" to promote the manufacture of clothes for the soldiers. This initiative was quite important in light of the difficulties in providing winter clothes. Small packets of food, clothing, tobacco, soap, toothpaste, pencils, paper, and other items were sent to soldiers at the fronts. Various campaigns were established to provide the solders with whatever they needed. The Antifascist Women's Organization (AMA) published a column in the press entitled "Soldier, What Do You Want? What Do You Need?" designed to ascertain the needs of the soldiers. Campaigns were subsequently developed to meet those needs.[92] Mujeres Libres formed a group dedicated to catering to the needs of the soldiers,[93] and all the women's organizations maintained direct contact with the front lines through visits and donations of clothes, food, flags, and other supplies. Boosting the morale of the soldiers constituted a primary objective of the women's organizations, and visits to the fronts were frequently arranged. These visits were at least partially politically motivated, as the AMA tended to visit predominantly communist and socialist battalions while Mujeres Libres visited anarchist troops.

These visits sometimes had objectives other than the political ones of maintaining morale, nurturing the soldiers' war spirit, and reassuring them of the fighting spirit at the homefront.[94] On some occasions, they served a more frivolous purpose–providing a momentary distraction for the soldiers with singing and dancing. The young JSU leader Teresa Pàmies later wrote that these occasions provided great fun and a lot of innocent amusement. However, such visits often resulted in problems when, as Pàmies described, soldiers mistakenly assumed that such contacts were a prelude to sexual relations.[95]

In Jativa, a visit to the front by Pepita García to see her two sons led to a campaign by the local branch of the AMA to provide sheets and clothes for the wounded at the fronts.[96] All of the women's groups organized visits to hospitals at the homefronts to look after the wounded and to provide general follow–up services for convalescent soldiers. Workshops were set up to make sweaters and other clothes for the soldiers, and sanitation supplies were collected to be forwarded to the fronts.[97]

Contact with the soldiers at the fronts generated a new form of personal relations, which became very popular in 1938. Women became Madrinas de Guerra (war godmothers) in this new role, and their task was to correspond with the soldiers at the fronts.[98] Yet the figure of the godmother was a traditional one, unlike that of the innovative *miliciana*, and its utilization betokened the endurance of traditional attitudes toward women. Thousands of letters were sent by soldiers who wanted to correspond with war godmothers. Many letters show that, despite the use of courtesy formulas such as "revolutionary salutations" or "Health and Republic," the soldiers tended to display very traditional attitudes toward women. Many letter exchanges were written as the beginning of a personal relationship that would lead to an engagement and marriage:

> The reason we are writing to you is the following: finding ourselves in the field of operations and not having anybody to write to nor any privacy, we turn to you in hopes that two young girls of your worthy organization will be kind enough to establish correspondence with us (with a view to marriage); we are disheartened with life and have decided to get married soon if we have an opportunity to do so, although you may take this as a joke.[99]

Of course, not all women were considered worthy of war godmother status; the soldiers asked that the *mujercitas* (little women) be the prettiest and most charming.[100] Other soldiers made a more conventional request, asking for proper girls or the possibility of a political discussion in their correspondence.[101] From the point of view of many soldiers, the institution of the Madrina de Guerra appeared to be a matrimonial agency or a social assistance service that provided a distraction from boredom at the fronts, such as laundering of clothes, domestic service, and motherly, sisterly, or wifely attention.[102] Such expectations, of course, were often disappointed, as the Madrinas de Guerra were designed just for correspondence. Moreover, because of the large number of responses from the soldiers, it was feared that, in such a mass of correspondence, strategic information might be revealed. That fear, together with the increasing difficulties endured by the republican army, conspired to prevent any substantial development of the figure of the Madrina de Guerra, which was eventually discarded by women antifascist activists.

The Cultural Militias were created in December 1936 as an initiative of the Federación Española de Trabajadores de la Enseñanza (FETE), the Spanish federation of teaching professionals, to fight the high level of illiteracy among the soliders at the war fronts.[103] This voluntary drive to raise cultural awareness among the soldiers at the fronts was given official backing in January 1937 by the Ministry of Public Instruction. The FETE's slogan, "Guns and books, two arms for victory," was representative of the republican and leftist cultural initiatives during the Civil War that exalted culture as a means for self-improvement and political awareness. At the inauguration of the Library of the First Mixed Brigade in January 1937, it was claimed that "nothing better than books will give these men the deep awareness [needed] in order to behave in the new life regime we propose."[104] Military vocabulary was used to describe the mobilization of former actors, poets, and writers who were converted into soldiers of culture.

The Cultural Militias provided soldiers with schools, newspapers, journals, books, library services, sports, cinema, and theater in order to broaden their cultural horizons. At the same time, their aim was to provide entertainment and escape from the tense situation in the trenches.[105] Although the Cultural Militia volunteers were mainly teachers, intellectuals, and writers already soldiering at the fronts, cultural interaction at the war fronts was another outlet for women.

The writer, actress, and theatre director María Teresa León was a prominent figure in these activities. She organized plays, poetry readings, song sessions, and other cultural activities at the fronts.[106] Since its foundation in 1935, María Teresa León and her husband, poet Rafael Alberti, had played a very active role in the development of the Alliance of Antifascist Intellectuals, and during the war she organized theater groups within the Alliance to further new theatrical experiences. Together with Alberti, she was co-director of the important cultural journal *El Mono Azul* (The Blue Overall), which fomented popular literature and poetry by recounting the experiences of life at the trenches.[107] As she tells in her writings, she was an active member of the "Theatre Guerrillas of the Center Army," a voluntary, itinerant theater group that held functions in villages and towns and at the fronts. León played a leading role in the organization, directing and even acting in some of the plays performed.[108] She was also active on the Board for the Defense and Protection of National Treasure and one of the key figures in the protection of Spanish art collections during the war.

A considerable number of women intervened in this arena, and actresses and women performers in variety and entertainment shows collaborated with popular cultural initiatives both at the homefront and the war fronts.[109] Although in Spain there was a centuries-old tradition of actresses, they were often identified as disreputable, indecent women or even as prostitutes. Significant changes had come about since the 1920's and the appearance of the renowned actress Margarita Xirgu, but in traditional Spanish society, women's appearance on the stage still represented a violation of the norms of gender conduct.

In her autobiography, *Memorias de la melancolía*, Maria Teresa León describes how the war opened up new possibilities for her to develop her potential on the stage as an actress and reciter of poetry, breaking with traditional norms of female decency imposed in Spanish society. She often had occasion to recite the poetry of her husband, Rafael Alberti, especially his *Cantata de los Héroes y la Fraternidad de los Pueblos* in honor of the International Brigades.[110] During the war, together with the wider acceptance of women in the world of theater and entertainment, working conditions improved somewhat due to tighter union control by anarchists and socialists.[111]

Other pioneering women assumed posts in the aviation and military administrations. Such was the case of Antonia García, a member of the communist youth organization who, during the initial phase of the war, was in training as a midwife in the Madrid Maternity Hospital and who later, in 1937, joined the general staff of the aviation administration as a photographer. Her job was to survey and photograph enemy territory in the areas occupied by the fascist troops. A non–combat position such as this was not subject to the usual gender job segregation.[112] Militia woman Rosario Sánchez is another example of a female member of the military staff even toward the end of the war. When Sánchez, as a *miliciana*, lost her hand in a bomb explosion, she was assigned the post of coordinator of the postal services in her division with the rank of sergeant.[113]

The antifascist women's organizations and the Ministry of Defense had planned from the beginning of the war to use female volunteers to provide ancillary services in the organization of military supplies and hospital services to the wounded. These plans, however, were not implemented until late 1938, toward the end of the war, when it was too late for them to be effective.[114]

Women's Proper Place: The Homefront

Women's primary contribution to the war effort was not in the trenches but rather at the homefront, where they made crucial, though less spectacular, contributions through traditional roles that were nonetheless absolutely essential in sustaining a country at war. In this non-combatant arena, women by the thousands threw themselves into wartime endeavors that ranged from working in munitions factories to volunteer work in social services, educational drives, cultural projects, and support activities for the combatants at the fronts. Furthermore, it was women who assumed the burden of maintaining the daily operations of the domestic sphere. And it was their mundane efforts, in the long run, that enabled the civilian population to survive and resist in the grim circumstances of war, bombardments, unemployment, shortages, restrictions, and hunger.

All the women's organizations saw women's proper place to be at the homefront. Propaganda in the women's press constantly referred to the gender division of the war effort. "Men to the War Fronts, Women to the Homefront" was a common slogan with which women of different ideological persuasions agreed. The predominant slogan within the arena of non-combatant activities at the homefront was "Women to Work." The urgent need to mobilize womanpower was expressed from the start of the war. The rhetoric used was militaristic and the message related to women's mobilization to work was loaded with political overtones. Women were constantly urged to join the "production front"[115] and were told to be soldiers at the homefront.[116] They had to occupy "production trenches" and become the "vanguard of production."[117]

War rhetoric referred to outstanding women workers as "heroines of production" or, using Russian terminology, women Stakhanovites. These women were frequently brought into the public eye.[118] Three shock–troop workers with high–level production in the garment industry, Adelina Canyelles, Obdulia Imbert, and Petronella Ladrón de Guevara, became popular production heroines in the summer of 1938 when the Generalitat of Catalonia awarded them the President Macià Medal for their "magnificent conduct and abnegation at work."[119] These workers were presented as proud examples of unwavering commitment, discipline, and worker productivity to be emulated by all antifascist women. Such women were genuine heroines, quite different from the then discredited model of *milicianas*. War vocabulary was focused upon the ideal of work. Female "work brigades," "cleaning soldiers," and female "shock troops" described different forms of women's mobilization in the work force. In factories, workshops, hospitals, relief work, and welfare, women's impact was often grouped through military rather than civil forms of organization in order to enhance the connection between civil and military resistance.

Hundreds of women identified with the transpolitical "Women to Work" drive. The women's press constantly repeated the slogan, and many women believed female integration into the labor market was vital to promoting male recruitment to the war fronts. Women believed that they were mobilized in the war effort. From a more specific feminist perspective, the war was seen as a crucial moment to break with traditional resistance to women's paid employment, but this attitude was not widespread. On the whole, access to work was couched in terms of war needs, which clearly linked women's work with war production and military recruitment; the statement "We are willing to work without rest at the homefront so that the men can go to the fronts" expressed the pervading mood in the early stages of the war.[120]

The policies of all the women's organizations were strikingly similar with regard to women's work. The anarchist Mujeres Libres and the antifascist women's organizations as well as women involved in the socialist and communist parties all endorsed the policy to incorporate women into production.[121] Ideological differences were put aside in this common drive to recruit and train women who could replace male workers; however, their strategies varied in accordance with political beliefs.

All the women's organizations saw the integration of the female work force into production as an essential ingredient in winning the war. They organized campaigns to entice women to work and, more importantly, to train women in skilled jobs. A front-page slogan in the Catalan communist newspaper *Treball* proclaimed, "Women must be urgently prepared to replace the men who have to go to the fronts."[122] A front page of the antifascist women's publication *Mujeres. Organo del Comité de Mujeres contra la guerra imperialista y el fascismo* (the organ of the Committee of Women Against Imperialist War and Fascism) depicted a woman working and proclaimed female professional training to be the most pressing need of the time.[123] Mujeres Antifascistas held popular assemblies accompanied by military bands to persuade women to join the work force,[124] while Mujeres Libres organized work sections within their local groups.[125]

In the early stages of the war, propaganda postulated that women were a reserve labor force trained to replace men. Women themselves purposively claimed, "We want to work. We want to be useful."[126] Not all this enthusiasm was a result of women's dedication to the war effort; on another level, they needed to work to support their families at a time when male breadwinners were away at the fronts. Unemployment and inflation were high, while scarcity and rationing of supplies were commonplace. Everyday survival under these conditions posed genuine problems to many working-class families.[127]

At the outbreak of the war, the female labor force was still a small percentage of the active population and was basically unskilled. According to the 1930 census, women represented only 12.65 percent of the work force; over 70 percent of women workers were single, and of these more than one–half were under twenty-six years of age. In other words, when the war began, female wage workers were scarce and mainly young single women. War pulled male workers who were not employed in priority war industries away from their jobs to the front. This displacement of manpower to trench warfare meant that many positions remained vacant, a dangerous situation because of the possibility of the paralyzation of industry.

The solution to this problem was the same as it had been during the First World War: women would have to take over jobs in the factories in order to maintain normal levels of production.[128] This idea was commonplace in the press and war propaganda, which compared the situation in Spain to that endured by European countries during World War I.[129] Another frequent reference point was the role of women workers in the Russian Revolution.[130] Such comparisons may indeed have served the purpose as effective propaganda at the time, but it would be simplistic to view the situation in Spain from this perspective.[131] The crisis in development of the Spanish economy and the tenacity of traditional mentality with regard to women's paid employment determined the slow changes in women's work experience during the Civil War years.

The Spanish economy suffered major problems because of the war.[132] In the region under republican control, there was a clear break with traditional systems of economic production. Significant economic difficulties were generated by the escalating lack of economic and financial resources; the increasing unavailability of primary goods, machinery, and commodities; the rapid reconversion in production goods geared for war needs; and the loss of national and international markets due both to the war and to the crisis in industries. The international political decision not to intervene in the war increased the financial and economic difficulties of the legitimate republican Spanish government. Furthermore, the emergence of new social questioning during the Civil War regarding capitalism and private property gave rise to new modes of production such as self-managed collectives in some regions of republican Spain. In the early months of the war, anarchist and radical socialists took over industries and farms and collectivized production.[133] This provoked national and international opposition and prevented, to a large extent, the importation of goods and the concession of financial credits to republican Spain.[134] With no credit forthcoming from Western powers, Spanish exports were insufficient to balance essential imports.

During the war years, scarcities and difficulties in adjusting available resources to war contingencies led to a surge in inflation and unemployment that was difficult to control. Thus, the Spanish economy was far from buoyant in this period; unemployment increased in most regions as factories closed due to shortages of goods or lack of market outlets. In the territory loyal to the Republic, industries were converted to respond to a war economy. War industries, such as munitions factories, grew while traditional sectors, such as the textile industries, suffered a crisis due both to the shortage of supplies and to the reduction of their traditional markets. Despite orders for uniforms from the Ministry of Defense, there was an overall reduction in production in the textile sector, which had traditionally occupied a major part of the actively employed female population.[135] Although there were some exceptions, such as in Alicante and Valencia, where the war economy reactivated productive activities,[136] the economy in most areas underwent serious reverses during the war.

Aside from economic problems, traditional resistance to women's paid labor was an additional obstacle to integrating females into the work force. Spanish workers continued to react negatively to women's paid employment. Even in the context of war, with thousands of male workers drafted to fight at the fronts, the integration of women into the work force failed to achieve general acceptance. Most male workers saw women's claim to their jobs as an encroachment on the traditional male prerogative of a preferential right to work.[137] Women's presence in the labor market was at best regarded as situational or just a temporary expedient imposed by wartime exigencies. Conventional views regarding women's paid labor pervaded the discussions, attitudes, and policies of wartime Spain. Traditional resistance of male workers, job segmentation, and wage discrimination endured, despite apparent changes in work conditions, such as in revolutionary collectivized industries.

From the start of the war, the women's organizations carried on a spirited campaign that encouraged women to work. They took the slogan "Women to Work" at face value and developed strategies and policies to implement it. However, faced with widespread male hostility and with the tenacity of conventional views on women's paid work that had been internalized by many women, even the women's organizations adopted somewhat ambivalent views on this issue. Nonetheless, both Mujeres Libres and the antifascist women's organizations officially advocated that women take up jobs to replace male workers. One of the major conclusions of the National Conference of the AMA in October 1937 was that women should be immediately incorporated into the labor market.[138] This was to be accompanied by a program for professional training, provided by the unions, that would allow women to occupy skilled jobs.

Women and Paid Work

The antifascist women's organizations had a pragmatic attitude and rarely developed any theoretical analysis of the general question of women's right to paid employment. On the contrary, they focused on accommodating women's work and professional training to war requirements. More significantly, they couched the justification of women's access to waged work in terms of war needs and not on the principle of women's rights. They drew attention to economic needs, production levels, or war front requirements that could be eased by women filling vacant jobs or freeing male workers for recruitment.

Little was said about women's right to work or about economic independence. What is more significant is that, in a constant effort to placate male apprehensions about female competition in the workplace, even the AMA was quick to indicate that women's work should never be conceived of as a threat to men's jobs, as it was never intended to replace men permanently. The communist leader Pasionaria frequently referred to this question in her political meetings, also trying to convince male workers that women did not threaten their jobs during or after the war. According to her, such an insinuation was ignoble and an insult to militant activists dedicated to antifascism.[139] The secretary general of the AMA, Emilia Elías, argued that the need to reconstruct industries after the war would mean that all the available labor force, including women, would be necessary.[140] Calls for women to work were thus supplemented by explanations aimed to allay male workers' fears.[141] Few stated the case as clearly as the Catalan communist leader Carme Julià, who openly stated at the First National Conference of the PSUC Catalan Communist Party Women that "men must not see their substitution as a desire for dualism or competition, as it is merely a transitory measure which will end once they return from the fronts."[142]

From its founding, the young antifascist women's organization Unión de Muchachas had been more energetic than its adult counterpart in demanding educational and cultural rights for women. Significantly, it expressed a greater degree of consciousness about women's condition and the limitations that traditional gender structures had imposed on women. The organization was articulate in affirming women's capacity and right to develop educational and professional skills on equal terms with men. In May 1937, at its conference in Madrid, the Unión de Muchachas adopted the policy to integrate women into the workplace as pivotal in its overall agenda: "Organize and develop our industrial, professional and technical training with the help of the Government, Unions and the Municipality, in order to be immediately incorporated into all kinds of agricultural and factory work."[143]

The work expectations of these young women were clearly not limited to the home. They, like many others, insisted on holding jobs in factories and in the areas of public transport, industry, medicine, and engineering as well as in aviation and other war-related fields. But these professional expectations were quickly frustrated when the women confronted overt hostility in male workers and resistance among unions and official entities in carrying out training programs. As they confronted these difficulties and reservations, their initial enthusiasm gave way to a more cautious declaration of their rights and expectations. In this sense, their discourse on work tended to become ambivalent because they linked their right to a job and their right to education and professional training to war requirements.

The issue of women and work was always phrased so as to avoid antagonizing male workers: "We want an organization where girls can be educated, acquire skills; one which deals with the task of setting up laundries to wash the soldiers' clothes, in sum, an organization capable of undertaking all the tasks the war has entrusted to women." Although the Unión de Muchachas proceeded to complain–"In spite of countless requests to our comrades in the unions, our professional training has not been carried out"–it reassured men about their good intentions regarding men's permanent jobs: "We do not want to displace you. We do not want to supplant you. We only want to learn; we want to learn in case some day, if the war obliges you to go to the trenches, we will be able to occupy your jobs and prevent the paralyzation of industry."[144]

This quotation echoes a number of ambiguities and leaves us wondering whether we can accept this argument at its face value and assume that these young women did not really intend to aggressively pursue their right to work. Or should we interpret it as a willful misrepresentation of their real attitude, crafted to appease male fears of female competition in the workplace and thus to ensure that male workers and unions would not withdraw their training programs? While a strong feeling existed among young women that the war heralded new job opportunities and some dreamed of being pilots, mechanics, or drivers, the traditional restrictions on female work options persisted, and strong sociocultural constraints prevented most women from formulating their demands to work without having to resort to exterior wartime justifications.

Although some women's organizations justified women's work as a necessary component in the war effort, the anarchist organization Mujeres Libres took a more overt position on women's right to work regardless of status, family situation, or political circumstances. Some members openly supported the unpopular view that women had a permanent right to hold a job, whether or not the country was at war. They also addressed the specific question of the relationship between economic independence and women's emancipation. For them, paid employment was a means by which women could acquire their economic independence, which they perceived to be the basis of individual freedom: "Women must be economically free....Only economic freedom makes all other freedom possible, both for individuals and for countries."[145] Thus, women's waged work could not be limited to circumstances of war. According to other members of Mujeres Libres, women's paid work was not only a right but also an obligation for all women. As schoolteacher Pilar Grangel formulated it:

> As a living being the first duty of a woman is work. Let it be clear that there cannot be any exceptions to this principle. It is an indispensable condition, the fulfillment of the biological condition of the human being. Work is the law of human progress, and he who refuses to carry out this law is a subversive element, a parasite and, like all parasites, a burden on everybody else.[146]

To avoid being labeled as social parasites, women had to work just like men; gender differences were not supposed to imply distinctions in this respect. In fact, the precept of universal obligatory work had been established by the Generalitat of Catalonia when, in June 1937, it obliged all citizens to possess a work certificate, a specific identity card that provided details on an individual's job status, wages, profession, and business. The Generalitat penalized those who did not carry this certificate, which was used to track the activities of the working population so as to identify those attempting to avoid conscription. Although the decree applied to workers of both sexes, some groups were exempt from carrying the obligatory identity card, including women who performed domestic work, the physically disabled, men over sixty-five, and members of the armed forces.[147] Thus, Grangel's position obliging all women to work irrespective of their domestic situation was, in fact, quite exceptional and not at all representative of the period's predominant attitudes.

Not only anarchists but a small number of women of other political persuasions proclaimed women's right and, indeed, their duty to work. The communist textile worker María Vendrell believed that labor rights acquired by women during the war should continue in its aftermath: "This incorporation of women to production must continue after the war. Once the temporary scarcity of labor has passed, women must not be allowed to find themselves once again as bereft of options as they were before the nineteenth of July."[148] However, as the war continued, specific gender demands appear to have been downplayed in favor of a more conciliatory male–female war effort that did not openly imply women's permanent right to work.

Political priorities and, from late 1937 on, war weariness led to the establishment of a non–conflictive position on women's access to wage work. Irrespective of partisan political differences, the issue of women's work was universally couched in terms that did not challenge prevailing forms of gender subordination and the sexual division of labor. Nonetheless, women did manage to articulate some gender-specific demands. For instance, it was common policy in all the women's organizations to demand wage parity and equal rights to professional training and skills. Women workers sought an end to injustice and inequality in the workplace, seeing this particular moment of potential social change as a time to redress traditional grievances.

Equal wages for equal work was clearly on the agenda of all the women's organizations,[149] and a good deal of coverage was given to it in the women's publications. The general press was much slower to publicize these demands. General coverage of these requests did not come until very late in the war when, by then, they had become a mere device to get women to participate in an economy that was disintegrating under the pressure of fascist advances.[150]

The women's organizations also advocated and tried to establish an infrastructure of child care services and collective restaurants to alleviate the domestic burden of working housewives. Nurseries and child care services became a feature of some factories and workshops that employed a significant female contingent.[151] However, even more important than wage hikes, parity, or job opportunities, what most interested women was that they be accorded greater dignity and social esteem.

Unions and Women's Work

Despite political differences, all the women's organizations had to overcome the indifference, hostility, and lack of cooperation of male–dominated unions–the anarcho–syndicalist CNT and the socialist and communist UGT–in the training of women workers.[152] The local group of the AMA in the town of Gandía presented an internal report to the Levante Provincial Committee expressing the pervasive frustration felt by women who wanted to work but were not admitted through established channels: "We have offered our unconditional support to the Defense Board but nobody takes us seriously! It is exasperating at this juncture! We don't know what the unions are waiting for to incorporate us into the workplace. They will only do so as a last resort."[153]

On record, both major unions favored women's recruitment into the work force but were slow to incorporate any specific policy into their agenda. Although women's organizations had been trying since the start of the war to persuade the unions to collaborate on training programs, as women stated publicly and even more openly in internal reports, there had been a decided lack of union collaboration. The antifascist organizations worked more closely with the UGT, while Mujeres Libres was involved with the CNT, but the same story was true of both unions: attempts to establish training programs were treated with indifference, frivolity, or open hostility.[154] In fact, the unions did not begin to implement the policy to incorporate women into the workplace until the spring of 1938. At that point, both the unions and the political parties paid more serious attention to the issue because of the unfavorable development of the war and because increased male recruitment had led to a dramatic reduction of the work force.[155]

By October 1937, the military offensive of the better equipped Franco troops—which had the backup support of German and Italian forces—led to the fall of the republican-held Northern Front, the Basque country, and Asturias. By the spring of 1938, severe republican losses in the Teruel area spoke of the growing weakness of the republican army, and in April 1938, Franco's troops reached the Mediterranean. The ongoing battle of the Ebro River during the summer and autumn of 1938 ended in November with the devastating defeat of the republican forces and the death of 60,000 republican soldiers.[156]

Although the UGT had agreed as early as October 1937 to include women's right to work in its agenda, it did not do so. In March 1938, at a meeting held by the Barcelona branch of the UGT, it was again decided to include this point in its program: "Train women for work. Help women have access to production. End the resistance of those comrades who think they are going to be displaced....Organize theoretical, and if possible, practical classes for women."[157] Months later, in late September 1938, the national committee of the UGT acknowledged that very little had actually been done in this area. It then proceeded to ratify the former agreement and invited all the branches of the UGT to implement it at the local level with the objective of not only replacing male workers but also intensifying production.[158] In the case of the CNT, women's work was finally incorporated into its official agenda in August 1938. At a meeting dealing with economic issues of the war and the revolution held in Valencia in October 1938, the CNT passed a number of resolutions concerning women's work and set up a complex program to coordinate and implement a major national program to train and integrate women into the labor market.

In 1938, the CNT did not break with its traditional acceptance of occupational segregation based on protective measures for working mothers. Furthermore, the war gave several unexpected twists to anarchist eugenics, which justified barring women from certain jobs on the dubious grounds that their capacity for reproduction might be affected and that they were temperamentally unsuited to work. Anarchist eugenics tended to be linked to issues such as sex reform, abortion and birth control, sanitation conditions, and lack of medical attention for working mothers.[159] The development of birth control and proper medical care for working mothers was one of the main points on the anarchist sex reform agenda. Moreover, anarchists tended to define eugenics through a class interpretation that legitimated its defense of birth control and improved sanitation and hygiene conditions for the working classes. It was quite exceptional for them to perceive eugenics in its traditional view as related to biological inheritance and the degeneration of the race.[160] Moreover, there was a clear division among anarchists. Sex reformers represented a minority group within Spanish anarchism that was part of a trend from which many mainstream anarchists disassociated themselves. Given the lack of interest on the part of the anarchist union CNT in prior manifestations of sex reform, it is indeed significant that the Pleno Nacional de Regionales, the national assembly of CNT union branches, subscribed to a traditional eugenics argument to prevent women from holding specific jobs. In the autumn of 1938, the assembly agreed to define as activities forbidden for woman "those that were biologically inadequate for her sexual condition and temperament which might give rise to race degeneracy."[161]

Gender hierarchy prevailed even among the anarchists, and, once again, women did not have the option to determine which jobs could be harmful to them or to their children. The CNT program also included the implementation of occupational segmentation, as male workers already in the workplace were taught new skills in order to occupy higher-level, specifically "male" jobs while female workers were trained to occupy the men's former jobs.[162]

The fact that one of the organizations dedicated to the revolutionary transformation of Spanish society should so explicitly uphold male prerogatives is, indeed, an indication of how deeply embedded traditional gender structures were in Spanish society and of how fiercely women had to battle to have their rights acknowledged, especially in the highly contentious area of work. Throughout the war years, both formal and informal instances of social control through gender discourse and labor regulations prevented acceptance of women's waged work. It is not surprising, then, that in the very last stages of the war it was still necessary to wage campaigns for a more general social acceptance of women's integration into the work force. As pressure from Franco's troops increased and the republican fronts were disintegrating, the appeals took on a more dramatic tone, but by then it was too late.[163]

Official Initiatives in Professional Training for Women Workers

It was in fact not the unions or the women's organizations but the local Catalan government that carried out the most successful of the initiatives for training women and improving their work situation, through its efforts to resolve production problems of the war economy. It is true that the Central Government had initially tried to mobilize women in the war effort by integrating the antifascist women's organizations into an official commission of female aid created by decree in August 1936, which was to be attached to the Ministry of Defense.[164] The Central Government's project, in fact, was to provide voluntary aid, relief work, and social assistance. General conscription to work was not officially mandated until the very end of the war when, in a late and desperate measure to confront Franco's advance, the president of the Republic, Manuel Azaña, signed a decree (January 1939) ordering obligatory mobilization of members of both sexes between the ages of seventeen and fifty-five who were not under military orders.[165] Here, gender differentiation was dropped when women as well as men were obliged to partake in any kind of work that might benefit republican defense strategies. However, by then it was too late; the disintegration of the republican institutions was well underway, and the decree was of little consequence. Even at this late stage, with Franco's troops in the vicinity of Barcelona, the Catalan government still maintained gender distinctions when it required all men under fifty-five to work in the fortifications of the city while women were registered only on a voluntary basis.[166]

Existing evidence suggests that in Catalonia there was great official interest in designing training programs for women and strategies for their integration into the workplace.[167] This can probably be attributed to several factors: Catalonia was not engaged in direct warfare as early as the other regions were, a process of social change had been underway there for some time, and a vigorous women's movement existed in the region. By November 1936, the Catalan government proposed to organize a service for the "training and professional preparation of women for men's occupations" under the auspices of the Ministry of Defense.[168] However, it took almost a year to develop a specific policy and adequate official structures to carry out this objective.

In July 1937, the Institut d'Adaptació Professional de la Dona (IAPD) (the Institute for the Professional Training of Women) was created by the Department of Labor and Public Works of the Generalitat.[169] The Institute was one of the most sophisticated and successful initiatives designed to foster women's professional training and to ensure their integration into the workplace; it was a concerted initiative by official bodies, unions, and political organizations. The characteristics of the Institute and the development of its program undoubtedly offer insight on the overall question of women and work during the Civil War, as it was such an unusual joint venture. Unions, official bodies, and women's organizations carried out other training programs, but they were more sporadic and less comprehensive initiatives.[170]

The IAPD reflected conventional attitudes and policies, as it introduced no new arguments to legitimize this official endeavor. The decree's preamble justifying its creation clearly reflects the prevailing discourse on the need to avoid the likely paralyzation of industry that could result from male conscription. The most effective means to avoid reduced production was to mobilize the reserve work force–women. The decree acknowledged women's historical capacity to adapt to moments of need and to undertake work hitherto carried out by men. It also went on to propose the creation of an institution that would undertake the task of "professionally preparing women for work at the homefront with the aim to replace men who have to leave their jobs in order to join the army."[171]

As a legislative measure, the decree was quite advanced compared to conventional practice, as some of its provisions had a more emancipatory focus on issues such as wages and job openings. It established the principles of wage parity ("for equal work, equal wage"), equal access to a job in conditions of equal physical aptitude, and equal job opportunities once a woman had passed a psychological and medical test. Some months later, in November 1937, further regulations were established in the organization and policies of the Institute. These endorsed the principle of wage parity by maintaining similar regulations for male and female workers and declared that the primary basis of women's mobilization was "to establish equality between men and women in their access to jobs in all kinds of occupations."[172]

To facilitate the selection of women candidates, some measures of affirmative action were introduced, such as reserving a percentage of apprenticeships for women and considering only women for certain occupations. However, it would be unwarranted to consider that such measures reflected an overall policy of affirmative action or definitive integration of women into the work force. In fact, the later standards regulating the Institute were much more cautious in their treatment both of women's right to paid work and their access to jobs. Indeed, parallel with popular belief, the decree quite clearly maintained the principle of labor differentiation by gender and the preferential right of men to work. Thus, it specified that all positions were temporary although they were to last for the duration of the war, and it was strictly forbidden to abandon one's job during that period. Furthermore, the decree guaranteed that the jobs of male workers who had been recruited would be reserved for them: "On returning from the fronts, the combatants will occupy the same jobs that they had before entering the Army."

Official policies clearly considered women's incorporation into wage work as a temporary exigency brought on by the war. The Institute actually established an order of priorities for access to jobs that openly favored unemployed male workers and skilled male refugees over women. To a large extent, access to work was also seen as compensation to reward dedication to the war effort. Thus, widows, wives, and daughters of workers who had disappeared at the fronts were given the first choice of jobs if these women had not yet received a pension or if they preferred to work instead of receiving their pension. Next in line were women who had been trained by the Institute, provided that they were wives and daughters of combatants who were in economic difficulties. So, in fact, Institute policy was not only designed to maintain production levels but also to alleviate economic destitution at the homefront. The policy to favor wives and daughters of combatants was not new and had been adopted throughout republican Spain.[173]

The female work force was composed mainly of younger women, and the Institute limited professional training to women between the ages of sixteen and thirty–five, despite the numerous applications by older women. Older women were directed to carry out voluntary activities in the women's organizations.[174]

In spite of its conventional stance on some policies, the IAPD was innovative in openly sponsoring training programs and job opportunities for women. Its policies were significant not only because they embodied official attitudes, but also those of an important cross–section of Catalan society. The IAPD represented a coordinated effort on the part of official institutions and political and union forces to provide women workers with new skills and place them in jobs; not only government entities, but also representatives of the major unions and political organizations, were involved in determining the direction and methods of administration. The Institute was guided by a complex power structure, which was made up of a plenary board, an executive commission, a workers' mobilization central section, a workers' mobilization county section located in each of the labor delegations in the Catalan constituencies, and a workers' mobilization local section in each of the Catalan municipalities (with the exception of Barcelona). It is important to underscore the geographical area the Institute covered–well beyond the city of Barcelona—and, more important still, the presence of political and union representatives at the different organizational levels.

The executive commission was the most powerful entity, as it proposed policy to the plenary board and directed the Institute's programs. Almost immediately after its creation, the government's representation on the commission was increased vis à vis the initial formula, which stipulated one representative each from the departments of Labor and Public Works, Culture, and Economy; this was changed to three representatives from the Department of Labor and Public Works and one each from the other departments.[175] The executive commission also had representatives from each of the major Catalan unions and political organizations.[176] Significantly, notwithstanding such broad representation, the Catalan women's organization, Unió de Dones, was not officially integrated into the Institute until July 1938, a year after its creation. Even then, the representative of Unió de Dones, Enriqueta Gallinat i Román, was not officially nominated until December 1938, shortly before the end of the war in Catalonia.[177] Two women were elected as members of the executive commission: the CNT representative, Carme Quintana i Villafranca, and the UGT representative, María Pérez i Enciso. The latter, a member of the Catalan Communist Party, was also one of the leaders of the Unió de Dones de Catalunya and to some extent enabled their voice to be heard among the affairs of the Institute.[178]

The plenary board was composed of the executive commission and the sections of the UGT and the CNT that had representatives from fourteen industrial groups: combustion and lubricants; metallurgy and mechanics; textiles; food industries; agricultural industries; chemicals; building industries; graphic arts; transport; gas and electricity; communications; irrigation; hygiene and health; and commerce, credit, and insurance.[179] Of the twenty union representatives nominated in February 1938, only three were women. Two were elected for the UGT as representatives for the textile and hygiene and health industries; the third was a CNT representative for the latter.[180] The Institute was an organization dedicated specifically to women; so it is paradoxical that women's overall representation in the Institute was so sparse. The Institute was run by men, initially by the eminent psychiatrist Dr. Emili Mira y López,[181] although later in the war María Pérez i Enciso was nominated as director. Notwithstanding the limited representation of women, the Institute was enthusiastically supported by the Unió de Dones and particularly by the communist women.[182]

Worker Control, Official Measures, and Women's Work

Although all women were obliged to join a union in order to take advantage of the Institute's facilities, the unions made few attempts to encourage female participation or to give women a wider voice in their proceedings. This apathy was generalized among the unions and not specific to the Institute, although it seems more blatant in this case since the Institute dealt specifically with women's issues.

The unions and the collectivized industries under worker control only rarely elected women representatives during the Civil War. An illustration is provided by looking at the 922 collectivized industries, many of which were textile industries with a strong contingent of women workers, in the four Catalan provinces of Barcelona, Tarragona, Gerona, and Lerida. In 1937, these 922 firms–most of them under worker control at a time when male workers were being recruited to serve in the army–presented the names of their delegate-supervisors, directors, and legal representatives to the Board of Syndical Economic Control of the Generalitat. A total of 2,854 representatives were elected, of which only 188, or 6.5 percent, were women. Furthermore, the majority of female delegates were elected to minor posts.

Women were directors of only 9 of the 922 collective industries documented, while only 18 women were supervisor-delegates.[183] This almost negligible female representation is highly significant because it indicates that there had been little change in the traditional gender hierarchy, despite notable social changes in industry. Revolutionary changes in factories did not automatically lead to the dismantling of gender hierarchy and power structures.

The IAPD was financed by the Generalitat, although it was run by voluntary groups that were to teach women new skills. Technical schoolteachers; industrial, commercial, and agricultural technicians; and skilled workmen taught crash courses at their schools and business centers and on shop floors. Schoolteachers provided women trainees with a general education. Classes given in schools and in factories provided training for work in war industries; food, health, and chemical industries; agricultural work; commerce; and administration.[184]

The IAPD training programs were very successful, although women's demands for professional training were so great that the Institute was overwhelmed with applicants. By July 1938, the IAPD had over 15,000 applicants for training, but only one-third of them had been admitted because of the lack of facilities.[185] In January 1939, the communist newspaper *Treball* reported that some 500 women had been trained at the Escola de Capacitació de la Dona (the Catalan School for Women's Training), a factory workshop affiliated with the IAPD, and that 420 trainees had been placed in munitions factories.[186] This achievement came late, however, for finding jobs for the 5,000 women workers who had trained there had always been difficult for the IAPD. Indeed, very few of these women found paid occupations.

It is true that the Institute placed some of its trainees in government jobs and influenced the passage of some official policies to guarantee women certain positions in the administration and management of female prisons.[187] Generally, however, it was ineffective in modifying overall state policy. Shortly before the occupation of Barcelona by Franco's troops in late January 1939, the Catalan newspapers initiated a drive to promote women's incorporation into wage work.[188] In late December 1938, when María Pérez i Enciso was director of the IAPD, she gave an interview concerning this campaign. She reminded her readers that the Institute had been advocating women's integration into the work force for a long time, although she welcomed any measures that would accelerate the process.[189] Not even official bodies like the Institute were able to modify traditional hostile attitudes toward women's work or to influence economic planning to utilize the reserve female work force in Catalonia.

The Institute's basic achievement was in providing training courses for thousands of women in Catalonia, although the inability for so many of these women to get jobs in which they could use their newly acquired skills was frustrating. Some work conditions did improve. For instance, domestic servants received considerable attention and were incorporated into the insurance system covering other wage workers, while local governments and municipalities gave wage increases to cleaning women.[190] In addition, in both Madrid and Barcelona, campaigns were established to train domestic servants for other occupations.[191]

One of the more innovative features of the Institute was its commitment to ensure wage parity once jobs were attained, a policy that marked a break with the traditional acceptance of wage inequality for female workers.[192] Nonetheless, the effectiveness of this policy in practice is difficult to ascertain; in fact, the IAPD seems to have been unable to enforce its wage equity policy. During the war years, wages were adjusted in most industries, but, as in former years, wage discrimination figured openly in the vast majority of wage agreements. In a selection of over fifteen wage agreements adopted after the creation of the IAPD in July 1937 that affected a variety of industries (commerce, textile, garment, horticulture, food, timber, and shoe industries and hostelry, restaurant, and shopping establishments) where gender differentials could be established for comparable professional categories, only one incorporated the principle of wage equality. This wage agreement, which applied equal wages for apprentices of both sexes, was made by the saddle and harness makers section of the Catalan branches of the garment, clothing, accessories, and similar industries.[193] Another agreement affecting shop assistants in the province of Gerona established a 10 percent wage differential between male and female employees,[194] but wage discrimination in similar professions was generally much higher than this.

All the agreements considered here supported wage discrimination and favored increased wage differentials in higher-level job categories.[195] If, for example, wages for male and female apprentices in their first year showed a differential ranging between 10 and 24 percent, by the fourth year these differentials reached more than 45 percent. In higher-level categories, figures show an average disparity of more than 43 percent, with differences ranging from 35 to 55 percent, depending on the trades involved. Of course, it is impossible to determine the degree of wage differentials in jobs where different professional categories were established for male and female workers, but wage increases were lower for women and their wages, on the whole, were substantially lower.[196]

The established wage agreements disregarded the principle of wage parity, and overt wage discrimination continued, despite some efforts to ameliorate the working conditions of women. What must be underscored is that most wage agreements were reached through union proposals, and, in fact, some of them affected collectivized industries. The negligible representation of women workers in the union structure and on bargaining teams indicates that women had no voice in demanding wage equity. In the collectivized Rivière metallurgical firm in Barcelona, women's remuneration was less than that of male workers in the same professional category,[197] while in the small town of Villanueva y Geltrú, where women comprised between 80 and 90 percent of the work force in the textile and clothing industries, women's wages were more than 48 percent lower than those of male workers.[198]

Wage discrimination was not unique to Catalonia, and, indeed, one of the characteristics of women's wage work during this period was that there continued to be a gender-based hierarchy in labor. In many areas of republican Spain where worker control had been established and capitalism and private property had been abolished, wage discrimination persisted even in collectivized industries and farms. For example, in Alicante, women's wages were generally about one-half those of male workers and in some instances even less, as was the case of the munitions factories where male workers earned 177 percent more than women workers.[199]

Despite wage hikes on farms, women workers still earned around 50 percent less than men, even on the farms run by official institutions.[200] The anarchist Miguel Chueca, in the Department of Labor of the Aragon Council, established a wage differential of ten pesetas for men and six pesetas for women workers even on the anarchist collectivized farms in Aragon.[201] Wages were, in fact, lowered by the employment of the reserve female work force, a practice that enabled some economically troubled industries to survive.

Although the women's organizations had espoused the principle of equal wages and acclaimed the official approval of wage parity, they did not lobby to enforce their application. Indeed, both Mujeres Libres and the Agrupación de Mujeres Antifascistas denounced wage discrimination, but they did so not because they hoped to further gender-specific demands but rather because they felt it might have negative effects on the war effort.[202] According to this viewpoint, more was at stake than wage hikes or equal wages, and the women's organizations took their militants to task for being too materialistic at a time when the crucial issue was the fight against fascism and for revolutionary change.[203] Specific demands had to yield to a unified strategy for victory. In fact, the women's organizations enthusiastically promoted a work ethic, emphasizing the idea of absolute commitment, Stakhanovism, self-sacrifice, and unselfishness as the correct approach to work. They disparaged slackers, resistance to work, struggles for improvement in working conditions, or questioning of the work ethic. Every effort was focused on the struggle against fascism or for revolutionary changes in Spanish society.

Despite the rhetoric of uncompromising dedication to work, at a rank-and-file level such complete dedication was not always forthcoming. Indeed, recent studies have documented that there was a growing resistance to work by both male and female workers.[204] Women were not always the docile and tractable labor force they were reported to be, but, in a larger sense, most women were not even in a position to develop strategies of resistance to work because they did not hold paying jobs.

Women's greatest contribution to the war effort was their voluntary unpaid labor in relief work, welfare, and everyday domestic work. Paid female employees were still a minority, and most of them were younger women, many of whom had already worked and had been retrained to meet war requirements.[205] However, some gains were achieved during the years of the war. For the first time, the question of women's incorporation into wage work was openly discussed, and government policies focused on training women workers and dealing with gender labor issues. There was also a greater degree of work mobility during these years, and many women joined the work force for the first time. Although in practice many women's work expectations were frustrated because they were unable to get jobs, women's wage work all over the country was projected as something new and exciting.

On the whole, the limited evidence available suggests that women wage earners were involved in a large variety of occupations. In Madrid, Barcelona, Cartagena, Alicante, and Valencia, women worked in war industries and metallurgical workshops that manufactured guns, munitions, cartridges, bullets, gas masks, bombs, grenades, flasks, mortar cases, and other items used for war purposes. In Madrid, women worked in more than thirty diverse war industries,[206] while in Barcelona several hundred women workers were employed in munitions factories.[207] By 1938, the metallurgical branch of the UGT had more than six thousand women affiliates.[208] It appears that women workers had the same work shifts as the men, which varied enormously from eight to ten or twelve hours per day, depending on the availability of primary material and market demand. In other towns and cities of republican Spain, women not only worked in the munitions plants but also in the aluminum, transport, medical, chemical, electrical, shoe, tanning, nougat, and food and flour industries, among others.

In big cities like Madrid and Barcelona, women assumed jobs in public transport, working as conductors, drivers, and even mechanics in the subway, bus, and trolley services. Over 80 percent of the staff of the Subway Company in Madrid was female, and a smaller number of women drove cars and trucks in transport, carrier, and provision services.[209] Women with higher education were employed in teaching, nursing, and the civil service. Women workers formed a majority mostly in the traditional sectors of textile and clothing, but also in new areas such as transportation. Despite this increase in women's participation in the labor force, their presence was still quite marginal.

Throughout republican Spain, women created sewing workshops. Together with major textile factories, hundreds of small sewing and knitting circles were established in factories, at the workplace, in neighborhoods, schools, shops, through unions, political parties, and women's organizations. Clothing workshops were run by women who played a major economic role throughout the war in providing supplies for the troops at the fronts. In fact, when war propaganda urged women to work, it was sewing and knitting workshops and textile factories, rather than heavy industry, that came to mind. Women were constantly bombarded with the message that it was their duty to provide the soldiers at the fronts with clothing. The front page of a local union magazine in Granada, for example, carried an illustration of a woman knitting in the foreground and another at a sewing machine in the background with the message: "Women! Prepare for winter! Remember that pneumonia kills like bullets. Work for the front."[210] A later message in the same magazine told women that their primary obligation was to supply the troops with the equipment necessary to survive the rigors of winter.[211] The items made included underwear, coats, jackets, socks, shirts, trousers, sweaters, caps, blankets, rucksacks, gloves, and scarves. Some of the workshops were large, like the one run by the Clothing Union of the UGT in Barcelona where more than two hundred people made shirts, underwear, nurses' uniforms, trousers, tunics, great–coats, jackets, rucksacks, gaiters, tents, and mattresses.[212] Some workshops collaborated directly with the military supplies administration, and the Agrupación de Mujeres Antifascistas had been offically charged by the government to provide part of the soldiers' equipment through their workshops.[213]

Although women workers in big textile industries were usually paid, it appears that the vast majority of women workers in clothing workshops were not. In fact, official entities promoted women's volunteer work. In Catalonia, the Department of Labor created a Women's Volunteer Work Board, which operated in conjunction with the IAPD and organized workshops and other relief activities. Every year major campaigns were organized by the women's groups to provide supplies for combatants. The "winter campaign" and the "Christmas campaign" were particularly successful when hundreds of women in sewing and knitting workshops produced clothes for the soldiers at the fronts. Clothing and supplying refugees, which was crucial for the overall welfare of those at the homefront, became another major activity for women activists. Although an official order in December 1936 declared that since the workshops were war industries workers should be paid, women in the workshops were mostly unpaid volunteers. During the war, unremunerated female labor in these workshops produced an extraordinary amount of goods and equipment for the soldiers as well as clothing for the refugees. Women were not only a cheap labor force but often a free one, and thus vital to the war economy. Free labor kept production costs low, which explains how the economy was sustained through such adverse circumstances.

The mass mobilization of women during the Civil War led to significant female protagonism in paid and volunteer work at the homefronts. Gender-appropriate roles were redefined to adjust to changing social, economic, and political circumstances. Political propaganda urged women to work, and women's integration into the work force was a central policy of the republican government, unions, and political groups. Despite such an innovative drive, the policy of integration was severely limited from the outset, as it was set within a gender discourse that reinforced traditional values regarding women's work. Readjustment to new working and economic conditions, but not the questioning of gender-defined roles, was the norm. Thus, restrictive ideological discourse based on a gender definition of work attenuated and eventually limited the changes proposed. Although women were eulogized as "Homefront Heroines," the redefinition of gender roles was restricted and women's identity and social roles were still constructed on the basis of traditional gender norms of conduct and the sexual division of labor. The openly unorthodox option of armed combat by the *milicianas* was even less admissible in a society that encouraged a transformation of social and economic structures but failed to confront changes in the patriarchal system.

The perseverance of traditional parameters of gendered division of labor and norms of social conduct impeded a significant turnaround in social roles. Therefore, women's proper place was quite clearly at the homefront. The economic, political, and social demands of the war, certain socioeconomical transformations, and the mass mobilization of women were all insufficient to produce significant changes in the overall power relations between men and women and thus circumscribed women's role to the usual gender-defined activities. Nonetheless, women's accomplishments at the homefront were vital to the survival of the civilian population, to the maintenance of the overall war economy, and to civil resistance. Finally, the demands of the war did expand, to some extent, personal, social, and professional options for many women.

▪ 5 ▪

Survival in Wartime: The Changing Boundaries of Public and Private

Hunger, rationing, interminable waiting lines, food scarcity, health and hygiene deficiencies, housing and fuel shortages, constant bombardments, and the evacuation of thousands of refugees constituted the everyday experiences of the civilian population at the homefront. Women embodied this struggle for survival, as the preservation and upkeep of their families was their primary responsibility. Although social disruption had precipitated some readjustments in gender roles, women held family duties paramount. With the onset of war, women continued in the traditional role of nurturer, but many of them also assumed responsibility for the basic means of subsistence for their children and dependents. Death, disappearance, or enlistment caused the absence of male breadwinners and women broke new ground by taking initiatives and overcoming traditional gender restrictions on their activities.

Women played a decisive role in civil resistance to fascism. The experience of surviving the war also brought a new dimension to the traditional roles of mother and housewife, as women's duties were projected onto the larger community and beyond the bounds of their immediate family to embrace, on numerous occasions, the civilian population. This collective dimension of women's nurturing role was groundbreaking and accurately reflected the blurring of the boundaries of public and private life at the republican homefront. Women's new role as community nurturers challenged the tradition of restricting female activity to the home, thus legitimizing women's access to the public sphere, albeit through supportive, gender-appropriate activities. In addition, political and trade union organizations endorsed women's activity in the public arena in an attempt to foster women's mobilization in the war effort.

Political and economic expediency explains the sanctioning of women's activities beyond the confines of the home, but, where women themselves were concerned, the sociocultural upgrading of their status along with the possibility to cultivate hitherto undeveloped potential bolstered their self-esteem and generated a new consciousness of their worth and capacity. It is true that, for many, the war represented a time of severe privations, yet for others it was also the most exciting time of their lives, one of deep commitment and of feverish activity. Shared interests in community survival at a time of revolutionary change and antifascist resistance gave a new legitimacy to women's demands for an acknowledged social role beyond the confines of the home.

Women's Role in Survival and Civil Resistance

The arduous, implacable effects of war on the homefront worsened as the initial revolutionary exuberance in the summer months of 1936 gave way to the harsh reality of a prolonged war and deteriorating economic and social conditions. Growing political instability resulted from the division and fragmentation of power, while economic problems were exacerbated by an escalating shortage of primary resources, loss of international markets, and economic difficulties.[1] After the first three months of the war, food and fuel shortages, constant bombardment, male enlistment or unemployment, and the escalating presence of refugees made everyday survival a struggle for a majority of the civilian population. Women bore the brunt of this burden when their traditional private reality of the home collapsed under the circumstances of the war.

Women's heightened visibility at the homefront became apparent in the early months of the war when their hitherto unappreciated skills in social work, nursing, and bartering for goods gained new importance. Women organized relief work and food supply when official channels collapsed. Veteran female activists of the war still recall women's versatility and wide-ranging skills, which enabled them to improvise solutions for the endangered family economy and welfare services.[2] Women's time has always been collective, whereas men's time has been both individual and collective. As a social group and as individuals, women developed a collective ethos of dedication to others, to children and family. Caring for the young, the old, and the vulnerable in society shaped women's perception of time in a collective way. Their traditional gender function as mothers and nurturers impeded the development of a notion of time as independent persons responsible for the distribution of their time according to their own specific interests. With the new circumstances of the war, women's time and work became even more community-oriented, as women collectively endeavored to overcome subsistence shortages and fulfill their obligation as nurturers to supply food, clothing, heating, hygiene, and basic sanitary services, thus fulfilling crucial strategies for civil resistance in war.

The parliamentary deputy for the republican Left, Victoria Kent, declared in a radio speech in the early days of the war that "women had to combat hunger in the cities."[3] The three years of the war were a time of galloping inflation, increased unemployment, and economic adversity. Food shortages and lack of provisions can be attributed to economic collapse and the fact that the grain-growing area of Spain remained under Francoist control. This situation was aggravated by speculation and hoarding. As early as the summer of 1936, Madrid was hit with supply shortages. Under siege and constant bombardments, it was the first of the major cities in republican Spain to endure the horrors of warfare. The civilian population was subjected to strict rationing of food. In December 1937, the Madrid socialist newspaper, *Claridad*, portrayed the appalling conditions under which women had to acquire food:

> For over a year now, in Madrid, food has been not only very scarce, but, in fact, unavailable except with heroic effort. The waiting lines suffered two threats: one, bombshells; the other, cold. At times, under freezing rain they were exposed to rough weather with temperatures of three to four degrees below zero [centigrade] from three or four o'clock in the morning to noon or late afternoon. And they put up with this suffering one day, and the next and the next.[4]

The desolate war food economy led to severe rationing, which was gradually introduced all over republican Spain. The civilian population suffered malnutrition, hunger, and illness. Official institutions were unable to cope with even supply distribution and rationing, thus aggravating food shortages.[5] Barcelona and Madrid, the two major cities, were the most heavily affected by scarcity in supplies. By October 1936, food rationing had been introduced in Barcelona and by March 1937, in Madrid. A medical prescription was required to obtain eggs, fish, meat, and milk. By the following summer, bread, the staple of the diet, was rationed to 150 grams per person and even then was not always available; water and coal were also in short supply.[6] The inefficiency of supply delegations, the political confrontations over economic models of distribution, and the steep decrease in production led not only to serious shortages but also to accelerating speculation and the development of a black market.[7]

In 1937, the collection "Higiene de la Guerra" (War Hygiene) of the Biblioteca Higia published a booklet containing basic advice on nutrition and food hygiene. This publication advised the civilian population about nutritional requirements and intake in times of wartime shortages.[8] Dr. Jesús Noguer-Moré, the author, established the following sliding scale of minimum calorie intake in time of rationing and restrictions:

Sedentary with moderate activity . . . . 2000–2300 calories

Homefront workers with regular job . . . . . 2500–2800 calories

Workers with work–intense jobs

or soldiers on campaign. . . . . 3000–3200 calories[9]

This scale was, in fact, quite close to the normal minimums established by Dr. Noguer-Moré, who calculated 2340 calories for an adult man with low activity and 3120 calories for work-intense situations.[10] Calculations based on the food supply in Madrid during the war years indicate a much lower average consumption of only 1060 calories per day from August 1937 to February 1939, with an even lower daily intake of 770 calories in December 1938.[11]

In the spring of 1938, chronic malnutrition touched off an epidemic of illnesses that devastated the adult population of Madrid.[12] Other areas in the direct line of trench warfare such as Asturias, the Basque country, and Aragón suffered immediately from supply shortages. Hunger and a scarcity of provisions plagued the entire homefront beginning in the autumn of 1936. The young communist activist Nieves Castro vividly describes the collective restaurant diet of black beans, popularly known as "Negrín's lentils," named after Prime Minister Juan Negrín.[13] However, most housewives did not have access to these soup kitchens. For the majority of women, providing food for their family and dependents became an activity so difficult that it took up most of the day and required great initiative and imagination. They stood from dawn to late evening in long waiting lines; and because of a poorly organized rationing system, they had to go from line to line in order to acquire different provisions. Medical prescriptions providing milk for babies or food such as vegetables and fish for the ill also required long hours of standing in lines. Even then, rationed goods were in short supply and insufficient to stave off hunger.

Women had to resort to other means to provide their families with basic provisions. They became experts in the black market and in bartering. Women who had never ventured beyond the boundaries of their immediate neighborhood took trains to the country and outlying villages to shop and exchange products.[14] Clothes, table linens, sheets, nails, candlesticks, and other goods were traded for oil, flour, eggs, beans, and potatoes. Housewives made soap, bleach, slippers, and clothes, which they then bartered for food. In Madrid, at dawn, women took the "hunger train" to nearby villages to barter with the peasants.[15] Others, who had nothing to exchange, took the risky option of stealing food and fruit from nearby farms. Many traveled long distances scavenging the countryside for food. The search for provisions was continual, time–consuming, dangerous, and demanding, as was the preparation of food without proper fuel. One woman in the small Catalan town of Granollers remembered:

> My life then consisted of looking for food....We went to Falset to look for oil, to Móra d'Ebre, to Monzón in Aragón, to Cambrils. Sometimes they confiscated our food. In Barcelona and Tarragona we were caught in heavy bombardments....Really, rationing did not give us enough food at all. We had no alternative but to go out looking for food. The majority of women had to do it.[16]

Providing nourishment and basic necessities was a full–time job for most women, who had to confront severe problems resulting not only from rationing and shortages but also from escalating inflation and unemployment. Economic initiatives to compensate the families of mobilized soldiers through subsidies were insufficient, and consumption of the civilian population dropped severely over the years of the war. As late as September 1938, the anarchist union, the Confederación Nacional del Trabajo (CNT), offered a proposal based on a "Family Subsidy for Military Mobilization" that it hoped the socialist union, the Unión General de Trabajadores (UGT), would adhere to.[17] However, by then, the economic situation at the homefront had been severely aggravated and daily survival was possible only through rationing, bartering, and dealing in the black market.

In Barcelona, from late November 1936 to May 1937, women resorted to other methods to meet their needs when they employed their traditional form of collective action and held numerous bread riots and protests.[18] Over the months, women led numerous protests and demonstrations in market lines and assaulted oil, soap, and food shops in a mass popular protest to demand basic supplies for the civilian population.[19] In the small village of Prat de Llobregat, near Barcelona, after seven days without bread, the village women occupied the town hall crying, "We want bread" and threatening to burn down the building and lynch the mayor.[20] Female mobilization in subsistence protests became politicized in early 1937 through political confrontations supporting models of economic management favored by communists, anarchists, and the POUM, which at different moments tried to direct the movement. Nonetheless, it was a genuine example of female collective action in defense of women's gender role as nurturers.[21] After the major political conflict that pitted communists against anarchists and dissident Marxists of the POUM in May 1937, female collective action through subsistence protests was ended when tighter control of ration lines was implemented under communist control.[22]

Problems with food rationing and market shortages were greatly aggravated from late 1936 on, when throngs of refugees from areas under direct attack sought shelter in other parts of republican Spain. Refugees were highly concentrated in the Catalan region. The Generalitat estimated that more than 300,000 refugees had entered Catalonia by the end of 1936, and a year later more than 1 million refugees from all over Spain had sought refuge there.[23] The evacuation of Malaga, Madrid,

Asturias, and the Basque country drew thousands of refugees to the safer regions of Murcia, Catalonia, and Valencia. The large increase in population made food supplies even more difficult to procure. This in itself was a tremendous challenge to everyday survival, but the requirements of refugees extended beyond food to encompass lodging, clothing, and medical services. Survival at the homefront thus required a complex distribution system for supplies and services.

Women in Social Welfare and Public Health

Voluntary relief work by women was a major contribution to the war economy and the functioning of civilian society. Women played a decisive role in managing different agencies that catered to the needs of refugees. The anarchist organization Mujeres Libres created pro-refugee committees, while in June 1938 the antifascist women's group Agrupación de Mujeres Antifascistas (AMA) was designated by the government to look after orphans of soldiers.[24] The Catalan antifascist group Unió de Dones de Catalunya (UDC) provided social assistance to war refugees that was highly commended by the government of the Generalitat, which in October 1938 nominated a representative of the UDC to serve on the official Consultive Commission on Aid for Refugees.[25] This commission had been created more than a year before, in August 1937, as an advisory body to the Commissariat for Assistance to Refugees, the official Catalan institution for refugees.[26] Although formal recognition of the services of the UDC came slowly, it is indeed indicative of the enormous contribution of the antifascist women's groups in organizing aid for refugees.

High-ranking official institutions had, with few exceptions, ignored women in the past, but a small number of women were named to official posts during the war, especially in social welfare, which was a more traditional area of activity for women in Spain. The well-known anarchist leader Federica Montseny was the first female minister in Spain. As a member of the government from November 1936 to May 1937 under the socialist prime minister Franciso Largo Caballero, she was in charge of the Ministry for Health and Social Assistance and thus was responsible for numerous initiatives in the field of social assistance, aid for refugees, and public health.[27] Joining a world governed by rules written by men, Montseny rejected traditional policies by placing women in high posts in her ministry.[28] Women such as Dr. Amparo Poch y Gascón, co-founder of Mujeres Libres, and women of other political affiliations—such as the socialist Dr. Mercedes Maestre—occupied important posts in her ministry.[29] Women were also appointed to direct numerous commissions of aid for Madrid and the Basque country;[30] Elàdia Faraudo i Puigdollers was nominated director general of evacuation and refugees at the Ministry of Work and Social Assistance in January 1938.[31]

Under Montseny's direction, social welfare institutions were modernized in republican Spain to align them with an earlier tradition in which charitable institutions had been redefined as modern social welfare establishments.[32] However, when official institutions were unable to absorb the sheer mass of the displaced, most of the daily assistance to refugees fell on housewives and families. In early 1937, refugees were billeted among families. Although they held "evacuation cards" that gave them a right to rations, providing food for these extra mouths fell, to a large extent, on the initiative of women.

Volunteer relief work for refugees was also channeled through different political parties and unions and was, for the most part, a female endeavor.[33] Women not only provided welfare assistance, food, and social services for refugees, but they also organized women refugees themselves to look after their own interests in a new environment. The Socialist Group of Asturian Refugees had its own Female Secretariat, which developed cultural and training activities among women refugees in Barcelona.[34] The Generalitat developed a department called "Voluntary Female Work" within the Ministry of Work, which, under the leadership of Justa Soto, coordinated multiple activities among women refugees in social work, training programs, workshops, and bomb raid rescue services.[35]

Attending to refugees in the circumstances of war was neither simple nor pleasant. Solutions to basic questions of food and hygiene were no easy matter, and the lack of resources in areas closer to the fronts made living conditions intolerable. In her memoirs, the British writer and antifascist activist Frida Knight vividly described the dreadful conditions of the refugee center "Pablo Iglesias," a huge dismantled factory where about 1,000 refugees were provisionally housed in the small town of Murcia, whose population had doubled after the influx of over 23,000 refugees from Malaga:

> The first impression of the center was quite unforgettable–the stench that assaulted you as you approached the entrance, the sight of the muck heaps and the piles of rubbish and refuse, that of the ragged people sitting and leaning in the doorway, the filthy bony children crawling in the semi-darkness of the interior. It was all like something out of Dickens at his most sordid, and one could hardly believe that it could exist in 1937.[36]

Volunteer relief work by women also concentrated on areas such as sanitation and medical assistance and the creation of nurseries for women workers and collective restaurants. Child welfare was one of the major areas of women's solidarity throughout the years of the war. Many families took refugee children into their care in the first months of the war and, as daily sustenance was increasingly difficult, the State Council for Children admitted that they represented a "heavy burden" because of the prolonged assistance they required.[37] The difficulties were so extreme that in some cases children were abandoned;[38]

however, most families and refugee children survived due to the enormous effort of housewives.

Women were also responsible on another level for child welfare as directors and staff of voluntary organizations and international entities such as the Red Cross and International Antifascist Solidarity. Official child refugee organizations existed, such as the Section for Child Hygiene of the Ministry of Health and Public Instruction, which attended to over 40,000 children in thirty-eight dispensaries in different parts of republican Spain,[39] and the National Council for Evacuated Children, which in Catalonia alone had seventy-four children's camps by December 1938.[40] In Catalonia, numerous official and volunteer organizations were dedicated to child welfare.[41] Some of these organizations had existed prior to the war, such as the international organization Segell Pro Infancia (Pro–Children's Stamps). Others, such as Ajut Infantil de Reraguarda (Child Aid at the Homefront), which had two nurseries, sixty-one residences, two farm schools, a sanatorium, and two camps by early 1938,[42] were created specifically as a response to the immediate requirements for child welfare generated by the war.

Official organizations were insufficient to meet all the needs in this field, so child relief was provided primarily by volunteers, most of whom were women.[43] Some women held significant directive posts in welfare organizations. Socialist lawyer Matilde Huici was a member of the Superior Council for the Protection of Minors and in 1937 was the Spanish delegate to the Children's Committee at the Society of Nations.[44] The former socialist and, by then, communist parliamentary deputy Margarita Nelken was a member of the executive committee of the Spanish Red Cross and an active figure in child relief.[45] However, most relief work was done on a local level by hundreds of anonymous female volunteers.

Volunteer relief work by women channelled support for child welfare by celebrating activities such as "Children's Week," an annual event held in early January to provide children with clothes and toys for the festive season. Women active in female organizations, political parties, and unions organized volunteer relief work, children's nurseries, and educational facilities for children.[46] Moreover, child welfare was an area in which political polarization among women was overcome. Joint ventures such as the creation of children's nurseries, camps, and other institutions were undertaken by women from rival political affiliations.[47] The initiative, skill, and dedication of anarchist, socialist, and communist women shortly after the outbreak of the war enabled the creation, in forty-eight hours, of a children's nursery that provided for more than 100 children belonging to antifascist militants' families.[48] In this case, as in many others, women improvised as teachers, nurses, cooks, dressmakers, and volunteers, running nurseries, day-care centers, and children's refugee centers. Women's activity in welfare was a decisive feature in the civil population's resistance to war between 1936 and 1939.

One of the characteristics of women's mobilization during the war years is that it broke down public and private barriers and launched female participation in the public arena. Thus, a basic premise of the ideology of domesticity—women's restriction to the private sphere—came to be questioned. The projection of women's social roles as wives and mothers into the public arena was quite overt in the field of social welfare. Women's volunteer work was the foundation of both official and unofficial social welfare institutions and vital to the survival of adult and child refugees. Women's areas of activity were clearly broadened during the years of the war, but the significance of this redefinition of women's roles must not be exaggerated. Women as social welfare workers were not professionalized during these years. Their dedication to child and refugee welfare appears to be a projection of their traditional gender role as nurturers, though nurturing now implied not only the sustenance of their immediate family but also of the community.

This new orientation defied traditional gender restrictions of women's activity to the home and opened new horizons for experience and work beyond the bounds of the family. This was a monumental step, especially as it affected thousands of housewives whose skills in this field had hitherto gone unacknowledged or untapped. To what extent did it signify a redefinition of gender relations or a decisive breakthrough in the collective strategy for equality and women's rights? In the case of the Spanish Civil War, it appears that the blurring of the public and private realms, although of profound social significance, did little to alter basic gender roles. However, it did broaden gender options for women and signified a certain readjustment in the cultural norms of gender conduct, as it allowed women to penetrate certain areas of the public world that were previously reserved for males.

This question raises the broader issue that concerns the actual redefinition of public and private and the terms in which it is enacted in different sociohistorical situations. To what extent is there a redefinition of the "public" when women occupy this terrain? Does the presence of women in public reconvert this sphere into a semi-public or intermediate area? Does the feminization of certain public arenas such as social welfare change the actual connotation of public and private? In the case of the Spanish Civil War, women's access to the public field of social welfare appears to have represented a decisive improvement in their social status. However, in terms of the construction of gender relations, it was articulated in regard to acknowledged gender differences and thus reinforced the gender basis of social relations. Access to the public sphere was legitimized on the basis of women's traditional roles as mother and spouse. Women's traditional status was upgraded–from that of a housewife to an unpaid community nurturer. The core ideological discourse on gender relations had not been challenged decisively, although it is true that women's participation in new fields of activity in a wider–based community context undoubtedly stimulated society's consciousness of women's rights and emancipation as well as women's own expectations concerning their role in society.

Under the aegis of these new activities in social welfare, traditional gender roles were carried out with little questioning of role adjustments, even in such innovative social circumstances. Child welfare was, precisely, a field in which new cultural values and role models could have been introduced. However, the socialization and education of child refugees followed traditional patterns. According to an account published in *Assistència Infantil* on the development of child welfare institutions in Catalonia, "Life in these homes is organized like life in a large, *patriarchal* family."[49] Reports and graphic documentation show quite clearly the sexual division of roles, with girls undertaking domestic work, such as sewing and cooking, and boys doing manual work.[50] While the development of a considerable number of non–segregated homes for boys and girls was an innovative step in social welfare, most children's homes and child welfare activities reinforced traditional gender norms of conduct and social values. Despite women's innovative step in working in social welfare, the perception of women's role and place in society did not change and thus was transmitted to the younger generations.

The outbreak of the war had a significant impact on the development of social and public health services. War conditions necessitated health services geared toward military health and hygiene and also implementation of departments specifically dedicated to social welfare. Furthermore, the adaptation of traditional medical and health services to the war effort was a response to new needs generated at the homefront. In the first year of the war, changes in public health and social welfare structures went far beyond technical sanitation modifications. The presence of two anarchists, Federica Montseny as minister of Health and Social Assistance in the republican government and Dr. Félix Martí Ibáñez as director general of Health and Social Assistance in the Catalan Health Services, gave impetus to a changing conceptualization of both public health and social welfare. The dual anarchist premises of antifascist war and revolutionary change had an initial transformative effect on public health, redesigned to "satisfy the needs of proletarian health."[51] A humanistic concept of medicine underpinned this new working–class orientation of public health policies, which also stressed the need to restructure medical services on a decentralized community basis that related health problems to the social environment.[52] Socialized medical welfare and preventive health measures were the keys to this new revolutionary focus on public health, which attempted to give a global sanitation and social response to the health needs of the population.

Women played a significant role in this process of restructuring medical, hygiene, and welfare services in the first months of the war. Félix Martí Ibáñez himself recognized the important role of women in the drive to implement new sanitation services:

> The creation of blood banks, dispensaries, and emergency clinics blossomed in the tragic hours of the 19th of July; when, women especially, dedicated to making a contribution to the revolutionary cause, in a romantic eager burst of creativity, structured a series of institutions which, while attending to the needs of wounded proletarians, also satisfied the desire of the people, so long repressed, to have sanitation centers created for and by them.[53]

Women's enthusiasm and initiative had indeed led to the creation of new health and welfare institutions all over Spain. The women's journals speak of blood banks, nursing and medical care centers, and welfare services established under the initiative of women's organizations. Nursing at the homefront and in the trenches was one of the major areas of female mobilization.

Although not categorized as *milicianas*, war nurses were also vital female figures at the fronts. A significant number of women were employed as war nurses in military hospitals. In some areas, war nurses were militarized, and many also worked in field hospitals at the fronts.[54] In her memoirs, Ana Pibernat, a young war nurse, described the tension, long hours, and dreadful conditions under which medical staff had to work. In 1938, she herself worked in a field hospital near the Ebro front, where unsanitary conditions led to a typhus outbreak that was even more threatening to staff and patients than war wounds or constant bombardment.[55] Nurses' dedication was crucial to maintaining needed medical services, and many nurses were killed in field and military hospitals.

The war generated an immediate need for trained nurses. Medical services were required for the escalating number of wounded soldiers at the war front and injured civilians and refugees at the bombarded homefront. Contributing to the shortage of nursing staff was the fact that nuns and religious institutions had formed the main core of nursing staff in many medical institutions.[56] As national catholicism had played a fundamental role in the political legitimization of the Franco regime and the church was a fundamental supporter of the "new state," most of the religious were anti–republican and abandoned their institutions in the territory under the Republic. Moreover, the popular reprisals against the religious in the republican zone also led nuns and priests to go into hiding; thus, educational and medical institutions had to be staffed by new lay workers.

As the war continued, in order to fill this need, women improvised by developing training programs for "war nurses" all over republican Spain. In January 1937 in Valencia, the national committee of Mujeres Antifascistas set up a school for nursing under the auspices of the Ministry of Public Instruction.[57] War nurses required training on two levels: technical health training, provided by the Faculty of Medicine at Valencia University, and political training in the principles of antifascism, provided by members of the antifascist women's organization. Other courses were established with official support, such as the Ministry of Health in the Basque country, where a school of nursing was created in Vizcaya, or in collaboration with military health services, as was the case of a series of intensive courses to train "people's nurses" in Madrid under the Central Army.[58]

Until the war years, a nursing career had been quite inaccessible to young women of the lower classes. The boom in intensive nursing courses opened this career as a popular option for many women. The need for immediate training of war nurses was such that academic and age requirements were waived, facilitating access to women whose social and educational backgrounds normally would have made it difficult for them to pursue such a career. Some of the women who had the opportunity to train as nurses were very young. The diary of a young Catalan tells of her training in Barcelona, her later experiences as a fourteen-year-old nurse in a small town during the war, and the difficulties her age and lack of experience posed.[59] In her memoirs, Ana Pibernat, a sixteen-year-old nurse from a small town in the province of Gerona in northern Catalonia, describes the rigorous practical training she was given as a health volunteer at the Military Hospital of Gerona.[60] She had just acquired her nursing diploma when the war broke out but had had very little practical training. Practical instruction and learning to improvise in situations in which traditional resources were unavailable was the focus of the war nurse training. After a brief period of practical training and another examination, Ana was awarded the title of military nurse and stationed in Tarragona and later, in 1938, in a military hospital in Valls, where the wounded from the Ebro battle were attended.

Enthusiasm, common sense, and application of their professional training eclipsed these young women's lack of experience and technical knowledge in the everyday practice of their profession. Long working hours under constant bombardment, a steady flow of wounded soldiers and civilian patients, shortages of food and general provisions, understaffing, and a lack of medical equipment and supplies all made working conditions for war nurses and for the medical corps particularly arduous and stressful.

Traditionally, nursing was a career that was seen to combine technical training with a broader humanistic education. The core training program of the prestigious Nursing School of the Generalitat, founded in 1935, was both technical and vocational. Student nurses were obliged to live in residence during their period of training in order to guarantee educational standards.[61] During the war, the Generalitat continued to offer residence grants to students, although other training programs had been established by then. Women's organizations such as Mujeres Libres and the Agrupación de Mujeres Antifascistas also formulated a vocational approach to nursing, but with a difference–the personal sacrifice and commitment of traditional nursing acquired more political connotations and, in some cases, a greater revolutionary undertone.

In fact, rivalry between more traditional approaches to nursing training and the new antifascist model of political and technical commitment came to the forefront on several occasions. The Basque antifascist women's journal *Mujeres* revealed such a conflict in April 1937 when it denounced the favorable treatment given to nurses trained under the traditional aegis of the Red Cross, described as a bastion of the middle class whose clientele were the *niñas de buena sociedad* (girls from high society).[62] The AMA alleged that the nursing titles of the Red Cross were immediately recognized by official institutions of the Basque Ministry, while nurses from a working-class background trained in the new intensive nursing courses had difficulties finding jobs. Nursing acquired a decisive political and class component during the war. For many women, the title of nurse represented a great achievement and an expansion of professional horizons.

Reservations about the popular training programs in nursing implemented by women's organizations, unions, and political institutions grew by the second year of the war when the initial need to provide nursing and welfare staff gave way to a more professional attitude toward training. Even then, official institutions were quick to point out the enormous benefit of women's skills and enthusiasm in the maintenance of essential medical and welfare services.[63] The Ministry of Health and Social Welfare of the Generalitat of Catalonia recognized the significance of women's role in sanitation and medical services:

> The women of our country offered themselves spontaneously to carry out these functions and many unions and organizations established short courses to train in the best way possible all the women who generously offered their collaboration. The valuable service which they gave in those days of peremptory needs must, indeed, be acknowledged.[64]

However, the Generalitat also emphasized that "the results were not always on the same level as the initial intention," as insufficient professional training eventually led to difficulties in the medical services. In June 1937, the Generalitat decreed that nursing titles acquired through unofficial channels had to pass an additional examination in order to receive an official certificate of competence, which superseded all other titles. The decree provided for further training facilities for those who failed to pass the required examination. The tightening of professional and academic control over the nursing profession undoubtedly affected the recognition of the academic qualifications of the hundreds of women nurses trained informally, although the actual circumstances of the war and the growing need for homefront medical and social welfare services allowed most women to continue their indispensable tasks in nursing.

The enthusiasm, dedication, and initiative of hundreds of women enabled health and sanitation services to function despite the extraordinary increase in demand because of the war. Military health services represented just one aspect of the new health policies that were geared toward preventive medicine and the improvement of public health in general. Health authorities dedicated much attention to health standards at the homefront, hoping to reduce epidemics and illness brought about by a low standard of living among both refugees and the civilian population. Other initiatives were developed in the field of social medicine as a part of an ongoing eugenic reform to combat infectious diseases such as tuberculosis and venereal diseases.

"The Fascism of Nature": Prostitution and Venereal Diseases

Prostitution and the spread of venereal diseases became highly visible, key issues of social and sanitation policies during the war. The new awareness of the virulence of "that loathsome sore"[65] was described in a well-known war poster as "the fascism of nature."[66] Through the creation of brothels and periodic medical examinations, hygienists, moral reformers, and social eugenicists of the nineteenth and twentieth centuries not only attempted to control prostitution and venereal disease[66] but also campaigned for public awareness.[67] Despite the existence of a small group of abolitionists who had advocated for an end to regulated prostitution since the mid-nineteenth century, official regulation was not abolished until June 1935, a year before the outbreak of the Civil War.

Traditionally, prostitution had been considered an example of "deviant" female sexuality and, as such, highly dangerous for society. From the latter part of the nineteenth century, the argument for controlling prostitution was based not only on the moral threat implied in its defiance of middle-class ideas of female respectability and religious virtue but, with increasing insistence, on the serious medical and sanitation problems it presented. By the early twentieth century, prostitution was seen as the primary cause of venereal disease–a social plague, like tuberculosis. The mobilization of social reform groups opposed to prostitution tended to center on hygienic, eugenic, and sanitary issues geared toward eliminating venereal disease. Of course, paternalistic ideological discourse was also based on the notion of the "fallen" woman and on a religious concept of the prostitute as the epitome of sin.

The struggle for the abolition of prostitution was always closely linked with anti–venereal campaigns. By the 1930's, in conjunction with the development of reform policies of the Second Republic and, more significantly, through the reform push of the eugenics movement,[68] the issue of the elimination of venereal diseases became a key feature in sociomedical reform politics. Social reform eugenicists were primarily concerned with hygiene, public health, and especially the spread of infectious diseases in Spain. While the threats of race degeneration and national decline had initially inspired them, of more immediate importance in the development of eugenics as a social movement was the drive for social reform, state modernization, and social welfare in Spain. The link between prostitution, venereal diseases, and race degeneration was a prominent feature in the health politics of the Second Republic, as the pamphlet *Un proyecto de la República. La abolición de la prostitución* implies:

> The infamous traffic in white slavery, the depraved despoiling of women in the life of prostitution, and, especially, the great and distressing problem of the propagation of venereal diseases, which is damaging the race, all make the abolition of the immemorial institution of the brothel a humanitarian imperative and a noble social and political principle.[69]

In the summer of 1935, different political constituencies agreed on the need to eliminate official regulation of prostitution, and the Minister of Labor, Health, and Welfare, the conservative Federico Salmón Amorín, finally regulated its abolition.[70] The Lucha Antivenérea (antivenereal campaign) was the core of the new legislation that considered "commercialized vice to be repugnant to the spirit, conscience and ideals of doctors, sociologists and legislators."[71] The gender bias of earlier state legislation, which had blamed the spread of venereal disease on prostitutes,[72] now gave way to a more egalitarian and technical orientation in the anti-venereal campaign based on "the equality of men and women in law, prophylaxis by therapy, and the health education of the people."[73] Only one article of the decree referred directly to prostitution, speaking of "suppressing the regulation of prostitution, not recognised in Spain as a licit way of life" (Article 1).[74] The rest of the legislation addressed the development of technical, medical, and sanitation policies for anti-venereal treatment. Despite the absence of an explicit gender bias in this legislative text, it was quite clear that the provision obliging infected persons to submit to periodical medical control would mainly affect women prostitutes.

The outbreak of the Civil War gave a new immediacy to the problem of venereal disease and prostitution. While public discussion of these issues was not new to Spanish society, what was new was the extraordinary popular interest it aroused. Debates about prostitution transcended the interest of minority groups such as social engineers, eugenicists, and sex reformers of previous decades. More significant still was the open connection made between prostitution, venereal disease, and gender power relations by women's groups hitherto silent on this subject. The fight against venereal disease was one of the few areas in which the positions of highly polarized political parties and unions coincided. Anarchists, socialists, communists, and republicans placed the elimination of venereal diseases high on their political agendas because of the public recognition of the devastating effects of venereal infection on soldiers.

The actual extent of prostitution during the war years cannot be estimated. Increased awareness of the perils of venereal disease does not necessarily signify a steep increase in the "commerce of love." However, there is no doubt that the anti-venereal campaign was a priority in sanitation policies during the war; an intense propaganda campaign using posters, radio, and pamphlets warned soldiers of the dangers of venereal disease. The press openly condemned recurrent frequenting of prostitutes by soldiers and constantly alleged that venereal infection caused almost as many casualties as the bullets of the enemy,[75] hence its symbolic representation as the "fascism of nature." War imagery in posters conveyed the message that soldiers must defend themselves against venereal disease as they did against the bullets of the fascist enemy:[76] "Avoid venereal ills like bullets" was the eloquent warning in a poster of the Council of War Health published by the Catalan government.[77] During the war, sanitation policies were not geared toward eliminating prostitution but toward controlling venereal disease.[78]

Prostitution was extensive in large cities such as Madrid, Barcelona, and Valencia, but its pervasive practice was also observed in smaller towns.[79] A 1934 report on prostitution in the city of Barcelona undertaken by the anti-venereal dispensaries estimated a total of 1,500 prostitutes in brothels and 1,000 street prostitutes.[80] By early 1937, the director general of Health and Social Assistance of the Generalitat, Dr. Félix Martí Ibáñez, estimated that there were approximately 4,000 prostitutes in Barcelona, representing an increase of 40 percent.[81]

War has generally been regarded as conducive to sexual laxity, and such was the case during the Civil War. According to one plea to soldiers for "moral equilibrium" and control over the flesh, "sexual madness" had overcome "honest proletarians" in arms.[82] It was also a period when soldiers on leave from the fronts had money to spend. Moreover, at a time when most women were dramatically afflicted by economic problems and thousands of women refugees were homeless, some may have become prostitutes as a provisional strategy for survival.

Even more important than the allegation that prostitution was on the increase was the contention that the spread of venereal disease represented a major health threat, especially to the military population. In fact, records of the Department of Dermato–Syphilography at the Hospital General de Catalunya, one of the major hospitals in Barcelona, show a significant increase in venereal disease with the inception of war. The Department, under the direction of Drs. Horta Vives and Noguer–Moré, registered a total of twenty patients discharged in July 1936.[83] A year later, in July 1937, the number of patients discharged had almost tripled, with a total of fifty-eight patients.[84] Of course, these records indicate the flow of patients at just one hospital center. Numerous other hospitals and anti-venereal dispensaries treated patients in Barcelona, while quacks and traditional home remedies also provided treatments.[85] Equally important is the high number of soldiers who were patients at this Department; more than 65 percent of the patients treated by Dr. Horta in July 1937 gave their profession as *milicianos* or soldiers.[86]

The anarchist women's organization Mujeres Libres stressed that the clientele of prostitutes were *milicianos* and antifascist soldiers: "Music-halls and houses of prostitution are packed with red and red and black scarves and all kinds of antifascist insignia."[87] Carmen Adell, in the small town of Villanueva y Geltrú, pointed out, "Now, in the midst of the Revolution, drunkenness and prostitution are rife; and it is not the former privileged class or the spoiled children of the upper classes who carry on this way; no, it is those who call themselves revolutionaries."[88]

A story told in the memoirs of the young nurse Ana Pibernat indicates how deeply prostitution was embedded in gendered cultural norms even in this time of radical social change. At a war hospital on the outskirts of Tarragona, a young ambulance driver had been operated on several times for a bullet wound to his genitals. All the hospital staff followed his case with great interest, and when it appeared that he had made a significant recovery, as a final test he was sent by the hospital to a "house of pleasure" in the nearby city of Tarragona to try out his "virile member" with "public girls." Pibernat describes the intense interest of both staff and patients–"All the hospital was as concerned as if it were his wedding night!"–and their jubilation on his success–"A miracle! It worked!"[89] Pibernat's ingenuous account of this experience indicates the extent to which prostitution appeared to be a commonplace experience, not only because it was prescribed medical treatment but because of her candid description and the language she uses to depict the event.

In conforming to the sanitation and social needs of the time, treatment of venereal disease in the context of war and revolution led to a complex public position on prostitution. The logistics of war imposed a strict discipline over the body and thus over sexual activity and hygiene. However, the logic of revolution provided a new focus on the ideological assumptions underlying conventional public views on prostitution. Discussion during this period revealed an overtly class-oriented interpretation of prostitution. Whereas prostitution had traditionally been stigmatized as a manifestation of female working-class sexual misconduct, in the war years the communist, socialist, and anarchist press propagated the view that prostitution was a degenerative social stigma inherited from capitalism.[90] Women's organizations echoed this line of analysis and argued that "prostitution was an absolutely necessary institution of capitalism."[91]

This view of prostitution presented two arguments: the most common was based on an economic contention, and the other on sexual politics. According to the standard economic line of argument, prostitutes were members of the proletariat, working-class women who sold their bodies for economic survival. This economic analysis made it quite clear that, at times, women from economically exploited working-class families had no other recourse for survival but to become prostitutes. Dire poverty and capitalist exploitation were the basic moving forces behind female working–class prostitution, which was seen as a temporary measure to assuage hunger:

> Women who sell their bodies are forced to do so for many reasons. The principal one is necessity. Working-class unemployment and the economic exploitation of women is characteristic of capitalism. In order to earn a miserable wage, working like slaves, many women, in their ignorance, prefer to prostitute themselves. In an unemployed family, prostitution can be a momentary solution. Masters, employers and all kinds of blackguards avail themselves of the destitution of the poor to prostitute their women.[92]

Although this discourse depicted prostitutes as victims of class oppression and sexual vulnerability, it also portrayed women's capacity for action and presented prostitution as a resistance strategy of destitute working-class women.

Revolutionary views on prostitution also offered another class argument based on the double sexual standards of the bourgeois and middle classes. Working-class women were convenient vehicles of sexual satisfaction for upper–class men that guaranteed the virginity and chastity of bourgeois women.[93] The Female Secretariat of the POUM followed the idea that the women of the upper classes maintained their virginal purity and expedient marriages through the prostitution of working-class women. In *Emancipación*, the dissident Marxist women argued that the elimination of prostitution would take place in the context of overall revolutionary social change that would transform both economic and social structures:

> The intolerance of free love, the form of matrimony and especially, all economic life on which bourgeois society is built, make this institution necessary. So, in order to make prostitution disappear, it is necessary to fight against all that....[94]

While the revolutionary views on prostitution addressed class oppression and the need for social change, public discourse was similarly constructed with a gender view of sexual politics. Unlike their male comrades, many women felt that a class view of prostitution was too simplistic.

In an article published in 1938, anarchist Ada Martí claimed that one of the primary duties of the revolution was to "end this foul and lamentable spectacle of a woman who, in the midst of a struggle for Freedom, is obliged to sell her body...for a piece of bread."[95] Along with most women's organizations, Martí argued that an economic solution to women's needs was to give her a decent job, which would then eliminate prostitution. More significant was her gender–specific argument that this could occur only when men had been reeducated in their gender relations with women; men had to overcome the cultural conditioning that had socialized them to consider women as "beasts of burden" and sexual objects. Only then could prostitution finally be abolished. Discussion of the sexual behavior of male clients had been peripheral to public debate on prostitution. The revolutionary circumstances of the war and, most significantly, women's sharpened feminist consciousness brought this issue to the forefront.

Mujeres Libres, the most articulate and active women's group fighting prostitution, denounced the fact that the clients of prostitutes were not bourgeois but working-class men. No ideological class barrier or revolutionary consciousness prevented the soldiers of the revolution from resorting to the "mercenary love" of their sisters in class:

> It is an incomprehensible moral incoherency that our *milicianos*—magnificent fighters at the fronts for well–beloved freedom—are those at the homefront who sustain and extend bourgeois deprivation in the worst of its forms of slavery: the prostitution of women. It cannot be explained how these spirits, disposed to all kinds of sacrifice at the trenches in order to win in a war to the death, foster the humiliating sale of the flesh of their sisters, in class and social condition, in the cities.[96]

This gender interpretation of the anarchist women continued, notwithstanding, to be class-defined in that this sexual misconduct was attributed to the influence of bourgeois moral values on working-class and even revolutionary men. The *milicianos'* behavior contradicted true revolutionary values and could be explained only as a result of their adoption of the "conduct of the masters."[97] According to this viewpoint, working-class men were seen as essentially innocent but tainted by bourgeois sexual values, which besmirched working-class women. Thus, a new reading of moral regeneration no longer critical of women but rather of working-class men was constructed.

Initially, a class perspective permeated women's views on prostitution, as in the case of Mujeres Libres, which first explained male working-class sexual misconduct as a consequence of bourgeois cultural values. Nonetheless, the anarchist women's organization gradually altered its focus. Its ideas on prostitution were heavily framed in class terms, but its gender-specific ideas became significant. Prostitutes were first and foremost victims of economic exploitation and sexual debasement by the capitalist system and bourgeois men. But they were also victims of sexual degradation by working-class men.

Mujeres Libres fiercely condemned interclass male sexual oppression of women, thus challenging the prevailing notion on the Left that prostitution was a bourgeois institution. These anarchist women understood prostitution to be a consequence of the double sexual standard that condoned premarital or extramarital sex for men while condemning it for women. According to Mujeres Libres, the double standard was a mechanism not only to protect the virtue of "decent" women but also to guarantee their safe pregnancies and wet nursing.[98] Mujeres Libres looked beyond the conventional leftist arguments that class–defined women as bourgeois or middle class and constructed a new category of women as a social collective. Thus, the politics of sexual difference defined its view of the prostitute, whose specific definition as a category it rejected. Collapsing the differences between "decent" women and prostitutes would create a gender bond among all women.

Generalizing the category of prostitute to include all women led Mujeres Libres to consider that no woman could be decent until prostitution had been eradicated. Its elimination was thus a gender-specific "liberating assignment" in which "all Spanish women immediately had to participate."[99] The more conventional construction of a female collective identity through the symbol of motherhood had been decisive in women's antifascist mobilization, as has been discussed in a previous chapter. In contrast, this vision of prostitution led to the theoretical formulation of an overall category of women that was not defined in terms of their traditional gender roles as mothers and spouses, but rather as sisters threatened by male sexual conduct.

Although groundbreaking in its theoretical formulation, the Mujeres Libres' discourse on prostitution found little response in Spanish society, where prostitution was enshrined in gendered cultural norms. Furthermore, anarchists' outlook on sexuality and prostitution took a different tack. Since the early twentieth century, the anarchist sex reform movement had aligned itself openly with the labor movement and sought to provide the working class, and particularly women, with medical counseling and information on birth control techniques, working-class eugenics, and reproduction and sex education.[100] Not surprisingly, it also proposed a countercultural view of sexual behavior that questioned many predominant traditional cultural norms and specifically promoted the "religious detoxification" of sex. Although the "new sexual ethics" proposed by anarchist sex reformers took into account the cultural construction of human sexuality, an essentialist view still predominated among some prominent sex reformers.[101] Sexuality was seen as an instinctive force and a basic biological mandate. Thus, the human sexual drive had to be fulfilled or physical degeneration might result.[102]

Although anarchist sex reformers were quite groundbreaking in their recognition of female sexual needs, their essentialist view of sexuality tended to be defined in male terms. The double-standard model of human sexuality permeated anarchist sex reform and led them to see male sexuality as uncontrollable.

The view that sexual desire was rampant in men and that its frustration was harmful led Mariano Gallardo to develop a new gender-specific explanation for prostitution, which blamed women for men's need to resort to prostitutes.[103] By inverting the terms of the double-standard model of human sexuality, Gallardo identified the cause of prostitution as women's adherence to the double standard of chastity and virginity. Women's refusal to have sexual liaisons in premarital and extramarital relations was what obliged men to resort to prostitutes and brothels. Gallardo demanded that female sexual virginity be treated as a "social crime, as an offence against the health and tranquility of men"[104] and claimed that "virginity is the reason why there are brothels, why many youths fall in the slime of prostitution and sexual vices, why there are sexual diseases and why men fall into depravity in brothels, in cabarets."[105]

Gallardo's beliefs were not representative of the anarchist sex reform movement, which had a less gendered bias toward women's sexuality and their social role. The sexual liberation of women had in fact figured prominently in the anarchists' program of sex education.[106] However, during the Civil War, the essentialist view of male sexuality as an uncontrollable drive once again displaced the more culturally constructed view of human sexuality of the mid–1930's, when anarchist sex reformers attributed the development of sexuality to cultural, religious, and social environments.

Nonetheless, the development of a new sexual culture was also a feature of anarchist eugenic reform during the war years. It was more in line with the earlier anarchist ideals of establishing a new sexual ethic based on a more natural, unprejudiced approach to human sexuality. The position of Federica Montseny, the anarchist minister of Health and Social Assistance, conceded the important need for a reform of sexual culture to conform to patterns of revolutionary change. Montseny herself admitted that her campaign in the Ministry of Health and Social Assistance to eradicate prostitution had failed. Regulation and the creation of rehabilitation centers for prostitutes were inadequate, according to her, if the basic sexual culture of Spanish society did not change. Montseny thus took up a theme common in anarchist sex reform, calling for a new sexual ethic unconditioned by religious prejudice, traditional sexual values, and sexual puritanism:

> While sexual morality is hypocritical and prudish, while the satisfaction of sexual needs is not considered something logical, as elementary as the satisfaction of the appetite, while changes in the mentality of men and women are not achieved, while Spain does not overcome its sexual morality,...the abolition of prostitution is impossible.[107]

The abolition of "mercenary love" was thus set in the context of social changes in cultural values and mentality. According to Montseny, and in line with anarchist sex reformers, both men and women had to construct a new sexual culture with different norms and values. Reflecting on her traditional non-gendered view of sexuality, Federica Montseny held quite a different view than the anarchist organization Mujeres Libres, which blamed male sexual misconduct for maintaining prostitution.[108]

Traditional views of prostitutes as deviant outcasts of society or as being sexually depraved were less prevalent in discussions during the war years when the revolution led to different views on prostitution. Nonetheless, this view was still purveyed through war imagery. The deployment of extensive propaganda in war posters reinforced the representation of the prostitute as dangerous female sexuality. A frequently portrayed image was that of a provocative nude woman enticing a fully clad soldier in battle dress to his destruction.[109] Another poster graphically portrayed a seductive woman leaning against a lamp post with the one word: "Danger!"[110] A striking poster by Rivero Gil shows a nude prostitute, whose arm is that of a skeleton, embracing a soldier; the message reads, "Attention! Venereal diseases threaten your health. Be alert against them!"[111] Two slatternly, semi–nude women seated at a table with a skeleton is another image that vividly illustrates the fact that official sources envisioned prostitutes as in league with death.[112]

This traditional view of prostitutes as deviant criminals permeated most official iconography intended to frighten soldiers into avoiding venereal disease. However, the message was at times quite ambiguous. The message on another war poster— "The hygiene of the militiaman is the weapon that we all need"—is not quite clear. Were men to refrain from contact with prostitutes or were they simply to adopt preventive hygienic measures to avoid infection? This view of the prostitute as a social outcast and an innate practitioner of a degenerate form of human conduct reinforced a gender-specific vision of women as the exclusive source of sexual misconduct and, as such, solely responsible for the propagation of venereal disease. Male complicity was disregarded in war imagery, and men were absolved of responsibility for any sexual "deviancy."

The perpetuation of this traditional view of prostitution despite contrary opinions can perhaps be attributed to the fact that official social and sanitation entities such as the Sanitation Council of War or ministerial departments controlled and produced the war posters. Republican war posters, however, have usually been regarded as representative of socialist realism and revolutionary values.[113] Most of the posters were printed by collectivized presses run by anarchist and socialist unions, which were supposedly subject to some degree of social control to reflect the new revolutionary values. Yet, revolutionary control did not imply challenging androcentric, sexist views. This powerful imagery highlights rather the continuity of gendered cultural norms and illustrates the sharp divergence between more innovative revolutionary rhetoric in other fields and the prevailing traditional patriarchal views in the construction of public attitudes and policies on prostitutes and, implicitly, on women as a social collective.

This traditional definition of prostitutes was not limited to imagery, however. In March 1937, a socialist newspaper ran an extensive article on prostitution that presented the classical characterization of the prostitute as a depraved woman who seduced innocent young soldiers of the revolution into degenerate sexual misconduct.[114] The predominant visual projection of "mercenary love" as gender-specific to women was crucial to the continuity of the traditional view of prostitution. As a visual representation, its impact was extraordinary. It was more effective, in the long run, in propagating a traditional view of prostitution than the more innovative written discussions were in changing this view.

Liberate the Prostitutes

The war prompted an innovative initiative by the women's organization Mujeres Libres to create *liberatorios de prostitución* (liberation homes for prostitutes). In contrast to official measures and conventional tradition in Spain, the prostitute, not venereal disease, was central to its policy.

Other women's organizations, such as the antifascist women's groups, also came to consider "the combat against prostitution as a fight for women's liberation"[115] and paid some sporadic attention to prostitution,[116] but it was the anarchist Mujeres Libres organization that gave the issue priority on its agenda: "The most urgent task to be carried out in the new social structure is the suppression of prostitution."[117] The organization's initiative also achieved greater social resonance because it found support from two high–level officials, Federica Montseny and Félix Martí Ibáñez. The co-founder of Mujeres Libres, Amparo Poch y Gascón, director of social assistance at the Ministry of Health and Social Assistance, was a close colleague of Minister Montseny. She was thus able to channel the initiative to create *liberatorios de prostitución* through this official institution.[118] In Catalonia, Félix Martí Ibáñez enthusiastically supported the project, but the ousting of anarchists from political power after the May 1937 conflict made the development of this new project impossible. Despite the intense campaigns launched by the anarchist women, the *liberatorios* were never backed by official institutions, which geared their policies toward a hygienic, sanitary approach to preventing venereal diseases and controlling the locus of infection rather than solving the problems of prostitutes.

Despite this failure, the *liberatorios* highlighted change and continuity in the development of discourse and policies on prostitution by women in a revolutionary project. The homes were designed as a transitory stage in the "social readaptation" of prostitutes to a "new life, society and work."[119] The *liberatorios* were rehabilitation homes where the "mercenaries of love" were to be given a comprehensive treatment consisting of health care, psychotherapy, and professional training centered on apprenticeship in trades.[120] The four-point program designed by Mujeres Libres had the following objectives: "Medical and psychiatric research and treatment; psychological and ethical care in order to give the pupils a sense of responsibility; professional guidance and training; and moral and material support at any time even after their rehabilitation."[121] The program emphasized the need to provide psychological resources to prostitutes so that they could be resocialized to embrace other cultural values and to adapt to "a world in which they lived, but from *outside*, never feeling it in their heart."[122]

In conjunction with this psychocultural focus, the program also recognized the importance of addressing the economic motivations related to prostitution, of supplying alternative options for earning a living. Professional training and alternative job options were crucial in anarchist proposals for the abolition of prostitution: "We cannot, in all justice, take away the *modus vivendi* of any human being, repugnant, painful if you like, but necessary for survival, without offering in exchange something else. It is neither pious nor human to offer words and discourse to those who lack even bread."[123] Economic independence was a critical component of the plan to eradicate prostitution.

The tightly conceived *liberatorios* program was technical in its approach and left little opportunity for the women themselves to take initiative. Although these places of respite were labeled "liberating homes," prostitutes were to be liberated not on their own initiative but on that of others. Félix Martí Ibáñez admitted that the "redemption of the mercenaries of love had to be their own doing," but he also made it quite clear that it would happen when they "accepted the means we offer them now to recommence a new life."[124] Despite the pervading social context of an ongoing revolutionary anarchist movement that advocated collectivized self–management, neither the Mujeres Libres nor Martí Ibáñez felt that prostitutes could rehabilitate themselves.

Implicit in the *liberatorios* proposal was the intention proclaimed by many previous reformist groups to *save* prostitutes. Although not openly pronounced, the idea of moral regeneration as a necessary part of the social adaptation of prostitutes was implicit in this program. Martí Ibáñez himself used the traditional term "redemption" to describe the aims of the *liberatorios*.

Lack of documentary sources prevents us from reconstructing prostitutes' views of the *liberatorios*. The question remains, however, as to whether prostitutes wanted to be saved and how to interpret the question of female initiative on this issue. Furthermore, the optimistic and perhaps naive account by the Catalan Left republican writer Aurora Bertrana in her memoirs describing life in District V, the red–light district in Barcelona, shows how prostitutes adapted to changing revolutionary times on their own initiative and modified their personal expectations in such a context:

> Some pimps...and madames of brothels had been assassinated; others had fled. The prostitution business was collectivized. In appearance, the narrow and secretive streets...all remained as before....But now, there were many armed men and with militian caps. The women joined them, free and light-hearted. They felt themselves mistresses of their acts, no longer subject to a master or an intermediary. In the drinking establishments they...went from table to table with a new light on their faces. They no longer looked at the men only as possible clients, but as a possible partner with whom to share a flight of triumph, a drop of happiness, a shadow of tenderness.[125]

In the initial months of the war, a small number of prostitutes adapted to revolutionary times and proceeded to change their life experience and become *milicianas*. However, they were still seen as prostitutes. This raises the question of closed analytical categories. Is a prostitute always to be defined solely as a prostitute? Does being a prostitute invalidate a genuine revolutionary antifascist stance? How do we deal with reformed prostitutes who fulfilled their obligations both in armed combat and in auxiliary duties at the fronts?[126]

The definition of a prostitute is a historical construction. Moreover, in revolutionary times people can be affected by the changes they witness and undergo political conversions.[127] Despite the changing collective experience of prostitutes during the war, what is significant is the persistent sameness of the discourse on prostitution in this specific context of trench warfare and revolutionary change. Prostitutes continued to be portrayed as unchanging deviants and a threat to the new social order. Revolutionary views still categorized prostitutes as a deviant species subject to social control to be kept apart from "respectable" women. Prostitutes attempted to redefine their status as *milicianas*; however, they failed to be categorized as anything other than whores. Changing revolutionary circumstances did nothing to challenge traditional definitions of female sexual misdemeanor or the social stigmatization of prostitutes.

The innovative *liberatorios* proposal was insufficient to change the overall mentality, gender conduct, and sexual standards of Spanish men. Hence, revolutionary ideas were buried under a morass of traditional patriarchal views on male sexuality and conduct, which remained unchanged despite the revolution and the innovative initiatives by women.

Revolution and the Legalization of Abortion

The Generalitat of Catalonia legalized abortion for the Catalan provinces in December 1936. The decree on the "Artificial Interruption of Pregnancy" of December 25, 1936 regulated abortion and authorized its practice in "hospitals, clinics and health institutions belonging to the Generalitat of Catalonia in which special services had been established to this effect."[128] By February 1937, abortion services had been established in four medical centers in Barcelona and in four regional hospitals in other parts of Catalonia.[129] For the first time in Spain, the legal practice of abortion was regulated.

The Soviet Union had been the first European country to legalize abortion, in 1920, but later introduced restrictive legislation in 1936. In the late 1930's, the Scandinavian countries also introduced abortion reform in the legislation of Finland (1934), followed by Sweden (1938), and Denmark (1939).[130]

Catalonia stands out as a watershed in Western Europe in the introduction of advanced abortion legislation. This initiative was even more surprising, as it took place in a country traditionally better known for its conservatism. However, the revolutionary circumstances of the Civil War impulsed social changes by anarchists who placed abortion reform high on their agenda.

Abortion had already emerged as a social problem in Spain in the early twentieth century when it came under public scrutiny in a complex controversy that focused not only on its moral and ideological implications but also on the public health consequences of its widespread practice.[131] A number of doctors and lawyers had justified the practice of therapeutic abortion if the mother's health was in grave danger. In this ongoing debate, only therapeutic abortion had been contemplated as legitimate, and many of these professionals distinguished precisely between criminal and therapeutic abortion.

Despite objections by more conservative colleagues, a small minority of lawyers and doctors, many of whom were associated with the eugenics reform movement, believed in the legitimacy of therapeutic abortion performed by specialized doctors. Their arguments were based on a reinterpretation of the Spanish Penal Code, jurisprudence, and medical evidence.[132] Given the pervasiveness of the Roman Catholic Church and of conservative ideology in Spain, it is indeed surprising that by the 1920's some well–known progressive and liberal doctors and lawyers endorsed voluntary therapeutic abortion. What is even more significant is that by the early 1930's therapeutic abortion came to be openly admitted as legitimate in lectures in such prestigious, traditional forums as the National Academy of Medicine.[133]

Public discussion on the issue of abortion had always been sharply gender-defined. Women had always remained silent in this ongoing debate, which had been limited to male professionals and the clergy. So despite the fact that abortion was essentially a female question, as it involved the control of women's reproductive capacities through the termination of pregnancy, abortion as a public issue was not addressed by Spanish women in the early twentieth century. Why did women fail to make a sustained challenge to the male monopoly of the public discussion of abortion? Women were absent from public debate on a variety of issues such as birth control and abortion because the gender-specific ideology of domesticity and the separation of the public and private spheres made it extremely difficult for Spanish women to gain representation in the public arena. Norms of social conduct deemed any female participation in a public debate on any issue a transgression against established gender rules of behavior, so very few women challenged the male monopoly of the public arena. Women participants in public forums belonged to an elite minority and certainly were not representative of Spanish women as a collective.

In a conservative society in which the Roman Catholic Church was the all-pervasive social institution whose role was to guard traditional moral values, the stigma attached to any discussion of sexuality or reproductive issues was enormous. Those topics were taboo, morally inadmissible, and, therefore, not open to debate to the general male public, and even less to women. Few women who conformed to standards of gender propriety could stand up in public to discuss any topic, much less scandalous issues such as abortion. It was considered inappropriate for females to show any sign of public interest in such matters. Such a concern was considered outrageous and a sign of wantonness, promiscuity, or indecency.

Even in private, with their own husbands, women did not openly discuss sexuality or reproductive issues because males considered any interest or knowledge in this field to be threatening and even a sign of dubious moral standards or unnatural desires.[134] Women were portrayed as asexual, ethereal, innocent beings, the "angels of the hearth," so practically any woman who subscribed to predominant cultural values and gender behavior patterns would not dream of discussing any of these issues in public and perhaps not even in private. Such an involvement could obviously bring about social ostracism and, more than likely, male rejection. So we find very few women who openly discussed these issues. Their isolation was even more acute because there were no female organizations that addressed this debate. And given the extremely low number of women doctors,[135] there were no groups of female medical professionals who could have justified their interest even on professional grounds.

Women's silence on the subject of abortion was due to gender constraints and moral and religious inhibitions. But there was also another reason—the predominance of traditional patriarchal views on women. The definition of female identity through motherhood and domesticity was still essentially an unquestioned social value. So it would have been difficult for women to articulate a public debate on reproductive rights that disassociated them from their primary role as mothers and reproducers of the species. When such topics gradually came to be considered appropriate for public discussion, they were not generated by an interest in female reproductive rights or self-determination but rather by concern for high mortality rates, hygiene, eugenics, public health, or even social change. Gender issues were mostly absent from discussion of abortion during this period. This omission, together with female silence, makes it difficult to ascertain the specific gender significance not only of the debate but of the actual practice of abortion in Spain at this time; the politics of abortion was indeed more discernible than its actual practice.

Evidence points to the existence of two different channels addressing the issue of abortion in Spanish society during the 1920's and 1930's. The first and most visible was the above-mentioned public interest by male professionals; the second, the private, silent, female, and pragmatic practice of abortion. These two channels did not intersect but developed along paths of separate views and practices. One belonged to the public professional arena of public health authorities, the eugenics movement, and the medical and law professions, the other to the domain of clandestine culture, female networks, and silent complicity.

Women aborted but did not publicly discuss the ethical, moral, or medical consequences of abortion. The professional elite discussed these issues and brought abortion under public scrutiny as a social problem. Furthermore, until the legalization of abortion in Catalonia in December 1936, abortion had been subject not just to moral and religious condemnation but also to legal prosecution. Its practice was clandestine, illegal, and underground. It tended to involve female networks for the diffusion of information on abortifacients, home remedies, addresses of practitioners, and moral and material support. Most practitioners were female, midwives or "wise women" whom women consulted when they wanted medical assistance from outsiders. So the actual practice of abortion had a decisive gender specificity, including women's experience. Abortion also had class connotations, as it was largely a social phenomenon that involved working–class women. Furthermore, the failure of the legalized abortion services available in Catalonia during the Civil War and women's inhibition in making use of them can be explained by the absence of women in the development of public policies and health services related to abortion.

The legalization of abortion in Catalonia in 1936 was not the outcome of the growing normalization of therapeutic abortion that had taken place since the turn of the century.[136] Rather, it was an anarchist initiative and must be understood in the framework of the ongoing anarchist sex reform movement and the specific sociopolitical context of the dual strategy of antifascist war and revolutionary struggle in Catalonia during the Civil War. In 1936, the issue of abortion was addressed from a social and class perspective that was very different from former medical discussions on the legitimacy of therapeutic abortion. Although some of the most assiduous anarchist writers and contributors to the debate on reproductive issues were doctors, they aspired to adopt a nonprofessional approach. Congruent with their anarchist outlook, they advocated self-help and so offered information and training on medical, hygienic, sexual, and reproductive issues as a means to achieve the development of full human potential, an old anarchist ideal. They identified with and addressed themselves primarily to a working-class audience.

By the late 1920's, anarchist sex reformers had introduced reproductive issues into their overall strategy for social change. Thus, in a logical progression, once they acquired political power in 1936 and were in a position to direct public health policies, they also addressed themselves to reproductive issues. So, for the small nucleus of anarchist sex reformers, strategies for social transformation also implied the development of reproductive rights.

Anarchist politics of reproduction had not historically focused on abortion but rather on birth control.[137] Abortion was always peripheral to anarchist sex reform and policy on sexual education and birth control. Reproductive strategies were dependent upon the use of contraceptives as a means to achieve family planning, while abortion was never seen in this light. Anarchists felt that informed educational policies on birth control would lead to the elimination of the need for abortion, so they concentrated on the diffusion of birth control information. Nonetheless, they did not ignore the social reality of abortion, and, although they did not condone it, abortion came to be accepted as a working-class resistance strategy to avoid family health and economic problems.

The 1936 legislation concerning abortion represented, to a large extent, an endorsement of the ongoing anarchist project to provide birth control and health services in the new climate of social change. So this legislation must be viewed against the background of the innovative health policies of the Catalan government and the development of new economic and revolutionary strategies throughout the country.[138] The key figure in the development of the new abortion policy was Dr. Félix Martí Ibáñez,[139] one of the most visible organizers of the anarchist sex reform movement. As director general of Health and Social Assistance of the Generalitat of Catalonia, he sponsored a public health policy to meet popular health needs in the areas of social and preventive medicine.[140] The eugenics reform was an important part of the overall restructuring of public health and social welfare policies. This reform focused primarily on the care of working-class women and children and centered on sex reform, birth control, maternity care, and prostitution.[141] The abortion legislation was just a part of the overall eugenics reform policy.

The "Eugenic Reform of Abortion," as the legislation was called, responded to a revolutionary eugenic, hygienic, class rationale. Dr. Félix Martí Ibáñez described it as a decisive step for the "glory of the revolution": "Abortion leaps from the dark incompetence in which it was held until today, and acquires a high social and biological category, on being converted to a eugenic instrument at the service of the proletariat."[142] The legalization of abortion can be considered primarily as a pragmatic hygienic measure designed to regulate its covert practice in Catalonia. The legislation established a series of goals that focused on eradicating clandestine abortion and infanticide, reducing illnesses and mortality due to abortive practices, and, finally, decreasing abortion in Catalonia through the establishment of birth control and family planning services, which would enable working-class mothers to avoid having to resort to abortion as a reproductive control strategy.[143]

The 1936 legislation was advanced for its day, as it placed few restrictions on those seeking an abortion. Abortions were approved in a wide variety of categories; therapeutic (mental or physical ill health of the mother), eugenic (paternal incest or the possibility of transmission of physical or mental defects), neo-malthusian (the conscious will to practice voluntary birth control), and personal (ethical or sentimental reasons to avoid unwanted maternity).

The overriding concern of the reform was to facilitate abortion for those whose pregnancy was a health hazard or when there was a danger of malformation or ill health of the fetus. Eugenic rationale constituted the main element of the politics of abortion promoted by the anarchist-oriented health authorities. This emphasis responded to the serious existing health problem of abortion malpractice by providing an immediate remedy to the situation. The eugenic focus also held to the traditional thinking within the anarchist sex reform movement, which had failed to address the issues of reproductive rights from the perspective of female autonomy and self-determination. Furthermore, a reproductive strategy that emphasized eugenics was undoubtedly seen to be more acceptable to the general population and, more specifically, to the medical profession.

The politics of abortion developed in this period was also an important component of the ongoing struggle for revolutionary change. For some people within the anarchist sex reform movement, reproductive rights were vitally linked to strategies for social transformation. The new legislation conceded a wide degree of individual autonomy on the decision to practice abortion. As had happened in prior birth control campaigns, "conscious motherhood" also became one of the slogans of the new public health policy; the woman now had the choice of maternity when economic and health conditions were optimum. Birth control was upheld as the mechanism to eliminate the "slavery of continuous motherhood," which ruined the health of many working-class mothers. Anarchist sex reformers urged workers to practice the "eugenic ideal" of "conscious generation" and, particularly, to postpone pregnancies until the end of the war when the "revolutionary victory" would allow the working class to procreate in idyllic conditions.[144]

The eugenic abortion reform also called for the construction of birth control clinics to inform and counsel on the use of birth control techniques. However, available sources indicate that these centers were never established, with the exception of the "School for Conscious Motherhood," which operated in the Casa de la Maternidad in Barcelona. Despite the fact that abortion was permitted on neo-malthusian grounds of voluntary restriction of the number of children, the new legislation did not classify abortion as a substitution for birth control. On the contrary, the policy focused on the actual elimination of the practice of abortion through the increased use of effective birth control techniques. The practice of abortion was, in fact, subjected to specific restraints to avoid its being used as a common birth control method. Under the law, a woman could have only one abortion a year except under special therapeutic circumstances that made the termination of a pregnancy advisable.

Historically, abortion had constituted a part of social reality in Catalonia. Despite the lack of systematic records on the incidence of abortion,[145] both quantitative and qualitative evidence drawn from medical, hospital, and public health records indicates quite clearly that there had been a high rate of clandestine abortion in Catalonia since the beginning of the century.[146] During the decade of the 1930's, the records of the departments of gynecology and obstetrics of the General Hospital of Catalonia in Barcelona registered high abortion rates, averaging 33.8 percent of all pregnant women in care at that facility.[147] This figure would seem to confirm a high abortion rate among women of the lower classes who were patients at the hospital.[148] As has been demonstrated for other European countries,[149] abortion appears to have been a fairly common method of birth control among the Catalan working class and a significant factor in the steep decline in overall fertility rates in Catalonia in this period.[150]

In the 1920's and early 1930's, the anarchist sex reform movement and the reformist eugenics movement[151] led to a more extensive discussion on birth control and contraceptive techniques. However, it is not at all clear that this discussion had, in fact, generated more widespread use of contraceptive methods among the overall population. Both eugenic and sex reform movements recommended a wide range of contraceptive methods,[152] but their use was conditioned by gender and class determinants.

Because contraceptives were commonly associated with prostitution,[153] the social stigma attached to them made it difficult for women to have easy access to them. Most women were unwilling to risk damaging their reputation by purchasing contraceptives. Another obstacle to women's use of effective birth control was that most techniques required prior medical consultation and constant supervision. Such a situation would have been quite unthinkable for many reasons. Women rarely consulted their doctors on reproductive issues, as these subjects were considered inappropriate for discussion. Moreover, the situation would remain unchanged as long as doctors themselves remained unsupportive of birth control and considered themselves the defenders of morality and traditional social values. Furthermore, if class distinctions are taken into consideration, very few working-class women would have been able to afford a doctor's consultation fees. In fact, the cheaper fees of midwives was one reason that they were a more attractive and realistic option as popular consultants for female ailments. As a consequence of social constraints, few women had access to information and medical guidance on the best contraceptive methods. A further obstacle for working-class women was undoubtedly the fact that all contraceptive devices and products were expensive and their purchase would not have been feasible for most working-class budgets.[154]

Despite a certain degree of access to birth control techniques through the popular diffusion of anarchist sex reform journals such as *Generación Consciente* and *Estudios* and the publication of numerous birth control tracts,[155] it is highly unlikely that a considerable portion of the Catalan or Spanish working class adopted them. Withdrawal and abortion appear to have been the more viable options for the reduction of family size. These two methods were quite different in their gender significance.

Withdrawal, which was apparently the most common form of birth control practiced in Spain in this period,[156] required the cooperation of the male partner, mutual agreement on its practice, and a previous decision on a strategy of family planning. Abortion, too, was part of a major strategy of family survival among working classes in Spain, but it appears to a large degree to have been a female decision that did not necessarily involve the male partner and tended to take place within the framework of a female network of practice and support.[157] Aspiring for recognition of their profession and status, midwives publicly denied any involvement in the practice of abortion, but they performed them for a moderate fee, which was more easily affordable to a working-class budget. Of course, women did not always have recourse to professional aid, and many home remedies were used. Female networking provided the necessary information on products, remedies, medical care, and general support.[158] Given women's ongoing experience of clandestine abortion, new health policies on abortion could appear to be a crucial point on a feminist agenda for revolutionary change. However, women did not consider abortion as a key feature in their mobilization during the Civil War.

Despite the enthusiastic drive by anarchist sex reformers to introduce the "eugenic reform of abortion" and the progressive gender dimension in the legislation itself, the implementation of the new regulation was a failure and the traditional practice of clandestine abortions continued. Significantly, the use of the official abortion service at the General Hospital of Catalonia was practically negligible. Records there show that only 5 percent of the 305 registered abortions between 1937 and 1938, the two years the decree was enforced, can be considered as voluntary abortions within the terms of the "eugenic reform of abortion."[159] The records of the Casa de la Maternidad, the former foundling home equipped to treat female refugees, registered a total of only 15 abortions.[160]

The disappearance of the records for the Hospital Clínico makes it difficult to assess the figures given by Dr. Félix Martí Ibáñez in a report claiming that more than 300 voluntary abortions had been performed there by June 1937.[161] It seems to be a high figure in comparison with the records of the other hospitals incorporated into this service. Martí Ibáñez himself performed abortions there,[162] and that may have facilitated a more favorable attitude by doctors and more efficient abortion services. However, even if the figure is accepted as being correct, most evidence points to an overall failure of the abortion reform and to the continuance of the practice of clandestine abortion, which shows a slight decrease in the General Hospital records for the war years, dropping from 184 cases in 1935 to 166 (1936), 163 (1937), and 142 (1938).[163]

From a gender perspective, there was a decided emancipatory content to the abortion legislation in that women held a significant degree of autonomy. Women were allowed to abort not just on the grounds of health or eugenics but also on the basis of self-determination. Women's reproductive rights were protected by the law, which stipulated that, in the case of a woman alleging sentimental or ethical reasons to abort, her opinion alone was to be considered and none of the members of her family had a right to object. This norm can also be seen as a measure instituted to protect the doctors involved in the clinical intervention. Nonetheless, such a possibility does not take away from the emancipatory content of the eugenics reform, which was overtly presented in this light by its promoter, Martí Ibáñez:

> The authorization to carry out abortion represents, then, a vigorous affirmation of maternity insofar as it affects women's responsibility. In the future, with regards to sexual life, women will be free from egoistic male tyranny and will have rights among which that of self-determination and the right to decide on their own maternity are the most significant....[164]

There was, then, a decided emphasis on female self-autonomy in this legislation, which was also presented as a tool to achieve overall women's emancipation. Despite the fact that the new legislation was not the outcome of women's pressure and mobilization, there was a high degree of sensitivity on the issue of women's reproductive rights. How, then, can the failure of this reform and particularly women's inhibition on the matter be explained?

Numerous factors must be taken into account in exploring the failure of this groundbreaking legislation. As has been said, the actual reform must be attributed to the co-existence of war and revolution in Catalonia. In another context, it would indeed have been unlikely for such a radical public health policy to be introduced by the health authorities at that time. The actual sociopolitical context of the war, while favoring this legislation, at the same time made its application particularly difficult. Public health services addressed what were considered the more urgent tasks of treating the wounded. Most hospitals were understaffed and under-equipped and had difficulty providing adequate medical attention. The organization and administration of any new health service would have been difficult to carry out under these circumstances. Moreover, the Catalan public health board tended to be more concerned with the development of their venereal disease prevention services. On the whole, the urgency to respond to immediate health problems caused by the war drew attention away from the abortion reform.

The hostile disposition of the medical profession toward the implementation of the new service is another key factor in explaining the weak impact of the abortion legislation. Doctors were unwilling to collaborate in the reform, although they were obliged to do so under the terms of the decree. The law did not establish a conscience clause that allowed for voluntary assignment to this service. The terms of the legislation were rigorous, as all specialists in gynecology were obliged to provide the service, but moral and ethical issues were not the only determinants in the hostile disposition of the medical profession. As has been discussed, an ongoing movement had been launched by a small number of doctors who had advocated legitimizing therapeutic abortion. Historically, then, the medical profession had not totally rejected abortion *per se*. The crucial question had been the doctors' control of the decision, which tended to be based on therapeutic grounds. The woman's right to decide to abort on personal, ethical, or neo-malthusian grounds recognized in the new legislation went far beyond the usual basis for legitimacy accepted by the medical profession. Abortion was no longer granted just on therapeutic grounds, and, more significant still, the right to decide was no longer confined to the doctors.

There were other decisive factors involved that did not derive from the question of abortion but had to do with the characteristics of public health policies. The abortion legislation was carried out under the initiative of Dr. Félix Martí Ibáñez and the anarchists who were influential in the Ministry of Health and Social Assistance. Thus, the new legislation was rejected by the core of the medical profession who resented interference in their affairs and were hostile to anarchist policies.[165] This animosity was quite decisive in the failure of the abortion services. It not only impeded clinical abortions but also the referral of patients to these services and to family planning centers. Doctors could have been decisive agents in normalizing the practice of abortion in hospitals, but Martí Ibáñez and the anarchist sex reformers failed to gain grassroots medical support for their project. Most doctors either ignored it or boycotted it.

In contrast to the extraordinary coverage the press gave to the anti-venereal disease campaign, it maintained a strikingly low profile on the whole issue of abortion. This can probably be attributed to the fact that the legalization was passed by decree. There was no prior political debate on the subject, and it came under little public scrutiny at the time. Despite the fact that the Generalitat had implemented a publicity campaign based on radio talks, lectures, and the publication of a tract,[166] public coverage of this health service was ineffective. Significantly, the women who knew about the eugenic reform tended to have some degree of politicization, whereas traditional female marginalization from politics may have caused unpoliticized women to be unaware of such issues and public policies. Thus, information appears to have circulated through closed channels and not necessarily to the public at large; most unpoliticized working-class women appeared not to have known about the legalization of abortion and the provision of clinical abortions.[167] The high level of illiteracy among women, the deficient publicity campaigns, and the actual circumstances of the war itself, together with the fact that the promoters of the abortion reform were an isolated handful of anarchist males with restricted resources, resulted in limited public awareness of the reform.

Finally, the marginalization of legal abortion reflects the gender dimension of the problem. Although the decree was the work of anarchists who advocated self-help, overall civil mobilization, and intervention in the dynamics of social change, it was nonetheless a regulation carried out by male doctors in the public administration. Women had no voice in its development or its implementation. Thus, even in this period of accelerated social transformation, legal regulation of abortion remained gender-defined. For the most part, women continued to function within the suppressive culture of the past rather than identify themselves with this public policy. Instead of availing themselves of the services, women continued to have clandestine abortions.

Even some women who were aware of the reform chose not to use the services. The crucial point here appears to be the survival of traditional social values with respect to abortion. Mental attitudes were slow to adapt, despite the accelerated tempo of change during the Civil War. Voluntary induced abortion continued to be socially unacceptable, and on a public level, condemned both on social and moral grounds. Women were slow to assert publicly their reproductive rights and were logically conditioned by the boundaries of their time and culture. Social and religious constraints and gender ideology still persisted and were very difficult to overcome. On a practical level, the excessive bureaucracy attached to the abortion services made it difficult for women to maintain anonymity, and so they feared the social repercussions of any public knowledge of their decision to abort.

More significantly, legal abortion did not become a public issue around which women mobilized. None of the major female organizations involved in the antifascist war effort included the subject of abortion on their agendas. The Female Secretariat of the dissident Marxist POUM was the only women's organization to openly discuss abortion. It welcomed the new reform, albeit with reservations. Interestingly, the organization's criticism focused on sexual politics, as it was perceived that the new facilities for abortion could have negative consequences for women, who would be even more greatly pressured into acquiescing to male sexual overtures.[168] According to its line of argument, predominant "revolutionary licentiousness" as practiced by male revolutionaries could easily lead to open sexual harrassment, because women could no longer allege fear of pregnancy to avoid sexual relations.

More significant still is the extraordinary silence of the anarchist women's organization Mujeres Libres on the "eugenic reform of abortion" sponsored by their fellow anarchists. The organization never discussed the new legislation in its journal and never raised the issue of abortion during the years of the war. Although Mujeres Libres was highly articulate and active in opposing prostitution, abortion was not a priority on its organizational agenda under any circumstance. The organization's silence underscores the continuing difficulties involved in women's public discussion of a topic that was still considered socially taboo and a threat to women's collective social cohesion.

The fact that abortion had historically been a public male issue was no doubt decisive in preventing women from identifying easily with this new health policy. Besides, the deficiencies and expense of the actual service, the disapproval of the medical profession and the community, and the alien hospital environment all contributed to preserving clandestine abortion as an attractive option for many women. Women's concentration on the ongoing antifascist struggle and the brief existence of the eugenic reform of abortion made it difficult for women to develop a reproductive strategy designed to break down traditional obstacles and to create a female-focused definition of their reproductive rights. Abortion continued to form part of clandestine culture; it remained a marginalized social reality despite the dynamics of social change of the period. Traditionally, abortion has been defined by historians as a women's issue and even as a feminist issue, but, in Spain, gender and moral restrictions remained so powerful that not even in this period of revolutionary change did it become part of women's agenda. Gender conditions still defined the issue of abortion as male, despite the expansion of gender options and roles for women during the years of the Civil War. Legal abortion was on the revolutionary agenda of the anarchists, but women did not identify with this goal. They made different choices regarding their priorities during the war and revolution.

▪ 6 ▪

The Battle Lost

War disrupted women's daily lives and traditional modes of living. It generated an immediate mass female response of active support against Franco and fascist aggression. It transformed women's lives in many ways, giving them greater autonomy of movement and decision that they immediately used. Despite the harsh conditions of war, many Spanish women lived the Civil War as an exciting, exhilarating experience that enabled them to develop their potential to an extent never before permitted by Spanish society. Women's novel participation in male jobs, trench warfare, volunteer work, community services, and social welfare was for many a liberating experience. Self-esteem and greater confidence in their own capacity led women to further expectations regarding their own role in society and to a broader awareness of their rights. They demanded greater recognition of their social status as women as well as the right to employment, professional training, and forthright involvement in all spheres of activity related to the war effort.

Women's agency was clear throughout the war, as when they undertook new social, economic, and military activities. They organized themselves on an unprecedented, vast scale. They created specific women's organizations with the political purpose of fighting fascism and were instrumental in promoting a new, mass female movement in villages, towns, and cities throughout unoccupied Spain. They demonstrated considerable organizational abilities and channeled the organized women's collective response to fascism, while at the same time identifying women's concerns and hitherto unattended needs.

Women became involved in the struggle against fascism and broke with their accustomed isolation from political and public life. They built barricades, nursed the wounded, and organized relief work and child welfare. They sewed uniforms and knitted sweaters and, through their unpaid labor, provided the soldiers at the fronts with uniforms, other clothing, and necessary equipment. Women worked in public transportation, in munitions factories, and on farms. Some women also broke completely with conventional gender roles by undertaking an active part in warfare as *milicianas*. They took up arms and strove to be accepted on a par with soldiers at the front. The *milicianas* initially symbolized the good fight against fascism and inspired others to participate in resistance activities. The choice to become a woman soldier also challenged social conventions because it actively defended the revolutionary cause. The *milicianas* fought at the fronts as well as providing necessary auxiliary services for the soldiers. However, their courage, tenacity, and dedication were insufficient to gain acceptance for a military role for women and failed to stave off the gradual discredit eventually associated with the *milicianas*. Their image tarnished, the women were obliged to retire to the homefront. But their role in daily survival there was crucial, too, in the maintenance of civil resistance to the onslaught of fascism.

Education and culture were identified as the keys to women's liberation and became the primary goal of a collective women's agenda. All the women's groups concerned themselves with the illiteracy of thousands of Spanish women. They collectively addressed the urgent demand for mass adult educational programs and, despite the difficulties of the war, enthusiastically provided these programs in thousands of centers in villages, small towns, and cities throughout republican Spain. Women gave classes and organized cultural and artistic activities and library services for adult women throughout the war. Schools, institutes, lectures, and courses were the means through which Mujeres Libres intended to fulfill their stated goal of emancipation from the triad of enslavement: their inherent status as women and workers and their fostered ignorance. Seizing the opportunity, activists from all the antifascist women's organizations challenged "male civilization" with the weapons of education and culture. Through their ongoing dedication to educational programs geared to women's specific needs, women's freedom and emancipation were diligently pursued.[1] One of the great achievements of the women's movement during the war and the revolution was the education and empowerment of women.

Women also overcame their historical silence as a social collective. They asserted their voice and publicly expressed their collective opinion on politics, the war, antifascism, feminism, and women's needs. They edited and published numerous journals and newspapers. Some were exclusively female endeavors, as was the case with *Mujeres Libres*, while others were in collaboration with male colleagues and comrades. *Companya, Emancipación, Muchachas, Mujeres* (Madrid), *Mujeres* (Bilbao), *Mujeres* (Valencia), *Mujeres Libres, Noies Muchachas, Pasionaria*, and *Trabajadoras* demonstrated women's organizational capacity as well as their initiative in the creation of literary platforms for their ideas and a concrete expression of a gendered reading of the war. Although this collective endeavor was feasible thanks to the assistance of trained professional journalists, it was the enthusiasm of novice women writers and editors finally permitted their own written forums that kept these journals and magazines alive. Women verbalized their commitment to the antifascist war effort–and their voices were heard.

These publications were also crucial tools in attracting other women to the cause. The range of articles and debates went far beyond the politics of antifascism, however, and women were frequently engaged in identifying their own interests regarding the war and the revolution, as well as providing resources for female cultural initiatives. This cultural interaction among readers, writers, and editors of the women's journals created a specific gender universe for women, an important, anchoring experience in a traditionally oral female culture.

Civil resistance and everyday survival in war can be accounted for through women's enormous energy and effort. Voluntary relief work by women was a major contribution to the war economy and the functioning of civilian society. Women played a decisive role in managing different social services agencies. They were involved in volunteer relief work in sanitation and medical assistance. They created nurseries for women workers, collective eating services, and child care and social welfare services for war refugees. Their dedication enabled health and social services to function despite the extraordinary increase in demand generated by the war.

Women's demands for an active role in work, civil resistance, welfare, and the antifascist fight forced reticent official institutions and political authorities to redefine gender roles that would permit the admission of women to the public arena. Right from the start of the war, the women's organizations carried on a spirited campaign for their access to paid employment. Faced with widespread male antagonism and tenacious conventional views hostile to female paid work, these women attempted, with a modicum degree of success, to develop professional training programs for women. Although the issue of women's paid work was addressed, it was still circumscribed to the needs of the war. Nonetheless, this experience sharpened the awareness of many women, particularly the younger generations, and helped redefine, to some extent, their expectations regarding women's right to a profession and a paid job.

Women held positions in social welfare and in public health. They were actively involved in the survival of society at the homefront, both in rural and urban areas. They played a crucial role in civil resistance and in the mass antifascist mobilization of the homefront. They resisted the advance of fascism by providing food, sustenance, welfare, health, and cultural services. As a result of this activism, they challenged the exclusive designation of women to the home and defied many traditional gender restrictions of Spanish society. Women's mobilization during the Civil War significantly expanded the parameters of public and private spheres and redefined the boundaries of domesticity.

The war experience brought a new dimension to the classic roles of mother, housewife, and nurturer because women now provided nourishment, welfare services, and the basic necessities for the entire civilian population's daily survival. This collective and public dimension of women's nurturing role was a watershed and an accurate reflection of the newly blurring boundaries between public and private spheres at the republican homefront. Shared interests in community survival gave new legitimacy to women's demands for an acknowledged social role beyond the confines of the home. Women's status was upgraded, albeit within gender limitations, from housewife to community nurturer with a significant role in civil resistance. However, the core ideological discourse on gender roles was never seriously challenged, although women's participation in a new, wider-based community context accelerated women's awareness of their rights.

Women's options certainly increased during the war years, signifying a certain readjustment in the cultural norms of gender conduct by allowing women access, for the first time, to some areas of the public world previously reserved for males. However, women's activities in that domain were legitimized through the adaptation of traditional gender models of social roles to the new circumstances of the war. This restructuring of the boundaries of public and private spheres and, more specifically, the redefinition of the public arena, were clearly limited. While it is true that women were no longer overtly denied access to the public sphere, the definition of what was public was still delimited according to gender. New patterns of gender behavior were elaborated in a modified discourse that established a role for women at the homefront but not in the trenches.

Gender roles were never redefined in a way that seriously challenged the division of the public and private spheres, despite women's tremendous energy and drive in new realms of activities. Although to some extent traditional norms of gender conduct and cultural values were challenged, a revolutionary view on public and private spheres never emerged. Women forged notable changes in their lives and expectations and, significantly, in their social status as women. Historical reality and processes of social and gender change are not linear and do not fit into neat interpretative frameworks of global transformation. Revolutionary change does not necessarily imply a breakdown in patriarchal relations or a deep challenge to "male civilization." In the case of the Civil War in Spain, women as a social collective gained significant ground in improving their gender status and opened up new horizons in their social, occupational, and personal options. Nevertheless, this progress occurred within the overall context of confining gender roles. Patterns of change and continuity with respect to women's overall situation during the time of the Civil War were still shaped by prevailing restrictions in gender norms, which severely limited changes in gender relations.

Women's apprenticeship in public experience during the war and the revolution highlighted the capacity of women to contribute to the fight against fascism. Their newly found collective identity as women in the antifascist fight and, for many, in the revolutionary cause, sharpened their political commitment. Women created their own unprecedented popular, mass women's movement that openly addressed political issues. Their cause was the antifascist fight–and for some, too, the revolutionary struggle in which they played a decisive role.

Women became highly politicized during the war and, for the first time, on a mass, grassroots basis, considered politics to be a significant concern for them. By challenging the traditional gender views that had always defended male monopoly of the political world, women not only voiced their political views on the war and the threat of fascism but also became committed political actors.

Women's pledge to the antifascist cause led them to undertake a wide range of political endeavors. They succeeded in mobilizing thousands of Spanish women into an active role in defense of democracy; in fact, their energetic antifascism was a decisive political apprenticeship in the values of democracy. For some, this apprenticeship was the first step in the recognition of the need for revolutionary changes in Spanish society. Women's forcible adherence to the antifascist battle sharpened their overall political commitment to the Second Republic, hence to democracy, freedom, and human rights. Some women activists challenged "male civilization" by openly questioning traditional male monopoly and hegemony in the world of politics, and exceptional figures such as Federica Montseny, Dolores Ibárruri, and Margarita Nelken achieved recognition of women in politics. However, what is more significant is that, on a collective level, women's historical apathy to the public arena of male politics changed during their attempt to design a new gender vision of politics during the war and the revolution.

Antifascist political commitment shaped women's experience of the war. However, it is also significant that women defined a female agenda connected to their social reality. Although many of their specifically formulated gender demands were lost in the compelling circumstances of the war, their growing capacity to pinpoint specific women's issues was crucial in enabling the development of their collective identity. They made choices concerning their agenda and established priorities concerning women's emancipation. Their feminist concerns evolved from their perception of women's circumstances and needs. Their route to women's emancipation passed through education, political commitment, the right to employment, and the recognition of their social worth. In the context of a devastating war, they nevertheless identified on their agenda the issue of prostitution as a priority concern.

Women's revolutionary, innovative views and actions related to prostitution provided a new theoretical vision framed by a notion of sisterhood that challenged traditional categorizations of women as either angels, madonnas, or whores. This vision led them to a decisive questioning of the gender discourse of domesticity. They refused to accept the traditional gender category of "Angel of the Hearth" and sought the recognition of women's respectability and decency. Women's views on prostitution also defied traditional sexist attitudes on sexuality by questioning men's right to mercenary sexual commerce with women. They openly discussed this component of "male civilization" and linked this issue to the need for revolutionary change in cultural values and personal conduct.

During the war and the revolution, women's feminist goals included women's education, professional training, paid employment, and political rights. As we have seen, solving the prostitute dilemma was a high priority. Yet other issues usually associated with women's rights, such as sex reform and abortion, were excluded from their agenda for social transformation and women's emancipation. At this time of radical change, the issues that concerned Spanish women were still shaped by their collective historical experience. Their social, gender, political, and cultural history inspired their resistance strategies, choices, and ways of conceiving feminist change. They defined their agenda on their own terms and, of course, were influenced by the extraordinary needs of the war. Despite the favorable context for the legalization of abortion, women excluded abortion and birth control from their list of priorities and never openly defined women's reproductive rights as their route to emancipation.

The richness and complexity of women's collective action in the fight against Franco highlights the numerous paths of contestation, revolutionary change, and emancipation. Women's social agency was very clear during the years of the war, as were the multiple fronts on which they challenged traditional Spanish society and "male civilization." Women's agency for social transformation, however, was also constantly shaped by interaction with tradition, mechanisms of gender control, and pressures of conventional gender roles and values. The ongoing cultural values generated conformity, impeded global challenges to "male civilization," and formed the limitations to women's feminist agenda. The boundaries of change in women's collective historical experience during the Civil War were shaped through gender consensus as well as dissonance. Even in times of revolutionary change, women's capacity for challenging the established patriarchal order was still constantly influenced by their historical experience and well-established sociocultural obstacles to gender changes. Women's new social apprenticeship, innovative experiences, and social endeavors during the war were a magnificent legacy for the future of the women's movement. The tragic outcome of the war prevented its development.

The final, devastating defeat of the republican forces on April 1, 1939 led to forty years of dictatorship under Franco. The Spanish republic was implacably crushed. Spain lost democracy, constitutional freedom, and political rights until the instauration of a democratic constitution in 1978. Brutal repression, the elimination of political and individual rights, and the abolishment of the Second Republic's democratic legislation characterized the new authoritarian regime. Franco created a state based on a strict hierarchical structure of society with national syndicalism and national catholicism as the pillars of the new Spain.

Francoist propaganda attempted to discredit the previous democratic regime with claims that it was a repository of political and cultural decadence. Prominent in this defamatory account were gender and cultural factors that blamed modifications in traditional cultural values, irreligiosity, and, most especially, the changed status of women. It was claimed that feminism and egalitarian demands had fully demonstrated women's growing corruption and denial of their natural biological mandate as mothers. The traditional female model of the Angel of the Hearth, the dedicated, submissive spouse and mother, had been disfigured when women were granted political rights. Women's emancipation was thus denounced as a sign of the moral decadence of the previous democratic regime.

Under Franco, women's primary social function was motherhood. Hence, women's aspirations related to work, education and self-betterment, social activity, and emancipation were perceived as a threat to their biological destiny as breeders of the nation's future generations. Women could be politicized only through the notion of fulfilling a common female destiny based on their reproductive function. Female sexuality, work, and education were regulated in accordance with this gender designation, while motherhood was idealized and considered a duty to the fatherland. Francoist ideology marked women off as a separate natural species, identifying them exclusively as mothers whose offspring would check the tendency toward declining birthrates and thus prevent the decadence of Spain.[2]

Women's path to emancipation was brutally closed by the repressive Franco dictatorship.[3] Women's voices were lost, their organizations disbanded, and their newly gained presence in the public arena disallowed. The new regime espoused a gender role of submission, docility, and unquestioning obedience to the traditional tenets of domesticity. As stressed by Pilar Primo de Rivera, the leader of the Sección Femenina, the only official Francoist women's organization, women's inevitable and absolute destiny was maternity. She qualified this role as "a biological, Christian and Spanish function."[4]

The new state endorsed the traditional view of the Catholic Church that proclaimed women's sacred duty to motherhood and family. A combination of traditional Catholic and Falangist, fascist values permeated the cultural fabric of Spanish society, framing and freezing gender roles for women. Traditional turn-of-the-century gender and religious discourse was recuperated to reinforce gender role models for women as mothers and housewives. With a gender code founded once again on the notion of women's differential nature, the new regime obliterated the egalitarian principles of the 1930's. Moreover, the Franco regime's newly defined features of women's gender identity–self-abnegation, resignation, sacrifice to children and spouse—severely undermined women's newly acquired values of self-esteem, collective identity, creativity, and female agency.

The obligatory social service training for all women under the Sección Femenina provided preparation and indoctrination for young adult women based on the canons of Francoist ideology and gender roles. Although the lives of some leaders of the Sección Femenina broke, in practice, with the norms of domesticity, young women were educated to formulate their gender identity and social expectations exclusively in terms of marriage and motherhood. Although women were permitted to be educated, the system transmitted educational gender models that socialized girls in the virtues of docility, submission, self-sacrifice, and modesty. The cultural prescriptions of the Franco regime fully disseminated the notion of self-effacement and the annulment of women's collective identity. These retrograde gender codes negated the achievements of women during the Civil War years.

Given the openly hostile male attitude toward any suggestion of female emancipation, women's status was immediately reduced. Francoist cultural norms once again redefined women as angels, madonnas, or whores. The feminine ideal of the model woman precluded any female agency in the public arena. Home and family were women's only entitled spaces. The gains of suffrage, political rights, and the social achievements for women under the Second Republic were denigrated and systematically obliterated. Women's hard-won conquests were snatched away. Their participation was no longer feasible in the public arena, in paid work, in politics, or in culture. As early as 1938, the Fuero del Trabajo, the most important legal declaration on work, dictated that the new state "will free married women from the workshop and the factory."[5] Work was again defined as a male monopoly, and the workplace, exclusive male territory. The accomplishments of the war years were lost when women were once again restricted to home and family.

In the tragic postwar period, many women were brutally repressed, imprisoned, or executed for their role in the Civil War. Yet, although the Franco regime cut off the path to freedom and emancipation, it did not succeed in completely undermining the social experience of the war years. Although repression impeded the development of collective consciousness, the experience women acquired during the war years enhanced their capacity to contest and to create resistance strategies against the dictatorship.[6] Political subjugation ended the mass organization of antifascist women and the open fight for democracy in Spain, but it did not quash women's democratic will or their goal of emancipation. Throughout the fascist decades, many women continued their political struggle in enforced exile; others within Spain played an active role in the clandestine democratic movement opposed to Franco.

Despite repressive legislation and systematic indoctrination by the Sección Femenina, many Spanish women refused to comply with the Franco model of a submissive mother. There is no evidence to suggest that women unquestioningly accepted their biological destiny as mothers according to the norms of the regime, nor that they identified with the ideological implications of the policies of the new state.[7] Despite the ironclad means at the disposal of the Franco state, its discourse and legislative policies were not always successful in enforcing fascist practices among Spanish women.[8] The women of the Civil War never lost sight of their rights and put to use the experience and skills acquired in the harsh circumstances of the war, practicing strategies for survival in the even more desolate postwar years.[9]

Under Franco, politics, culture, and the economy were exclusively male domains. Women's voices were silenced during the years of the dictatorship. The regime fostered historical amnesia regarding women's past and their capacity for social change. The new generations of Spanish women born and educated under the dictatorship lost the benefit of the experience of their foremothers. For over thirty-five years they were educated and socialized in the gender codes of the feminine ideal of the Francoist woman and in ignorance of the democratic experience of the past. However, women's genealogy in the fight against fascism and "male civilization" was not totally lost. In the early seventies, the burgeoning feminist movement, women activists in the political opposition to Franco, and historians in women's history managed to reconstruct the lost link and recuperate women's visibility and role in war and revolution in the 1930's. The discovery of their foremothers' commitment to democracy and women's rights shaped the awareness of the new generations of Spanish women and inspired them to seek an active role in establishing democracy, freedom, and women's liberation.

Chronology of the Spanish Civil War

1936

July 18–19   The military uprising under Franco spreads from Morocco to the Peninsula.

July   Arms are handed over to the people, who organize militias to fight against the rebel troops.

The military rebellion is successful in Galicia, León, and parts of Andalusia. Spain is divided into two military zones, republican and fascist.

In Barcelona, the Central Committee of Antifascist Militians is created.

The PCE in Madrid founds the Fifth Regiment.

In Burgos, the military rebels create the National Defense Council. Burgos becomes the seat of rebel power.

In Berlin and Rome, the rebel generals obtain military aid from fascist leaders Hitler and Mussolini.

August   France and Great Britain propose an agreement on non–intervention in Spain by European countries.

The rebel troops begin the offensive on Irún.

Rebel General Yagüe occupies Badajoz and carries out a brutal repression there.

187

August   A decree by the republican prime minister creates the Commission of Women's Aid in Madrid.

The Council for the Defence of Vizcaya is founded in Bilbao.

Poet García Lorca is assassinated in Viznar.

Franco installs his headquarters in Cáceres.

September   The government under republican Giral resigns. Left socialist Francisco Largo Caballero is prime minister of a new government with members of the different Popular Front organizations.

The Female Secretariat of the POUM is founded.

The rebel government prohibits the political parties of the Popular Front and all political and union activities.

A new government is formed in the Generalitat in Catalonia with the participation of the anarchosyndicalist union, the CNT.

October   Francisco Franco is proclaimed head of the government of the Spanish state and supreme commander of army, navy, and air forces.

The republican Parliament approves the Basque Statute of Autonomy.

The battle of Madrid begins.

A decree on collectivizations and worker control is promulgated by the Generalitat.

November   Largo Caballero forms a new government with the participation of anarchists.

Anarchist leader Federica Montseny becomes the first woman minister in Spain, as minister of Health and Social Assistance.

The republican government moves to Valencia, and the Council of Defense is created in Madrid.

Intense combat occurs in the area of Madrid. The first attempts to take over Madrid by the rebel troops fail.

Germany and Italy officially recognize Franco as head of the Spanish state.

December   The councils of Aragón, Asturias, and Santander–León are officially created.

December	Voluntary abortion is regulated in Catalonia with the Decree on the Artificial Interruption of Pregnancy legislated by the Generalitat.

1937

January	The rebels attack Málaga.
February	The Battle of the Jarama takes place.
	Franco troops occupy Málaga, which is followed by savage reprisals.
	The Second National Committee of the Agrupación de Mujeres Antifascistas is created in Bilbao.
	Women are granted civil parity by the republican government.
March	The battle of Guadalajara begins. Italian troops take part in the attack.
	The battle of Guadalajara ends. The rebel offensive fails.
	The First Conference of the Female Secretariat of the POUM is held.
	Rebel General Mola initiates the offensive on the Northern Front.
April	Severe air attacks are launched in the north. Guernica is destroyed by the German Condor Legion.
May	Political crises in Barcelona include violent clashes among the anarchists and dissident Marxists and the communists. Federica Montseny acts as a mediator in the conflict. Anarchists and the POUM lose political power after the conflict.
	A new government is formed in the Generalitat.
	The Largo Caballero government falls. Federica Montseny loses her post as minister.
	The Conference of the Unión de Muchachas is held in Madrid.
	Socialist Juan Negrín forms a new government. Communists play a significant role in state policies.
	Almeria is bombarded by the Franco air force.
June	Franco nominates ambassadors in Berlin and Rome.
	War industries are nationalized in the republican zone.

June	Bilbao is occupied by Franco troops. The Basque country falls to the rebels.
	Franco suppresses the economic regime established in the Basque country.
July	Political polarization occurs within the Spanish socialist party.
	Spanish bishops prepare a collective pastoral letter supporting Franco.
	The Institute for the Professional Training of Women is created by the Generalitat.
	The International Conference of Antifascist Writers is held in Valencia.
August	The First National Conference of Mujeres Libres is held in Valencia.
	The government of the Republic authorizes the celebration of religious services in private.
	The Council of Aragón is dissolved.
	The battle of Belchite begins.
September	The Vatican nominates Monsignor H. Antoniutti as head of its delegation to the Franco government.
October	Franco troops conquer Gijón and Avilés. The Northern Front falls.
	The government of the Republic is moved to Barcelona.
	The Second National Conference of the Agrupación de Mujeres Antifascistas is held in Valencia.
November	The Unió de Dones de Catalunya is formed.
	The First National Congress of the Unió de Dones de Catalunya is held.
	Sir R. Hodgson, the British representative, arrives in Burgos.
	Japan gives official recognition to Franco.
December	Republican troops begin the offensive on Teruel.
	Rafael Alberti and Miguel Hernández write the poems *De un momento a otro* and *Viento del pueblo*. Artist Pablo Picasso paints Guernica.

1938

January   Prices rise sharply at the homefront.

The republican army takes Teruel.

February   Teruel is reconquered by Franco troops.

March   Franco suppresses the 1932 laws of the Second Republic on divorce and civil matrimony.

The Fuero de Trabajo is proclaimed by Franco.

Offensive on the Aragon Front begins.

A demonstration in Barcelona protests against attempts to negotiate an end to the war.

Barcelona is bombarded by the Franco air force.

April   Lerida is occupied by Franco troops.

Franco abolishes the Catalan Statute of Autonomy.

The new republican government is in political crisis. A new government is formed by Negrín, who is also minister for defense.

The rebel troops reach the Mediterranean.

Valencia is attacked by Franco troops.

Prime Minister Negrín publishes the Thirteen Points Program of the new government, which has the support of all the Popular Front organizations.

May   Portugal recognizes the Franco government.

June   France closes its borders.

The Papal Nuncio, Monseigneur Cicognani, arrives in Burgos, and the Franco ambassador presents his credentials to Pope Pius XI.

The Agrupación de Mujeres Antifascistas is appointed by the government to look after the welfare of the orphans of soldiers.

July   The Non–Intervention Committee approves the plan for the withdrawal of the International Brigades.

July	The battle of the Ebro begins.
August	The republican troops stage a counter attack in Extremadura.
	A republican decree militarizes industries.
September	Mujeres Libres applies unsuccessfully for recognition as an official branch of the libertarian movement.
	Negrín announces the withdrawal of the International Brigades to the Society of Nations.
October	The Unió de Dones de Catalunya is appointed a member of the Consultative Commission on Aid for Refugees.
	The International Brigades leave from Barcelona.
November	Republican troops lose to Franco in the battle of the Ebro.
December	Catalonia is attacked by Franco troops.

1939

January	Barcelona is occupied by Franco troops.
February	The last meeting of the Parliament of the Republic is held in Figueras.
	The occupation of Catalonia is concluded.
	Manuel Azaña resigns as president of the Republic.
	Great Britain and France officially recognize the Franco government.
March	In Madrid, Coronel Casado forms the National Council of Defense.
	The Negrín government abandons Spain.
	Casado attempts to negotiate with Franco.
	The Franco army enters Madrid.
	Franco and Mussolini troops occupy Alicante.
April 1	The Civil War ends, resulting in exile and repression of republicans.
April	The United States recognizes the Franco government.

Notes

INTRODUCTION

1. Suceso Portales, "Necesitamos una moral para los dos sexos," *Mujeres Libres,* Num. 10. Reproduced in Mary Nash, *Mujeres Libres, 1936–1939* (Barcelona: Tusquets, 1975).

2. R. Bridenthal and C. Koonz, *Becoming Visible: Women in European History* (Boston: Ed. Houghton Mifflin, 1977); Gerda Lerner, *The Majority Finds Its Past. Placing Women in History* (New York: Oxford University Press, 1981); K. Offen, R. Roach Pierson, and J. Rendall, *Writing Women's History: International Perspectives* (London: Macmillan, 1991).

3. For this debate, see "Politics and Culture in Women's History," *Feminist Studies,* vol. 6, num. 1 (Spring 1980). For a discussion of this debate, see Mary Nash, "Nuevas dimensiones en la historia de la mujer," in Nash (ed.), *Presencia y protagonismo: aspectos de la historia de la mujer* (Barcelona: Serbal, 1984).

4. C. Dauphin, A. Farge, et al., "Women's Culture and Women's Power: Issues in French Women's History," in Offen, Roach Pierson, and Rendall (eds.), *Writing Women's History.* See also the discussion of this debate in *Journal of Women's History,* Vol. 1, Num. 1 (Spring 1989).

5. Gerda Lerner, *The Creation of Patriarchy* (New York: Oxford University Press, 1986).

6. J. Bennet, "Feminism and History," *Gender and History,* Vol. 1, Num. 3 (1989) and "Women's History: A Study in Change and Continuity," *Women's History Review,* Vol. 2, Num. 2 (1993). Also: B. Hill, "Women's History: A Study in Change and Continuity or Standing Still?," *Women's History Review,* Vol. 2, Num. 1 (1993).

7. Mary Nash, *Mujeres Libres: España 1936–1939* (Barcelona: Tusquets, 1976) and *Mujer y movimiento obrero en España, 1931– 1939* (Barcelona: Fontamara, 1981).

8. J. Alvarez Junco and M. Pérez Ledesma, "Historia del movimiento obrero ?Una segunda ruptura?," *Revista de Occidente,* num. 12 (March–April 1982).

9. Mary Nash, "Two Decades of Women's History in Spain: A Reappraisal," in Offen, Roach Pearson, and Rendall (eds.), *Writing Women's History.*

10. Roger Chartier, "De la historia social de la cultura a la historia cultural de lo social," *Historia Social,* Num. 17 (otoño 1993).

CHAPTER 1

1. A. M. Aguado, R. Capel, et al., *Textos para la historia de las mujeres en España* (Madrid: Cátedra, 1994); chapter: "Una mirada española," in Georges Duby and Michelle Perrot, *Historia de las mujeres en Occidente*, vols. 4 and 5 (Madrid: Taurus, 1993); Mary Nash, *Mujer, familia y trabajo en España (1875–1936)* (Barcelona: Anthropos, 1983); Mary Nash (ed.), *Més enllá del silenci. Historia de les dones a Catalunya* (Barcelona: Generalitat de Catalunya, 1988); M. Dolores Ramos, *Mujeres e Historia. Reflexiones sobre las experiencias vividas en los espacios públicos y privados* (Málaga: Universidad de Málaga, 1993); Geraldine Scanlon, *La polémica feminista en la España Contemporánea (1868–1974)* (Madrid: Siglo XXI, 1976); 2nd ed., Madrid: Akal, 1986).

2. Miguel Artola, *Antiguo Régimen y revolución liberal* (Barcelona: Ariel, 1978); Josep Fontana, *Cambio económico y actitudes políticas en la España del siglo XIX* (Barcelona: Ariel, 1973) and *La crisis del Antiguo Regimen. 1808–1833* (Barcelona: Critica, 1979); Jordi Nadal, *El fracaso de la revolución industrial en España (1814–1913)* (Barcelona: Ariel, 1975).

3. José M. Jover Zamora, et al., *La Era Isabelina y el Sexenio Democrático. Historia de España de Menéndez Pidal. XXXIV* (Madrid: Espasa–Calpé, 1981); Clara E. Lida and Iris M. Zavala, *La revolución de 1868. Historia, Pensamiento, Literatura* (New York: Las Américas Publishing Co., 1970); M. Victoria López Cordón, *La revolución de 1868 y la I Republica* (Madrid: Siglo XXI, 1976) and "La situación de la mujer a finales del Antiguo Régimen," in Capel (ed.), *Mujer y sociedad en España. 1700–1975* (Madrid: Dirección General de Juventud y Promoción Socio–cultural, 1982); Concepción Saiz, *La Revolución del 68 y la cultura femenina. Apuntes al natural. Un episodio nacional que no escribió Pérez Galdós* (Madrid: Librería General de Victoriano Pérez, 1929).

4. José Francos Rodríguez, *La mujer y la política españolas* (Madrid: Pueyo, 1920), 146.

5. Giuliana di Febo, "Orígenes del debate feminista en España. La escuela krausista y la Institución Libre de Enseñanza (1870–1890)," *Sistema. Revista de Ciencias Sociales* 12 (January 1976).

6. J. N. Burstyn, *Victorian Education and the Ideal of Womanhood* (London: Croom Helm, 1980); Carmela Covato and M. Cristina Leuzzi (eds.), *"E l'uomo educò la donna* (Rome: Ed. Reuniti, 1989); Carol Dyehouse, *Girls Growing Up in Late Victorian and Edwardian England* (London: Routledge and Kegan Paul, 1981); Françoise Mayeur, *L'Education des filles en France au XIXé siècle* (Paris: Hachette, 1979).

7. José M. Jover Zamora, "La época de la Restauración. Panorama político–social, 1875–1902," in Manuel Tuñón de Lara, et al., *Revolución burguesa, oligarquía y constitucionalismo* (Barcelona: Labor, 1981); José Luis Garcia Delgado, et al., *La España de la Restauración: política, economía, legislación y cultura* (Madrid: Siglo XXI, 1985).

8. G. Bonacchi and A. Groppi (eds.), *Il dilemma della cittadinanza. Diritti e doveri delle donne* (Rome: Laterza, 1993); Ellen Carol Dubois, *Feminism and Suffrage. Independent Women's Movement in America 1848–1869* (Ithaca: Cornell University Press, 1978); S. S. Holton, *Feminism and Democracy: Women's Suffrage and Democracy in Britain, 1900–1918* (Cambridge: Cambridge University Press, 1986); Jane Rendall, *Equal or Different: Women's Politics, 1800–1914* (Oxford: Basil Blackwell, 1987).

9. For a discussion of gender discourse, see: Mary Nash, "Identidades, representación cultural y discurso de género en la España Contemporánea," in P. Chalmeta, F. Checa Cremades, et al., *Cultura y culturas en la historia* (Salamanca: Universidad de Salamanca, 1995).

10. M. Carmen Simón Palmer, "Libros de religión y moral para la mujer española del siglo XIX." Paper presented Primeras Jornadas de Bibliografía de la Fundación Universitaria Española, Instituto Milà y Fontanals, Consejo Superior de Investigación Científica, Barcelona 1977.

11. Augusto Jerez Perchet, *La mujer de su casa* (Barcelona: Librería de J. y A. Bastinos, Eds., 1886), 6.

12. Leonor Serrano de Xandri, "El trabajo intelectual y el trabajo manual de la mujer moderna," in Carmen Karr, *Educación femenina (Cursillo de conferencias celebrado en el Ateneo Barcelonés, los días 31 de enero y 1, 3, 4 y 5 de febrero de 1916)* (Barcelona: Librería Parera, 1916).

13. Gener Pompeyo, "De la mujer y sus derechos en las sociedades modernas," *La Vanguardia,* 26 February 1889.

14. Dolors Monserdà, *Estudi feminista. Orientacions per a la dona catalana* (Barcelona: LLuis Gili, 1909), 63; Dolors Monserdà de Macià, *Tasques socials. Recull d'articles, notes i conferències.* Pròleg del Pare Isnasi Casanovas S. J. (Barcelona: Miguel Parera Llibreter, 1916).

15. See: Nash, *Mujer familia y trabajo,* 11–21; and Geraldine Scanlon, *La polémica feminista en la España Contemrporánea* (Madrid: Siglo XXI, 1976), 161–194.

16. Francesc Tusquets, *El problema feminista* (Barcelona: Imp. Elzerirana i Llibrería Camí, 1931), 85.

17. Gener Pompeyo, "De la mujer y sus derechos en las sociedades modernas," *La Vanguardia,* 26 February 1889.

18. Gregorio Marañón, *Tres ensayos sobre la vida sexual. Sexo, trabajo y deporte, maternidad y feminismo, educación sexual y diferenciación sexual* (Madrid: Biblioteca Nueva, 1927) and *Biología y feminismo* (Madrid: Imp. Suc. Enrique Teodoro, 1920). For further discussion, see: Mary Nash, "Naternidad, maternología y reforma eugénica en España," in Georges Duby and Michelle Perrot, *Historia de las mujeres en Occidente,* Vol. 5 (Madrid: Taurus, 1993).

19. Dr. Polo y Peyrolon, *Apostolado de la mujer en las sociedades modernas (Discurso leído en la solemne junta que la Juventud Católica de Valencia dedicó a María Santísima de los Dolores el día 31 de marzo de 1882)* (Valencia: Imprenta Manuel Alufre, 1882), 8–10.

20. Joan Gaya, "Què li farem fer, a la nena?," *Catalunya Social,* núm. 13 (June 1936).

21. Concepción Arenal, "La educación de la mujer," in *La emancipación de la mujer en España,* edited by Mauro Armiño (Madrid: Biblioteca Jucar, 1974), 67.

22. Lucia Sánchez Saornil, "La cuestión femenina en nuestros medios," *Solidaridad Obrera,* 15 October 1935. This series of articles is reproduced in Mary Nash, *Mujeres Libres. España 1936– 1939* (Barcelona: Tusquets, 1976). For a discussion of Lucia Sánchez Saornil's view on the woman question, see Mary Nash, "Dos intelectuales anarquistas frente al problema de la mujer: Federica Montseny y Lucia Sánchez Saornil," *Convivium* 44–45 (1975).

23. See: Temma Kaplan, "Politics and Culture in Women's History," *Feminist Studies* 6,1 (Spring 1980); Mary Nash, "Nuevas dimensiones en la historia de la mujer," in Mary Nash (ed.), *Presencia y protagonismo. Aspectos de la historia de la mujer* (Barcelona: Serbal, 1984), 45–50 and *Mujer y movimiento obrero en España. 1931– 1939* (Barcelona: Fontamara, 1981); Marta Bizcarrondo, "Los orígenes del feminismo socialista en España," in *La mujer en la historia de España. (siglos XVI–XX)* (Madrid: Universidad Autónoma de Madrid, 1984).

24. Mary Nash, "Control social y trayectoria histórica de la mujer en España." Roberto Bergalli and Enrique E. Mari (eds.), *Historia ideológica del control social (España– Argentina, siglos XIX y XX)* (Barcelona: Promociones y Publicaciones Universitarias, 1989).

25. Emilia Pardo Bazán, "La mujer española," *La España Moderna* XVII (May 1890).

26. In either case her wages were to be dedicated to the needs of the home. For a discussion of labor legislation and women, see: María Glória Núñez Pérez, *Trabajadoras en la Segunda República. Un estudio sobre la actividad económica extradoméstica (1931–1936)* (Madrid: Ministerio de Trabajo, 1989).

27. "LLei sobre la capacitat jurídica de la dona i dels cónyuges," *Butlletí Oficial de la Generalitat de Catalunya,* 20 June 1934.

28. Concepción Arenal, "Estado actual de la mujer en España," *Boletin de la Institución Libre de Enseñanza,* 31 August 1895.

29. Carmen Karr, *Cultura femenina (Estudi y orientacions). Conferencies donades en l'"Ateneu Barcelonès" els dies 6, 13 y 20 d'abril de 1910* (Barcelona: L'Avenç, 1910). See also the case of Suceso Luengo in Andalusia: Rosa M. Badillo Baena, *Feminismo y educación en Malaga: el pensamiento de Suseso Luengo de la Figuera (1892–1920)* (Malaga: Universidad de Malaga, 1992).

30. Esther Cortada Andreu, *Escuela mixta y coeducación en Cataluña durante la Segunda República* (Madrid: Instituto de la Mujer, 1988).

31. Antonio Pirala, *El libro de oro de las niñas* (Madrid: 1–915), reproduced in J. L. Peset, et al., *Ciencias y enseñanza en la revolución burguesa* (Madrid: Siglo XXI, 1978), 136.

32. Karr, *Cultura femenina,* 23.

33. Emilia Pardo Bazan, "La educación del hombre y la de la mujer. Sus relaciones y diferencias (Memoria leída en el Congreso pedagógico el día 16 de octubre de 1892.)," *Nuevo Teatro Crítico* 22 (October 1892). Reproduced in Leda Schiavo (ed.), Emilia Pardo Bazan, *La mujer española y otros artículos feministas* (Madrid: Ed. Nacional, 1976), 92.

34. See: François Furet and Jacques Ozouf, *Reading and Writing. Literacy in France from Calvin to Jules Ferry* (Cambridge: Cambridge University Press, 1982); Mayeur, *L'Education des filles*. The case of Italy was much more similar to Spain. See Carmela Covato, *Sapere e pregiudizio. L'Educazione delle donne fra '700 d '800* (Rome: Archivio Guido Izzi, 1991).

35. Rosa M. Capel, *El trabajo y la educación de la mujer en España. 1900–1936* (Madrid: Dirección General de la Juventud y Promoción Socio–cultural, 1982) 361–379; Jordi Monés, *El pensament escolar i la renovació pedagògica a Catalunya (1833–1938)* (Barcelona: La Magrana, 1977); M. Samaniego Moneu, *La política educativa de la II República* (Madrid: C.S.I.C., 1977).

36. See: J. Anadón Fernández, "El profesorado femenino de la Escuela Normal Central de Maestras de Madrid. 1858–1900," in Jornadas de Investigación Interdisciplinaria, *El trabajo de las mujeres. Siglos XVI–XX* (Madrid: Universidad Autonoma de Madrid, 1987); Capel, *El trabajo;* M. Luisa Barrera Peña and Ana López Peña, *Sociología de la mujer en la Universidad. Análisis histórico– comparativo. Galicia–España 1900–1981* (Santiago de Compostela: Universidad de Santiago de Compostela, 1983).

37. Francisco De Luis, *Cincuenta años de cultura obrera en España. 1890–1940* (Madrid: Funcación Pablo Iglesias, 1994); L. Litvak, *Musa libertaria. Arte, literatura y vida cultural del anarquismo español* (Barcelona: Antoni Bosch, 1981); Carmen Peñalver, "Les associacions populars a Barcelona, 1923–1930" (M. A. diss., University of Barcelona, 1985).

38. Mary Nash, *Mujer y movimiento obrero en España 1931–19–39,* (Barcelona: Fontamara, 1981), 143–146.

39. See: *Reglamentación de la Agrupación Femenina Socialista de Madrid* and the *Libro de Actas de las Reuniones Generales de la Agrupación Femenina Socialista 1906–1915.*

40. José Alvarez Junco, *La ideología política del anarquismo español (1868–1910)* (Madrid: Siglo XXI, 1976); Pere Solà, *Educació i moviment llibertari a Catalunya (1901–1939)* (Barcelona: Edicions 62, 1980).

41. Quoted in Clara E. Lida, "Educación anarquista en la España del ochocientos," *Revista de Occidente* 97 (1971), 38.

42. "Circular a los obreros federados," 8 August 1878. Quoted in Lida, "Educación anarquista."

43. Maria Luisa Cobos, "A la mujer ¡No! A vosotros proletarios," *Solidaridad Obrera*, 8 October 1935.

44. Lucia Sánchez Saornil, "La cuestión femenina en nuestros medios," *Solidaridad Obrera*, 26 September 1935.

45. Mercedes Comaposada, "Origen y actividades de la agrupación de Mujeres Libres," *Tierra y Libertad,* 27 March 1937.

46. Joan Gaya, "Les dones al treball i els homes en atur," *Catalunya Social,* July 1936.

47. Joan Gaya, "Què li farem fer a la nena?," *Catalunya Social,* June 1936.

48. Mary Nash, "Identidad de género, discurso de la domesticidad y la definición del trabajo de las mujeres en la España del siglo XIX," in Georges Duby and Michelle Perrot, *Historia de las mujeres en Occidente,* Vol. 4 (Madrid: Taurus, 1993).

49. Quoted in Anselmo Lorenzo, *El proletariado militante* (Madrid: Alianza, 1974), 255.

50. See: Nash, *Mujer y movimiento obrero,* 61–68, 106–109, 146–153, 181–186.

51. Capel, *El trabajo,* 199–297; and Nash, *Mujer, familia y trabajo,* 40–60.

52. Mary Nash, "Treball, conflictivitat social i estratègies de resistència: la dona obrera a la Catalunya contemporània"; Mary Nash (ed.), *Més enllà del silenci. Les dones a la història de Catalunya* (Barcelona: Generalitat de Catalunya, 1988).

53. The strikes in the Magin Quer and Centro Cooperativo Industrial factories began in June and September, respectively, and the general strike in the sector lasted from the end of September to November. Nash, "Treball, conflictivitat social."

54. See: Jordi Maluquer, "La estructura del sector algodonero en Catalunya durante la primera etapa de la industrialización (1832– 1861)," *Hacienda Publica Española* 38 (1976) and "Los orígenes del movimiento obrero español 1834–1874," in Jover Zamora, et al., *La Era Isabelina.*

55. Pilar Pérez–Fuentes Hernández, *Vivir y morir en las minas. Estrategias familiares y relaciones de género en la primera industrialización vizcaína: 1877–1913* (Bilbao: Editorial de la Universidad del Pais Vasco, 1993).

56. Enriqueta Camps i Cura, "Ells nivells de benestar al final del segle XIX. Ingrés i cicle de formació de les famílies a Sabadell (1890)," *Recerques,* num. 24 (1991).

57. Joan W. Scott and Louise A. Tilly, *Women, Work and Family* (New York: Holt, Rinehart and Winston, 1978).

58. See: Josep Benet and Casimiro Martí, *Barcelona a mitjan segle XIX. El moviment obrer durant el Bienni Progressista (1854–1856)* (Barcelona: Curial, 1976), 356, 422, 669–670.

59. See also: Paloma Villota, "Los motines de Castilla la Vieja de 1856 y la participación de la mujer. Aproximación a su estudio," in *Nuevas perspectivas sobre la mujer. Actas de las Primeras Jornadas de Investigación Interdisciplinaria* (Madrid: Universidad Autónoma, 1982) and "La mujer castellano–leonesa en los orígenes del movimiento obrero (1855)," in *La mujer en la Historia de España. Siglos (XVI–XX). Actas de las Segundas Jornadas de Investigación Interdisciplinaria* (Madrid: Universidad Autónoma, 1984).

60. Alejandro Sanmartin, *Trabajo de las mujeres. (Respuesta al grupo XIV del Cuestionario). Comisión de Reformas Sociales. Información oral y escrita, practicada en virtud de la Real Orden del 5 de diciembre de 1883 en Madrid.* Text reproduced in Nash, *Mujer, familia y trabajo,* 315–342.

61. Nash, "Treball, conflictivitat social."

62. Silvia Puertas i Novau, *Artesanes i obreres. Treballadores de l'agulla a la Barcelona contemporània* (Lerida: Diario La Mañana, 1994); Mary Nash, "Trabajadoras y estrategias de sobrevivencias económica: el caso del trabajo a domicilio," in Jornadas de Investigación Interdisciplinaria, *El trabajo de las mujeres. siglos XVI–XX* (Madrid: Universidad Autonoma de Madrid, 1987).

63. See: Pilar Pérez–Fuentes Hernández, "El trabajo de las mujeres en la España de los siglos XIX y XX: Algunas consideraciones metodológicas," in *Mujer, Trabajo y Reproducción. III Congreso del ADEH. 22–24 de abril de 1993.* Universidad do Minho, Braga. (forthcoming); A. Soto Carmona, "Cuantificación de la mano de obra femenina. 1860–1930," in *La mujer en la historia de España* and Núñez, *Trabajadoras en la Segunda República.*

64. From *Breve Relació* by Fray Joan Serrahima in *LLibre de resolucions de la M.Rt. comunitat y varias notas (1647–1834)* quoted by Josep Fontana, *Cambio económico y actitudes políticas en la España del siglo XIX* (Barcelona: Ariel, 1973), 80.

65. Francisco Raull, *Historia de la Conmoción de Barcelona de la noche 25 al 26 de julio de 1835. Causas que la produjeron y sus efectos, hasta el día de esta publicación* (Barcelona: Imp. A. Bergnes, 1835), 53.

66. For an account of the revolt, see: Anna M. Garcia Rovira, "Burgesia liberal i poble menut. La revolta popular de l'estiu de 1835," *L'Avenc* 87 (November 1985) and *La revolució liberal a espanya i les classes populars (1832–1835)* (Vic: Eumo, 1989).

67. Bando del Mariscal de Campo, José María de Pastors, Barcelona, 31 July 1835; *El Diario de Barcelona,* 31 July 1835.

68. Cayetano Barraquer y Roviralta, *Los religiosos en Cataluña en la primera mitad del siglo XIX* (Barcelona: Francisco J. Altés y Alabert, 1915) 2: 482–287.

69. Barraquer y Roviralta, *Los religiosos en Cataluña,* 3: 823.

70. Villota, "Los motines de Castilla la Vieja."

71. Villota, "Los motines de Castilla la Vieja."

72. Villota, "Los motines de Castilla la Vieja."

73. For a discussion of female involvement in collective action, see: Temma Kaplan, "Female Consciousness and Collective Action: The Case of Barcelona 1910–1918," *Signs* 7 (Spring 1982) and *Red City, Blue Period: Social Movements in Picasso's Barcelona* (Berkeley: University of California Press, 1992); Louise A. Tilly, "Women's Collective Action and Feminism in France, 1870–1914" in Louise A. Tilly and Charles Tilly (eds.), *Class Conflict and Collective Action* (London: Sage Publications, 1981), 207–231.

74. Claude Morange, "De 'Manola' a obrera" (La revuelta de las cigarreras de Madrid en 1830. Notas sobre un conflicto de trabajo)," *Estudios de Historia Social* 12–13 (January–June 1980).

75. "El motin de las cigarreras," *La Bandera Social,* núm. 5.

76. Letter by Francisco Tomás addressed to the Women's Sector in Bolonia. Reproduced in M. T. Martínez de Sas (ed.), *Cartas, Comunicaciones y Circulares de la Comisión Federal de la Región Española* (Barcelona, Universidad de Barcelona, 1979), 175.

77. See: Temma Kaplan, *Anarchists of Andalusia. 1860–1903* (Princeton, NJ: Princeton University Press, 1977), 86–87 and "Other Scenarios: Women and Spanish Anarchism," in Renate Bridenthal and Claudia Koonz, *Becoming Visible. Women in European History* (Boston: Houghton Mifflin, 1977).

78. See *La Publicidad,* 25 April 1891.

79. Teresa Claramunt, *La mujer. Consideraciones sobre su estado ante las prerrogativas del hombre* (Mahon: Biblioteca El Porvenir del Obrero, 1905).

80. See: Nash, *Mujer y movimiento obrero en España,* 24–28.

81. Alvaro Soto Carmona, "La participación de la mujer en la conflictividad laboral (1905–1921)," in Maria Carmen García–Nieto Paris (ed.), *Ordenamiento jurídico y realidad social de las mujeres* (Madrid: Universidad Autónoma de Madrid, 1986).

82. According to official figures, 78 percent of male workers participated in strikes, while female participation reached 87 percent. Soto Carmona, "La participación."

83. See Albert Balcells, "La mujer obrera en la industria catalana durante el primer cuarto del siglo XX" in *Trabajo industrial y organización obrera en la Catalunya Contemporánea (1900–1936)* (Barcelona: Ed. Laia, 1974), 27–30; Temma Kaplan, "Female Consciousness." Balcells gives the figure of over 22,000 women strikers.

84. Carlos Forcadell, *Parlamentarismo y bolchevización del movimiento obrero español (1914–1918)* (Barcelona: Crítica, 1978); Gerard H. Meaker, *The Revolutionary Left in Spain 1914–1923)* (Stanford: Stanford University Press, 1974). Santiago Roldán, José Luis Delgado, and Juan Muñoz, *La formación de la sociedad capitalista en España. 1914–1920,* 2 Vols. (Madrid: Confederación Española de Cajas de Ahorros, 1973).

85. Kaplan, "Female Consciousness"; Lester Golden, "Les dones com avantguarda: Els rembomboris del pà del gener de 1918," *L'Avenç.* 44 (December 1981); Maria Dolores Ramos, "Realidad social y conciencia de la realidad de la mujer: obreras malagueñas frente a la crisis de subsistencias (1918)," in García–Nieto Paris (ed.), *Ordenamiento jurídico.*

86. Carmen de Burgos, *La mujer moderna y sus derechos* (Valencia: Ed. Sempere, 1927) and *Misión social de la mujer.* Conferencia pronunciada el día 18 de febrero de 1911 (Bilbao: Imp. José Rojas Núñez, 1911) and *La flor de la playa y otras novelas cortas* (introduction by C. Núñez Rey) (Madrid: Castália, 1989).

87. See: Rosa Maria Capel Martínez, *El sufragio femenino en la Segunda Republica* (Granada: Universidad de Granada, 1975); Esperanza García Mendez, *La actuación de la mujer en las Cortes de la Segunda Republica* (Madrid: Ministerio de Cultura, 1979); Concha Fagoaga, *La voz y el voto de las mujeres. 1877–1931* (Barcelona: Icaria, 1985); Scanlon, *La polémica.*

88. Antonio Elorza, "Feminismo y socialismo en España (1840–1868), *Tiempos de Historia* 1:3 (February 1976) and *El Fourierismo en España* (Madrid: Ed. Revista del Trabajo, 1975).

89. In the 1860's, a later publication–*La Buena Nueva*–continued somewhat along the same lines, although by then the women involved were also identified with spiritism.

90. Pere Sánchez i Ferré, "Els orígens del feminisme a Catalunya. 1870–1920," *Revista de Catalunya* 45 (October 1990).

91. For example, an unidentified program demanding suffrage for women of "integrity," their participation in the "destiny of the nation," women's administration of property, the extinction of celibacy, the promotion of conjugal union, and the establishment of criminal regulations against "coquettes" appeared in *La Unión Liberal* on September 16, 1854. See Fagoaga, *La voz,* 45–49.

92. Karen Offen, "Defining Feminism. A Comparative Historical Approach," *Signs: Journal of Women in Culture and Society* 14, 1 (1988).

93. Fagoaga, *La voz;* Scanlon, *La polémica.*

94. Dolors Monserdà, *Estudi feminista. Orientacions per a la dona catalana* (Barcelona: Luis Gili, 1907), 4.

95. Elisenda Macià i Encarnación, "L'Institut de Cultura: un model de promoció cultural per a la dona catalana," *L'Avenç.* 112 (February 1988); Mary Nash (ed.), *Més enllà del silenci. Les dones a la història de Catalunya* (Barcelona: Generalitat de Catalunya, 1988); Mercedes Ugalde Solano, *Mujeres y nacionalismo vasco. Génesis y desarrollo de Emakume Abertzale Batza (1906–1936)* (Bilbao: Universidad del País Vasco, 1993).

96. For a discussion of the construction of historical feminism in Spain, see: Mary Nash, "Experiencia y aprendizaje: la formación histórica de los feminismos en España," *Historia Social* 20 (Autumn 1994).

97. Monserdà. *Estudi Feminista,* 4.

98. Sánchez i Ferré, "Els orígens del feminisme."

99. Maria Carmen Sierra Perrón, "Lerrouxismo femenino. El papel de las Damas Rojas en la política del Partido Radical" (Master's diss., Universidad Autónoma de Barcelona, 1984).

100. Maria de Echarri, "Acción Social de la Mujer" and "Conferencia a las Señoras de Pamplona." Reproduced in Amalia Martín–Gamero, *Antologia del feminismo* (Madrid: Alianza, 1975), 185–187.

101. Cristina Dupláa, "Les dones i el pensament conservador català contemporani," in Nash (ed.), *Mes enllá del silenci.*

102. Maria Aurelia Capmany, *El feminisme a Catalunya* (Barcelona: Nova Terra, 1973); Montserrat Duch i Plana, "La LLiga Patriòtica de Dames: un projecte del feminisme nacional conservador," *Quaderns d'Alliberament* 6 (1981) and "El paper de la dona en el nacionalisme burguès," *Estudios de Historia Social* 28–29 January–June 1984); Maria Luddy and Cliona Murphy, *Women Surviving. Studies in Irish Women's History in the 19th and 20th Centuries* (Swords: Poolbeg, 1990); Margaret Ward, *Unmanageable Revolutionaries. Women and Irish Nationalism* (London: Pluto Press, 1983).

103. On nationalism during the Second Republic, see: J. González Beramendi and R. Maiz (eds.), *Los nacionalismos en la España de la segunda república* (Madrid: Siglo XXI, 1991).

104. Mary Nash, "La Dona moderna del segle XX: la 'Nova Dona' a Catalunya," *L'Avenç.* 112 (February 1988).

105. *Or y Grana. Setmanari autonomista per a les dones, propulsor d'una Lliga Patriòtica de Damas,* 6 October 1906.

106. Elisenda Macià i Encarnación, "L'Institut de Cultura: un model de promoció cultural per a la dona catalana," *L'Avenç.* 112 (February 1988) and "Ensenyament professional i orientació católica d'una nova professió femenina: la dona oficinista (1909–1936) (Master's diss., Barcelona University, 1986).

107. See: Nash, "Trabajadores y estrategias de sobrevivencias económica."

108. Junoy, *Or y Grana,* Any 1, Num. 13.

109. Scanlon, *La polémica.* Fagoaga, *La voz.*

110. Elisabeth Starcevic, *Carmen de Burgos. defensora de la mujer* (Almería: Editorial Cajal, 1976).

111. Mary Nash, "La mujer en las organizaciones de izquierda en España" (1931–1939), Vol. 1 (Ph.D. diss., University of Barcelona, 1977), 372–390.

112. See Nash, *Mujer y movimiento obrero.*

113. Offen, "Defining Feminism."

114. Capel, *El sufragio femenino*; Fagoaga, *La voz;* Scanlon, *La polémica feminista.*

115. P. Villalaín García, "Mujer y política. La participación de la mujer en las elecciones generales celebradas en Madrid durante la II República (1931-1936)." (Ph.D. diss., Universidad Autónoma de Madrid, 1993).

116. M. J. González Castillejo, *La nueva historia: Mujer, vida cotidiana y esfera pública en Málaga, 1931–1936* (Málaga: Universidad de Málaga, 1991); Jean Louis Guereña, "La réglementation de la prostitution en Espagne aux XIX–XXe siècles," in R. Carrasco (ed.), *La prostitution en Espagne de l'époque des Rois Catholiques à la II République* (Paris: Annales Littéraires de l'Université de Besançon, 1994); M. Samaniego Boneu, *Los seguros sociales a debate. la Segunda República* (Madrid: Ministerio de Trabajo y Seguridad Social, 1988).

CHAPTER 2

1. For a historiographical overview of the Second Republic and the Civil War, see: Juan García Durán, *La Guerra Civil española. Fuentes (Archivos, bibliografía y filmografía)* (Barcelona: Crítica, 1985); María Gloria Nuñez Pérez, *Bibliografía comentada sobre la II República española (1931–1936). Obras publicadas entre 1940 y 1992* (Madrid: Fundación Universitaria Española, 1993); Stanley G. Payne, "Recent Historiography on the Spanish Republic and Civil War." *The Journal of Modern History,* vol. 60, num. 3 (September 1988); Hilari Raquer, "L'Església i la Guerra Civil (1936–1939). Bibliografía Recent (1975–1985)." *Revista Catalana de Teología* XI/1 (1986): 119– 252.

2. See the papers presented at the following conferences: Historia y Memoria de la Guerra Civil. Encuentro en Castilla y Leon. Salamanca, September 1986; 11 Col.loqui Internacional sobre la Guerra Civil espanyola (1936–1939): La Guerra i la Revolució a Catalunya. Barcelona, November 1986. The Spanish Television series on the Spanish Civil War did not include any women among the panel of historians and scarcely reflected women's experience in its content. The notable exception was the Conference and Exhibition on Women in the Civil War, Salamanca, October 1989. See: *Las mujeres en la Guerra Civil* (Madrid: Ministerio de Cultura, 1989).

3. The specific development of Spanish historiography over the past two decades also influenced the development of women's history and its focus. Mary Nash, "Two Decades of Women's History in Spain: A Re–Appraisal"; K. Offen, R. Pierson, R. Rendall (eds.), *Writing Women's History: International Perspectives* (London: Macmillan, 1991). On current social history in Spain, see the journal *Historia Social;* also Santiago Castillo (ed.), *La historia social en España. Actualidad y perspectivas* (Madrid: Siglo XXI, 1991).

4. José Alvarez Junco and Manuel Pérez Ledesma, "Historia del movimiento obrero. ¿Una segunda ruptura? *Revista de Occidente* 12 (March–April 1982).

5. The celebration of the fiftieth anniversary of the Civil War and the subsequent publications aroused a degree of debate and controversy: E. Malefakis (Dir.), *1936–1939. La Guerra de España* (Madrid: Ed. El País, 1986); M. E. Nicolás, Pedro García, Inmaculada López, et al., "La 'Historiografía de la reconciliació': La Guerra d'Espanya de *El País,*" L'Avenç 104 (April 1987); Enric Ucelay da Cal, "Socialistas y comunistas en Cataluña durante la Guerra Civil: un ensayo de interpretación," in Santos Juliá (ed.), *Socialismo y Guerra Civil. Annales de Historia* 2 (1987); Josep M. Cobos, Maribel Ollé, and Carles Santacana, "Col.lectivitzacions industrials, un debat que resta obert,"*L'Avenç* 105 (June 1987); Claudio Venza, "Convegni sulla guerra civile spagnola. Nuove problematiche," *Qualestoria* 1 (April 1987). On Anglo–American historiography, see: Martin Blinkhorn, "Anglo–American Historians and the Second Spanish Republic: The Emergence of a New Orthodoxy," *European Studies Review* 3, 1 (1973); Paul Preston, *Revolution and War in Spain. 1931–1939* (London: Methuen, 1984). During the Franco regime, Anglo–American historiography dominated interpretations of the Civil War. Since the mid–1970's there has been a vast production of local, monographical, and general studies by Spanish historians.

6. Enric Ucelay Da Cal, *La Catalunya populista. Imatge, cultura i política en l'etapa republicana (1931–1939)* (Barcelona: La Magrana, 1982), 295.

7. José Luis García Delgado (ed.), *La Segunda Republica española: El Primer Bienio. 111 Colloquio de Segovia sobre la Historia Contemporánea de España* (Madrid: Siglo XXI, 1987).

8. Raymond Carr, *España 1801–1975* (Barcelona: Ariel, 1982), 580. English version, *Spain 1801–1939* (Oxford: Oxford University Press, 1966).

9. See: Slomo Ben–Ami, *The Origins of the Second Republic in Spain* (Oxford: Oxford University Press, 1978); Gabriel Cardona, *El poder militar en la España Contemporánea hasta la Guerra Civil* (Madrid: Siglo XXI,1983); Gabriel Jackson, *The Spanish Republic and the Civil War 1931–1939* (Princeton: Princeton University Press, 1972); Martin Blinhorn, *Spain in Conflict, 1931–1939* (London: Sage, 1986) and *Democracy and Civil War in Spain, 1931–1939* (London: Methuen, 1988); J. Fontana and M. Tuñón de Lara, et al., *La II República, una esperanza frustrada. Actas del congreso Valencia Capital de la República (abril 1986)* (Valencia: Edicions Alfons el Magnànim, 1987); José Luis García Delgado (ed.), *La II República española.*

Bienio rectificador y frente popular (1934–1936) (Madrid: Siglo XXI, 1988); Frances Lannon and Paul Preston (eds.), *Elites and Power in Twentieth–century Spain. Essays in Honor of Sir Raymond Carr* (Oxford: Oxford University Press, 1992); Paul Preston, *The Coming of the Spanish Civil War. Reform, Reaction and Revolution in the Second Republic* (London: Routledge, 1994) (Spanish Ed., Turner, 1974); Antonio Mazuecos Jimenez, "La política social socialista durante el primer bienio republicano: trabajo, previsión y sanidad," *Estudios de Historia Social* 14 (July–September 1980); Santiago Varela, *Partidos y parlamento en la II República* (Barcelona: Ariel–Fundación Juan, March 1978).

10. Mercedes Cabrera Calvo–Sotelo, *La patronal ante la II República: Organización y estrategia (1931–1936)* (Madrid: Siglo XXI, 1983); José R. Montero, *La C.E.D.A.: el catolicismo social y político en la II Republica* (Madrid: Ediciones de la Revista de Trabajo, 1977); Martin Blinkhorn, *Carlism and Crisis in Spain, 1931–1939* (Cambridge: Cambridge University Press, 1975).

11. John Brademas, *Anarcosindicalismo y revolución en España (1930– 1937)* (Barcelona: Ariel, 1974). English version: "Revolution and Social Revolution. A Contribution to the History of the Anarcho– Syndicalist Movement in Spain, 1930–1937" (Ph.D. diss., University of Oxford, 1953). Pierre Broué, *La revolución española 1931–1939* (Barcelona: Peninsula, 1977); Santos Juliá, *La Izquierda del P.S.O.E. (1935–1936)* (Madrid: Siglo XXI, 1977); Richard Gillespie, *The Spanish Socialist Party. A History of Factionalism* (Oxford: Clarendon, 1989); Helen Graham, *Socialism and War. The Spanish Socialist Party in Power and Crisis, 1936–1939* (Cambridge: Cambridge University Press, 1991).

12. Paul Preston, "Spain's October Revolution and the Rightist Grasp for Power," *Journal of Contemporary History* 10, Num. 4 (1975); Adrian Schubert, *The Road to Revolution in Spain: The Coal Mines of Asturias, 1860-1934* (Champaign: University of Illinois, 1987).

13. Santos Juliá Díaz, *Madrid, 1931–1934. De la fiesta popular a la lucha de clases* (Madrid: Siglo XXI, 1984).

14. Da Cal, *La Catalunya populista.*

15. M. Alexander and H. Graham (eds.), *The French and Spanish Popular Fronts: Comparative Perspectives* (Cambridge: Cambridge University Press, 1988); Santos Juliá, *Origenes del Frente Popular en España. 1934–1936* (Madrid: Siglo XXI, 1979) and "Sobre la formación del Frente Popular en España." *Sistema. Revista de Ciencias Sociales* 73 (July 1986); Ricard Vinyes, *La Catalunya Internacional. El Front populisme en l'exemple Català* (Barcelona: Curial, 1983).

16. Paul Preston, *The Coming of the Spanish Civil War;* Manuel Tuñon de Lara, "Origenes lejanos y próximos," in Tuñon de Lara, Aróstegui, And Viñas, et al., *La Guerra Civil española 50 años después.*

17. Santos Juliá, "Il Fronto popolare nella guerra civile spagnola." Claudio Natoli and Leonardo Rapone (eds.), *A cinquant'anni dalla Guerra di Spagna* (Milan: Franco Angeli, 1987).

18. See Tuñon de Lara, *La guerra civil española; Studia Histórica* 111 (1985); Juliá (ed.), "Socialismo y Guerra Civil"; Julio Aróstegui, *Historia y memoria de la guerra civil. Encuentro en Castill y León* (Salamanca: Junta de Castilla y León, 1988) and "La República en guerra y el problem del poder," *Studia Histórica,* vol. 3, num. 4 (1985); W. Bernecker, *Colectividades y revolucion social: el anarquismo en la guerra civil española, 1936–1939* (Barcelona: Crítica, 1982); Graham, *Socialism and War.*

19. Roger Chartier, "Différénces entre les sexes et domination symbolique. Note critique," *Annales, ESC.,* Num. 4 (July–August 1993); Thomas Laqueur, *Making Sex. Body and Gender from the Greeks to Freud* (London: Harvard University Press, 1990); Mary Nash, "Identidades, representación cultural y discurso de género en la España Contemporánea," in P. Chalmeta and F. Checa Cremades, et al., *Cultura y culturas en la Historia* (Salamanca: Universidad de Salamanca, 1995).

20. George Orwell, *Homage to Catalonia* (Harmondsworth: Penguin, 1983).

21 Several works were published about her. See: *Lina Odena. Heroína del pueblo* (Madrid: Ediciones Europa America, 1936); Angel Estivill, *Lina Odena. La gran heroína de las juventudes revolucionarias de España* (Barcelona: Ed. Maucci, s.d.).

22. Miguel Hernández, "Rosario, Dinamitera," in "Viento del Pueblo 1937," *Obra poética completa,* comp. by Leopoldo de Luis and Jorge Urrutia (Madrid: Ed. Zero, 1976). On Rosario la Dinamitera, see: Tomasa Cuevas, *Cárcel de mujeres. 1939–1945)* (Barcelona: Sirocco Books, 1985), 153–164.

23. See "La camarada Lina Odena ha mort gloriosament," *Treball,* 26 September 1936, or "Els herois de la Pàtria," *Companya,* 1 April 1937.

24. Arteche, 1936. (144x100cm) Fundación Figueras. Centro de Estudios de Historia Contemporánea, Barcelona.

25. See the collection of war posters at the Fundación Figueras, Centro de Estudios de Historia Contemporánea and the Centre d'Estudis Històrics Internacionals, University of Barcelona. Also: Carmen Grimau, *El cartel republicano en la Guerra Civil* (Madrid: Ediciones Cátedra, 1979). Inmaculada Julián, *Les avantguardes pictòriques a Catalunya* (Barcelona: La Frontera, 1986), 57–75.

26. F. Borkenau, *The Spanish Cockpit* (London: Ed. Faber and Faber, 1937); Mika Etchebéhère, *Mi guerra en España* (Barcelona: Plaza y Janés, 1976); H. E. Kaminski, *Los de Barcelona* (Barcelona: Cotal, 1976); John Langdon–Davies, *La setmana tràgica de 1937. Els fets de maig* (Barcelona: Edicions 62, 1987); Mary Low and Juan Breá, *Red Spanish Notebook. The First Six Months of the Revolution and the Civil War* (San Francisco: City Lights, 1979).

27. Orwell, *Homage to Catalonia,* 9.

28. Orwell, *Homage to Catalonia,* 9.

29. See also Sonia Orwell and Ian Angus (eds.), *The Collected Essays. Journalism and Letters of George Orwell* (Middlesex: Penguin, 1970).

30. *El Hogar y la Moda,* January–December 1937. *Modas Nuevas. Album de Confecciones y Labores para el Hogar. Revista Mensual,* October 1936–January 1937. See also the antifascist youth magazine *Noies Muchachas,* published by Aliança Nacional de la Dona Jove and Unión de Muchachas, 16 August 1938.

31. Teresa Pàmies, *Quan érem Capitans (Memòries d'aquella guerra)* (Barcelona: Dopesa, 1974), 94. See also Teresa Pàmies, *Crònica de la vetlla* (Barcelona: Editorial Selecta, 1975).

32. "De Solidaridad Obrera. La frivolidad en los frentes y la retaguardia. La guerra es una cosa más seria," *Diari oficial del Comité Antifeixista i de Salut Pública de Badalona,* 3 October 1936.

33. Da Cal, *La Catalunya populista,* 299.

34. Inmaculada Julián, "La imagen de la mujer en el período 1936– 1938 a través de los carteles de guerra republicanos," paper presented Primer Col.loqui d'Historia de la Dona, Centre d'Investigació Històrica de la Dona, University of Barcelona, October 1986.

35. Mary Nash, "'Milicianas' and Homefront Heroines: Images of Women in Revolutionary Spain (1936–1939)," *History of European Ideas* 11 (1989).

36. Julián, "La imagen de la mujer."

37. Rosa Maria Capel, *El sufragio femenino en la II República* (Granada: Universidad de Granada, 1975). Mary Nash, "Les dones i la Segona República: la igualtat de drets i la desigualtat de fet," *Perspectiva Social* 26 (1988).

38. Membership card of the Agrupación de Mujeres Antifascistas in the name of Salud de Rubio Nazarino, a dressmaker by profession.

39. "La incorporación de la mujer a la industria de guerra. Necesidad de escuelas de capacitación," *Mundo Obrero* (Edición para los frentes), 29 October 1937.

40. "Missió de la mare a l'avantguarda i de la futura mare a la reraguarda," *Treball,* 12 January 1937.

41. The slogan continued: "Glory to the combatants of the Popular Army. Mother: we are not fighting this war for others. THIS IS OUR WAR." *Companya* 9 (15 August 1937).

42. See Maxine Molyneux on combative motherhood in the context of Nicaragua: "Mobilization without Emancipation? Women's Interests, the State and Revolution in Nicaragua," *Feminist Studies* 11, 2 (Summer 1985).

43. "¡Madres y mujeres del mundo!," *Frente Rojo,* 26 October 1938.

44. El Comité, "Pedimos un puesto en la lucha contra el fascismo," *Mujeres,* Edición de Bilbao, March 1937.

45. Teresa Cherta, "Oídme todos...los que me queráis oir," *Lluita. Organ del Partit Socialista Unificat i de la U.G.T.,* 25 February 1937.

46 "¡Madres y mujeres del mundo! Un llamamiento de las mujeres de España," *Frente Rojo,* 26 October 1938.

47. "Nuestra camarada "Pasionaria" se dirige, en vibrante manifiesto, a todas las mujeres del mundo," *Mundo obrero* (Edición para los frentes), 18 July 1937.

48. "La mujer en la Revolución," *Tierra y Libertad,* 5 November 1936.

49. See Federación de Mujeres Libres, "La mujer factor indispensable para el triunfo de la guerra y de la revolución." Hoja volante, s.d.

50. "No es mejor madre la que más aprieta al hijo contra su pecho que la que ayuda a labrar para él un mundo nuevo," *Mujeres Libres 4 Utopías. 4 Realizaciones* (s.d.s.l.).

51. "Las mujeres en los primeros dias de la lucha," *Mujeres Libres,* Num. 10 (July 1987).

52. L. Viola, "Fermesa i endevant," *Treball,* 9 August 1936.

53. "Mujeres libres en Madrid. *Mujeres Libres.* VIII Mes de la Revolución," "Agrupación de Mujeres.A todas las mujeres," *Fragua Social,* 9 December 1936.

54. "Editorial. ¡Mujeres!" *Mujeres Libres.* VIII Mes de la Revolución.

55. See Mary Nash, *Mujer y movimiento obrero en España. 1931–1939* (Barcelona: Fontamara, 1981), 21–84.

56. See Dolores Ibarruri, *En la lucha* (Moscow: Ed. Progreso, 1968) and *El Unico camino* (Barcelona: Bruguera, 1979); Marie Marmo Mullaney, *Revolutionary Women. Gender and the Socialist Revolutionary Role* (New York: Praeger, 1983); Teresa Pàmies, *Una española llamada Dolores Ibarruri* (Barcelona: Martinez Roca, 1975).

57. Miguel Hernandez, "Pasionaria," in Viento del Pueblo, 1937. *Obra poética completa.*

58. Federica Montseny, *Mis primeros cuarenta años* (Barcelona: Plaza y Janes, 1987); Carmen Alcalde, *Federica Montseny. Palabra en rojo y negro* (Barcelona: Argos Vergara, 1983); Shirley Fredricks, "Feminism: The Essential Ingredient in Federica's Montseny's Anarchist Theory," in Jane Slaughter and R. Kern (eds.), *European Women on the Left. Socialism, Feminism and the Problems Faced by Political Women, 1880 to the Present* (Westport, CT: Greenwood Press, 1981); Mary Nash, "Dos intelectuales anarquistas frente al problema de la mujer; Federica Montseny y Lucia Sanchez Saornil," *Convivium. Filosofía, Psicología, Humanidades* 44–45 (1975); Agustí Pons, *Converses amd Federica Montseny: F. Montseny, sindicalisme i acràcia* (Barcelona: Laia, 1977).

59. It was the Grupo Femenino Sindical Socialista Margarita Nelken from El Bonillo in Albacete.

60. Robert Kern, "Margarita Nelken: Women and the Crisis of Spanish Politics," in Slaughter and Kern, *European Women on the Left.* Victoria Kent, "Una experiencia penitenciaria," *Tiempo de Historia* 17 (April 1976) and *Cuatro años de mi vida, 1940–1944* (Barcelona: Bruguera, 1978). Margarita Nelken, *Tres tipos de virgenes* (Madrid: Ed. Cuadernos Literarios, 1929); *La condición social de la mujer en España* (Madrid: Ed. C.V.S., 1975); *La mujer ante las Cortes Constituyentes* (Madrid: Ed. Castro, 1931); and *Las escritoras españolas* (Barcelona: Ed. Labor, 1930).

CHAPTER 3

1. Nash, *Mujer y movimiento obrero en España,* 243–244.

2. Encarnación Fuyola, *Mujeres Antifascistas. Su trabajo y su organización* (Valencia: Gráficas Gesovia, 1937), 6.

3. Letter from the Comité Nacional de Mujeres Antifascistas to the Comité Nacional de Mujeres Antifascistas de Euskadi. Valencia, 1 March 1937.

4. This is an approximate figure derived from both the internal documentation of the organization located and the press. Due to the loss of much documentation and its fragmentary nature, the overall figure is probably considerably higher.

5. Fuyola, *Mujeres Antifascistas,* 8.

6. Emilia Elías, *Por qué luchamos las mujeres antifascistas* (Valencia: Agrupación de Mujeres Antifascistas, s.d.), 4–14.

7. Ramón Casteras, *Las JSUC: ante la guerra y la revolución (1936– 1939)* (Barcelona: Nova Terra, 1977); Jesus López Santamaría, "Juventud y guerra civil. El caso de las juventudes libertarias," *Sistema* 47 (March 1982).

8. Fuyola, *Mujeres Antifascistas,* 10.

9. Fuyola, *Mujeres Antifascistas,* 11.

10. Fuyola, *Mujeres Antifascistas,* 11.

11. Letter from the Comité Provincial de Valencia of the Agrupación de Mujeres Antifascistas. Valencia, 12 April 1937.

12. One member has an illegible political affiliation. *Relación completa de afiliadas. Agrupación de Mujeres Antifascistas.* Godella. (Manuscript)

13. With the exception of a schoolteacher affiliated with the schoolteachers' union, the remaining 56 members of the Rafelcofer AMA were UGT members. *Relación de afiliadas con expresión de la edad, profesión y organización a que pertenencen. Agrupación de Mujere Antifascistas de Rafelcofer.* 2 March 1938. (Manuscript). With the exception of two CNT members, the remaining 63 members were UGT at tha Sagunto branch of the AMA.

14. See Nash, *Mujer y movimiento obrero,* 248–249.

15. Nash, *Mujer y movimiento obrero,* 248–249.

16. *Report from the Comité de Mujeres Antifascistas de Requena,* 8 June 1938; *Report from the Comité de Mujeres Antifascistas de Museros to the Comité Provincial de Mujeres Antifascistas,* 19 October 1937; *Acta de constitución de la Agrupación de Mujeres Antifascistas de Godella,* 1 July 1937.

17. *Relación nominal de la Agrupación de Mujeres Antifascistas de esta ciudad de Pedralba, con expresión de Partidos, o Agrupación a que pertenece cada una de ellas; Acta de la reunión del Comité de la Agrupación de Mujeres Antifascistas de la barriada de Ruzafa,* 10 May 1938 and 16 May 1938.

18. Fuyola, *Mujeres Antifascistas*; Emilia Elías, *Por qué luchamos.*

19. On the Spanish Left, the orthodox communist party was the one that paid least attention to women's issues. On communist policy, see: Nash, *Mujer y movimiento obrero,* 175–206.

20. Angelita Santamaría, *Tareas de la mujer en el partido y en la producción. Conferencia provincial del Partido Comunista. Informe de la camarada Angelita Santamaría.* (Madrid: Publicaciones de la Comisión de Agit–Prop del Comité Provincial del Partido Comunista, 1938), 15. According to Catalan communist leader Dolors Piera, the female membership of the Catalan communist party, *P.S.U.C.,* represented 5 percent of its total membership by July 1937. Dolors Piera, *La aportación femenina en la Guerra de la Independencia. Informe presentado a la Primera Conferencia Nacional del Partido Socialista Unificado de Cataluña (I.C.) por la camarada Dolors Piera* (Barcelona: Ediciones del Departamento de Agitación y Propaganda del P.S.U., 1937). A recent figure by Piera gives the rather inflated number of 10,000 women affiliated with the Catalan communist party in 1938. Manuscript Report by Dolors Piera to Mary Nash, 2 April 1986.

21. Letter from the Comité Provincial de Mujeres Antifascistas de Cuenca to the Comité Nacional de Mujeres Contra la Guerra y el Fascismo en Valencia. Signed: Carmen Arias, 13 July 1937; Letter from the Secretaria Femenina de las Juventudes Socialistas Unificadas, Comité de Madrid al Comité de Mujeres Antifascistas de la Barriada Norte. Signed: Margarita Sanchez, 25 November 1937.

22. Santamaría, *Tareas,* 7. Not italicized in original text.

23. Manuscript report by Dolors Piera to Mary Nash, 2 April 1986. Her estimate is approximate, as the UDC did not have membership cards or membership fees.

24. A substantial number of housewives figure in the lists of members of local branches of the AMA, and it would seem that many of the women were neighbors, living at the same address.

25. Agrupación de Mujeres Antifascistas, *Acta del Comité Ejecutivo,* Valencia, 5 December 1938.

26. Carmen Calderón, *Matilde de la Torre y su época* (Santander: Ediciones Tantin, 1984).

27. On socialist women's activities prior to and during the war, see: Nash, *Mujer y movimiento*

obrero, 137–173. María Cambrils, *Feminismo socialista*. Prólogo de Clara Campoamor (Valencia: Tip. las Artes, 1925); Regina García García, *Yo he sido marxista. El cómo y porqué de una conversión* (Madrid: Editora Nacional, 1946); María Martínez Sierra, *La mujer española ante la República* (Madrid: Ediciones de Esfinge, 1931); Patricia W. O'Connor, *Gregorio and María Martínez Sierra* (Boston: Twayne Publishers, 1977); Antonina Rodrigo, *María Lejárraga. Una mujer en la sombra* (Barcelona: Círculo de Lectores, 1992).

28. *Reglamento. La Estrella de la Civilización. Agrupación Socialista Femenina de Navas de San Juan* (Jaen), 29 November 1931.

29. Letter to Camarada Secretario de la Comisión Ejecutiva del Partido Socialista Obrero Español from the Presidenta de La Estrella de la Civilización, Agrupación Femenina Socialista de Navas de San Juan, Antonia Morales. Navas de San Juan, 24 August 1938.

30. Junta General Ordinaria del Grupo Femenino Socialista de Elche, 29 May 1938. Signed by president Francisca Vazquez and secretary Rita García.

31. "Para nuestras lectoras," *Claridad*, 24 April 1937.

32. Santos Juliá (ed.), *Socialismo y Guerra Civil* (Madrid: Editorial Fundación Pablo Iglesias, 1987). Helen Graham, *Socialism and War. The Spanish Socialist Party in Power and Crisis, 1936–1939* (Cambridge: Cambridge University Press, 1991).

33. Marta Bizcarrondo, "Los orígenes del feminismo socialista en España," *La mujer en la Historia de España (siglos XVI–XX)* (Madrid: Universidad Autonoma de Madrid, 1984).

34. The representations were from PSUC, UGT, CNT, Partido Sindicalista, Esquerra Republicana, Acció Catalana Republicana, Estat Català, Unió de Rabassaires, Ajut Infantil de Reraguarda, Comité Nacional de la AMA, Socorro Rojo de Cataluña (sección del SRI), Dona a la Reraguarda y Aliança Naçional de la Dona Jove, and El Partido Federal Ibérico. "Programa del Primer Congrés Naçional de la Dona," *Companya*, 6 November 1937.

35. Enriqueta Gallinat and Teresa Gispert (E.R.C.); Reis Bertral and Angelina d'Ors (Estat Catala); Angelina Comte, Teresa Vallejos, Teresa Palau, María Pala, Dolors Piera, and Llibertat Picornell (P.S.U.C.), together with Bernadeta Cataneu, Secretary General of the World Committee of Antifascist Women, were the members of the Committee. Data given by Dolors Piera. Manuscript report to Mary Nash, 2 April 1986. The Estat Català representative, Reis Bertral, is considered by some sources to represent PSUC interests.

36. Manuscript report by Dolors Piera to Mary Nash, 2 April 1986.

37. Manuscript report by Dolors Piera to Mary Nash, 2 April 1986.

38. Interview with Teresa Pàmies of the Aliança Naçional de la Dona Jove and the J.S.U., Barcelona, June 1974. See also: Antonia Sánchez, *Hacia la unidad de las muchachas. Discurso pronunciado en el Congreso Alianza de la Juventud Socialista Unificadas* (Madrid: Editorial Juventud Unión Poligráfica, s.d.); Juventudes Socialistas Unificadas. Secretariado Femenino, *Jóvenes trabajadoras* (Valencia: Estudi Gráfic, s.d.). See: M. López del Castillo, "Testimonios acerca de la Aliança Nacional de la Dona Jove," in *Las mujeres y la Guerra Civil española. III Jornadas de estudios monográficos. Salamanca, octubre 1989* (Madrid: Ministero de Cultura, 1991).

39. "Conclusiones de la Conferencia de las Muchachas de Madrid," *Muchachas*, 20 May 1937.

40. "Primera Conferéncia Nacional de l'Aliança de la Dona," *Companya*, 15 August 1937.

41. See, for example: *Lista de afiliadas a la Agrupación de Mujeres Antifascistas en Benifayá*; *Afiliadas en 1937 en Foyos*; *Relación completa de afiliadas de la Agrupación de Mujeres Antifascistas de Godella*; *Relación de afiliadas con expresión de la edad, profesión y organización a que pertenecen Agrupación de Mujeres Antifascistas*, Rafelcofer, 2 March 1938; *Lista de Mujeres Antifascistas de Monte Olibete*; *Nombres de las afiliadas*, Gandia. (Manuscripts)

42. Primer Congrés Nacional de la Dona. (Typed Manuscript)

43. The composition of the National Committee in October 1937 was: Dolores Ibarruri, Dra. Arroyo, Isabel de Palencia, Irene de Falcon, Matilde Cantos, Matilde Huici, Trinidad Torrijos, Emilia Elías, Gloria Morell, Constancia de Hidalgo de Cisneros, L. Alvarez del Vayo, Margarita Nelken, Eloina Malesechevarría, Aurora Arnáiz, Victoria Kent, Gertrudis Araquistain, Roberta Ramón, and delegates from the following factories and workshops: Ferrobéllum, Hutchinson, Quirós and Carmena. Primer Congrés Nacional de la Dona. (Typed Manuscript)

44. Decreto del 29 de agosto creando el Comité de Auxilio Femenino. *Mujeres,* 2 September 1936. See Nash, *Mujer y Movimiento Obrero,* 254–255.

45. *Comisión Nacional de Auxilio del Ministerio de Defensa Nacional de la República* (s.l.: Comité Nacional de Mujeres Antifascistas, 1938).

46. Prologue, *Comisión de Auxilio Femenino.*

47. El Comité, "Pedimos un puesto en la lucha contra el fascismo," *Mujeres* (Ed. Bilbao), 17 April 1937.

48. Febus, "Se clausura la 11 Conferencia de Mujeres Antifascistas," *Claridad,* 2 November 1937. See also *Acta de la Asamblea celebrada el dia 20 de abril en la Agrupación de Ruzafa.* Valencia, 23 April 1938.

49. Fuyola, *Mujeres Antifascistas,* 7.

50. Piera, *La aportación femenina en la Guerra de la Independencia.* Also: *Acta de la Asamblea celebrada en la Agrupación de Mujeres Antifascistas de la Barriada de Ruzafa el día 29 de abril de 1938.* On the War of Independence, see: J. R. Aymes, *La Guerra de la Independencia en España. 1808–1814* (Madrid: Siglo XXI, 1974).

51. Elías, *Por qué luchamos,* 4–14.

52. Fuyola, *Mujeres antifascistas,* 7.

53. Elías, *Por qué luchamos,* 4–14.

54. Astrea Barrios, "Feminismo," *Mujeres* (Ed. Bilbao), 8 March 1937.

55. Matilde Huici, "Los derechos civiles de la mujer y su ejercicio," *Mujeres* (Ed. Valencia), October 1937.

56. Nash, *Mujer y movimiento obrero,* 175–206.

57. Nash, *Mujer y movimiento obrero,* 175–206.

58. Nash, *Mujer y movimiento obrero,* 175–206.

59. Febus, "Se clausura la 11 Conferencia de Mujeres Antifascistas," *Claridad,* 2 November 1937.

60. Astrea Barrios, "¡Hombres a la vanguardia! ¡Mujeres en la retaguardia!," *Mujeres* (Ed. Bilbao), 17 April 1937.

61. *Acta de la Asamblea celebrada el dia 20 de abril de la Agrupación de Ruzafa,* Valencia, 23 April 1938.

62. Fuyola, *Mujeres Antifascistas,* 13.

63. Piera, *La aportación femenina en la guerra de la Independencia,* 5.

64 Mary Nash, "La donna nella guerra civile," in C. Natoli and L. Rapone (eds.), *A cinquant'anni dalla Guerra di Spagna* (Milan: Franco Angeli, 1987).

65. Many generations of women from teenagers to older women in their fifties were members of the AMA, although the available lists of affiliates show a predominance of younger women in their twenties, thirties, and forties.

66. *Estatutos de Mujeres Libres. Carnet de afiliación.*

67. For example, this is the figure given in *Informe que esta Federación eleva a los comités Nacionales del Movimiento Libertario y a los delegados del Pleno del mismo. Federación Nacional de Mujeres Libres.* Signed by the Comité Nacional de Mujeres Libres. La Secretaria. Barcelona, September 1938. For a discussion of the various figures and their sources, see Nash, *Mujer y movimiento obrero,* 87.

68. This figure has been compiled from internal documents, press reports, interviews, etc. However, it undoubtedly undervalues the total number of local groups, which have been impossible to locate due to the disappearance of documentation. For an indicative list of groups, see: Nash, *Mujeres Libres,* 233–236.

69. José Alvarez Junco, *La ideología política del anarquismo español (1868–1910).* Lucienne Domergue, "La féminisme dans la "Revista Blanca" 1898–1905): La femme vue par les anarchistes," in Equipe de philosophie ibérique et ibero–americaine, *La femme dans la penseé espagnole* (Paris: C.N.R.S., 1984); Nash, *Mujer y movimiento obrero,* 21–84.

70. In anarchist terminology, *compañero* cannot be translated as comrade as the latter–*camarada*–was associated with communists.

71. A. Morales Guzmán, "Libertad y cultura. Aspiraciones," *Tierra y Libertad,* 13 March 1936.

72. A. Morales Guzmán, "Ocupémonos de la mujer. Tema del momento," *Tierra y Libertad,* 12 July 1935.

73. María Luisa Cobos, "A la mujer, no; a vosotros proletarios," *Solidaridad Obrera,* 8 October 1935; Trinidad Urien, "Con, de, en, por, sin sobre, tras la mujer en el campo anarquista. Para el compañero Berbegal," *Tierra y Libertad,* 10 December 1935.

74. Nash, *Mujer y movimiento obrero,* 68–76. See also: Francisco De Luis, *Cincuenta años de cultura obrera en Espana. 1890–1940* (Madrid: Fundación Pablo Iglesias, 1994).

75. For a discussion of Sánchez Saornil's viewpoint, see Mary Nash, "Dos intelectuales anarquistas frente al problema de la mujer: Federica Montseny y Lucía Sánchez Saornil," 71–99. For a selection of Sánchez Saornil's articles, see Nash, *Mujeres Libres.*

76. Anarchists did not tend to refer to their spouses as husbands or wives but as their *compañeros/as.* Such terms indicated their rejection of official or church intervention in personal relationships although in practice most maintained monogamic, conventional personal relationships. Unconventional free lovers, followers of E. Armand or Han Ryner, naturists, etc. were a very small minority among mainstream anarchists, who, in fact, were rather puritanical and traditional within their lay cultural models and customs. See Alvarez Junco, *La ideología política* and Nash, "El neomaltusianismo español y los conocimientos populares sobre el control de la natalidad en España," in Nash (ed.), *Presencia y protagonismo,* 307–340; and Mary Nash, "Riforma sessuale e 'nuova morale' nell'anarchismo spagnolo," in G. Di Febo and C. Natoli (eds.), *Spagna anni Trenta. Società, culura, istituzioni* (Milan: Franco Angeli, 1993).

77. María Luisa Cobos, "A la mujer, no, a vosotros proletarios," *Solidaridad Obrera,* 8 October 1935.

78. Lucia Sánchez Saornil, "La cuestión femenina en nuestros medios," 26 September 1935 and "Resumen al margen de la cuestión femenina para el compañero M.R. Vazquez," *Solidaridad Obrera,* 8 November 1935.

79. For a discussion of the development of *Mujeres Libres,* see Martha A. Ackelsberg, *Free Women of Spain. Anarchism and the Struggle for the Emancipation of Women* (Bloomington: Indiana University Press, 1991) and Nash, *Mujeres Libres,* 12–22 and *Mujer y Movimiento obrero,* 85–87.

80. Lucía Sánchez Saornil, *Horas de revolución* (Barcelona: Sindicato del Ramo de Alimentación, 1937) and *Versos sobre Durruti* (Madrid: Ed.Comisión de Propaganda Confederal y Anarquista CNT– AIT., s.d.); Mercedes Comaposada, *Esquemas* (Pub. Mujeres Libres, s.l., s.d.); Amparo Poch y Gascón, *Niño* (Pub. Mujeres Libres, s.l., s.d.) and *La vida sexual de la mujer* (Valencia: Cuadernos de lectura, 1932).

81. Letter from Mujeres Libres to Emma Goldman, 17 April 1936.

82. Emma Goldman, "Situación social de la mujer," *Mujeres Libres,* Semana 21 de la Revolución.

83. Letter from Mujeres Libres to Antonio Escorihuela, 30 May 1936.

84. In a letter to Maria Luisa Cobos, she was told that the journal "did not receive sponsorship or financial aid from anybody" and that they proposed "to publish it by themselves" (2 April 1936).

85. Letter from Mujeres Libres to Josefa Terra, 23 April 1936.

86. Although much changed in content and format, *Mujeres Libres* continued to be published in exile during the Franco dictatorship by Mujeres Libres members Suceso Portales, Sara Guillen, and Mary Stevenson.

87. Mercedes Comaposada, "Origen y actividades de la agrupación de Mujeres Libres," *Tierra y Libertad,* 27 March 1937.

88. See: Alvarez Junco, *Ideología política del anarquismo español*; Lucienne Domergue, "Le feminisme dans la "Revista Blanca" (1898–1905); Temma Kaplan, *Anarchists of Andalusia. 1868–1903* (Princeton: Princeton University Press, 1977); Nash, *Mujer y movimiento obrero,* 21–37; Ackelsberg, *Free Women of Spain;* Sara Berenguer, *Entre el sol y la tormenta. Treinta y dos meses de guerra (1936–1939)* (Barcelona: Seuba Ediciones, 1988).

89. Emma Goldman, "Situación social de la mujer," *Mujeres Libres,* Semana 21 de la Revolución.

90. Suceso Portales, "Necesitamos una moral para los dos sexos!," *Mujeres Libres,* 10.

91. Editorial, "Mujeres en la transformación revolucionaria," *Tierra y Libertad,* 26 December 1936.

92. Mujeres Libres, "Finalidades," *Estructuración. Finalidades.* Reproduced in Nash, *Mujeres Libres,* 73.

93. Estatutos de Mujeres Libres.

94. Estatutos de Mujeres Libres. The anarchosyndicalist union, the Confederación Nacional del Trabajo(CNT), and the radical political organization Federación Anarquista Ibérica (FAI), together with the youth organization—Federación Ibérica de Juventudes Libertarias (FIJL)— formed the anarchist movement. See: W. Bernecker, *Colectividades y revolución social: el anarquismo en la guerra civil española. 1936–1939* (Barcelona: Crítica, 1982); Javier Paniagua, *La sociedad libertaria. Agrarismo e industrialización en el anarquismo español, 1930–1939* (Barcelona: Crítica, 1982); M. T. Smyth, *La CNT al País Valencià, 1936–1939* (Valencia: Edicions Alfons el Magànim, 1987).

95. Interview with Suceso Portales, Montady, summer 1973 and 1974. Also, manuscript: "Apuntes biográficos" by Sara Guillen on Suceso Portales, Montady, 17 March 1975. Lola Iturbe, *La mujer en la la lucha social. La guerra civil de España* (Mexico: Ed. Mexicanos Unidos, 1974). Interview with Lola Iturbe, Barcelona, November 1981. Also: Berenguer, *Entre el sol y la tormenta.*

96. For example, Federica Montseny was most articulate in her rejection of feminism. See Nash, "Dos intelectuales anarquistas frente al problema de la mujer: Federica Montseny y Lucía Sánchez Saornil."

97. Suceso Portales, "Necesitamos una moral para los dos sexos," *Mujeres Libres,* 10.

98. Ilse, "La doble lucha de la mujer," *Mujeres Libres,* VIII Mes de la Revolución.

99. Ilse, "La doble lucha de la mujer," *Mujeres Libres,* VIII Mes de la Revolución.

100. Mariano R. Vazquez, "Por la elevación de la mujer. Avance," *Solidaridad Obrera,* 10 October 1935.

101. For a discussion of Mujeres Libres' view on feminism, see Nash, *Mujer y movimiento obrero,* 91–97.

102. Nash, "Dos intelectuales anarquistas frente al problema de la mujer: Federica Montseny y Lucia Sánchez Saornil." Federica Montseny, *El problema de los sexos* (Toulouse: Ed. Universo, s.d.); *La mujer, problema del hombre* (Barcelona: Ediciones de la "Revista Blanca," 1932); and her fictional works: *La Victoria. Novela en que se narran los problemas de orden moral que se le presentan a una mujer de ideas modernas* (Barcelona: Ediciones de "La Revista Blanca," 1925), *El hijo de Clara* (Segunda parte de La Victoria) (Barcelona: Ediciones de "La Revista Blanca," 1927), and *La indomable* (edition by Maria Alicia Langa Laorga) (Madrid: Castália, 1991).

103. Although there were some sporadic moves by the anarcho– syndicalist union CNT to recruit women, other more minority groups of Spanish anarchism such as the sex reform movement were more aware of women's issues. See Mary Nash, *Mujer y movimiento obrero,* 61–68. "El neomaltusianismo español y los conocimientos populares sobre el control de la natalidad en España" and "La reforma sexual en el anarquismo español." Mary Nash, "La reforma sexual en el anarquismo español." Paper presented at the International Symposium on the Cultural Traditions of Spanish Anarchism. Institute for Social History. Amsterdam, June 1988; and "Riforma sessuale e 'nuova morale' nell'anarchismo spagnolo."

104. Federica Montseny, "La mujer, problema del hombre," *La Revista Blanca* 86 (15 December 1926). For a discussion of Montseny's view of feminism, see Friedricks, "Feminism: The Essential Ingredient in Federica Montseny's Anarchist Theory." Also, Nash, "Dos intelectuales anarquistas frente al problema de la mujer: Federica Montseny y Lucia Sánchez Saornil"; Alcalde, *Federica Montseny. Palabra en rojo y negro.*

105. Federica Montseny, "La mujer, problema del hombre," IV, *La Revista Blanca* 94 (15 April 1927). Federica Montseny, *El problema de los sexos* (Toulouse: Ed. Universo, s.d.) and *La mujer, problema del hombre* (Barcelona: Ediciones de la "Revista Blanca," 1932).

106. Nash, "Dos intelectuales anarquistas frente al problema de la mujer. Federica Montseny y Lucia Sánchez Saornil."

107. Such was the case of the communist and socialist women's groups. See Nash, *Mujer y Movimiento obrero.*

108. Lucia Sánchez Saornil, "La cuestión femenina en nuestros medios," *Solidaridad Obrera,* 2 October 1935.

109. H. E. Kaminski, *Los de Barcelona* (Barcelona: Ediciones del Cotal, 1976), 62.

110. *Informe que esta Federación eleva a los Comités Nacionales del Movimiento Libertario y a los delegados del Pleno del mismo.* Signed by the Comité Nacional de Mujeres Libres. La Secretaria. Barcelona, September 1938. For a discussion of these petitions and the reaction of the anarchist movement, see: Nash, *Mujer y movimiento obrero,* 98–106.

111. *Acta de la Reunión extraordinaria celebrada por este sub– comité el día 11 de febrero de 1939.* Las regionales: Centro– Levante. Locales: Madrid–Valencia. Delegaciones del comité peninsular FAI y subcomité nacionales CNT. Also: Agustí Pons, *Converses amb Frederica Montseny. Sindicalisme i acrácia,* 20.

112. *Exposición del problema de las relaciones de las Secretarías Femeninas de la FIJL con "Mujeres Libres," que presenta a estudio de las Regionales la Secretaría Femenina Peninsular,* 8 September 1938; *Informe que presenta la Secretaría Femenina del Comité Peninsular sobre el sexto punto del orden del día del próximo pleno nacional de Regionales de la FIJL que ha de celebrarse en Barcelona.* Secretaria Femenina, Comité Peninsular Federación Ibérica de Juventudes Libertarias, Barcelona, 1 October 1938.

113. *Acta de la Reunión extraordinaria celebrada por este Subcomité el día 11 de febrero de 1939.*

114. The Executive Committee of the Catalan Libertarian Movement was created in April 1938 and the National Liaison Committee of the Libertarian Movement in October 1938. Jesús López Santamaria, "Formació i evolució de les Joventuts Llibertàris," *l'Avenç.* 75 (October 1984), 24–29; and "El desario a la 'Trinidad' Libertaria: feminismo y afeminismo en el seno del anarquismo hispano. El caso de las JJ.LL," in *Las mujeres y la Guerra Civil española.*

115. Pons, *Conversa amb Frederica Montseny,* 19.

116. "Informe que esta Federación eleva."

117. *Acta de la Reunión Extraordinaria.*

118. *Sub–Comité Nacional de Mujeres Libres, estructuración en Secretarías. Desenvolvimiento de las mismas entre si. Sec. General, Sec. Organización, Sec. Propaganda y Cultura y Cultura y Prensa, Sec. Asistencia Social (Ayuda moral al Combatiente)* (s.l.: s.e., s.d.).

119. In interviews with 56 women of diverse social extraction, mostly non–politicized or of rank and file, the pattern of closed circuits became quite clear. Women of a specific political affiliation remained within it and were either unaware of or hostile to women's organizations of a different political tendency. Mary Nash, Oral History Project: *The Family in Autonomous Catalonia,* University of Barcelona, 1982–1984.

120. Martha Ackelsberg, "Mujeres Libres: Individuality and Community. Organizing Women during the Spanish Civil War," 11–12; and L. Berger and C. Mazer, *De Toda la Vida.* (Video)

121. Mary Nash, Oral History Project: *The Family in Autonomous Catalonia.*

122. Interview with Isabel Gonzalez Sugrañes, October 1981.

123. "La interviu de hoy. Mercedes Comaposada, Secretaria del Comité Nacional de Propaganda de Mujeres Libres dice," *CNT,* 20 August 1938.

124. The translation of *capacitación* is not "empowerment," as M. Ackelberg suggests, and it is not at all specific to anarchist women. It was a common term used by communists, socialists, and the antifascist women's organizations with the more technical connotation of professional, educational and political training. Martha A. Ackelsberg, "Separate and equal"? Mujeres Libres and Anarchist Strategy for Women's Emancipation," *Feminist Studies* (Spring 1985), 74.

125. Such an interpretation was suggested implicitly to me by Sara Guillen, a member of *Mujeres Libres.* Interview with Sara Guillen, Montady, Summer 1975.

126. Mary Nash, "L'Avortement legal a Catalunya. Una experiencia fracassada," *L'Avenç.* (March 1983); "Marginality and Social Change: Legal Abortion in Catalonia during the Civil War." William D. Phillips, Jr. and Carla Rahn Phillips (eds.), *Marginated Groups in Spanish and Portuguese History* (Minneapolis: Society for Spanish and Portuguese Historical Studies, 1989) and "Género, cambio social y la problemática del aborto," *Historia Social* 2 (Autumn 1988).

127. Amparo Poch y Gascon, *La vida sexual de la mujer* (Valencia: Cuadernos de Lectura, 1932) and *Niño* (s.l.: Publicaciones Mujeres Libres, s.d).

128. Interview with Sara Guillen, Montady, Summer 1975. This was stated with respect to

Lucia Sánchez Saornil and Amparo Poch y Gascón. Pepita Carnicer referred openly to Lucía Sánchez Saornil as a lesbian in the documentary video by Lisa Berger and Carol Mazer, *De toda la vida.*

129. Etta Federn, *Mujeres de la revolución* (Barcelona: Publ. Mujeres Libres, s.d.); Mujeres Libres, *Actividades de la Federación de Mujeres Libres* (Barcelona, s.d.); Mujeres Libres, *Cómo organizar una agrupación Mujeres Libres* (s.d., s.e.).

130. On women in the dissident Marxist parties prior to the Civil War, see Nash, *Mujer y movimiento obrero,* 207–225.

131. On the unification process of the dissident Marxist parties, see: Pagés, *Andreu Nin y su evolución política* (Madrid: Ed. Zero, 1975), 179–187. On the BOC, see Francesc Bonamusa, *El Bloc Obrer i Camperol (1930–1932)* (Barcelona: Curial, 1974).

132. Letter to Mary Nash from Maria Teresa Andrade, Paris, 27 May 1975.

133 *Resoluciones aprobadas en el Pleno Ampliado del Comité Central del POUM celebrado en Barcelona los días 12 al 16 de diciembre de 1936* (Barcelona: Ed. Marxista, 1936), 18. (I would like to thank Pelai Pagés for drawing my attention to this document.)

134. Interview with Maria Teresa Andrade, Madrid, October 1984.

135. "Tesis de la organización del Partido. Proyecto del Ponente E.A. (Enric Adroher?)," *Boletín Interior de discusión del 11 Congreso del POUM,* Num. 1 (February 1938), p. 8. (I would like to thank Pelai Pagés for drawing my attention to this document.)

136. The POUM had grown from 6,000 members in July 1936 to 30,000 by December 1936. "Informe sobre la situación política presentado por Andreu Nin al Comité Central Ampliado del POUM celebrado en Barcelona 12–16 de diciembre de 1936," *Boletin Interior. Organo de Información y discusión del Comité Ejecutivo del POUM,* Num. 1 (15 January 1937).

137. Pelai Pagés, *Andreu Nin;* and "Le mouvement trotskyste pendant la guerre civile d'Espagne," *Cahiers Léon Trotsky* 10 (June 1982).

138. "Después de los sucesos," *Emancipación,* 29 May 1937. For an analysis of May 1937, see: Juliá, *Socialismo y Guerra Civil.* Da Cal, *La Catalunya Populista,* 304–309. Manuel Cruells, *Els fets de Maig. Barcelona 1937* (Barcelona: Joventud, 1970).

139. "El comunismo y la familia," *Emancipación,* 29 May 1937.

140. Interview with María Manonelles, Barcelona, September 1984.

141. *La mujer ante la Revolución,* 21.

142. Interview with Maria Teresa Andrade, Madrid, October, 1984. Significantly, even before her exile in France, María Teresa Andrade did not follow the Spanish convention of women maintaining their own surnames. She used her husband's surname, Andrade, instead of her own, García Banus.

143. "Tesis de la organización del Partido. Proyecto del Ponente E. A. (Enric Adroher?)," *Boletín Interior de discusión del II Congreso del POUM,* Num. 1 (February 1938), 8.

144. Interview with Teresa Andrade, Madrid, October 1984.

145. "Tesis de la Organización del Partido. Proyecto del Ponente E. A. (Enric Adroher?)."

146. "Qué es y qué quiere el Secretariado Femenino del POUM," *Emancipación,* 20 February 1937.

147. *La Mujer ante la Revolución* (Barcelona: Publicaciones del Secretariado Femenino del POUM Ed. Marxista, 1937), 3.

148. *Emancipación. Organo Quincenal del Secretariado Femenino del P.O.U.M.,* Num. 1 (20 February 1937).

149. "Qué es y qué quiere el Secretariado Femenino del POUM," *Emancipación,* 20 February 1937.

150. Letter from Maria Teresa Andrade, Paris, 25 May 1975. This social composition also coincides with data on male leadership in the POUM. Ucelay da Cal, "Socialistas y comunistas en Cataluña durante la guerra civil: Un ensayo de interpretación." Santos Juliá (ed.), *Socialismo y Guerra civil.*

151. María, "Emancipación," *Emancipación,* 29 May 1937.

152. *La mujer ante la Revolución,* 7.

153. Alejandra Kollontai, *La Juventud comunista y la moral sexual* (Barcelona: Ed. Marxista. Publicación del Secretariado Femenino del POUM, 1937).

154. Orwell describes this training in *Homage to Catalonia.*

155 "Por una potente Alianza Nacional de Mujeres," *Pasionaria,* October 1937.

156. *Informe que esta Federación eleva a los Comités Nacionales del Movimiento Libertario y a los Delegados del Pleno del Mismo. Federación de Mujeres Libres.* Signed by the Comité Nacional de Mujeres Libres. La Secretaria. Barcelona, September 1938, 3.

157. "Contra todo propósito de intención inconfesable Mujeres Libres reafirma su vigorosa personalidad revolucionaria," *Tierra y Libertad,* 20 August 1938.

158. Lucía Sánchez Saonril, "Por la Unidad. Actitud clara y consecuente de Mujeres Libres. En respuesta a Dolores Ibárruri," *Solidaridad Obrera,* 14 August 1938.

159. *Informe que esta Federación eleva a los Comités Nacionales del Movimiento Libertario y a los Delegados del Pleno del mismo. Federación Nacional de Mujeres Libres.* Signed by the Comité Nacional de Mujeres Libres. La Secretaria. Barcelona, September 1938, 3.

160. For a discussion of these proposals, see Mary Nash, *La mujer en las organizaciones de Izquierda en España (1931–1939).* (Ph.D. diss., University of Barcelona, 1977), 714–723.

161. "Contra todo propósito de intención inconfesable Mujeres Libres reafirma su vigorosa personalidad revolucionaria," *Tierra y Libertad,* 20 August 1938.

162. *Informe que esta Federación eleva a los Comités Nacionales del Movimiento Libertario y a los Delegados del Pleno del mismo. Federación Nacional de Mujeres Libres,* 2.

163. "La interviu de hoy. Mercedes Comaposada, Secretaria del Comité Nacional de Propagnada de 'Mujeres Libres,' dice," *CNT,* 20 August 1938. Pàmies, *Quan érem Capitans,* 77–79.

164. "El míting femení U.G.T.–C.N.T. celebrat anit passada, amb gran èxit, a l 'Olympia," *Treball,* 2 May 1937.

165. Consuelo García, *Las cárceles de Soledad Real. Una vida* (Madrid: Alfaguara, 1983), 53–54.

166. The youth organization Unión de Muchachas considered the disparaging remarks on the Girls' Conference (described "as an orgy like those celebrated by the bourgeoisie" by the anarchist newspaper *Castilla Libre*) to be an affront. It referred to the same event as the "healthy gaiety of the girls at the party which ended the Conference." A.S. "¡Cuidado con los plumíferos incontrolables!," *Muchachas,* Num. 2.

167. See the inclusion of an article from the anarchist newspaper in its pages: "La mujer en la revolución," published originally in *Tierra y Libertad. Mujeres* (Ed. Bilbao), 6 March 1937.

168. *Mujeres Libres ante el Congreso Regional de Mujeres Antifascistas que se celebra en Barcelona los días 6,7 y 8 del corriente.* Also, letter from Teresa Andrade, Paris, 27 May 1975.

169. Pàmies, *Quan érem Capitans,* 36–37.

170. Pàmies, *Quan érem Capitans,* 40–41.

171. Mercedes Abril, "Alerta mujeres proletarias," *La Batalla* (Diario), 28 April 1937.

172. "Mujer trabajadora," *Emancipación,* 20 February 1837. M. Abril, "Alerta mujeres proletarias," *La Batalla* (Diario), 28 April 1937. Isabel Peiró, "Por el frente de mujeres revolucionarios," *Emancipación,* 24 April 1937.

173. Isabel Peiró, "Por el frente de Mujeres Revolucionarias," *Emancipación,* 24 April 1937. The Female Secretariat of the youth organization of the JCI also developed the proposal to set up a revolutionary front for working–class girls. Secretariado Femenino del J.C.I., "Jovenes proletarias! Por el Frente Revolucionario de muchachas trabajadoras," *Juventud Obrera,* Second Week in October 1937; and "Ante la Conferencia Nacional de la Mujer Joven de Cataluña," *Juventud Obrera,* Second Week in August 1937.

174. Letter from the Comité Provincial de Mujeres Antifascistas, Madrid, to Emilia Elias, Madrid, 6 August 1937.

175. Nash, *Mujer y movimiento obrero,* 348–250, 265–269.

CHAPTER 4

1. A minority of women in the republican zone did not support the antifascist cause. Of these some were open fascist supporters. However, most appear to have collaborated in what was known as *socorro blanco* (white aid), assisting right–wing supporters and clergy in escaping from revolutionary leftist justice. Interview with Mercedes Marquillas, Barcelona, 22 July 1981. On religious persecution in the republican zone, see: Gabriel Ranzato, "Dies Irae. La persecuzione religiosa nella zona repubblicana durante la Guerra Civile Spagnola (1936–1939)," *Movimiento Operario e Socialista* 2 (May–June 1988) and the critique by Enric Ucelay da Cal, "Gabriel Ranzato: 'Ira di Dio,' ma rabbia di chi," *Movimiento Operario e Socialista*, Vol. XII. Nova serie (January–August 1989). Also: Bruce Lincoln, "Revolutionary Exhumations in Spain. July 1936," *Comparative Studies in Society and History* 2 (1985).

2. Nash, *Mujer y movimiento obrero,* 243

3. For a discussion of women's resistance to militarism in the First World War, see: Joahanna Alberti, *Beyond Suffrage. Feminists in War and Peace, 1914–1928* (London: Macmillan, 1989); Mary Nash and Susana Tavera, *Experiencias desiguales. Conflictos sociales y respuestas colectivas (Siglo XIX).* (Madrid: Sintesis, 1994); Joan Montgomery Byles, "Women's Experience of World War One: Suffragists, Pacifists and Poets," *Women's Studies International Forum* 8, 5 (1985); Claire M. Tylee, "Maleness Run Riot"–The Great War and Woman's Resistance to Militarism," *Women's Studies International Forum* 11, 3 (1988).

4. "Les catalanes mai no hem parit covards: que els nostres fills no manquin a llur deure"–deia una pancarta de la gran manifestació celebrada ahir," *Treball* (26 February 1937).

5. "La incorporación de la mujer a la industria de guerra. Necesidad de escuelas de capacitación," *Mundo Obrero (Para Frentes),* 29 October 1937; "Misió de la mare a l'avantguarda i de la futura mare a la reraguarda," *Treball,* 12 January 1937. "Mares, també al poble necessita del vostre heroïsme!," *LLuita,* 26 November 1936.

6. "Defensa de Madrid. Tribunas. Vigilancia. Las mujeres. Tres sugestiones en torno a una necesidad urgente," *Claridad,* 7 October 1936; Report from the Sociedad de Trabajadores de Oficios Varios "Adelante," *Chiva,* 10 April 1938. Signed by the Secretary General, Mariá Molines. (Manuscript)

7. "Les dones de Catalunya és manifestaren diumenge per una política enèrgetica de guerra. Vibrants parlaments de les camarades Dolors Piera i Margarida Nelken," *Treball,* 15 March 1938; "Dona! Descobrint un emboscat o denunciant un feixista contribuixes a anihilar l'enemic contra el qual lluita el teu fill combatent i acceleres la victòria i el seu retorn," *Treball,* 22 March 1938.

8. "Dones antifeixistes de_Catalunya!," *Treball,* 27 April 1938.

9. "'Pasionaria' Comandante Honorario del Quinto Regimiento," *A.B.C. Diario de la Guerra Civil,* Fascículo 9.

10. "Discurso de 'El Campesino' ante las Mujeres Antifascistas del Sector Este," *Claridad,* 20 September 1937.

11. "Manifiesto de la Agrupación Mujeres Libres," *Mujeres Libres,* VIII Mes de la Revolución.

12. "No regaleis juguetes bélicos a los niños," *Boletin de Información. CNT–AIT–FAI,* 1 January 1936.

13. Reports from the Female Branch of the Sociedad de Trabajadores de Oficios Varios, "Adelante," *Chiva* 10 (April 1938), signed by the Secretaria General, Maria Moliner. (Two Typed Manuscripts)

14. For example, the Antifascist Committee of a small village in Gerona obliged one of the villagers to deposit one thousand pesetas as a guarantee that his wife would cease her right–wing activities in the village. Comité Antifeixista. Comissió de Treball addressed to Sr. Rossend Puigvert i Estrach, Vilobí d'Onyar, 4 August 1936. Signed by the Executive Committee, Front Antifeixista Viloví D'Onyar. Also, Receipt. Comité Antifeixista. Comissió de Treball, Vilobí d'Onyar, 5 August 1936. Signed Luis Salagras, Salvador Comas, and Josep (P?, signature illegible) (Typed Manuscript). I would like to thank Joaquim Puigvert for making these documents available to me.

15. Literally the "Baby–bottle Levy."

16. Teresa Pàmies, *Quan érem Capitans (Memòries d'aquella guerra)* (Barcelona: Dopesa, 1974), 63.

17. "Por una vida alegre y optimista," *Muchachas,* 4 September 1937.

18. Federica Montseny, *Acción de la mujer en la paz y en la Guerra,* Conferencia de Federica Montseny, dada en el local de "Mujeres Libres" el día 14 de agosto de 1938." (Typed Manuscript)

19. Montseny, *Acción de la mujer en la paz y en la guerra,* 23–24.

20. "Maria Gazquez Lopez, "Escribe una mujer española," *Ruta,* 21 January 1937. Other anarchists voiced the problem that the war and revolution represented for pacifists, although they rejected inhibition and conscientious objection in this specific context. Félix Martí Ibañez, "Alerta a los pacifistas. La objeción de conciencia y la revolución," *Hombres Libres,* 10 September 1937.

21. Interview with Conchita Pérez Collado, Barcelona, 16 June 1981.

22. Testimony of Rosario Sánchez (La Dinamitera) in Maite Goicoechea, "Mujer y Guerra Civil: la historia que no se contó. Milicianas del 36: las olvidadas," *Vindicación Feminista* 26–27 (September 1978), 52.

23. Interview with Conchita Pérez Collado, Barcelona, 16 June 1981.

24. Pàmies, *Quan érem Capitans,* 40.

25. Luis Maria Jiménez de Aberasturi, *Casilda, miliciana. Historia de un sentimiento* (San Sebastian, Editorial Txertoa, 1985), 25, 41.

26. J. Baliús, "Elisa García ha muerto en el frente de Aragón," *Solidaridad Obrera,* 3 September 1936.

27. Aurelio Jerez Santa–Maria, "En los frentes de la Libertad. Táta, mujer anarquista, interviene en un golpe de mano contra los facciosos de Aravaca," *Hombres Libres,* 9 July 1937.

28. Jiménez de Aberasturi, *Casilda, miliciana,* 41.

29. Pàmies, *Quan érem capitans,* 35–41.

30. Josep Massot i Muntaner, "Diario de la miliciana," *El desembarcament de Bayo a Mallorca. Agost–setembre de 1936* (Barcelona: Publicacions de l'Abadía de Montserrat, 1987), 402, 405.

31. Amadeu Bernadó, "La dona i la revolució. Caritat Mercader, nervi de la frustrada Olimpíada Popular de Barcelona, parla als seus companys del P.S.U. i als lectors de Treball," *Treball,* 1 September 1936.

32. "Las mujeres en los primeros días de la lucha," *Mujeres Libres,* 10 July 1937.

33. Interview with Conchita Pérez Collado, Barcelona, 16 June 1981.

34. Interview with Conchita Pérez Collado, Barcelona, 16 June 1981.

35. Manuscript reproduced by Massot i Muntaner, "Diario de la miliciana," 393–410.

36. Manuscript reproduced by Massot i Muntaner, "Diario de la miliciana," 396–397.

37. M. Eiroa San Francisco, "La participación de la mujer en la Guerra Civil en Málaga," *Congreso de Andalucismo Histórico* (Granada, September 1987); Antonio Nadal, "Experiencias psíquicas sobre mujeres marxistas malagueñas," (Malaga, 1939). *Baetica,* Num. 10 (1987).

38. H. E. Kaminski, *Los de Barcelona* (Barcelona: Ediciones del Cotal, 1976), 210.

39. Mika Etchebéhère, *Mi guerra de España* (Barcelona: Plaza y Janes, 1987).

40. Els herois de la Pàtria," *Companya,* 1 April 1937; Etchebéhère, *Mi guerra de España;* Massot, "Diario de la miliciana." Oral testimonies and ichnographic collections show that the majority of *milicianas* were girls and young women.

41. Interview with Conchita Pérez Collado, Barcelona, 16 June 1981; Massot, "Diario de la miliciana," 403.

42. "Artur Cussó, secretari d'Organització Femenina del P.S.U.C. ha fet, per ràdio, una crida propugnant la formació de les Milicies femenines," *Treball,* 30 July 1936.

43. "Batalló femení, *Treball,* 8 August 1936; G. Viana, "La collaboració de la dona contra el feixisme. El Batalló femení de Catalunya," *Treball,* 16 August 1936.

44. Massot i Muntaner, "Diario de la Miliciana," 393–410.

45. See *Diario del Quinto Regimento de Milicias Populares,* Madrid, 26, 28 July and 11 September 1936.

46. Carme Manrubia, "Per què les dones no podan ingressar a l'Escola de Comissaris de Guerra?," *Companya,* Num. 12 (16 December 1937).

47. Jiménez de Aberasturi, *Casilda, miliciana,* 56–57.
48. Massot, "Diario de la miliciana," 393.
49. I refer to Argentina García,"Nuestras milicianas," *Mujeres* (Bilbao), 6 March 1937.
50. Margarita Nelken, "Mujeres de España," *Frente Rojo,* 19 July 1938.
51. Nadal, "Experiencias psíquicas," 369.
52. Interview with Conchita Pérez Collado.
53. Etchebéhère, *Mi guerra de España,* 56–57.
54. Etchebéhère, *Mi guerra de España,* 57.
55. Kaminski, *Los de Barcelona,* 210.
56. Els herois de la Pàtria," *Companya,* 1 April 1937.
57. "Las mujeres en los primeros días de la lucha," *Mujeres Libres,* 10 July 1937.
58. Kaminski, *Los de Barcelona,* 209; John Tisa, *Recalling the Good Fight. An Autobiography of the Spanish Civil War* (Massachusetts: Bergin and Garvey Publishers, 1985), 120.
59. "Rosario, dinamitera,/puedes ser varón y eres/la nata de las mujeres,/la espuma de la trinchera." Miguel Hernández, "Rosario, Dinamitera," *Obra poética completa* (Madrid: Ed. Zero, 1976), 312.
60. "L'Assemblea de la 'Unió de Dones' del districte IV. 'A la reraguarda – digué Dolors Piera – cada dona ha d'ésser un soldat,'" *Treball,* 8 June 1938.
61. George Orwell, *Homage to Catalonia* (Harmondsworth: Penguin, 1983).
62. Geraldine Scanlon refers to this as a bill, but I have been unable to locate it as such in the official *Gaceta Oficial del Estado.* Such an order appears to have existed, although it may have been formulated as an internal military one. Geraldine Scanlon, *La polémica feminista en la España contemporánea (1864–1975)* (Madrid: Siglo XXI, 1976), 294.
63. Ronald Fraser, *Recuérdalo tú y recuérdalo a otros. Historia Oral de la Guerra Civil española* (Barcelona: Crítica, 1979), 1, 400 (English version, *Blood of Spain. The Experience of Civil War, 1936–1939* (London: Allen Lane, Penguin Books Ltd., 1979).
64. "Aviso a los compañeros de Francia," *Boletin de Información CNT.AIT.FAI.,* 3 December 1936.
65. Comité Local, "A les dones de Catalunya. Organitzem els Grups de Reraguarda!," *Treball,* 12 September 1936.
66. Interview with Conchita Pérez Collado, Barcelona, 16 June 1981.
67. Jiménez de Aberasturi, *Casilda, miliciana,* 53–54.
68. "El Comité, "Pedimos un puesto en la lucha contra el fascismo," *Mujeres* (Bilbao), 17 April 1937.
69. "¡Las mujeres en los primeros días de la lucha!," *Mujeres Libres,* 10 July 1937.
70. "Una dona en el front," *Combat.* Diari de la J.C.I. P.O.U.M., 24 August 1936.
71. *La mujer ante la Revolución.* Publicaciones del Secretariado Femenino del POUM (Barcelona: Ed. Marxista, 1937), 7.
72. Interview with Conchita Pérez Collado. See also the memoirs of Captain Mika Etchehébère, which describe the efforts of militia women to get the men to explain how to handle a gun. *Mi guerra de España* (Barcelona: Plaza y Janés, 1987), 22.
73. "Las mujeres en los primeros días de la lucha," *Mujeres Libres,* 10 July 1937.
74. "La prostitución, el arma principal de la Quinta Columna," *Claridad,* 4 March 1937.
75. Many former militia women at the Conference on Women in the Civil War denounced this situation and the need to recuperate the good name of *milicianas. Homenatge a la Dona a la Guerra Civil,* University of Barcelona, October 1987. Also interviews with Conchita Pérez Collado (Barcelona, 1981) and Rosario Sánchez (Barcelona, 1987). See also: Jiménez de Aberasturi, *Casilda, miliciana,* 43–45; Goicoechea, "Milicianas del 36"; and Mary Nash, "Women in War: Milicianas and Armed Combat in Revolutionary Spain, 1936–1939," *The International History Review,* Vol. XV, Num. 2 (May 1993).
76. Kaminski, *Los de Barcelona,* 210. Etchebéhère, *Mi guerra de España;* Félix Martí Ibáñez, *Tres Mensajes a la mujer* (Barcelona: Ediciones y Reportajes, 1937).
77. I have not been able to locate any direct documentation on this point, although oral testimonies and written sources refer to it. Pàmies, *Quan érem capitans,* 45; and Kaminski, *Los de Barcelona,* 210.
78. Félix Martí Ibáñez, *Tres Mensajes a la mujer* (Barcelona: Ediciones y Reportajes, 1937).

79. Massot, "Diario de la miliciana," 396–410.

80. Interviews with Conchita Pérez Collado and Rosario Sánchez (la Dinamitera). Also Jiménez de Aberasturi, *Casilda, miliciana,* 44.

81. Fraser, *Recúerdalo tú,* 400.

82. Jiménez de Aberasturi, *Casilda, Miliciana,* 49–50.

83. Fraser, *Recuérdalo tú,* 400.

84. Nash, *Mujer y movimiento obrero,* 37–61, 73–75. Also "La reforma sexual en el anarquismo español." Paper presented at the International Conference on the Cultural Traditions of Spanish Anarchism. Amsterdam, June 1988; and "L'avortement legal a Catalunya: una experiència fracassada," *L'Avenç.,* num. 58 (marzo 1983) and "Riforma sessuale e 'nuova morale' nell'anarchismo spagnolo."

85. Martí Ibáñez, *Tres Mensajes a la mujer.*

86. Martí Ibáñez, *Tres Mensajes a la mujer.*

87. Massot, "Diario de la miliciana," 396, 404.

88. Pàmies, *Quan érem capitans,* 45.

89. Pàmies, *Quan érem capitans,* 45.

90. Pàmies, *Quan érem capitans,* 45–46.

91. Interview with Antonia García, Barcelona, December 1983.

92. "Soldat: Que desitges? Que Necessites? Les dones contesten a la crida del Comité Nacional de Dones Antifexisistes," *Treball,* 28 March 1938.

93. "Mujeres Libres, LLeva a las trincheras el calor de su voz fraternal," *Tierra y Libertad,* 30 July 1938.

94. "A todos los combatientes del ejercito del pueblo," Federación de Mujeres Libres. (Typed Manuscript)

95. Pàmies, *Quan érem capitans,* 42–46.

96. *Informe de las Mujeres Antifascistas de Jativa. A las Mujeres antifascistas de Jativa os mandan un saludo y un abrazo fraternal a todas las compañeras aquí reunidas.* Signed by the Secretary, A. García. (Typed Manuscript)

97. "La Unión de Muchachas ante la campaña de invierno," *Claridad,* 10 September 1938; "Manifest de les dones del P.S.U. Jornada Internaional de la Dona. Per la Unitat antifeixista de les dones de Catalunya," *Treball,* 7 March 1937.

98. War godmothers were also used on the Franco side, and some of the *madrinas* provided intense emotional relationships for soldiers.

99. Letter by Casimiro Mártinez and Eustaquia López. (Manuscript). See also letter by Alejandro (signature illegible) (Manuscript), who suggests that if he gets on well with his war godmother they could fall in love.

100. Letter by Manuel Abajo, 5 May 1937. (Manuscript)

101. Letter signed by Francisco Martin and Emilio Miranda, 19 July 1938. (Manuscript); Letter signed Paulino Huertas, L. Marin, M. Tercero, Esteban Garcia, R. (signature illegible), and V. (signature illegible) (Manuscript), 21 July 1938.

102. For example: Letter by Angel Garcia Bermejo (Manuscript), 20 July 1938; Letter by Solariego Perez and Angel Mendez Sanchez (Manuscript), 27 July 1938; Letter by Francisco Mérida (Manuscript), 4 August 1938; Letter by R. Garcia (Manuscript), 18 June 1938; Letter by Rafael Pérez Calero (Manuscript), 18 July 1938.

103. Juan M. Fernández Soria, "El frente de la cultura en el Ejército," *Historia 16,* num. 17.

104. Cited in M. Tuñon de Lara, "La cultura durante la Guerra Civil," *Historia 16,* num. 27, 18.

105. Juan M. Fernández Soria, "Política de Bibliotecas en la República durante la Guerra Civil," *Perspectiva Contemporánea. España. Siglo XX* 1, 1 (October 1988); Manuel Tuñón de Lara (ed.), *Comunicación, cultura y política durante la II República y la Guerra Civil* (Bilbao: Servicio de Publicaciones de la Universidad del País Vasco, 1990).

106. Maria Teresa León, *Memoria de la melancolía* (Sant Vicenç dels Horts: Círculo de Lectores, 1979), 38.

107. Serge Salaün, "Poetas 'de oficio'y vocaciones incipientes durante la Guerra de España," *Creación y público en la literatura española* (Madrid: Castalia, 1974) and *La poesía de la guerra de España* (Madrid: Castalia, 1985).

108. María Teresa León, *Memoria de la melancolía* and *Juego Limpio* (Barcelona: Seix Barral, 1987). See also: M. Inmaculada Monforte Gutiez, "La labor cultural de María Teresa León," *Las mujeres y la Guerra Civil Española. 111 Jornadas de estudios monográficos, Salamanca, octubre 1989* (Madrid: Ministerio de Cultura, 1991); Antonina Rodrigo, *Mujeres de España. Las silenciadas* (Barcelona: Plaza y Janés, 1979).

109. Rosario Calleja Martín, "Mujeres de la industria de espectáculos. Madrid (1936–1939)," *Las mujeres y la Guerra Civil española.*

110. León, *Memoria de la melancolía*, 38–41.

111. Calleja Martín, "Mujeres de la industria de espectáculos."

112. Interview with Antonia García, Barcelona, 29 December 1983.

113. Interview with Rosario Sánchez, Barcelona, October 1987..

114. Nash, *Mujer y movimiento obrero*, 254–256. "L'Enquesta de TREBALL a les dones de Catalunya," *Treball*, 28 December 1938.

115. Margarita Nelken, "Del front i de la reraguarda," *Treball*, 19 April 1938.

116. "A la reraguarda – digué Dolors Piera – cada dona ha d'ésser un soldat." L`Assemblea de la 'Unió de Dones' del Districte IV, *Treball*, 8 June 1938.

117. Alvar Bernado,"Les dones a les trinxeres de la producció. Imperatius de l'hora present," *Treball*, 7 July 1938. "Les dones a l'avantguarda de la producció," *Treball*, 12 April 1938.

118. "Mujeres stajanovistas y municiones," *Claridad*, 30 April 1937; "El front del treball, Unió de Dones de Catalunya homenatja a tres heroïnes de la producció," *Treball*, 31 July 1938. Maruixa Ortiz, "Tallers de guerra: llurs obreres," *Noies Muchachas*, 16 August 1938. On the Russian Stakhanovite Movement, see: Vladimir Shlapentokh, "The Stakhanovite Movement: Changing Perceptions over Fifty Years," *Journal of Contemporary History* 23 (1988).

119. "Decrets," *Diari oficial de la Generalitat de Catalunya*, 23 July 1938; "Obreras de choque. Las muchachas en el camino de la victoria. Tres conductas ejemplares," *Noies Muchachas*, Num. 4 (16 August 1938).

120. "Les dones, en peu de guerra," *Treball*, 26 February 1937.

121. Maribel Larrañaga, "La mujer debe vivir el momento presente," *Mujeres* (Bilbao), 24 April 1937; "100,000 Dones," *Companya*, 15 June 1937; "La incorporación de las mujeres al trabajo," *Mujeres Libres*, Num. 12.

122. *Treball. Organ Central del Partit Socialista Unificat de Catalunya*, 26 February 1937.

123. "Imperiosa necesidad del momento: ¡Capacitación femenina!," *Mujeres* (Bilbao), 22 May 1937.

124. Letter addressed to Sr. Coronel Comte. Militar de la Plaza de Madrid by *Mujeres Antifascistas*. Sector Norte. Madrid, 30 September 1937. (Manuscript)

125. "Las compañeras de la "Agrupación de Mujeres Libres" piden que se las adiestre en el trabajo para, llegada la ocasión, poder substituir a los hombres en los lugares de producción," *Tierra y Libertad*, 5 December 1936; "¡Mujeres! Por la defensa de Madrid. Por la defensa de la Revolución," *Tierra y Libertad*, 5 November 1936.

126. "Editorial," *Companya*, Num. 18.

127. "A las mujeres antifascistas," *Claridad*, 3 September 1936.

128. Jean Bethke Elshtain, *Women and War* (Brighton: The Harvester Press, 1987); Anna Bravo, "Per una storia delle donne: donne contadine e prima guerra mondiale," *Società Historia*, Num. 10. 1980. F. Thébaud, *La femme au temps de la guerre de 14* (Paris: Stock, 1986); J. Montgomery Byles, "Women's Experience of World War One: Suffragists, Pacifists and Poets."

129. See images on women and work in war posters and propaganda in Mary Nash, *Las mujeres en la Guerra Civil* (Madrid: Ministerio de Cultura, 1989), 75–93.

130. "Los trabajadores de G. M. colectivizada a las mujeres antifascistas." (Pamphlet)

131. G. Braybon, *Women Workers of the First World War* (London: Croom Helm, 1981); S. Gilbert, "Gender–charged Munitions: The Language of World War I Munitions Reports," *Women's Studies International Forum*, Vol. 11, Num. 2 (1988); Richard Wall and Jay Winter, *The Upheaval of War. Family, Work and Welfare in Europe, 1914–1918* (Cambridge: Cambridge University Press, 1988).

132. Josep María Bricall, *Política económica de la Generalitat (1936–1939)* (Barcelona: Ed. 62, 1970) and "La economía española (1936–1939)," in Manuel Tuñon de Lara, et al., *La guerra*

civil española. 50 años después; M. González Portilla and J. M. Garmendia, *La guerra civil en el País Vasco. Política y Economía* (Madrid: Siglo XXI, 1988).

133. W. Bernecker, *Colectividades y revolución social: el anarquismo en la guerra civil española. 1936–1939* (Barcelona: Crítica, 1982); J. Casanova, "Las colectivizaciones," *Historia 16,* Vol. 16; A. Monjo and C. Vega, *Els treballadors i la guerra civil. Història d'una indústria catalana col. lectivitzada* (Barcelona: Ed. Empúries, 1986).

134. Bricall, *Política económica;* and "La economía española." J. M. Santacreu Soler, "Cambio económico y conflicto bélico. Transformaciones económicas en la retaguardia republicana (Alicante 1936–1939)." (Ph.D. diss., University of Alicante, 1988) and *L'economia valenciana durant la guera civil. Protagonisme industrial i estancament agrari* (Valencia: Edicions Alfons el Magnànim, 1992).

135. Alvaro Soto Carmona, "Cuantificación de la mano de obra femenina (1860–1930)," *La mujer en la Historia de España (siglos XVI–XX)* (Madrid: Universidad Autónoma, 1984); Antoni Castells, "La colectivización y socialización de la industria y los servicios en Barcelona Ciudad y Provincia. Las agrupaciones o concentraciones de empresa," Juan García Durán Prize, University of Barcelona, 1986; María Gloria Núñez Pérez, *Trabajadoras en la Segunda República.*

136. Santacreu Soler, "Cambio económico" and *L'economia Valenciana.*

137. Dolors Piera, *La aportación femenina en la guerra de la independencia,* 5; Angelita Santamaría, *Tareas de la mujer en el partido y en la producción,* 6–7; "Les dones exigim el llloc que ens pertoca en la producció, *Treball,* 1 March 1938.

138. "Conclusiones aprobadas sobre el tema: Trabajos realizados por la mujer para la guerra e incorporación al trabajo mediante su capacitación," *Mujeres* (Bilbao), num. 23 (13 November 1937).

139. "Discurs de 'Pasionaria' en la Gran Assemblea d'Informació del P.S.U.," *Treball,* 1 March 1938.

140. "Informa Emilia Elías. Nosotros debemos decir al Gobierno que vamos a darle todo por el trabajo y por la guerra!," *Pasionaria,* 13 November 1937. This was also the point of view expressed by the Catalan communist leader Dolors Piera: "El Front del Treball Unió de Dones de Catalunya homenatja tres heroïnes de la producció," *Treball,* 31 July 1938.

141. Angelita Santamaría, *Tareas de la mujer en el partido y en la producción,* 6–7.

142. "Aliança Nacional de Dones de Catalunya. La primera Conferéncia Nacional de Dones del PSUC," *Treball,* 16 March 1937.

143. "Contribuyamos a la victoria. Nuestra Conferencia nos ha marcado el camino a seguir," *Muchachas,* Num. 2.

144. "Conferencia de las muchachas de Madrid. Intervención de los sectores. Sector Oeste," *Muchachas,* Num. 2.

145. "Acciones contra la prostitución," *Mujeres Libres,* Num. 11.

146. Pilar Grangel, "En vez de crítica, soluciones," *Mujeres Libres,* num. 13.

147. Decree of the sixteenth of June 1937 signed by Luis Companys, president, and Rafael Vidiella, minister of Labor and Public Works. *Diari Oficial de la Genralitat de Catalunya,* 18 June 1937.

148. Rosa Robert, "La dona i els problemes de la guerra," *Treball,* 26 January 1938.

149. "Vers l'alliberaciò definitiva de la dona," *Companya,* Num. 8 (19 July 1937); "Conclusiones aprobadas sobre el tema: Trabajos realizados por la mujer para la guerra e incorporación al trabajo mediante su capacitación," *Pasionaria,* Num. 23 (13 November 1937). "¿Hasta cuando?," *Mujeres Libres,* Num. 10. "Por nuestra incorporación a la vida activa y productora," *Muchachas,* 4 September 1937.

150. "A igual treball, igual salari," *Treball,* 30 January 1938.

151. "Editorial. Consignes de la Uniò de Dones de Catalunya en el dia del nen. Trenta–vuit guarderies per al 8 de març," *Companya,* Num. 13; Letter: Comité de Mujeres Antifascistas. Cartagena. Signed by Luz Lafuente, Secretaria General, 4 May 1937 (Manuscript). In Catalonia there were also official initiatives to provide nurseries: "Decreto," Barcelona, 20 January 1936. Signed by the Governor General of Catalonia, Fèlix Escalas, and the minister of Health and Social Assistance, Felip Bertran i Guëll. *Diari Oficial de la Generalitat de Catalunya,* 23 February 1936.

152. J. C., "La incorporació de la dona a les indústries de guerra," *Treball,* 17 June 1938.

153. *Informe presentado por la Agrupación de Mujeres Antifascistas de Gandía l C. Provincial.* Signed. Por el Comité. La Secretaria General, Gloria Morell. Gandía, 9 April 1938. (Manuscript)

154. *Acta de la Reunión extraordinaria celebrada por este sub– comité del dia 11 de febrero de 1939. Las regionales: Centro– Levante, Locales: Madrid–Valencia. Delegaciones del comité peninsular FAI y sub–comités nacionales CNT* (Typed Manuscript); Mujeres Libres, *Informe que esta Federación eleva a los Comités Nacionales del Movimiento Libertario y a los Delegados del Pleno del mismo. Federación Nacional de Mujeres Libres.* Signed: Comité Nacional de Mujeres Libres. La Secretaria, Barcelona, September 1938 (Typed Manuscript); Report: "Las Mujeres Antifascistas de Jativa os mandan un saludo y un abrazo fraternal a todas las compañeras aquí reunidas," *Jativa,* July 1938. Signed: La Secretaria. A. Garcia (Typed Document). "Conferencia de las Muchachas de Madrid. Intervención de los Sectores. Sector Oeste," *Muchachas,* num. 2. Also, Nash, *Mujer y movimiento obrero,* 97–109.

155. For example, in Alicante by the end of 1938, over 40 percent of the active population had been conscripted: Santacreu Soler, "Cambio económico y conflicto bélico," 64–67.

156. Gabriel Cardona, "Las operaciones militares"; Tuñón de Lara, Aróstegui, Viñas, et al., *La guerra civil española 50 años después.*

157. Lucia Sauger, "La incorporación de la mujer al trabajo y los sindicatos," *Trabajadoras,* Num. 2 (1 April 1938).

158. "La reunión del Comité Nacional de la U.G.T. En la resolución aprobada sobre el segundo punto – Industrias de guerra – se abordan los problemas básicos de la producción," *Claridad,* 30 September 1938.

159. As has been mentioned above, the war also provoked a new line of eugenics arguments such as the alleged argument to oblige women militians to withdraw from the fronts, proposed by Félix Martí Ibáñez. On sex reform, see: Thomas Glick, "Psicoanálisis, reforma sexual y política en la España de entre guerras," *Estudios de Historia Social,* Num. 16–17 (January–June 1981); Mary Nash, "El neomaltusianismo anarquista y los conocimientos populares del control de natalidad en España" and "Social Eugenics and Natonalist Race Hygiene in Early Twentieth Century Spain," *History of European Ideas,* Vol. 15, Nums. 4–6 (1992).

160. Mark B. Adams (ed.), *The Wellborn Science. Eugenics in Germany, France, Brazil and Russia* (Oxford: Oxford University Press, 1990); William H. Schneider, *Quality and Quantity. The Quest for Biological Regeneration in Twentieth–century France* (Cambridge: Cambridge University Press, 1990); Richard A. Soloway, *Demography and Degeneration. Eugenics and the Declining Birthrate in Twentieth Century Britain* (London: The University of North Carolina Press, 1990); Paul Weindling, *Health, Race and German Politics between National Unification and Nazism 1870–1945* (Cambridge: Cambridge University Press, 1991).

161. Mariano Cardona Rosell, "En torno a los acuerdos del Pleno Nacional de Regionales de la CNT," in section "Incorporación de la mujer al trabajo," *Tierra y Libertad,* 8 October 1938.

162. Mariano Cardona Rosell, "En torno a los acuerdos del Pleno Nacional de Regionales de la CNT."

163. The communist newspaper *Treball* ran a series of articles on women's work in late December 1938 and early January 1939: "L'enquesta de TREBALL a les dones de Catalunya," *Treball,* 28 and 30 December 1938, 4 January 1939.

164. "Decreto de 29 de agosto creando el Comité de Auxilio Femenino," *Mujeres* (Madrid), 2 September 1936; Comité Nacional de Mujeres Antifascistas, *Comisión de auxilio femenino del Ministerio de Defensa Nacional de la República* (s.l., 1938). For a discussion, see Nash, *Mujer y Movimiento obrero,* 254–256.

165. Decree signed by Manuel Azaña, president of the republican government, and Juan Negrín López, minister of national defense. *Gaceta de la República,* 14 January 1939.

166. Decree published: *Diari Oficial de la Generalitat.* Signed by the Conseller d'Economía, Joan Comorera, 21 January 1939.

167. The Basque Government also developed some training programs. However, they were not on the scale of the Catalan experience. See: "El problema femenino visto por nuestros Consejeros del Gobierno Provisional de Euzkadi," *Mujeres. Organo del Comité de Mujeres*

Contra la Guerra y el Fascismo (Bilbao), 24 April 1937.

168. Decree signed by the First Chancellor and Interim Minister of Culture, Josep Tarradellas, the Chancellor of Defence, Felip Díaz i Sandino, and the Chancellor of Labor and Public Works, Miquel Valdés. *Diari Oficial de la Generalitat,* 22 November 1936.

169. Decree signed by the president of the Generalitat, LLuís Companys, and the Chancellor of Labor and Public Works, Rafael Vidiella. *Diari Oficial de la Generalitat,* 13 July 1937.

170. See, for example, the mixed School of Apprenticeship and Professional Formation in Baluarte organized by the Metallurgy Union of the UGT. "Enseñanza popular. Cómo se capacitan profesionalmente los metalúrgicos del mañana," *Claridad,* 28 November 1938. See also the School for Army Gunsmiths, which trained twenty–five women apprentices in Madrid, or the School for Mechanics in Aviation, which was to give nine–month courses to women: Lorenzo, "La capacitación de la mujer en la guerra. Como nuestras muchachas madrileñas aprendan para ocupar un puesto en la fábrica," *Claridad,* 20 December 1937; *Circular No.1 A los Comités Provinciales y Locales.* Signed: Por el Comité Regional "Mujeres Libres" de Levante, La Delegada de Trabajo, Concha Miñana. (Typed Manuscript)

171. Decree signed by LLuís Companys, president of the Generalitat, and Rafael Vidiella, Minister of Labor and Public Works, 10 July 1937. *Diari Oficial de la Generalitat de Catalunya,* 13 July 1937.

172. Decree signed by the Minister of Economy in charge of the Department of Labor and Public Works, Joan Comorera. Barcelona, 3 November 1937. *Diari Oficial de la Generalitat de Catalunya,* 11 November 1937.

173. For example, unions in the Turrón (nougat) industry in Alicante favored wives, widows, and daughters to substitute the male workers at the warfronts. Santacreu Soler, "Cambio económico y conflicto bélico."

174. For example, only women aged between seventeen and twenty–four were allowed to register for courses in the School of Aviation Mechanics: *A los Comités Provinciales y Locales.* Signed: El Comité Regional "Mujeres Libres" de Levante. La Delegada de Trabajo. Concha Miñana. (Typed Manuscript)

175. Decree signed by the president of the Generalitat, Lluís Companys and the Minister of Labor and Public Works, Rafael Vidiella. Barcelona, 21 July 1937. *Diari Oficial de la Generalitat de Catalunya,* 23 July 1937.

176. Representatives were from the following organizations: Confederación Regional del Trabajo de Cataluña, Secretariat de Cataluña de la Unión General de Trabajadores, Partido Socialista Unificado de Cataluña, Esquerra Republicana de Catalunya, Unió de Rabassaires, and Acció Catalana.

177. "Ordres," *Diari Oficial de la Generalitat de Catalunya,* 14 December 1938.

178. See Nash, *Mujer y movimiento obrero,* 185.

179. *Diari Oficial de la Generalitat de Catalunya,* 11 November 1937.

180. The women representatives were: Maria Rubí i Tarrasa (Textile), Pietat Ferrer i Garriga (Hygiene and Health) for the UGT, and Aurea Cuadrado Castillón as the CNT representative for Hygiene and Health. *Diari Oficial de la Generalitat,* 22 February 1938.

181. Dr. Emili Mira i López was nominated president, Ignasi Juvés i Mariol, treasurer, and Carles Sala i Franqueza, secretary of the Institute in July 1937. *Diari Oficial de la Generalitat de Catalunya,* 28 July 1937.

182. "Conselleria de Treball i Obres Públiques. Ha estat creat l'Institut d'Adaptació Professional de la Dona," *Treball,* 14 July 1937; "Educació professional de la dona," *Treball,* 15 July 1937; "Amb un formidable entusiasme, les dones responen a la mobilització del treball," *Treball,* 13 April 1938; "En un mes es necessiten vint mil dones," *Companya,* 1 July 1937. "L'Institut d'Adaptació Professional de la Dona," *Companya,* 6 November 1937.

183. Data from *Diari Oficial de la Generalitat de Catalunya,* 6 January 1927; 24 January 1937; 5 February 1937; 18 February 1937; 11 March 1937; 7 April 1937; 15 April 1937; 2 May 1937; 23 May 1937; 22 June 1937; 27 June 1937; 15 July 1937; 7 August 1937; 20 August 1937; 10 September 1937.

184. Enriqueta Gallinat,"Una visita al Instituto de Adaptación Profesional de la Mujer," *Mi Revista,* 1 January 1938.

185. "A l'Institut d'Adaptació Professional de la Dona. Quinze mil noies disposades a subsitutir l'home a la reraguarda," *Treball,* 7 July 1938; "Cinco mil mujeres movilizadas por el "Institut d'Adaptació Professional de la Dona," *Trabajadoras,* 8 March 1938.

186. Amadeu Bernadó, "Dones que treballaran per a la guerra. Una visita a la Primera Escola de Capacitació de la Dona a Catalunya," *Treball,* 10 January 1939.

187. The Minister of Justice, Andreu Nin, ordered women to be in charge of the female penitentiary organizations in Catalonia. "Ordre," *Diari Oficial de la Generalitat de Catalunya,* 15 December 1936. Several vacancies were covered between 1937 and 1938, and some women were also introduced into the administration of Justice.

188. L'Assemblea de Barcelona de la Unió de Dones de Catalunya," *Treball,* 15 January 1939.

189. "La dona catalana de cara a la guerra," *Treball,* 29 December 1938.

190. *Diari Oficial de la Generalitat de Catalunya,* 18 November 1938; 10 January 1939.

191. "Las obreras del hogar al servicio de la guerra," *Claridad,* 20 September 1937; "A las camaradas del servicio doméstico," *LLuita,* 3 March 1937.

192. Under the Second Republic, in the thirties, legislative measures had been passed to avoid wage discrimination. However, in practice, it was hardly applied. See Nash, "Treball, conflictivitat social i estratègies de resistència"; Núñez Pérez, *Trabajadoras en la Segunda República.*

193. "Ordres," *Diari Oficial de la Generalitat de Catalunya,* 16 June 1938.

194. "Jurats Mixtos de Treball de les Comarques Gironines," *Diari Oficial de la Generalitat,* 20 August 1937.

195. See "Bases de Treball" published in the *Butlletí Oficial de la Generalitat de Catalunya,* 1938.

196. For example, in retail industries women workers, shop assistants, and telephone operators were awarded a 25 percent wage hike while wages for male occupations were increased 30 percent. See: "Treball. Ordres," *Diari Oficial de la Generalitat de Catalunya,* 5 March 1938.

197. Anna Monjo and Carme Vega, *Els treballadors i la guerra civil. Història d'ùna indústria catalana collectivitzada* (Barcelona: Editorial Empúries, 1986), 87.

198. Blanca Deusdad, "La dona obrera durant la Guerra Civil a Vilanova," *Primera Edició,* Num. 2 (July 1988).

199. Santacreu Soler, "Cambio económico y conflicto bélico," 82–83.

200. For example, in the government–run farms under the Agrarian Reform Institute, wage differentials of almost 50 percent were maintained. Santacreu Soler, "Cambio económico y conflicto bélico," 83. See also: María Chicote Serna, "El trabajo de las mujeres en el ámbito rural de la provinicia de Madrid, 1930–1945," in *Las mujeres y la Guerra Civil española.*

201. Julian Casanova, "Las colectivizaciones," La Guerra Civil, *Historia 16,* Vol. 16. Bernecker, *Colectividades y revolución social;* Luis Garrido, *Colectividades agrarias en Andalucía: Jaen, 1931–1939* (Madrid: Siglo XXI, 1979).

202. "¿Hasta cuando?," *Mujeres Libres,* Num. 10; "Conclusiones aprobadas sobre el tema trabajos realizados por la mujer para la guerra e incorporación al trabajo mediante su capacitación," *Pasionaria,* 13 November 1937; Febus, "Clausura de la Segona Conferencia Nacional de Dones Antifeixistes," *Treball,* 3 November 1937.

203. "La incorporación de las mujeres àl trabajo," *Mujeres Libres,* num. 12.

204. Michael Seidman, "Towards a History of Workers' Resistance to Work: Paris and Barcelona during the French Popular Front and the Spanish Revolution, 1936–1938," *Journal of Contemporary History* 23 (April 1988); Monjo and Vega, *Els treballadors i la guerra civil,* 166–168.

205. Alvar Bernado, "Imperatius de l'hora present. Les dones a les trinxeres de la producció," *Treball,* 7 July 1938; Joan Vallespinos, "Isabel Cais, l'única dona que treballa amb oxigen i gas d'acetilè," *Treball,* 3 November 1938.

206. Maria Carmen García Nieto, "Las mujeres en la defensa y en la resistencia de Madrid." (Unpublished Paper)

207. Alvar Bernado, "Imperatius de l'hora present. Les dones a les trinxeres de la producció," *Treball,* 7 July 1938; "Tallers de guerra: llurs obreres," *Noies Muchachas,* 16 August 1938; Joan Vallespinos, "Isabel Cais, l'única dona que treballa amb oxigen i gas d'acetilè," *Treball,* 3

November 1938. Interview with Concha Pérez, Barcelona, 16 June 1981; Interview with Petra Cuevas, Madrid, 4 October 1981.

208. "Llibertat Picornell. Davant la Segona Conferència de Dones del P.S.U. Metallúrgiques, de cara a la guerra," *Treball,* 29 September 1938. A newspaper report gave the unlikely figure of over 60 percent females in the textile industry and 40 percent in the chemical, sugar, and tanning industries by November 1937. Official figures are not available to document the number of women workers in industries. Lorenzo, "Las muchachas madrileñas trabajan para la guerra," *Claridad,* 23 November 1937.

209. García Nieto, "Las mujeres en la defensa y en la resistencia de Madrid."

210. Illustration on the first page of *Hombres Libres. Organo de la Federación Provincial de Sindicatos Unicos de Granada,* 20 August 1937.

211. "Urge realizar la 'auténtica' política de guerra que señaló la C.N.T.," *Hombres Libres,* 24 September 1937.

212. The U.G.T. had two other big workshops in Barcelona. Francesc de F. Sòria, "Una visita als tallers del vestit de guerra de la U.G.T.," *Treball,* 29 November 1936; Antoni Ballester, "La dona i la guerra. Les dones del Sindicat de l'Art del Vestir, model i exemple de la reraguarda," *Treball,* 26 February 1937.

213. Nash, *Mujer y movimiento obrero,* 254–255.

CHAPTER 5

1. Josep Maria Bricall, *Política económica de la Generalitat (1936– 1939). Evolució i formes de la producció industrial* (Barcelona: Edicions 62, 1970) and "La economia española (1936–1939)," in Tuñon de Lara, Aróstegui, Viñas, et al., *La guerra civil española. 50 años después;* González, Portilla, and Garmendia, *La guerra civil en el País Vasco. Política y Economia;* J. M. Santacreu Soler, "Cambio económico y conflicto bélico. Transformaciones económicas en la retaguardia republicana."

2. Testimony by Carmen Rodriguez, Salamanca, October 1989.

3. "Victoria Kent fa una crida emocionant a les dones," *Treball,* 29 July 1936.

4. "Ropa de abrigo para los combatientes," *Claridad,* 28 December 1937.

5. Maria de los Angeles Arranz, "Los abastos en la Guerra Civil," *Historia 16,* Num. 16; José Miguel Santacreu Soler, "Cambio económico y conflicto bélico. Transformaciones económicas en la retaguardia republicana.

6. Ramona Via, *Nit de Reis. Diari d'una infermera de 14 anys* (Barcelona: Club Editor, 1984), 34. Also: Maria Carmen García Nieto, "El trabajo 'no pagado' de las mujeres madrileñas durante la Guerra Civil." Paper presented at the I Colloqui d'Història de la Dona, Barcelona, October 1986.

7. Arranz, "Los abastos en la Guerra Civil."

8. Jesús Noguer–Moré, *Nuestra alimentación en tiempos de escasez* (Barcelona: Biblioteca Higia, 1937).

9. Noguer–Moré, *Nuestra alimentación,* 14.

10. Noguer–Moré, *Nuestra alimentación,* 13.

11. F. Grande Covián, "Deficiencias vitamínicas en Madrid durante la Guerra Civil: una reminiscencia," *Los médicos y la medicina en la Guerra Civil española* (Madrid: Monografías Beecham, 1986), 63.

12. Grande Covián, "Deficiencias vitamínicas en Madrid," 64.

13. Nieves Castro, *Una vida para un ideal. Recuerdos de una militante comunista* (Madrid: Ediciones de la Torre, 1981), 46.

14. Juli Canut i Capdevila, "Les memòries de Josepa Puig," *L'Erol, Revista Cultural del Berguedà,* 6 September 1983; Blanca Deusdad, "La dona obrera durant la Guerra Civil a Vilanova," *Primera Edició* 2 (July 1988).

15. García Nieto, "El trabajo 'no pagado' de las mujeres madrileñas durante la Guerra Civil."

16. Interview with L. A. by Elisabet Ibáñez, Lucia Liria, Mireiea Ribera, and Goretti Triquell, Granollers, June 1988.

17. *Proyecto de Reglamento para la Fundación y Funcionamiento de la "Caja Nacional de Subsidio Familiar por Movilización Militar,"* Barcelona, 21 September 1938. (Typed Manuscript)

18. Temma Kaplan, "Female Consciousness and Collective Action: The Case of Barcelona, 1910–1918." Mary Nash, "Treball, conflictivitat social i estratègies de resistència: la dona obrera a la Catalunya Contemporània," in Mary Nash (ed.), *Més enllà del silenci. Les dones a la història de Catalunya.*

19. Enric Ucelay da Cal, "El concepte de 'vida quotidiana'i l'estudi de la Guerra Civil," *Acàcia,* Num. 1 (1990), 67.

20. Via, *Nit de Reis,* 34.

21. Angel Samblancat, "La República de los Comités," *Mi Revista,* 1 March 1937.

22. Manuel Cruells, *Els fets de Maig. Barcelona 1937* (Barcelona: Editorial Joventut, 1970).

23. Josep Maria Bricall, *Política econòmica de la Generalitat (1936–1939),* 33–35.

24. Ejercito de tierra. Subsecretaria. Order num. 11523. Signed by Negrín, Barcelona, 11 June 1938.

25. Decree 19 October 1938 signed by El Conseller de Governació i Assistència Social, Antoni M°. Sbert. *Diari Oficial de la Generalitat de Catalunya,* Monday, 24 October 1938. The other members of the Commission were: Assistencia Infantil (Institut d'Acció Social universitària i escolar de Catalunya), Assistència Municipal de Barcelona, Socors Roig Internacional, Ajut Infantil de Reraguarda, and Pro Infància Obrera.

26. "Decret que organitza l'assistencia integral dels refugiats de guerra." Signed by Lluis Companys, El Conseller de Governació i Assistència Social, Antoni María Sbert, El Conseller de Cultura, Carles Pi i Sunyer, el Conseller de Finances, Josep Tarradellas, El Conseller de Treball i Obres Públiques, Rafael Vidiella. Barcelona, 14 August 1937.

27. Federica Montseny, *Mi experiencia en el Ministerio de Sanidad y asistencia Social. Conferencia pronunciada el 6 de junio de 1937 en el Teatro Apolo* (Valencia: Comisión de Propaganda y Prensa del Comité Nacional de la C.N.T. Valencia, 1937).

28. Federica Montseny, "La sanidad y la asistencia social durante la Guerra Civil," *Los médicos y la medicina en la Guerra Civil española* (Madrid: Monografías Beecham, 1986), 95.

29. Dr. Amparo Poch y Gascón was director of Social Assistance and Dr. Mercedes Maestre was subsecretary at the Ministry.

30. For example, Gloria Prades was the vice president of the Catalan Committee of Aid for the Basque Country. See: Antonina Rodriguez, "Estudio de una mujer sindicalista," in *Las mujeres y la Guerra Civil española.*

31. Decree signed by Lluis Companys, Barcelona, 18 January 1938. *Diari Oficial de la Generalitat de Catalunya,* 20 January 1938.

32. Cristina Rimbau i Andreu, "L'Obra assistencial de la Generalitat de Catalunya. 1931–1936" (M.A. diss., University of Barcelona, 1985); and "Una aportació a la reflexió sobre l'organització dels serveis socials," *Revista de Treball Social,* vol. 107, num. 9 (1987).

33. "Les dones del P.S.U. i el problema dels refugiats," *Treball,* 23 January 1938; Maria Teresa Andrade, "Las colonias de refugiados del Socorro Rojo del P.O.U.M.," *Socorro Rojo,* 15 December 1936.

34. *Agrupación de Refugiados Asturianos. Secretariado Femenino.* Signed *Por el Comité* Purificación Tomàs. (Typed Manuscript)

35. "El treball voluntari femení. Les refugiades han d'aportar el seu ajut a aquesta gran obra antifeixista," *Treball,* 23 May 1937; Llorença García de Riu, " L'actuació de la dona en la guerra. 'Treball voluntari femení'. Departament de la Generalitat de Catalunya," *Treball,* 5 November 1938.

36. Frida Knight, Memoirs, 125 (Typed Manuscript). I would like to thank Jon Arrizabalaga for drawing my attention to this manuscript. Frida Knight (Stewart) was later an active member of the underground resistance movement in France during World War II. See: Frida Stewart, *Dawn Escape* (London: Everybody's Books, s.d.).

37. "Copia de los oficios remitidos por la Delegación Centro–Sur del Consejo Nacional de la Infancia evacuada al Presidente de este Consejo en Barceña." Signed: El Delegado, Madrid, 26

September 1938. (Typed Manuscript)

38. "Copia de los oficios remitidos por la Delegación Centro–Sur del Consejo Nacional de la Infancia evacuada al Presidente de este Consejo en Barceña." Signed: El Delegado, Madrid, 26 September 1938. (Typed Manuscript)

39. "Sección de Higiene Infantil. Al Director General de Sanidad." Signed: El Jefe de la Sección de Higiene Infantil, Isidoro Bajo Mateos, Barcelona, 27 June 1938. (Typed Manuscript)

40. "Informe de mi gestión al frente de la Secretaria General del consejo Nacional de la Infancia Evacuada." Signed: Fran (Gómez?), Barcelona, 5 December 1938. (Typed Manuscript)

41. *Institut d'Acció Social Universitaria i Escolar, Pro Infancia Obrera, Segell Pro– Infancia,* and *Ajut Infantil de Reraguarda.*

42. Maria Dolors Lasalle, "Que fa la República pels infants," *Companya,* 29 January 1938.

43. The head of the section of child hygiene denounced the desperate state of his institution in June 1938. "Sección de Higiene Infantil. Al Director General de Sanidad." Signed: El Jefe de la sección de higiene Infantil, Isidoro Bajo Mateos, Barcelona, 27 June 1938. (Typed Manuscript)

44. Tanischka, "Parlant amb Matilde Huici. Com compren l 'infant els pobles nous," *Companya,* 1 July 1937.

45. Margarita Nelken, *Niños de hoy, hombres de mañana* (Madrid: Ediciones del S.R.I., s.d.).

46. M.P.E., "La dona que treballa en el transport," *Companya,* Num. 18.

47. "L'Assistència Revolucionaria. La Llar de l'Infant. Una obra modèlica de les dones de la U.G.T. i de la C.N.T.," *Treball,* 16 August 1936; see also, *Revista S.I.A.S.,* Nums. 2 and 3 (April–May, June–July 1937).

48. M., "La Casa del Nen, obra de solidaritat conjunta entre les dones de la U.G.T. i de la C.N.T.," *Treball,* 13 August 1936; "L'Assistència Revolucionaria. La Llar de l'Infant. Una obra modèlica de les dones de la U.G.T. i de la C.N.T.," *Treball,* 16 August 1936.

49. "Les llars per a infants creades per Assistència Infantil," *Foc Nou. Revista Mensual publicada sota el patronatge de l'Ateneu Obrer,* January 1938. (Italics are not in original text.)

50. Institut D'Acció Social Universitaria i Escolar de Catalunya, *Assistència Infantil. L'obra realitzada i l'obra a realitzar* (Barcelona: Institut d'Acció Social Universitaria i Escolar de Catalunya, s.d.).

51. Dr. F. Martí Ibáñez, "Sanidad, Asistencia social y Eugenesia en la Revolución española," *Estudios,* Num. 160 (January 1937).

52. Ramón Jordi González, "Puntos de vista y conceptos anarquistas sobre sanidad durante el período 27 de setiembre 1936 al 24 de marzo de 1938," *Offarm,* Vol 4, Num. 5 (May 1985) and Vol 4, Num. 6 (June 1985); Dr. F. Martí Ibáñez, "Sanidad, Asistencia social y Eugenesia en la Revolución española," *Estudios,* Num. 160 (January 1937); Frederica Montseny, *Mi experiencia enel Ministerio de Sanidad y Asistencia Social.*

53. Martí Ibáñez, "Sanidad, Asistencia social y Eugenesia."

54. Ana Pibernat, "Mis Memorias." (Manuscript)

55. Ana Pibernat, "Mis Memorias." (Manuscript)

56. "Sanitat i Assistència Social. Decret," *Diari Oficial de la Generalitat de Catalunya,* 12 June 1937.

57. E. H., "La Escuela de Enfermeras del Comité Nacional de Mujeres Antifascistas en la Facultad de Medicina de Valencia," *Mujeres. Revista Mensual del Comité Nacional de Mujeres Antifascistas,* (Valencia), October 1937.

58. "Recogiendo una inspiración. Enfermeras de guerra," *Mujeres. Organo del Comite de Mujeres antra la Guerra y el Fascismo* (Bilbao), 17 April 1937; "!Haceos enfermeras populares. Los cursillos de enfermeras de Sanidad Militar," *Claridad,* 15 May 1937.

59. Ramona Via, *Nit de reis.*

60. Ana Pibernat, *Mis Memorias.* (Manuscript)

61. Generalitat de Catalunya, *Les noves institucions jurídiques i culturals per a la dona. Setmana d'activitats femenines. Febrer 1937* (Barcelona: Departament de Cultura, Generalitat de Catalunya, 1937).

62. "Recogiendo una inspiración. Enfermeras de guerra," *Mujeres. Organo del Comité de Mujeres contra la Guerra y el Fascismo* (Bilbao), 17 April 1937.

63. "Sanitat i Assistència Social. Decret," *Diari Oficial de la Generalitat de Catalunya,* 12 June 1937.

64. "Sanitat i Assistència Social. Decret," *Diari Oficial de la Generalitat de Catalunya,* 12 June 1937.

65. Ramiro Ramos, "Combatamos la prostitución. Buscando la raíz del problema," *Hombres Libres,* 3 December 1937.

66. Eduardo Vicente, "Las enfermedades venéreas son el fascismo de la naturaleza." Milicias de la Cultura. Ministerio de Instrucción Pública y Sanidad. This poster also circulated as a postcard.

67. Matilde Cuevas de la Cruz and Luis Otero Carvajal, "Prostitución y legislación en el siglo XIX. Aproximación a la consideración social de la prostituta." Maria Carmen García–Nieto Paris, (ed.), *Ordenamiento jurídico y realidad social de las mujeres. Siglos XVI a XX* (Madrid: Universidad Autónoma de Madrid, 1986), 247–258; Mary Nash, *Mujer, familia y trabajo en España. 1875–1936* (Barcelona: Anthropos, 1983), 29–39, 255–296. Jean Louis Guereña, "La réglementation de la prostitution en Espagne aux XIX– XXe siècles" in Carrasco, *La prostitution.*

68. Antonio Peyri, *La lluita anitvenèria a Catalunya l'any 1934* (Barcelona: Generalitat de Catalunya, s.d.), 6; Nash, "Social Eugenics and Nationalist Race Hygiene in Early Twentieth Century Spain"; R. Alvarez Peláez and R. Huertas García–Alejo, *Criminales o locos? Dos peritajes psiquiátricos del Dr. Gonzalo R. Lafora* (Madrid: CSIC, 1987); Glick, "Psicoanálisis, reforma sexual y política en la España de entre guerras."

69. *Un proyecto de la República. La abolición de la prostitución* (S.L. Imp. M. Pérez de Rozas, s.d.), 13.

70. Federico Salmón Amorín was a member of the conservative party, Confederación Española de Derechas Autónomas.

71. Decreto, 28 June 1935. Gaceta Oficial del Estado, 30 June 1935.

72. The 1934 Catalan legislation on antivenereal dispensaries had already developed a technical sanitary approach to venereal health policies that treated both male and female patients, although in practice, most of the female patients were prostitutes. See: Peyri, *La Lluita antivenèria.*

73. Decreto, 28 June 1935. Gaceta Oficial del Estado, 30 June 1935.

74. Decreto, 28 June 1935. Gaceta Oficial del Estado, 30 June 1935.

75. Isabel Romero, "La prostitución ante la guerra. Un peligro que hay que atajar rapidamente," *Castilla Libre,* 2 March 1937; "Prostitució, vergonya del mon," *Companya,* Num. 10; "La prostitución el enemigo principal de la Quinta Columna," *Claridad,* 4 March 1937.

76. Eduardo Vicente, "Las enfermedades venéreas son el fascismo de la naturaleza." (Poster)

77. "Guarda't dels MALS VENERIS com de les BALES." Consell de Sanitat de Guerra de la Generalitat de Catalunya. (Poster)

78. Report by Dn. Miguel Madroñero y Pascual y Dn. Hector Martínez Ibañez, Médicos de Asistencia Pública Domiciliaria de Barbastro on "Las casas de lenocinio de esta ciudad y de sus derivaciones para la salud publica," 3 June 1937 (Typed Manuscript). Reports on antivenereal health policies during the war found they were much more effective when dealing with controlled rather than clandestine prostitution.

79. The dispensary of the antivenereal campaign in the small Catalan town of Lerida had treated well over one hundred soldiers by early 1937. "Perfil de la vida local," *Acracia,* 12 February 1937.

80. Peyri, *La lluita antivenèria.*

81. Félix Martí Ibáñez, "Mensaje a la mujer obrera. Conferencia en el Palacio de la Música Catalana en ocasión de la 'Semana de la Mujer,'" in *Tres mensajes a la mujer* (Barcelona: Coll. Nueva Era. Ediciones y Reportajes, 1937), 21.

82. Valle. Delegado de Prensa, "De la moral," *El Guerillero,* 6 May 1937. I would like to thank Michel Froidevaux for drawing my attention to this document.

83. "Moviment hospitalari del mes de julio de 1936," *Annual de L'Hospital General de Catalunya,* November 1936.

84. Estadística del malalts sortits el mes de Julio de 1937. Visita del Dr. Horta. Hospital General de Catalunya (Manuscript) and Estadística del malalts sortits el mes de Juliol de 1937. Visita del Dr. Noguer–Moré. Hospital General de Catalunya (Manuscript). (The only documentation located is based on hospital discharge.)

85. A constant preoccupation of the antivenereal campaign was the unusual degree of intrusion by non–professionals in the treatment of venereal diseases. The control of quack interference was a major item in the 1935 Decree on the Abolition of Prostitution.

86. *Estadística del malalts sortits el mes de Juliol de 1937*. Visita del Dr. Horta. Hospital General de Catalunya (Manuscript). Of the 43 patients treated, 23 gave their profession as *milicianos* and 5 as soldiers. Professions are not recorded in the documentation by Dr. Noguer–Moré.

87. Manifiesto, Mujeres Libres, *Ruta,* 21 January 1937.

88. Carmen Adell, "En nombre de la Revolución, más moralidad," *Vida Nueva,* 20 February 1937. I would like to thank Michel Froidevaux for drawing my attention to this article.

89. Ana Pibernat, "Mis Memorias." (Manuscript)

90. Isabel Romero, "La prostitución ante la guerra."

91. "Prostitución," *Emancipación,* 29 May 1937.

92. Frederic Fernández, "Prostitució moral i revolució," *Treball,* 9 September 1936.

93. Frederic Fernández, "Prostitució moral i revolució," *Treball,* 9 September 1936.

94. "Prostitución," *Emancipación,* 29 May 1937.

95. Ada Martí, "Dice una mujer," *Ruta,* 25 March 1938.

96. Agrupación de Mujeres Libres. C.N.T. – F.A.I., "Prostitución." (Poster)

97. Agrupación de Mujeres Libres. C.N.T. – F.A.I., "Prostitución." (Poster)

98. "Liberatorios de prostitución," *Mujeres Libres,* 65 días de la Revolución.

99. "Liberatorios de prostitución," *Mujeres Libres,* 65 días de la Revolución.

100. Mary Nash, "Riforma sessuale e 'nuova morale' nell'anarchismo spagnolo."

101. For a detailed analysis, see Nash, "Riforma sessuale e 'nuova morale' nell'anarchismo spagnolo."

102. Mariano Gallardo, "Experimentación sexual," *Estudios,* October 1935; Félix Martí Ibáñez, "Eugenesia y moral sexual. Carta a una muchacha española sobre el problema sexual," *Estudios*, February 1935.

103. Mariano Gallardo, *El sexo, la prostitución y el amor* (Toulouse: Ed. Universo, s.d.).

104. Gallardo, *El sexo, la prostitución.*

105. Gallardo, *El sexo, la prostitución.*

106. Un médico rural, "A modo de Programa," *Estudios,* June 1931.

107. Federica Montseny, *Mi experiencia en al Ministerio de Sanidad y Assistencia Social,* 27.

108. For a detailed discussion of divergencies, see Mary Nash, "Dos intelectuales anarquistaas frente al problema de la mujer: Federica Montseny y Lucía Sánchez Saornil," *Convivium,* Nums. 44–45 (1975).

109. "Guarda't dels Mals veneris...." (Poster)

110. "¡Peligro!" Sanidad. I. G. Seix i Barral, Barcelona. (Poster)

111. Rivero Gil, "¡Atención! Las enfermedades venéreas amenazan tu salud. ¡Prevente contra ellas!" Jefatura de Sanidad del Ejercito. Lit. U.G.T.–C.N.T. (Poster)

112. Eduardo Vicente, "Las enfermedades venéreas son el fascismo de la naturaleza." (Poster)

113. Grimau, *El cartel republicano en la Guerra Civil;* Julián, *Les avantguardes pictòriques a Catalunya.* For reproductions of war posters: Jaume Miravitlles and Josep Termes, *Carteles de la República y de la Guerra Civil* (Barcelona: La Gaya Ciencia, 1978) and *Las mujeres en la Guerra Civil* (Madrid: Ministerio de Cultura, 1989).

114. "La prostitución, el aliado principal de la Quinta Columna," *Claridad,* 4 March 1937.

115. "Prostitució vergonya del mon," *Companya,* Num. 10.

116. For example, it was discussed in a paper at the First National Conference of the Catalan Antifascist Women's Movement. "Programa del Primer Congrés Nacional de la Dona que tindrá lloc els dies 6,7 i 8 de novembre del 1937."

117. "Liberatorios de prostitución," *Mujeres Libres,* 65 días de la Revolución.

118. Federica Montseny, "La sanidad y la assistencia social durante la guerra Civil," 100.

119. Félix Martí Ibáñez, "La abolición del amor mercenario." *Estudios,* March 1937.

120. "Liberatorios de Prostitución," *Mujeres Libres,* 65 Días de la Revolución; "Acciones contra la prostitución," *Mujeres Libres,* Num. 11; Félix Martí Ibáñez, "La abolición del amor mercenario," *Estudios,* March 1937.

121. "Liberatorios de Prostitución," *Mujeres Libres,* 65 Días de la Revolución.

122. Martí Ibañez, "La abolición del amor mercenario."

123. Ada Martí, "Dice una mujer," *Ruta,* 25 March 1938.

124. Martí Ibáñuz, "La abolición del amor mercenario."

125. Aurora Bertrana, *Memòries del 1935 fins al retorn a Catalunya* (Barcelona: Editorial Portic, 1978), 64–65.

126. Etchebéhère, *Mi guerra de España,* 22.

127. María Teresa Andrade, *Dinamita con su tenedor* (Manuscript). This is a semi–fictional account by Andrade, who claimed it was based on a real case.

128. This legislation was later developed in the Order of the Ministry of Health and Social Assistance of the 1st of March 1937.

129. The hospitals were: Hospital General de Catalunya, Hospital Clínico, Hospital de la Maternidad, and Hospital Dr. Cardenal in Barcelona; Hospital del Municipio in Puig Alt de Ter, Hospital Comarcal in Berga, Centro Sanitario Comarcal in Igualada, and Centro Sanitario Comarcal de Granollers. *Lista de las instituciones que practican la interrupción artificial del embarazo.* Signed Martí Ibáñez. (Typed Manuscript)

130. Malcolm Potts, Peter Diggory, and John Peel, *Abortion* (Cambridge: Cambridge University Press, 1977), 377–385.

131. Mary Nash, "Marginality and Social Change. Legal Abortion in Catalonia during the Civil War." William D. Phillips and Carla Rahn Phillips (eds.), *Marginated Groups in Spanish and Portuguese History* (Minneapolis: Society for Spanish and Portuguese Historical Studies, 1989) and "Género, cambio social y la problemática del aborto," *Historia Social,* Num. 2 (Autumn 1988).

132. Mary Nash, "Ordenamiento jurídico y realidad social del aborto en España: una aproximación histórica," in Garcia–Nieto Paris (ed.), *Ordenamiento jurídico.*

133. V. Aza, *Derechos y deberes biológicos de la mujer. Discurso de recepción del Doctor Vital Aza, Academia Nacional de Medicina* (Madrid: Imprenta Rot, 1934), 46.

134. Oral testimony by women interviewed underscored this point of view. Mary Nash, Oral History Project, *La Familia a la Catalunya Autònoma.*

135. Women were not granted university degrees until 1910.

136. Mary Nash, "L'avortement legal a Catalunya. Una experiéncia fracassada," *L'Avenç.* (March 1983).

137. Mary Nash, "El neomaltusianismo anarquista y los conocimientos populares sobre el control de natalidad en España," in Mary Nash (ed.), *Presencia y protagonismo. Aspectos de la Historia de la mujer* (Barcelona: Serbal, 1984).

138. This innovative health policy had already begun in the early thirties. See Cristina Rimbau, *L'Assistencia Social de la Generalitat de Catalunya 1931–1936* and "Una aportació a la reflexió sobre l'organització dels serveis socials."

139. See the biographical profile by Ignasi Vidal in the Prologue to F. Martí Ibañez, *Consultorio psiquico–sexual* (Barcelona: Tusquets, 1975).

140. Felix Martí Ibáñez, *Diez meses de labor en Sanidad y Asistencia Social* (Barcelona: Ed. Tierra y Libertad, 1937), 24.

141. Martí Ibañez, *Diez meses de labor en Sanidad,* 69–79. Also, D. Bellmunt, *La revolució i l'Assistencia Social* (Barcelona: Imp. Clarasó, 1937).

142. Martí Ibáñez, *Diez meses de labor en Sanidad,* 151–152.

143. For a detailed analysis of this legislation, see Nash, "L'avortement legal a Catalunya."

144. Martí Ibañez, *Diez meses de labor en Sanidad,* 125.

145. For a discussion of documentary sources, see: Mary Nash, "La documentación hospitalaria; un ejemplo de su estudio para la historia de la mujer. La incidencia del Decreto de Interrupción Artificial del Embarazo en los Departamento de Ginecología y Obstetricia del Hospital de la Santa Cruz y San Pablo," 11 Jornadas de Metodología y Didáctica de la Historia, Universidad de Cáceres, December 1981.

146. A. Brossa, "Mortalitat fetal i infantil a Catalunya. Treballs estadístics," Sisé Congrés de Metges de Llengua Catalana, *Butlletí de la Societat Catalana de Pediatría* 1 (1930); H. Puig i Sais, *El problema de la natalitat a Catalunya. Un gravíssim perill per a la nostra pátria*

(Barcelona: Imp. Viuda Badía Oantenys, 1915), 58.

147. *Registro de Salidas. Estadística de enfermas salidas (1936– 1938).* Departments of Gynecology and Obstetrics, Hospital de la Santa Cruz y de San Pablo (Hospital General de Catalunya), *Resumenes mensuales y anuales,* (1936–1939), Department of Obstetrics. I would like to express my thanks to Sra. Larusea for her collaboration in making available the archives of the Hospital de la Santa Cruz y San Pablo.

148. Records on abortion are very problematical and tend to distort the real figures, as the data tends to include only those abortions that were non–routine, usually due to medical complications. So hospital records on the one hand probably show a higher ratio of pregnancy–abortion than normal but at the same time underestimate the overall number of abortions, as basically only those which had produced complications would have been registered in the hospital. Public hospitals were also class defined, as wealthy patients would either go to private clinics or have home medical attention.

149. See Patricia Knight, "Women and Abortion in Victorian and Edwardian England" and Angus McLaren, "Women's Work and Regulation of Family Size. The Question of Abortion in the Nineteenth Century," *History Workshop Journal* 4 (1977). Also, Angus McLaren, "Abortion in France: Women and the Regulation of Family Size, 1800– 1914," *French Historical Studies* 10 (Spring 1970); K. Luker, *Abortion and the Politics of Motherhood* (Berkeley: University of California Press, 1985); A. McLaren, *Birth Control in Nineteenth Century England* (London: Croom Helm, 1978).

150. See Jordi Nadal, *La población española.(siglos XVI–XX)* (Barcelona: Ariel, 1984).

151. See Raquel Alvarez Peláez, "Introducción al estudio de la eugenesia española (1900–1936)," *Quipu,* vol. 2, num. 1 (January– April 1985); Glick, "Psicoanálisis, reforma sexual y política en la España de entre guerras"; Nash, "El neomaltusianismo anarquista" and "Social Eugenics and Nationalist Race Hygiene in Early Twentieth Century Spain."

152. For a detailed account, see Nash, "El neomaltusianismo anarquista."

153. This is a common pattern found in interviews with women of different social extraction. Mary Nash, Oral History Project, *La familia a la Catalunya Autònoma.*

154. For example, some vaginal cones advertised represented two days' wages of a garment worker.

155. See Nash, "El control de la natalidad y la difusión de los medios de contracepción. El debate en el Movimiento Eugénico español." Paper presented 1 Congrés Hispano Luso Italià de demografia Històrica, Barcelona, April 1987.

156. Nash, "El neomaltusianismo anarquista y los conocimientos populares sobre el control de natalidad en España."

157. This is the tendency observed in my oral history sources, *La familia a la Catalunya Autònoma.*

158. Nash, Oral History Project, *La familia a la Catalunya Autònoma.*

159. Nash, "L'avortement legal a Catalunya."

160. The sources used for the Casa de la Maternidad are the following: Registro de abort/Molas. 1914–1933. Registro de Abortos – Ginecología 1936–1956. Historia de los partos de la segunda quincena de diciembre de 1963 (misplaced documents) and Historias Clínicas. I would like to express my thanks to Carmen Delgado and Drs. Perez del Pulgar y Guilera for their collaboration in making available the archives of the Casa de la Maternidad.

161. Martí Ibañez, *Diez meses de labor en Sanidad,* 46.

162. Interview with C. P., Barcelona, 16 June 1981, who had actually been attended by Martí Ibáñez in her abortion.

163. See complete data for the period 1931–1938 in Mary Nash, "L'avortement legal a Catalunya: una experiència fracassada," *L'Avenç., num. 58 (March 1983).

164. Martí Ibañez, *Diez meses de labor en Sanidad,* 73.

165. Interview with Dr. Ramon Casañellas, Barcelona, 15 February 1982. Dr. Casañellas had worked in the Gynecology Department of the Hospital General de Catalunya during this period.

166. *La reforma eugénica del aborto* (Barcelona: Ed. Consellería de Sanitat i Assistencia Social Generalitat de Catalunya, s.d.).

167. This is the general pattern that has emerged from the interviews in the oral history

project, *La familia a la Catalunya Autonoma.*

168. Lie, "Por la creación de Consultorios para la propaganda y práctica de los medios preventivos," *Emancipación,* 29 May 1937.

CHAPTER 6

1. "El Casal de la Dona Treballadora. Una obra magnífica de Mujeres Libres," *Tierra y Libertad,* 28 May 1938; Carmen Meana, "La mujer y los sindicatos," *Trabajadoras,* 8 March 1938; 14 August 1937; "Nuestros amigos," *Muchachas,* 7 November 1937.

2. Mary Nash, "Pronatalism and Motherhood in Franco's Spain," in Gisela Bock and Pat Thane, *Maternity, Visions of Gender and the Rise of the European Welfare States, 1890–1950* (London: Routledge and Kegan Paul, 1991).

3. Maria Teresa Gallego Méndez, *Mujer, Falange y franquismo* (Madrid: Taurus, 1983); M.I. Pastor i Homs, *La educación femenina en la postguerra (1939–1945): el caso de Mallorca* (Madrid: Ministerio de Cultura, 1984); Rosario Sánchez López, *Mujer española, una sombra de destino en lo universal: trayectoria histórica de Sección Femenina de Falange (1934–1977* (Murcia: Universidad de Murcia, 1990).

4. Resumen del Discurso de Pilar Primo de Rivera, *La Vanguardia,* 11 January 1940.

5. *Fuero del Trabajo,* 9 March 1938.

6. Tomasa Cuevas, *Mujeres de la cárceles franquistas,* 2 vols. (Barcelona: Sirocco, 1986); Juana Doña, *Desde la noche y la niebla. Mujeres en las cárceles franquistas* (Madrid: Ed. La Torre, 1978); Giuliana di Febo, *Resistencia y movimiento de mujeres en España 1936–1939* (Barcelona: Icaria, 1984); Fernanda Romeu, *Voces silenciadas. Las mujeres en el franquismo* (Valencia: Edición propia, 1994).

7. Nash, "Pronatalism and Motherhood in Franco's Spain."

8. For a recent fictional account, see: Josefina R. Aldecoa, *Historia de una maestra* (Barcelona: Anagrama, 1990) and *Mujeres de negro* (Barcelona: Anagrama, 1994).

9 Maria Carmen García–Nieto París, "Trabajo y oposición popular de las mujeres durante la dictadura franquista," in Georges Duby and Michelle Perrot, *Historia de las mujeres en Occidente,* Vol. 5 (Madrid: Taurus, 1993).

Glossary

Agrupación de Mujeres Antifascistas (AMA) – an umbrella antifascist women's organization under communist control.

Ajut Infantil de Reraguarda – an organization supporting child welfare at the homefront.

Aliança Nacional de la Dona Jove (ANDJ) – the Catalan young women's antifascist organization.

Ancien Regime – refers to the absolutist monarchy based on divine right, a feudal system, and a highly stratified society ruled by the two estates of the landed aristocracy and the clergy. In Spain, the first attempt to abolish the absolutist monarchy occurred during the War of Independence against Napoleon when the first liberal constitution of Cadiz was established in 1812. The definitive transition from the ancien regime to a constitutional, liberal monarchy was not achieved until the 1837 constitution.

Asociación Nacional de Mujeres Españolas (ANME) – the feminist organization created in 1918 that demanded women's civil rights and later included suffrage in its agenda.

Asturian Revolt – the insurrection and revolt in October 1934 of the mining community in Asturias, which attempted to implement a social revolution.

Ateneo – a popular working–class cultural center.

Bienio Progresista (1854–1856) – the two–year period of progressive government characterized by social conflict and an improvement in constitutional rights.

Bloc Obrer i Camperol (BOC) – the working and peasant dissident communist party in Catalonia which amalgamated with Izquierda Comunista Española in 1935 to create the POUM.

Bourbon Restoration – refers to the restoration of the monarchy under the Bourbon dynasty in 1875.

Collective – refers to farms and industries that were collectivized during the Civil War. They represented an alternative model to capitalism and espoused the collectivization of property, goods, production, and benefits. They were run on a non–hierarchical organization of labor in which all the members of the collective took part in management and production. Most of the collectives were developed by anarchists, although a small number were created by leftist socialists.

Compañero – the term used in anarchist circles to refer to a fellow member of the anarchist movement or to a husband/wife or partner. The term comrade was not used, as it evoked communist connotations.

Confederación Nacional del Trabajo (CNT) – the anarcho–syndicalist trade union.

Cortes – refers to the Spanish Parliament. Cortes Constituyentes refers to the constituent assembly.

Cultural Militia – created in December 1936 under the initiative of the socialist federation of teaching professionals, it provided schools and educational and cultural programs to the soldiers at the fronts through the initiative of educated volunteers.

Cumann na mBan – the Irish nationalist women's organization.

Emakume Abertzale Batza – the Basque nationalist women's organization linked with the Basque Nationalist Party.

Esquerra Republicana de Catalunya (ERC) – the Catalan nationalist center–left republican party.

Estat Català – the Catalan nationalist separatist party.

Eugenic Reform of Abortion – refers to the regulation of voluntary abortion in the region of Catalonia in December 1936. This measure was developed under the initiative of anarchist sex reformer Dr. Félix Martí Ibáñez, then director general of the Ministry of Health and Social Assistance of the Generalitat.

Falange Española – the Spanish fascist organization founded in 1933 on which Franco constructed the only official party of the regime. After 1945, the political base of the Franco regime was known as the Movimiento Nacional.

Federación Anarquista Ibérica (FAI) – the radical vanguard of the anarchist movement that espoused insurrectionary tactics to achieve the anarchist revolution.

Federación Ibérica de Juventudes Libertarias (FIJL) – the anarchist youth federation.

Female Secretariat of the POUM (FSPOUM) – the women's bureau of the dissident Marxist party, the Partido Obrero de Unificación Marxista.

Feminal – the women's journal published monthly in Catalonia from 1907 to 1917 as a supplement to *Illustració Catalana*. Catalan feminist Carme Karr was its director.

Fifth Columnists – Franco supporters who acted as informers, spies, and saboteurs at the republican homefront.

First Republic (1873–1874) – the republican regime that substituted the monarchy during a brief period in the nineteenth century.

Fourierists – followers of French social utopian Charles Fourier.

Generalitat – the autonomous government of Catalonia created with the Autonomous Statute in September 1932.

Institut d'Adaptació Professional de la Dona (IAPD) – an official Catalan organism to promote professional training for women.

Institut de Cultura i Biblioteca Popular de la Dona (1919–1936) – the library and educational and professional training center for women run by the women of the Catalan bourgeoisie.

International Brigade – refers to the international volunteers who fought in the Spanish Civil War.

International Workingmen's Association (IWA) – the first international association of working men created by Karl Marx in 1864 to promote proletarian emancipation.

Izquierda Republicana – the center-left republican party.

Juventudes Socialistas Unificadas (JSU) – the amalgamated socialist and communist youth movement under communist control.

Krausista – the Spanish followers of German philosopher Krause who represented a modernizing force dedicated particularly to educational reform in the nineteenth century and became a major influence in the development of Spanish liberalism.

Latifundio – large landed estates to be found in central and southern Spain.

Liberatorio de Prostitución – an initiative proposed by the anarchist women's organization Mujeres Libres to create liberation homes for the rehabilitation of prostitutes.

Libertarian Communism – communist anarchism, a trend within the Spanish anarchist movement.

Lucha Antivenérea – sanitation campaigns against venereal diseases.

Madrina de guerra – refers to the figure of the "war godmother" who sponsored a soldier at the front and corresponded with him.

Miliciana – militia woman, a member of the popular militia.

Militia – refers to the popular militia, "the people in arms." The armed civil population emerged during the first days of the Civil War to defend republican Spain from fascism. The militia was not a regular army and provided, under anarchist, dissident communist leadership and the initiative of unions, a collective, non–hierarchical armed resistance to fascism at the fronts. It also tended to favor the social revolution.

Mono – the blue working–class overalls that became a sign of revolutionary attire in the first stage of the war.

Movimiento Libertario Español (MLE) – the Spanish Libertarian Movement, which collectively represented the different branches of Spanish anarchism–the CNT, the FAI, and the FIJL–in 1938.

Mujeres – refers to the three journals published by the Agrupación de Mujeres Antifascistas in Madrid (1936), Valencia (1937), and Bilbao (1937).

Mujeres Libres – the anarchist women's organization that defended anarcho–feminism and antifascism.

Partido Comunista de España (PCE) – the mainstream orthodox communist party.

Partido Obrero de Unificación Marxista (POUM) – the dissident Marxist communist party.

Partido Socialista Obrero Español (PSOE) – the Spanish Socialist Party.

Partido Socialista Unificado de Cataluña – the Catalan communist party founded in July 1936 through the amalgamation of socialists and communists.

Pasionaria – refers to the name by which communist leader Dolores Ibárruri was popularly known.

Pronunciamento – the traditional initiative by a military leader to carry out a coup d'etat with the complicity of other military.

Republican forces – refers to the army of the legitimate democratic Second Republic opposed to the rebel, nationalist forces under Franco.

Republican regime – refers to a republican political system, as opposed to a monarchy. The first experience of a republic in Spain, known as the First Republic, lasted from 1873 to 1874. The second republican period was initiated in 1931 with the democratic Second Republic.

Second Republic (1931–1939) – refers to the democratic republican regime established after the abdication of King Alfonso XIII when the republicans won the elections in the major cities of Spain in April 1931.

Segell Pro–Infancia – an organization to promote children's welfare.

Sexenio Democrático (1868–1874) – the revolutionary period in the nineteenth century that fostered the democratization of the political system. The reigning Bourbon dynasty was substituted by King Amadeo of Savoy. In 1873, the constitutional monarchy was substituted for the first time by a constitutional republic, the First Republic (1873–1874).

Third International – refers to the International founded by Lenin and Trotsky in 1919 to develop the communist revolution. In 1935, under Stalin, its tactics changed to collaboration with other political parties in a united popular front against fascism.

Unió de Dones de Catalunya (UDC) – the Catalan women's antifascist organization.

Unión de Muchachas (UM) – refers to the antifascist women's youth organization under communist control.

Unión General de Trabajadores (UGT) – the socialist trade union.

Bibliography

Primary Sources

ARCHIVES, LIBRARIES, AND DOCUMENT COLLECTIONS

Archivo de la Audiencia Territorial, Barcelona.
Archivo de la Casa de la Maternidad, Barcelona.
Archivo de la Diputación de Barcelona.
Archivo General del Hospital de la Santa Cruz y San Pablo, Barcelona.
Archivo Histórico Nacional, Madrid.
Archivo Histórico Nacional, Sección Guerra Civil, Salamanca.
Archivo del Partido Comunista de España, Madrid.
Arxiu Nacional de Catalunya, Barcelona.
Biblioteca Arus, Barcelona.
Biblioteca del Ateneo de Barcelona.
Biblioteca Francesca Bonnemaison, Barcelona.
Biblioteca Nacional, Madrid.
Biblioteca Nacional de Catalunya, Barcelona
Biblioteca de Renée Lamberet, Paris.
Biblioteca Universitaria, Valencia.
Bibliothèque Nationale, Paris.
British Library, London.
Centre d'Estudis Històrics Contemporánis, Fundació Figueras, Barcelona.
Centre d' Estudis Històrics Internacionals, Universidad de Barcelona.
Centre de Documentació d'Història de la Medicina, Barcelona.
Centre de Documentació Històrica–Social, Ateneu Enciclopèdic Popular, Barcelona.
Centre International de Recherches sur l'Anarchisme, Geneva.
Fundación Pablo Iglesias, Madrid.
Fundación Primero de Mayo, Madrid.
Hemeroteca Municipal, Madrid.
Hemeroteca Nacional, Madrid.

233

Instituto Municipal de Historia, Barcelona.
International Institut Voor Sociale Geschiedenis, Amsterdam.
Library of Congress, Washington, D.C.

CORRESPONDENCE

Correspondence from the Local Groups and Committees of the Agrupación de Mujeres Antifascistas.
Correspondence by Mujeres, "Organo del Comité Nacional contra la Guerra y el Fascismo," Bilbao.
Correspondence by the journal Mujeres.
Correspondence by Socorro Rojo Internacional to the Agrupación de Mujeres Antifascistas.
Correspondence from different local groups, committees, and federations of Mujeres Libres.
Correspondence by Federica Montseny.
Correspondence between Lucía Sanchez Saornil and María Luisa Cobos.
Correspondence from Mujeres Libres in exile.
Correspondence of the journal "Mujeres Libres."
Correspondence of the Group of Asturian Refugees.
Correspondence and report by Dolors Piera to Mary Nash, April 1986.
Correspondence by María Teresa Andrade to Mary Nash, May 1975.

NEWSPAPERS, JOURNALS, PERIODICAL PUBLICATIONS

Acción Sindical. "Portavoz de CNT en la comarca de Valls, Montblanch." Periódico bilingüe. Valls, 1936.
Adelante. "Diario obrero." Barcelona. 1933–1934.
Adelante. "Organo del POUM de Lérida." 1937.
Alba Roja. "Organo del Sindicato Unico de Trabajadores de Premià de Mar." Portavoz de CNT, FAI, AIT. Premià de Mar, 1937.
Almanaque de El Socialista para 1930. Madrid, 1929.
Almanaque de el Socialista para 1932. Madrid, 1931.
Almanaque Tierra y Libertad. 1933.
Annual de L'Hospital General de Catalunya. 1936–1937.
Avant. "Organ del POUM." Barcelona, 1936.
Boletín de Información del Comité Regional del Pais Valenciano del POUM. s.d.
Boletín de la Agrupación Socialista Madrileña. Madrid, 1929–1936.
Castilla Libre (CNT– AIT). "Diario órgano de la Confederación Regional del Trabajo del entro." 1937–1939.
Catalunya Roja. "Organ del Partit Comunista de Catalunya (adherit al P.C. de España SE de la Internacional Comunista)." Semanario. Barcelona, 1932–1934.
Ciudad y Campo. "Organo confederal y anarquista de la Comarca de Tortosa." Tortosa, 1937.
Claridad. "Diario de la Noche." Later "Portavoz de la UGT." Madrid, 1936–1939.
Claridad. "Revista política." Bimensual. Barcelona, 1932–1933.
Claridad. "Semanario Socialista de Crítica e Información." Madrid, 1935–1936.
CNT. "Organo de la Confederación Nacional del Trabajo." "Diario de la tarde." Barcelona, 1938.
Combat. "Diari de la J.C.I." 1936.
¡Compañera! "Organo de las mujeres trabajadoras de la ciudad y del campo." Madrid, 1934.
Companya. "Revista de la Dona." Barcelona, 1937–1938.
Cultura Libertaria. "Semanal." Barcelona, 1931–1933.
Democracia. "Semanario Socialista." Madrid, 1935.
Diari Oficial de la Generalitat de Catalunya. 1936–1938.

Diari Oficial Del Comité Antifeixista i de Salut Pública de Badalona. 1936.

El Comunista. Madrid, 1931.

El Hogar y la Moda, 1937.

El Liberal. Madrid, 1935.

El Luchador. "Periódico de Sátira, Crítica, Doctrina y Combate." Semanal. Barcelona, 1931–1933.

El Socialista. "Diario." Madrid, 1931–1938.

Ellas. "Semanario de las mujeres españolas." Madrid, 1932.

Emancipación. "Organo del Secretariado Femenino del POUM." Quincenal. Barcelona, 1937.

Estampa. "Revista gráfica." Madrid, 1935–1937.

Estudios. "Revista eclectica." Mensual. Valencia, 1929–1938.

Estudios. "Portaveu de la Comisió de Cultura de la Cooperativa Obrera La Lealtad." Barcelona, 1932–1933.

Etica. "Revista de educación industrial, filosófica, literatura y arte y naturismo." Mensual. Barcelona, 1927–1928.

Euskadi Roja. "Semanario Comunista. Organo provincial del Partido comunista (SE–IC). Portavoz de los Sindicatos Revolucionarios." San Sebastián, 1933–1934.

Feminal. 1907–1917.

Femmes dans l'action mondiale. "Revue editée par le Comité Mondial des Femmes contre le guerre et le fascisme." 1937.

Foc Nou. "Revista mensual publicada sota el patronatge de l'Ateneu Obrer." 1938.

Fragua Social. "Organo de la Confederación Regional del Trabajo de Levante. Portavoz de la Confederación Nacional del Trabajo de España." Valencia, 1936–1937.

Frente. "Periódico del Frente de Combate." 1938.

Frente Rojo. "Organo central del Partido Comunista (SEIC). Diario de la Noche." Madrid, 1932.

Front. "Organ del POUM." Tarrasa, 1936.

Front. "Organ del BOC de Manresa–Berga." Manresa, 1934.

Front. "Organ del BOC de Sitges." Sitges, 1934–1937.

Generación Roja. "Revista de la Juventud Comunista Ibérica." Mensual. Barcelona, 1937.

Heraldo Obrero. "Organo de la Federación Catalano–Balear del Partido Comunista de España (SE de la IC). Semanario." Barcelona, 1931.

Hombres Libres. "Organo de la Federación Provincial de Sindicatos Unicos de Granada." Granada,1937.

Horitzons. "Organ del Partit Socialista Unificat de Catalunya, d'Igualada i Comarca adherit a la Internacional Comunista." Igualada, 1937.

Ideas. "Portavoz del Movimiento Libertario de la comarca del bajo Llobregat, CNT, AIT, FAI." Hospitalet, 1937.

Impuls. "Organ del POUM." Sabadell, 1937.

Justicia. "Organo de la Federación Catalana de la UGT." Barcelona, 1928.

Justicia Social. "Setmanari social. Organ de la Unió Socialista de Catalunya." Barcelona, 1931–1936.

Juventud. "Organo de la Comisión Nacional de Unificación F.J.S." Madrid, 1936.

Juventud Comunista. "Organo central de la JCI (POUM). Semanal." Barcelona, 1936–1937.

Juventud Libre. "Organo de la Federación Ibérica de Juventudes Libertarias." Madrid, 1937.

Juventud Obrera. "Organo de la Juventud Comunista Ibérica (POUM)." Barcelona, 1937.

La Antorcha. "Organo de la Juventud Comunista Ibérica de Madrid (POUM)." Madrid, 1936.

La Batalla. "Organo del Partido Obrero de Unificación Marxista." 1936–1937.

La Batalla. "Semanario Comunista." Later "Organo de la Federación Comunista Ibérica y Portavoz del BOC" and "Semanario Obrero de Unificación Marxista." Barcelona, 1931–1937.

La Dona Catalana. 1925–1938.

La Humanitat. "Diario de Barcelona." Barcelona, 1931–1933.

La Nueva Era. "Revista mensual de Doctrina e Información." Barcelona, 1936.

La Revista Blanca. "Revista quincenal." Barcelona, 1923–1936.
La Victoria. "Organ de la Federació d'Agrupacions Professionals Obreres de Catalunya." (2ª etapa.) Badalona, 1935.
La Voce delle donne. (Le voix des femmes). "Revue mensuelle." s.l., 1936–1937.
Las Noticias. "Portavoz de la Unión General de Trabajadores." s.l., 1937.
L'Estudiant. "Setmanari estudiantil portaveu de la Federació Nacional d'Estudiants de Catalunya. FNEC y UGT." Tortosa, 1937.
Leviatán. "Revista mensual de Hechos e Ideas." Madrid, 1934–1936.
L'Hora. "Setmanari d'Avançada." Barcelona, 1930–1931; 1934–1936.
Liberación. "Revista mensual sociológica, económica, arte, literatura." Barcelona, 1935–1936.
Liberación. "Periódico Comunista del P.C. de Catalunya." Barcelona, 1934.
Llibertat. Tarragona, 1936–1937.
Llibertat. "Organo del Comité local de Salud Pública." Mataró, 1936–1938.
Lluita. "Periòdic del Partit Comunista de Catalunya." Barcelona, 1934.
Lluita. "Organ del Partit Socialista Unificat i de la U.G.T." 1937.
Lucha Social. "Organo mensual de la Delegación local de Subsidios." Lérida, 1934.
Más allá. "Portavoz de la División Francisco Ascaso." Frente de Huesca, 1937.
Mi Revista. "Ilustración de actualidades." Barcelona, 1937.
Modas Nuevas. "Album de Confecciones y Labores para el Hogar. Revista Mensual." 1936–1937.
Muchachas. "Portavoz de las jóvenes madrileñas." Later "Portavoz de la Alianza de las Muchachas." Published by the Unión de Muchachas Madrileñas. Madrid, 1937. Barcelona, 1938.
Mujer. "Revista semanal ilustrada." Madrid, 1931.
Mujeres. Madrid. s.d.
Mujeres. "Portavoz de las mujeres antifascistas." Madrid, 1936.
Mujeres. "Periódico de las mujeres que luchan por la paz, la libertad y el progreso." Madrid, 1936.
Mujeres. "Organo del Comité Nacional femenino contra la guerra y el fascismo. Semanario antifascista." Bilbao, 1937.
Mujeres. "Revista mensual del Comité Nacional de Mujeres antifascistas." Valencia, 1937.
Mujeres Libres. "Bulletín d'Information." s.d., s.l.
Mujeres Libres. Madrid; later Barcelona, 1936–1938.
Mundo Obrero. "Defensor de los trabajadores de la ciudad y el campo." Madrid, 1930–1933.
Mundo Obrero. "Edición de la mañana para los Frentes. Organo Central del Partido Comunista (SEIC)." Madrid, 1937–1938.
Mundo Obrero. "Organo del Partido Comunista de España (SE de la IC). Semanal." Madrid, 1931.
Mundo Obrero. "Organo Central del Partido Comunista (SEIC). Diario." Madrid, 1938.
Mundo Proletario. "Semanario Comunista." Madrid, 1931.
Noies Muchachas. "Editado por la Aliança de la Dona Jove y de Muchachas." Barcelona, 1938.
Nosotras. "Revista Femenina." Madrid, 1931.
Nosotros. "Revista mensual anarquista." Valencia, 1937.
Oceal. "Ministerio de Trabajo y Asistencia Social. Periódico quincenal gratis a refugiados." Valencia, 1937.
Or y Grana. "Setmanari autonòmic per les dones, propulsor d'una Lliga Patriótica de Dones." Barcelona, 1906–1907.
Orientaciones Nuevas (CNT–AIT). Granollers, 1937.
Pasionaria. "Revista de las Mujeres Antifascistas de Valencia." Valencia, 1937.
Pentalfa. "Magazine moderno de la ciencia de la alimentación y natura desnudista." Barcelona, 1936.
Rebelión. Madrid, 1934.
Renovación. "Organo de la Federación de Juventudes Socialistas de España." Madrid, 1934.
Ruta. "Organo de las Juventudes Libertarias de Cataluña." Barcelona, 1936–1938.
Sembra. "Organo semanal de los sindicatos de la comarca Vigatana, Ter y Fresser, CNT." Vich, 1932–1933.

Sembrador. "Organo comercial de las Juventudes Libertarias del Ter y del Fresser." Puigcerdà, 1936.
Socorro Rojo. POUM. "Organo oficial del Comité Central del Socorro Rojo del POUM." Barcelona, 1936.
Solidaridad Obrera. "Organo de la Confederación Regional del Trabajo de Cataluña." Barcelona, 1931–1939.
Superación. "Organo de la CNT y FAI de Sabadell y su comarca." Sabadell, 1937.
Tiempos Nuevos. Barcelona, 1935–1938.
Tierra y Libertad. "Semanario Anarquista." Barcelona, 1932–1938.
Timón. "Revista. Síntesis de orientación político–social." Barcelona, 1938.
Trabajadoras. "Editado por la delegación del Comité Central del Partido Comunista (SE de la JC)." Madrid, 1938.
Trabajadoras. "Periódico quincenal del PCE y del PSUC Comité Nacional Femenino del PC." Barcelona, 1938.
Treball. "Diari dels treballadors de la ciutat i del camp." Later "Organ Central del Partit Socialista Unificat de Catalunya." Barcelona, 1936–1939.
La Tribuna Socialista. "Organo diario de la Agrupación Socialista de Barcelona (PSOE)." Barcelona, 1931.
Umbral. "Semanario de la Nueva Era." Valencia, 1937–1939.
Vanguardia. "Portavoz Juvenil Marxista." Zaragoza, 1935–1936.
Vida Nueva. 1937

PAMPHLETS

AZA, Vital. *Derechos y deberes biológicos de la mujer. Discurso de recepción del Doctor Vital Aza, Academia Nacional de Medicina.* Madrid: Imprenta Rot, 1934.
BELLMUNT, Domènec. *La revolució i l'assistència social.* Barcelona: Imp. Clarassó, 1937.
CANTO IBAÑEZ, F. *La mujer ante el problema sexual.* Conferencia leida en el Ateneo Racionalista el día 28 de enero de 1937. Castellón: Pub. Instituto de Higiene, 1937.
CLARAMUNT, Teresa. *La mujer. Consideraciones sobre su estado ante las prerrogativas del hombre.* Mahón: Bib. El Porvenir del Obrero, 1905.
COMAPOSADA, Mercedes. *Esquemas.* Pub. Mujeres Libres. s.d., s.l.
Comisión Nacional de Auxilio del Ministerio de Defensa Nacional de la República. s.l.: Comité Nacional de Mujeres Antifascistas, 1938.
El POUM ante los problemas de la Revolución Española. Presented by M. Solano. Barcelona: Ed. La Batalla, 1936.
ELÍAS, Emilia. *Por qué luchamos las mujeres antifascistas.* Valencia: Agrupación de Mujeres antifascistas, s.d.
ESTIVILL, A. *Lina Odena. La gran heroína de las juventudes revolucionarias de España.* Barcelona: Ed. Maucci, s.d.
ESTIVILL y ABELLÓ, A. *Sexo, moral y familia. Contra los conceptos burgueses, la concepción proletaria.* Prologue by Jaime Miravitlles. Barcelona: Ed. CIB. Documentos sociales, s.d.
FEDERN, Etta. *Mujeres de la revolución.* Barcelona: Pub. Mujeres Libres, s.d.
FUYOLA, Encarnación. *Mujeres antifascistas. Su trabajo y su organización.* Valencia: Ed. mujeres antifascistas, 1937.
GENERALITAT DE CATALUNYA. *La reforma eugénica del aborto.* Barcelona: Generalitat de Catalunya, 1937.
GENERALITAT DE CATALUNYA. *Les noves institucions jurídiques i culturals per a la dona. Setmana d'activitats femenines. Febrer 1937.* Barcelona: Generalitat de Catalunya, 1937.
GOLDMAN, Emma. *La prostitución.* Ed. G.G.LL. del Ramo de Alimentación. s.d., s.l.
GONZÁLEZ, Virginia. *A las obreras.* Madrid, s.d. s.e.
GUSTAVO, Soledad. *A las proletarias. Propaganda emancipadora entre las mujeres.* Buenos

Aires: Biblioteca de la Cuestión Social, s.d.

GUSTAVO, Soledad. *El amor libre (en plena anarquía)*. Montevideo: Biblioteca "El Obrero," 1904.

GUSTAVO, Soledad. *La Sociedad Futura*. Conferencia organizada por la Agrupación Republicana "Germinal" de Madrid el 2 de abril de 1899. Barcelona: Ed. La Revista Blanca, 1931.

GUSTAVO, Soledad. *El Sindicalismo y la Anarquía*. Barcelona: Ed. de la Revista Blanca, 1932.

IBÁRRURI, Dolores. *Las heroicas mujeres de España. Discursos*. Valencia: Ed. Nuestro Pueblo, 1937.

IBÁRRURI, Dolores. *¡A las mujeres madrileñas!* Editado por el Comité Provincial de Madrid del Partido Comunista, s.d., s.e.

IBÁRRURI, Dolores. *¿Qué deberá ser el partido único del Proletariado?* Extracto del Informe pronunciado ante el Pleno del CC del PC. "Es hora ya de crear el Partido Unico del Proletariado." Ed. del PCE. s.d., s.l.

Manifiesto del Pleno Amplio del Comité Central del PC. Murcia: Secretaría de Agitación y Propaganda del PC de Murcia, s.d.

IMBERT, Obdulia. *Promoción Obdulia Imbert*. Sarrià: Talleres C.D.J.C., s.d.

INSTITUT D'ACCIÓ SOCIAL UNIVERSITARIA I ESCOLAR DE CATALUNYA. *Assistència Infantil. L'obra realitzada i l'obra a realitzar*. Barcelona: Institut d'Acció Social Universitaria i Escolar de Catalunya, s.d.

INSTITUT DE CULTURA I BIBLIOTECA POPULAR DE LA DONA. *Crónica retrospectiva: Noces d'Argent*. Barcelona: Institut de Cultura i Biblioteca Popular de la Dona, 1934.

JUVENTUD SOCIALISTA UNIFICADA DE ESPAÑA. *Conferencia Nacional, 1937*. Valencia: Ed. Obrera Guerra, 1937.

JUVENTUDES SOCIALISTAS UNIFICADAS. SECRETARIADO FEMENINO. *Jovenes trabajadoras*. Valencia: Estudi gràfic, s.d.

KOLLONTAI, Alejandra. *La Juventud comunista y la moral sexual*. Barcelona: Ed. Marxista, 1937.

KOLLONTAI, Alejandra. *El comunismo y la familia*. Barcelona: Ed. Marxista. Publicación del Secretariado Femenino del POUM, 1937.

La guerra i la revolució a Catalunya en el terreny econòmic. Barcelona: Ed. Marxista, 1937.

La mujer ante la revolución. Barcelona: Pubs. del Secretariado Femenino del POUM. Ed. Marxista, 1937.

Lina Odena. Heroina del pueblo. Madrid: Ed. Europa–América, 1936.

MARTÍ IBÁNEZ, Félix. *Grandezas y Miserias de la Revolución social española*. Barcelona: Oficinas Propaganda CNT–FAI, 1937.

MARTÍ IBÁÑEZ, Félix. *Ensayos sobre el amor*. Barcelona: Col. "Nueva Era," 1937.

MARTÍ IBÁÑEZ, Félix. *Mensaje eugénico a los trabajadores*. s.l., s.d.

MARTÍ IBÁÑEZ, Félix. *Tres mensajes a la mujer*. Barcelona: Col. "Nueva Era," 1937.

MARTÍ IBÁÑEZ, Félix. *Victoria. Mensaje eugénica a la mujer*. Barcelona: Generalitat de Catalunya, s.d.

MARTÍ IBÁÑEZ, Felix. *Diez meses de labor en Sanidad y Asistencia Social*. Barcelona: Ed. Tierra y Libertad, 1937.

MARTÍNEZ, Montserrat. *Aliança Nacional de la Dona Jove. Pla General de Treball*. s.d., s.l.

MAYMON, Antonia. *Humanidad Libre. Esbozo Racionalista*. Valencia: Bib. Juventud Libertaria, s.d.

MIRA, Dr. *El problema sanitario ante la Revolución proletaria*. Barcelona: Ed. Marxista, 1937.

MONTSENY, Federica. *El problema de los sexos*. Toulouse: Ed. Universo, s.d.

MONTSENY, Federica. *La mujer, problema del hombre*. Barcelona: Ediciones de la "Revista Blanca," 1932.

MONTSENY, Federica. *Cien días en la vida de una mujer*. Toulouse: Ed. Universo, s.d.

MONTSENY, Federica. *Mi experiencia en el Ministerio de Sanidad y asistencia Social. Conferencia pronunicada el 6 de junio de 1937 en el Teatro Apolo*. Valencia: Comisión de Propaganda y Prensa del Comité Nacional de la C–N.T. Valencia, 1937.

MUJERES LIBRES. *Actividades de la Federación de Mujeres Libres.* Barcelona, s.d.

MUJERES LIBRES. *Cómo organizar una agrupación Mujeres Libres.* s.d., s.e.

MURIÀ, Anna. *El 6 de octubre y el 19 de julio.* Paris: Association Hispanophile de France, 1937.

NELKEN, Margarita. *La epopeya campesina.* Texto íntegro pronunciado ante el micrófono del Ministerio de la Guerra, el 27 de agosto de 1936. Madrid: s.e., 1936.

NELKEN, Margarita. *Niños de hoy, hombres de mañana.* Madrid: Ediciones del S.R.I., 1937.

NOGUER–MORÉ, Jesús. *Nuestra alimentación en tiempos de escasez.* Barcelona: Biblioteca Higia, 1937.

OLIVER, Juan A. *Importancia capital del feminismo en la obra del progreso humano.* Discurso leído en el acto de inauguración de la Biblioteca Pública Femenina en la institución para la enseñanza de la mujer. Valencia: Talleres Tipográficos "Las Artes," 1932.

PCE COMITÉ CENTRAL. *Pleno Ampliado 1937. Valencia. Lo que el PC considera indispensable para ganar la guerra. Informe del día 5 de marzo de 1937.* Barcelona: Ed. PCE, 1937.

PÉREZ HERVAS, J. *El hombre, problema de la mujer.* Barcelona: Bib. "La Revista Blanca," 1933.

PEYRI, Antonio. *La lluita antivenèria a Catalunya l'any 1934.* Barcelona: Generalitat de Catalunya, s.d.

PI de FOLCH, Maria. *Una visió femenina del moment present.* Barcelona: Ed. Lyceum Club, 1932.

PIERA, Dolors. *La aportación femenina en la guerra de la independencia. Informe presentado a la Primera Conferencia Nacional del Partido Socialista de Cataluña (I.C.).* Barcelona: Ediciones del Departamento de Agitación y Propaganda del PSUC, 1937.

POCH y GASCON, A. *Niño.* Pub. Mujeres Libres. s.l., s.d.

POCH y GASCON, A. *La vida sexual de la mujer.* Valencia: Cuadernos de lectura, 1932.

POLO Y PEYROLON, Dr. *Apostolado de la mujer en las sociedades modernas. (Discurso leído en la solemne junta que la Juventud Católica de Valencia dedicó a María Santísima de los Dolores el día 31 de marzo de 1882).* Valencia: Imprenta Manuel Alufre, 1882.

PSUC (I.C.) *Conferencia Nacional 1937. Resolución política aprobada por la Primera Conferencia Nacional celebrada el 24 al 26 de julio de 1937.* Ed. PSU. s.d., s.l.

PUIG I SAIS, H. *El problema de la natalitat a Catalunya. Un gravíssim perill per a la nostra pátria.* Barcelona: Imp. Viuda Badía Oantenys, 1915.

Resoluciones aprobadas en el Pleno Ampliado del Comité Central del POUM celebrado en Barcelona los días 12 al 16 de diciembre de 1936. Barcelona: Ed. Marxista, 1936.

SALUD ALEGRE, Dra. *La creencia en la mochila.* Barcelona: Pub. Mujeres Libres, s.d.

SÁNCHEZ, Antonia. *Hacia la unidad de las muchachas. Discurso pronunciado en el Congreso Alianza de la Juventud Socialista Unificada.* Madrid: Ed. Editorial Juventud Unión Poligráfica, s.d.

SÁNCHEZ SAORNIL, Lucía. *Horas de revolución.* Barcelona: Sindicato del Ramo de Alimentación, 1937.

SÁNCHEZ SAORNIL, Lucía. *Versos sobre Durruti.* Madrid: Ed. Comisión de Propaganda Confederal y Anarquista CNT–AIT., s.d.

SANTAMARÍA, A. *Tareas de la mujer en el partido y en la producción. Conferencia Provincial del Partido Comunista.* Madrid: Publicaciones de la Comisión de Agit–Prop. del Comité Provincial del Partido Comunista, 1938.

Un proyecto de la República. La abolición de la prostitución. s.l. Imp. M. Pérez de Rozas, s.d.

BOOKS, ARTICLES, MEMOIRS, DOCUMENTS, CONTEMPORARY ACCOUNTS

ANDRADE, María Teresa. *Dinamita con su tenedor.* (Manuscript)

ARENAL, Concepción. "Estado actual de la mujer en España." *Boletín de la Institución Libre de Enseñanza.* 31 August 1895.

ARENAL, Concepción. *La emancipación de la mujer en España.* Edited by M. Armiño. Madrid: Ed. Júcar, 1974.

ASOCIACIÓN INTERNACIONAL DE TRABAJADORES. *Actas de los Consejos y Comisión Federal de la Región Española (1870–1874).* 2 vols. Transcription and preliminary study by Carlos Seco Serrano. Barcelona: Universidad de Barcelona, 1970.

ASOCIACIÓN INTERNACIONAL DE TRABAJADORES. *Cartas. Comunicaciones y circulares del III Congreso Federal de la Región Española.* Transcription and preliminary study by Carlos Seco Serrano. Barcelona: Universidad de Barcelona, 1972.

AZAÑA, Manuel. *Memorias políticas y de guerra.* 2 vols. Barcelona: Crítica, 1978.

BARRAQUER I ROVIRALTA, Cayetano: *Los religiosos en Cataluña en la primera mitad del siglo XIX.* Barcelona: Francisco J. Altés y Alabert, 1915.

BERENGUER (GUILLEN), Sara. "Biographical profile of Suceso Portales." Manuscript. March 1975.

BERENGUER, Sara. *Entre el sol y la tormenta. Treinta y dos meses de guerra (1936–1939).* Barcelona: Seuba Ediciones, 1988.

BERTRANA, Aurora. *Memòries del 1935 fins al retorn a Catalunya.* Barcelona: Editorial Portic, 1978.

Boletín Interior de discusión del 11 Congreso del POUM. Num. 1. February 1938. (Unpublished Manuscript)

BORKENAU, Franz. *The Spanish Cockpit.* London: Ed. Faber and Faber, 1937.

BROSSA, A. "Mortalitat fetal i infantil a Catalunya. Treballs estadístics." Sisé Congrés de Metges de Llengua Catalana. *Butlletí de la Societat Catalana de Pediatría.* Num. 1. 1930.

CAMBRILS, María. *Feminismo socialista.* Prólogo de Clara Campoamor. Valencia: Tip. las Artes, 1925.

CAMPOAMOR, Clara. *La situación jurídica de la mujer española.* s.l., 1938.

CAMPOAMOR, Clara. *Mi pecado mortal. El voto femenino y yo.* Madrid: Librería Beltrán, 1936.

CAMPOAMOR, Clara. *La Révolution espagnole vue par une republicaine.* Paris: Imp–Edit. Plon, 1937.

CAMPOAMOR, Clara. *El derecho femenino en España.* s.l., 1936.

CASTRO, Nieves. *Una vida para un ideal. Recuerdos de una militante comunista.* Madrid: Ediciones de la Torre, 1981.

CUEVAS, Tomasa. *Cárcel de mujeres. (1939–1945).* Barcelona: Sirocco Books, 1985.

DE BURGOS, Carmen. *La mujer moderna y sus derechos.* Valencia: Ed. Sempere, 1927.

de BURGOS, Carmen. *Misión social de la mujer.* Conferencia pronunciada el día 18 de febrero de 1911. Bilbao: Imp. José Rojas Núñez, 1911.

de BURGOS, Carmen. *La flor de la playa y otras novelas cortas.* Introduction by C. Núñez Rey. Madrid: Castália, 1989.

DE LA MORA, Constancia. *In Place of Splendour.* New York: Harcourt, Brace and Co., 1939.

DOÑA, Juana. *Desde la noche y la niebla. (Mujeres en las cárceles franquistas. Novela testimonio.* Madrid: Ediciones de la Torre, 1978.

ETCHEBÉHÈRE, Mika. *Mi guerra en España.* Barcelona: Plaza y Janés, 1976.

FORMICA, Mercedes. *Visto y vivido, 1931–1937. Pequeña historia de ayer.* Barcelona: Planeta, 1983.

FRANCOS RODRÍGUEZ, José. *La mujer y la política españolas.* Madrid: Pueyo, 1920.

GALLARDO, Mariano. *La Libertad de la Mujer.* (Manuscript sent to the journal Mujeres Libres for publication)

GARCÍA, Consuelo. *Las cárceles de Soledad Real. Una vida.* Madrid: Alfaguara, 1982.

GARCÍA GARCÍA, Regina. *Yo he sido marxista. El cómo y porqué de una conversión.* Madrid: Editora Nacional, 1946.

HILDEGART. *La rebeldía sexual de la juventud.* Barcelona: Ed. Anagrama, 1977.

HUERTA, Luis. *Prostitución, abolicionismo y mal venéreo.* Valencia: Bib. Orto, 1933.

IBÁRRURI, Dolores. *Pour la Victoire. Articles et discours. 1936–1938.* Paris: Ed. Sociales Internationales, 1938.

ITURBE, Lola. *La mujer en la la lucha social. La guerra civil de España.* Mexico: Ed. Mexicanos Unidos, 1974.

JEREZ PERCHET, Augusto. *La mujer de su casa.* Barcelona: Librería de J. y A. Bastinos, Eds., 1886.

JIMÉNEZ DE ABERASTURI, Luis Maria. *Casilda, miliciana. Historia de un sentimiento.* San Sebastian: Editorial Txertoa, 1985.

KAMINSKI, H. E. *Los de Barcelona.* Barcelona: Ediciones del Cotal, 1976.

KARR, Carmen. *Cultura femenina. (Estudi i orientacions). Conferencies donades en l'Ateneu Barcelonès" els dies 6, 13 y 20 d'abril de 1910.* Barcelona: L'Avenç, 1910.

KARR, C., SERRANO. L., and DOMENENCH, M. *Educación femenina. (Ciclo de conferencias celebrado en el Ateneo Barcelonés, los días 31 de enero y 1, 3, 4 y 5 de febrero de 1916).* Barcelona: Librería Parera, 1916.

KENT, Victoria. *Cuatro años de mi vida. 1940–1944.* Barcelona: Bruguera, 1978.

KENT, Victoria. "Una experiencia penitenciaria." *Tiempo de Historia* 17 (April 1976).

KNIGHT, (STEWART) Frida. *Memoirs.* (Typed Manuscript)

LANGDON–DAVIES, John. *La setmana tràgica de 1937. Els fets de maig.* Barcelona: Edicions 62, 1987.

LEÓN, Maria Teresa. *Memoria de la melancolía.* Sant Vicenç dels Horts: Círculo de Lectores, 1979.

LORENZO, Anselmo. *El proletariado militante.* Madrid: Alianza, 1974.

LOW, Mary, and BREA, Juan. *Red Spanish Notebook. The First Six Months of the Revolution and the Civil War.* San Francisco: City Lights, 1979.

MARAÑÓN, Gregorio. *Tres ensayos sobre la vida sexual. Sexo, trabajo y deporte, maternidad y feminismo, educación sexual y diferenciación sexual.* Madrid: Biblioteca Nueva, 1927.

MARAÑÓN, Gregorio. *Biología y feminismo.* Madrid: Imp. Suc. Enrique Teodoro, 1920.

MARTÍ IBÁÑEZ, Félix. *Consultorio psíquico–sexual.* Edited by Ignasi Vidal. Barcelona: Ed. Tusquets, 1975.

MARTÍNEZ SIERRA, María. *La mujer española ante la República.* Madrid: Ediciones de Esfinge, 1931.

MARTÍNEZ SIERRA, María. *Una mujer por los caminos de España.* Buenos Aires: Losada, 1952.

MONSERDÀ, Dolors. *Estudi feminista. Orientacions per a la dona catalana.* Barcelona: Lluis Gili, 1909.

MONSERDÀ de MACIÀ, D. *Tasques socials.* Recull d'articles, notes i conferències. Pròleg del Pare Ignasi Casanovas S. J. Barcelona: Miguel Parera Llibreter, 1916.

MONTSENY, Federica. *La Victoria. Novela en que se narran los problemas de orden moral que se le presentan a una mujer de ideas modernas.* Barcelona: Ediciones de "La Revista Blanca," 1925.

MONTSENY, Federica. *El hijo de Clara. (Segunda parte de La Victoria).* Barcelona: Ediciones de "La Revista Blanca," 1927.

MONTSENY, Federica. *Acción de la mujer en la paz y la guerra.* Lecture given at the Mujeres Libres center, 14 August 1938. (Manuscript)

MONTSENY, Federica. *Presente y porvenir del anarquismo en España.* 1931. (Manuscript)

MONTSENY, Federica. *Mis primeros cuarenta años.* Barcelona: Plaza y Janes, 1987.

MONTSENY, Federica. *La indomable.* Edition by Maria Alicia Langa Laorga. Madrid: Castália, 1991.

NELKEN, Margarita. *Tres tipos de vírgenes.* Madrid: Ed. Cuadernos Literarios, 1929.

NELKEN, Margarita. *La condición social de la mujer en España.* Madrid: Ed. C.V.S., 1975.

NELKEN, Margarita. *La mujer ante las Cortes Constituyentes.* Madrid: Ed. Castro, 1931.
NELKEN, Margarita. *Las escritoras españolas.* Barcelona: Ed. Labor, 1930.
ORWELL, George. *Homage to Catalonia.* Harmondsworth: Penguin, 1983.
ORWELL, Sonia, and ANGUS, Ian eds. *The Collected Essays. Journalism and Letters of George Orwell.* Middlesex: Penguin, 1970.
PÀMIES, Teresa. *Quan érem Capitans. (Memòries d'aquella guerra).* Barcelona: Dopesa, 1974.
PÀMIES, Teresa. *Crònica de la vetlla.* Barcelona: Editorial Selecta, 1975.
PARDO BAZÁN, Emilia. *La mujer española y otros artículos feministas.* Edited by Leda Schiavo. Madrid: Ed. Nacional, 1976.
PARDO BAZÁN, Emilia. "La mujer española". *La España Moderna* XVII (May 1890).
PIBERNAT, Ana. *Mis Memorias.* (Manuscript)
PRIEGO, Victoria. *La mujer ante las urnas.* Madrid: Col. Inquietudes de nuestro tiempo, 1933.
PUIG I SAIS, H. *El problema de la natalitat a Catalunya. Un gravíssim perill per a la nostra pátria.* Barcelona: Imp. Viuda Badía Oantenys, 1915.
RAULL, Francisco. *Historia de la Conmoción de Barcelona de la noche 25 al 26 de julio de 1835. Causas que la produjeron y sus efectos, hasta el día de esta publicación.* Barcelona: Imp. A. Bergnes, 1835.
SAÍZ, Concepción. *La revolución del 68 y la cultura femenina. Apuntes al natural. Un episodio nacional que no escribió Pérez Galdós.* Madrid: Librería General de Victoriano Pérez, 1929.
STEWART, (KNIGHT) Frida. *Dawn Escape.* London: Everybody's Books, s.d.
TUSQUETS, Francesc. *El problema feminista.* Barcelona: Imp.Elzerirana i Llibrería Camí, 1931.
VALENTÍ CAMP, Santiago. *La mujer ante el amor y frente a la vida. (Teorías, sistemas y opiniones de feminófilos, antifeministas y feminofosios).* Prólogo de A. Castro. Barcelona: Ed. Llibreria Sortes, 1932.
VALENTÍ CAMP, Santiago. *Las reivindicaciones femeninas.* Prólogo de R. Lamo. Barcelona: Ed. T. Ruiz, 1927.
VALVIDARES, Manual. *A las mujeres y jóvenes de Ciaño. Santa Ana.* (Manuscript sent to the journal *Mujeres Libres* for publication). 10 June 1936.
VIA, Ramona. *Nit de Reis. Diari d'una infermera de 14 anys.* Barcelona: Club Editor, 1984.

Secondary Sources

BOOKS AND ARTICLES

ABELLA, Rafael. *La vida cotidiana durante la guerra civil.* Barcelona: Planeta, 1974.
ACKELSBERG, Martha. "Mujeres Libres: Individuality and Community. Organizing Women during the Spanish Civil War." *Radical America.* 18.1 (1984).
ACKELSBERG, Martha A. "'Separate and Equal?' Mujeres Libres and Anarchist Strategy for Women's Emancipation." *Feminist Studies* (Spring 1985).
ACKELSBERG, Martha A. *Free Women of Spain. Anarchism and the Struggle for the Emancipation of Women.* Bloomington: Indiana University Press, 1991.
ADAMS, Mark B. ed. *The Wellborn Science: Eugenics in Germany, France, Brazil and Russia.* Oxford: Oxford University Press, 1990.
AGUADO, A. M., and CAPEL, R., et al. *Textos para la historia de las mujeres en España.* Madrid: Cátedra, 1994.
ALBERTI, Johanna. *Beyond Suffrage. Feminists in War and Peace,* 1914–1928. London: Macmillan, 1989.
ALCALDE, Carmen. *La mujer en la guerra civil española.* Ed. Cambio 16. Madrid, 1976.
ALCALDE, Carmen. *Federica Montseny. Palabra en rojo y negro.* Barcelona: Argos Vergara, 1983.
ALDECOA, Josefina. *Historia de una maestra.* Barcelona: Anagrama, 1990.

ALDECOA, Josefina. *Mujeres de negro*. Barcelona: Anagrama, 1990.

ALEXANDER, M., and GRAHAM, H., eds. *The French and Spanish Popular Fronts: Comparative Perspectives*. Cambridge: Cambridge University Press, 1988.

ALVAREZ JUNCO, José. *La ideología política del anarquismo español (1868–1910)*. Madrid: Siglo XXI, 1991.

ALVAREZ JUNCO, José, and PÉREZ LESDESMA, Manuel. "Historia del movimiento obrero. ¿Una segunda ruptura? *Revista de Occidente*. Num. 12 (March– April 1982).

ALVAREZ PELÁEZ, Raquel. "Introducción al estudio de la eugenesia española (1900–1936)." *Quipu*. Num 2 (1985).

ALVAREZ PELÁEZ, R., and HUERTAS GARCÍA–ALEJO, R. *¿Criminales o locos? Dos peritajes psiquiátricos del Dr. Gonzalo R. Lafora*. Madrid: CSIC, 1987.

ARÓSTEGUI, Julio. *Historia y memoria de la Guerra civil. Encuentro en Castilla y León*. Salamanca: Junta de Castilla y León, 1988.

ARÓSTEGUI, Julio. "La República en guerra y el problem del poder." *Studia Histórica*. vol.3, num. 4 (1985).

ARRANZ, Maria de los Angeles. "Los abastos en la Guerra Civil." *Historia 16*. Num. 16.

ARTOLA, Miguel. *Antíguo Régimen y revolución liberal*. Barcelona: Ariel, 1978.

AYMES, J. R. *La Guerra de la Independencia en España*. 1808–1814. Madrid: Siglo XXI, 1974.

BADILLO BAENA, Rosa M. *Feminismo y educación en Malaga: el pensamiento de Suceso Luengo de la Figuera (1892–1920)*. Malaga: Universidad de Malaga, 1992.

BALCELLS, Albert. *Trabajo industrial y organización obrera en la Cataluña contemporánea (1900–1936)*. Barcelona: Ed. Laia, 1974.

BARRERA PEÑA, M. Luisa, and LÓPEZ PEÑA, Ana. *Sociología de la mujer en la Universidad. Análisis histórico–comparativo. Galicia–España 1900–1981*. Santiago de Compostela: Universidad de Santiago de Compostela, 1983.

BEN–AMI, Slomo. *The Origins of the Second Republic in Spain*. Oxford: Oxford University Press, 1978.

BENET, Josep, and MARTÍ, Casimiro. *Barcelona a mitjan segle XIX. El moviment obrer durant el Bienni Progressista (1854–1856)*. Barcelona: Curial, 1976.

BENNET, J. "Feminism and History". *Gender and History*. Vol.1, Núm. 3 (1989).

BENNET, J. "Women's History: A Study in Change and Continuity." *Women's History Review*. Vol. 2, Núm. 2 (1993).

BERNECKER, W. *Colectividades y revolución social: el anarquismo en la guerra civil española. 1936–1939*. Barcelona: Crítica, 1982.

BETHKE ELSHTAIN, Jean. *Women and War*. Brighton: The Harvester Press, 1987.

BLINKHORN, Martin. *Carlism and Crisis in Spain, 1931–1939*. Cambridge: Cambridge University Press, 1975.

BLINKHORN, Martin. *Spain in Conflict, 1931–1939*. London: Sage, 1986.

BLINKHORN, Martin. *Democracy and Civil War in Spain. 1931–1939*. London: Methuen, 1988.

BLINKHORN, Martin. "Anglo–American Historians and the Second Spanish Republic: The Emergence of a New Orthodoxy." *European Studies Review* 3, 1 (1973).

BOADO, Emilia. "Las milicias del 36" en *Historia Internacional*, num. 1 (Abril, 1975).

BOCK, Gisela, and THANE, Pat. *Maternity, Visions of Gender and the Rise of the European Welfare States, 1890–1950*. London: Routledge and Kegan Paul, 1991.

BONACCHI, G., and GROPPI, A., eds. *Il dilemma della cittadinanza. Diritti e doveri delle donne*. Rome: Laterza, 1993.

BONAMUSA, Francesc. *El Bloc Obrer i Camperol (1930–1932)*. Barcelona: Curial, 1974.

BOSCH, Aurora. *Ugetistas y libertarios, Guerra Civil y Revolución en el País Valenciano*. Valencia: Edicions Alfons el Magnànim, 1983.

BRADEMAS, John. *Anarcosindicalismo y revolución en España*. (1930– 1937). Barcelona: Ariel, 1974.

BRAVO, Anna. "Per una storia delle donne: donne contadine e prima guerra mondiale." *Società Historia*, Num. 10 (1980).

BRAYBON, G. *Women Workers of the First World War*. London: Croom Helm, 1981.

BRICALL, Josep Maria. *Política econòmica de la Generalitat (1936– 1939). Evolució i formes de la producció industrial*. Barcelona: Edicions 62, 1970.
BRIDENTHAL, R., and KOONZ, C. *Becoming Visible. Women in European History*. Boston: Ed. Houghton Mifflin, 1977.
BROUÉ, Pierre. *La revolución española 1931–1939*. Barcelona: Peninsula, 1977.
BURSTYN, J. N. *Victorian Education and the Ideal of Womanhood*. London: Croom Helm, 1980.
CABRERA CALVO–SOTELO, Mercedes. *La patronal ante la II República. Organización y estrategia, (1931–1936)*. Madrid: Siglo XXI, 1983.
CALDERÓN, Carmen. *Matilde de la Torre y su época*. Santander: Ediciones Tantin, 1984.
CAMPBELL, Ann. *Women at War with America. Private Lives in a Patriotic Era*. Cambridge, MA: Harvard Press, 1984.
CAMPO ALANGE, Condesa de. *La mujer en España. Cien años de su historia*. Madrid: Ed. Aguilar, 1964.
CAMPS I CURA, Enriqueta. "Ells nivells de benestar al final del segle XIX. Ingrés i cicle de formació de les famílies a Sabadell (1890)." *Recerques*, Num. 24 (1991).
CANUT I CAPDEVILA, Juli. "Les memòries de Josepa Puig." L'Erol, *Revista Cultural del Berguedà*, 6 September 1983.
CAPEL, Rosa M. *El sufragio femenino en la II República española*. Granada: Ed. Universidad de Granada, 1975. (2nd.Ed. Madrid: Horas y Horas Editorial, 1992).
CAPEL, Rosa M. *El trabajo y la educación de la mujer en España (1900– 1930)*. Madrid: Ministerio de Cultura, 1982.
CAPEL, Rosa Mª., ed. *Mujer y sociedad en España. 1700– 1975*. Madrid: Dirección General de Juventud y Promoción Socio–cultural, 1982.
CAPMANY, M. A., and ALCALDE, C. *El feminismo ibérico*. Barcelona: Ed. Oikos–Tau, 1970.
CAPMANY, María Aurelia. *El feminisme a Catalunya*. Barcelona: Nova Terra, 1973.
CARDONA, Gabriel. *El poder militar en la España Contemporánea hasta la Guerra Civil*. Madrid: Siglo XXI, 1983.
CARR, Raymond, ed. *The Republic and the Civil War in Spain*. London: Macmillan, 1971.
CARR, Raymond. *España 1801–1975*. Barcelona: Ariel, 1982. (English version, Spain 1801–1939. Oxford: Oxford University Press, 1966).
CARRASCO, Raphael, ed. *La prostitution en Espagne de l'époque des Rois Catholiques à la II République*. Paris: Annales Littéraires de l'Université de Besançón, 1994.
CASANOVA, Julián. "Las colectivizaciones." La Guerra Civil. *Historia 16*, Vol. 16.
CASTERAS, Ramón. *Las JSUC: ante la guerra y la revolución (1936– 1939)*. Barcelona: Nova terra, 1977.
CASTILLO, Santiago, ed. *Estudios de historia de España. Homenaje a Manuel Tuñón de Lara*. 2 vols. Madrid: Universidad Internacional Menéndez Pelayo, 1981. 2 vols.
CASTILLO, Santiago, ed. *La historia social en España. Actualidad y perspectivas*. Madrid: Siglo XXI, 1991.
CHARTIER, Roger "Différénces entre les sexes et domination symbolique." Note critique". *Annales, ESC*, Num. 4 (July–August 1993).
CHARTIER, Roger. "De la historia social de la cultura a la historia cultural de lo social." *Historia Social*, Núm. 17 (Autumn 1993).
COBOS, Josep Mª, OLLÉ, Maribel; and SANTACANA, Carles. "Collectivitzacions industrials, un debat que resta obert." *L'Avenç*. 105 (June 1987).
CORTADA ANDREU, Esther. *Escuela mixta y coeducación en Catalunya durante la Segunda República*. Madrid: Instituto de la Mujer, 1988.
COVATO, Carmela, and LEUZZI, M. Cristina, eds. *E l'uomo educò la donna*. Rome: Ed. Reuniti, 1989.
COVATO, Carmela. *Sapere e pregiudizio. L'Educazione delle donne fra `700 e `800*. Rome: Archivio Guido Izzi, 1991.
CRUELLS, Manuel. *Els fets de Maig. Barcelona 1937*. Barcelona: Editorial Joventut, 1970.
DE LUIS, Francisco. *Cincuenta años de cultura obrera en España. 1890–1940*. Madrid: Fundación Pablo Iglesias, 1994.

DEUSDAD, Blanca. "La dona obrera durant la Guerra Civil a Vilanova." *Primera Edició* 2 (July 1988).

DI FEBO, Giuliana. "Orígenes del debate feminista en España. La Escuela Krausista y la Institución Libre de Enseñanza (1870–1890)." *Sistema*. Madrid, 1976.

DI FEBO, Giuliana. *Resistencia y movimiento de mujeres en España, 1936–1939*. Barcelona: Icaria, 1984.

DI FEBO, Giuliana, and NATOLI, Claudio., eds. *Spagna anni Trenta. Società, cultura, istituzioni*. Milan: Franco Angeli, 1993.

DÍAZ SÁNCHEZ, P., and DOMINGUEZ PRATS, P. *Las mujeres en la historia de España. Bibliografía comentada*. Madrid: Instituto de la Mujer, 1988.

DUBY, GEORGES, and PERROT, Michelle. *Historia de las mujeres en Occidente*. Vols. 4 and 5. Madrid: Taurus, 1993.

DUCH I PLANA, Montserrat. "La LLiga Patriòtica de Dames: un projecte del feminisme nacional conservador." *Quaderns d'Alliberament* 6 (1981).

DUCH I PLANA, Montserrat. "El paper de la dona en el nacionalisme burguès." *Estudios de Historia Social* 28–29 (January–June 1984).

DYEHOUSE, Carol. *Girls Growing Up in Late Victorian and Edwardian England*. London: Routledge and Kegan Paul, 1981.

EIROA SAN FRANCISCO, M. "La participación de la mujer en la Guerra Civil en Málaga." *Congreso de Andalucismo Histórico*. Granada. September 1987.

ELORZA, A. *Socialismo utópico español*. Alianza Editorial. Madrid, 1970.

ELORZA, Antonio. "Feminismo y socialismo en España (1840–1868)." *Tiempos de Historia*, Num. 3 (February 1976).

ELORZA, Antonio. *El Fourerismo en España*. Madrid: Ed. Revista del Trabajo, 1975.

EQUIPE DE PHILOSOPHIE IBÉRIQUE ET IBERO–AMERICAINE. *La femme dans la penseé espagnole*. Paris: C.N.R.S., 1984.

FAGOAGA, Concha. *La voz y el voto de las mujeres. 1877–1931*. Barcelona: Icaria, 1985.

FAGOAGA, C. and SAAVEDRA, P. *Clara Campoamor. La sufragista española*. Madrid: Dirección General de Juventud y Promoción Socio– Cultural, 1981.

FERNÁNDEZ SORIA, Juan M. "Política de Bibliotecas en la República durante la Guerra Civil." *Perspectiva Contemporánea*, num. 1 (October 1988).

FOLGUERA, P., ed. *El feminismo en España: dos siglos de historia*. Madrid: Fundación Pablo Iglesias, 1988.

Fondos bibliográficos, sobre la II República, la Guerra Civil y el franquismo. Zaragoza: Cortes de Aragón, 1989.

FONTANA, Josep. *Cambio económico y actitudes políticas en la España del siglo XIX*. Barcelona: Ariel, 1973.

FONTANA, Josep. *La crisis del Antiguo Régimen. 1808–1833*. Barcelona: Crítica, 1979.

FONTANA, J., and TUÑóN DE LARA, M., et al. *La II República, una esperanza frustrada. Actas del congreso Valencia Capital de la República (abril 1986)*. Valencia: Edicions Alfons el Magnànim, 1987.

FORCADELL, Carlos. *Parlamentarismo y bolchevización del movimiento obrero español. (1914–1918)*. Barcelona: Crítica, 1978.

FRANCO, Gloria A. *La incorporación de la mujer a la administración del Estado, Municipios y Diputaciones. 1918–1936*. Madrid: Dirección General de Juventud y Promoción Sociocultural, 1981.

FRASER, Ronald. *Recuérdalo tú y recuérdalo a otros. Historia Oral de la Guerra Civil española*. Barcelona: Crítica, 1979. (*Blood of Spain. The Experience of Civil War, 1936–1939*. London: Allen Lane, Penguin Books Ltd., 1979).

FURET, François, and OZOUF, Jacques. *Reading and Writing. Literacy in France from Calvin to Jules Ferry*. Cambridge: Cambridge University Press, 1982.

GABRIEL, Pere. *Escrits polítics de Frederica Montseny*. Barcelona: Centre d'Estudis d'Història Contemporània, 1979.

GALLEGO MÉNDEZ, Maria Teresa. *Mujer, Falange y franquismo*. Madrid: Taurus, 1983.

GARCÍA DELGADO, José Luis, ed. *La Segunda Republica española: El Primer Bienio. 111 Colloquio de Segovia sobre la Historia Contemporánea de España*. Madrid: Siglo XXI, 1987.

GARCÍA DELGADO, José Luis, ed. *La II República española. Bienio rectificador y frente popular. (1934–1936)*. Madrid: Siglo XXI, 1988.

GARCÍA DELGADO, José Luis, et al. *La España de la Restauración: política, economía, legislación y cultura*. Madrid: Siglo XXI,   1985.

GARCÍA DURÁN, Juan. *La Guerra Civil española. Fuentes (Archivos, bibliografía y filmografía)*. Barcelona: Crítica, 1985;

GARCÍA MÉNDEZ, Esperanza. *La actuación de la mujer en las Cortes de la Segunda República*. Madrid: Ministerio de Cultura, 1979.

GARCÍA–NIETO PARIS, M. C. "Movimientos sociales y nuevos espacios para las mujeres, 1931–1939." *Bulletin du Département de Recherches Hispaniques*, num. 29 (June 1984).

GARCÍA–NIETO PARIS, M. C., ed. *Ordenamiento jurídico y realidad social de las mujeres*. Madrid: Universidad Autónoma de Madrid, 1986.

GARCÍA–NIETO, Maria Carmen. "El trabajo 'no pagado' de las mujeres madrileñas durante la Guerra Civil." Paper presented I Colloqui d'Història de la Dona. University of Barcelona, October 1986.

GARCÍA ROVIRA, Anna M. "Burgesia Liberal i poble menut. La revolta popular de l'estiu de 1835." *L'Avenç* (November 1985).

GARCÍA ROVIRA, Anna M. *La revolució liberal a Espanya i les classes populars,(1832–1835)*. Vic: Eumo, 1989.

GARRIDO, Luis. *Colectividades agrarias en Andalucía: Jaen, 1931–1939*. Madrid: Siglo XXI, 1979.

GILBERT, S. "Gender–charged Munitions: the Language of World War I Munitions Reports." *Women's Studies International Forum*, Vol. 11, Num. 2 (1988).

GILLESPIE, Richard. *The Spanish Socialist Party. A History of Factionalism*. Oxford: Clarendon, 1989.

GLICK, Thomas. "Psicoanálisis, reforma sexual y política en la España de entre guerras." *Estudios de Historia Social*, Num. 16–17 (January– June 1981).

GOICOECHEA, Maite. "Mujer y Guerra Civil: la historia que no se contó. Milicianas del 36: las olvidadas." *Vindicación Feminista* 26–27 (September 1978).

GOLDEN, Lester. "Les dones com avantguarda: Els rembomboris del pà del gener de 1918." *L'Avenç*, Num. 44 (December 1981).

GONZÁLEZ BERAMENDI, J., and MAIZ, R., eds. *Los nacionalismos en la España de la segunda república*. Madrid: Siglo XXI, 1991.

GONZÁLEZ CASTILLEJO, M. José. *La nueva historia: Mujer, vida cotidiana y esfera pública en Málaga, 1931–1936*. Málaga: Universidad de Málaga, 1991.

GONZÁLEZ PORTILLA, M., and GARMENDIA, J. M. *La guerra civil en el País Vasco. Política y Economía*. Madrid: Siglo XXI, 1988.

GRAHAM. Helen. *Socialism and War. The Spanish Socialist Party in Power and Crisis, 1936–1939*. Cambridge: Cambridge University Press, 1991.

GRANDE COVIAN, F. "Deficiencias vitamínicas en Madrid durante la Guerra Civil: una reminiscencia." *Los médicos y la medicina en la Guerra Civil española. Madrid: Monografías Beecham*, 1986.

GRIMAU, Carmen. *El cartel republicano en la Guerra Civil*. Madrid: Ediciones Cátedra, 1979.

HAUSE, S. C. *Women's Suffrage and Social Politics in the French Third Republic*. Princeton: Princeton University Press, 1984.

HERNÁNDEZ, Miguel. *Obra poética completa*. Edited by Leopoldo de Luis and Jorge Urrutia. Madrid: Ed. Zero, 1976.

HILL, Bridget. "Women's History": A Study in Change and Continuity or Standing Still?" *Women's History Review*, Vol. 2, Núm. 1 (1993).

HOLTON, S. S. *Feminism and Democracy: Women's Suffrage and Democracy in Britain, 1900–1918*. Cambridge: Cambridge University Press, 1986.

IBÁRRURI, Dolores. *En la lucha*. Moscow: Ed. Progreso, 1968.

IBÁRRURI, Dolores. *El único camino*. Barcelona: Bruguera, 1979.

IFACH, María Gracia. *Miguel Hernández. El escritor y la crítica*. Madrid: Taurus, 1975.

JACKSON, Gabriel. *The Spanish Republic and the Civil War, 1931–1939*. Princeton: Princeton University Press, 1972.

JORDI GONZALEZ, Ramon. "Puntos de vista y conceptos anarquistas sobre sanidad durante el período 27 de setiembre 1936 al 24 de marzo de 1938." *Offarm*, Vol. 4, Num. 5 (May 1985) and Vol 4, Num. 6 (June 1985).

Jornadas de Investigación Interdisciplinaria. *El trabajo de las mujeres. siglos XVI–XX*. Madrid: Universidad Autonoma de Madrid, 1987.

JOVER ZAMORA, José M., et al. *La Era Isabelina y el Sexenio Democrático. Historia de España de Menéndez Pidal. XXXIV*. Madrid: Espasa–Calpe, 1981.

JULIÁ, Santos. *La Izquierda del P.S.O.E. (1935–1936)*. Madrid: Siglo XXI, 1977.

JULIÁ, Santos. "Sobre la formación del Frente Popular en España." *Sistema. Revista de Ciencias Sociales* 73 (July 1986).

JULIÁ, Santos, ed. *Socialismo y Guerra Civil*. Madrid: Editorial Fundación Pablo Iglesias, 1987.

JULIÁ, Santos. *Manuel Azaña. Una biografía política. Del Ateneo al Palacio Nacional*. Madrid: Alianza, 1990.

JULIÁ DÍAZ, Santos. *Orígenes del Frente Popular en España. (1934– 1936)*. Madrid: Siglo XXI, 1979.

JULIÁ DÍAZ, Santos. *Madrid, 1931–1934. De la fiesta popular a la lucha de clases*. Madrid: Siglo XXI, 1984.

JULIÁN, Inmaculada. *Les avantguardes pictòriques a Catalunya*. Barcelona: La Frontera, 1986.

JULIÁN, Inmaculada. "La imagen de la mujer en el período 1936–1938 a través de los carteles de guerra republicanos." Paper presented Primer Col.loqui d'Historia de la Dona. University of Barcelona, October 1986.

KAPLAN, Temma. *Anarchists of Andalusia. 1868–1903*. Princeton: Princeton University Press, 1977.

KAPLAN, Temma. "Politics and Culture in Women's History," *Feminist Studies* 6,1 (Spring 1980).

KAPLAN, Temma. "Female Consciousness and Collective Action: The Case of Barcelona, 1910–1918." *Signs. Journal of Women in Culture and Society* 7,3 (1982).

KAPLAN, Temma. *Red City, Blue Period: Social Movements in Picasso's Barcelona*. Berkeley: University of California Press, 1992.

KNIGHT, Patricia. "Women and Abortion in Victorian and Edwardian England." *History Workshop Journal* 4 (1977).

KRADITOR, Aileen. *The Ideas of the Woman Suffrage Movement, 1890– 1920*. New York: Columbia University Press, 1965.

LACALZADA DE MATEO, M. J. *Mentalidad y proyección social de Concepción Arenal*. Ferrol: Cámara Oficial de Comercio, Industria e Navegación, 1994.

"La Guerra Civil," nums. 1– 24 *Historia* 16 (1986).

La mujer en la Historia de España. (siglos XVI–XX). Actas de las Segundas Jornadas de Investigación Interdisciplinaria. Madrid: Universidad Autónoma de Madrid, 1984.

LAMBERET, Renée. "Soledad Gustavo, sa place dans la pensée anarchiste espagnole." *Convivium*. Nums. 44-45 (1975).

LANNON, Frances, and PRESTON, Paul, eds. *Elites and Power in Twentieth–century Spain. Essays in Honor of Sir Raymond Carr*. Oxford: Oxford University Press, 1992.

LAQUEUR, Thomas. *Making Sex. Body and Gender from the Greeks to Freud*. London: Harvard University Press, 1990.

Las mujeres y la Guerra Civil española. III Jornadas de estudios monográficos. Salamanca, octubre 1989. Madrid: Ministero de Cultura, 1991.

LERNER, Gerda. *The Creation of Patriarchy*. New York: Oxford University Press, 1986.

LEVINE, Phillipa. *Feminist Lives in Victorian England. Private Roles and Public Commitment*. Oxford: Blackwell, 1990.

LIDA, Clara E. *Anarquismo y revolución en la España del siglo XIX*. Madrid: Ed. Siglo XXI, 1973.

LIDA, Clara E. "Educación anarquista en la España del ochocientos." *Revista de Occidente*, num. 97 (1971).

LIDA, Clara E., and ZAVALA, Iris M. *La revolución de 1868. Historia, Pensamiento, Literatura*. New York: Las Américas Publishing Co., 1970.

Liddington, J., and Norris, J. *One Hand Tied Behind Us: The Rise of the Women's Suffrage Movement*. London: Virago, 1978.

LINCOLN, Bruce. "Revolutionary Exhumations in Spain. July 1936." *Comparative Studies in Society and History*, num. 2 (1985).

LITTLE, Douglas. *Malevolent Neutrality. The United States, Great Britain and the Origins of the Spanish Civil War*. Ithaca: Cornell University Press, 1985.

LITVAK, L. *Musa libertaria. Arte, literatura y vida cultural del anarquismo español*. Barcelona: Antoni Bosch, 1981.

LLATES, Rossend. *Francesca Bonnemaison de Verdaguer i la seva obra*. Barcelona: Ed. Fundació Salvador Vives Casajuana, 1972.

LÓPEZ CORDÓN, Mª Victoria. *La Revolución de 1868 y la I República*. Madrid. Siglo XXI, 1976.

LÓPEZ SANTAMARÍA, Jesus. "Juventud y guerra civil. El caso de las juventudes libertarias." *Sistema* 47 (March 1982).

LÓPEZ SANTAMARÍA, Jesús. "Formació i evolució de les Joventuts Llibertàris." *L'Avenç*. 75 (October 1984).

Los estudios sobre la mujer: de la investigación a la docencia. VIII Jornadas de Investigación Interdisciplinaria. Madrid: Universidad Autónoma, 1990.

Los médicos y la medicina en la Guerra Civil española. Madrid: Monografías Beecham, 1986.

LUDDY, Maria, and MURPHY, Cliona. *Women Surviving. Studies in Irish Women's History in the 19th and 20th Centuries*. Swords: Poolbeg, 1990.

LUKER, Kristen. *Abortion and the Politics of Motherhood*. Berkeley: University of California Press, 1985.

MACIÀ I ENCARNACIÓN, Elisenda. "L'Institut de Cultura: un model de promoció cultural per a la dona catalana." *L'Avenç*., Num. 112 (February 1988).

MALEFAKIS, Edward. *Reforma agraria y revolución campesina en la España del siglo XX*. Barcelona: Ariel, 1971. (*Agrarian Reform and Peasant Revolution in Spain*. New Haven, 1970).

MALEFAKIS, Edward (Dir.). *1936–1939. La Guerra de España*. Madrid: Ed. El País, 1986.

MALUQUER, Jordi. "La estructura del sector algodonero en Catalunya durante la primera etapa de la industrialización (1832–1861)." *Hacienda Publica Española*, num. 38 (1976).

MANGINI, Shirley. "Memories of Resistance: Women Activists from the Spanish Civil War." *Signs. Journal of Women in Culture and Society* 17 (Autumn 1991).

MARMO MULLANEY, Marie. *Revolutionary Women. Gender and the Socialist Revolutionary Role*. New York: Praeger, 1983.

MARTÍN GAMERO, Amalia. *Antologia del feminismo*. Madrid: Ed. Alianza, 1975.

MARTÍN I RAMOS, Josep LLuis. *Els origens del Partit Socialista Unificat de Catalunya (1930–36)*. Barcelona: Ed. Curial, 1977.

MARTÍN NÁJERA, Aurelio (Dir.) *Fundación Pablo Iglesias, Catálogo de los archivos de la guerra civil de las comisiones ejecutivas del PSOE y UGT*. Madrid: Fundación Pablo Iglesias, 1988.

MARTINEZ DE SAS, M. T., ed. *Cartas, Comunicaciones y Circulares de la Comisión Federal de la Región Española*. Barcelona: Universidad de Barcelona, 1979.

MASSOT I MUNTANER, Josep. "Diario de la miliciana." *El desembarcament de Bayo a Mallorca. Agost–setembre de 1936*. Barcelona: Publicacions de l'Abadía de Montserrat, 1987.

MATHEU, Roser. *Quatre dones catalanes*. Barcelona: Ed. Fundació Salvador Vives Casajuana, 1972.

MAYEUR, Françoise. *L'Education des filles en France au XIXé siècle*. París: Hachette, 1979.

MAZUECOS JIMENEZ, Antonio. "La política social socialista durante el primer bienio republicano: trabajo, previsión y sanidad". *Estudios de Historia Social* 14 (July–September 1980).

McLAREN, Angus. "Women's Work and Regulation of Family Size. The Question of Abortion in the Nineteenth Century." *History Workshop Journal* 4 (1977).

McLAREN, Angus. *Birth Control in Nineteenth Century England*. London: Croom Helm, 1978.

MEAKER, Gerard H. *The Revolutionary Left in Spain 1914–1923*. Stanford: Stanford University Press, 1974.

MIRAVITLLES, Jaume, and TERMES, Josep. *Carteles de la República y de la Guerra Civil*. Barcelona: La Gaya Ciencia, 1978.

MOLYNEUX, Maxine. "Mobilization without Emancipation? Women's interests, the State and Revolution in Nicaragua." *Feminist Studies* 11,2 (Summer 1985).

MONÉS, Jordi. *El pensament escolar i la renovació pedagògica a Catalunya (1833–1938)*. Barcelona: La Magrana, 1977.

MONJO, Anna, and VEGA, Carme. *Els treballadors i la guerra civil. Història d'ùna indústria catalana col.lectivitzada*. Barcelona: Editorial Empúries, 1986.

MONTERO, José R. *La C.E.D.A.: el catolicismo social y político en la II Republica*. Madrid: Ediciones de la Revista de Trabajo, 1977.

MONTGOMERY BYLES, J. "Women's Experience of World War I: Suffragists, Pacifists and Poets." *Women's Studies International Forum*. 8, 5 (1985).

MONTSENY, Federica. *"Problemas del Anarquismo español."* In *Anarchi e anarchia nel mondo contemporaneo* Atti del Convegno promosso della Fondazione Luigi Einaudi. Torino 5.7 diciembre 1969. Turin: Fondazione Einaudi, 1971.

MORANGE, Claude. "De 'Manola' a 'obrera.' (La revuelta de las cigarreras de Madrid en 1830. Notas sobre un conflicto de trabajo)." *Estudios de Historia Social*, nums. 12–13 (January–June 1980).

NADAL, Antonio. "Experiencias psíquicas sobre mujeres marxistas malagueñas. Malaga 1939." *Baetica*, Num. 10 (1987).

NADAL, Jordi. *La población española. (siglos XVI–XX)*. Barcelona: Ariel, 1984.

NADAL, Jordi. *El fracaso de la revolución industrial en España. (1814–1913)*. Barcelona: Ariel, 1975.

NASH, Mary. "Dos intelectuales anarquistas frente al problema de la mujer: Federica Montseny y Lucía Sánchez Saornil." *Convivium*. Nums. 44-45 (1975).

NASH, Mary. *Mujeres Libres: España 1936–1939*. Barcelona: Tusquets, 1976.

NASH, Mary. *Mujer y movimiento obrero en España. 1931–1939*. Barcelona: Fontamara, 1981.

NASH, Mary. "L'avortement legal a Catalunya: una experiència fracassada." *L'Avenç.*, num. 58 (March 1983).

NASH, Mary. *Mujer, familia y trabajo en España (1875–1936)*. Barcelona: Anthropos, 1983.

NASH, Mary. *Presencia y protagonismo. Aspectos de la historia de la mujer*. Barcelona: Serbal, 1984.

NASH, Mary. "Las mujeres en la Guerra Civil." *Historia 16* (May 1987).

NASH, Mary. "Le donne protagoniste durante la Guerra Civile." *Storia e Dossier*, Num. 11 (October 1987).

NASH, Mary. "Le donne nella Guerra Civile." In Claudio Natoli and Leonardo Rapone (eds.). *A Cinquant'anni dalla Guerra di Spagna*. Milan: Franco Angeli, 1987.

NASH, Mary (ed.). *Més enllá del silenci. Historia de les dones a Catalunya*. Barcelona: Generalitat de Catalunya, 1988.

NASH, Mary. "Género, cambio social y la problemática del aborto." *Historia Social*, Num. 2 (otoño 1988).

NASH, Mary. "La Dona moderna del segle XX: La "Nova Dona" a Catalunya." *L'Avenç.*, Num. 112 (February 1988).

NASH, Mary. "Les dones i la Segona República: la igualtat de drets i la desigualtat de fet." *Perspectiva Social* 26 (1988).

NASH, Mary. "Control social y trayectoria histórica de la mujer en España." In Roberto Bergalli and Enrique E. Mari (eds.). *Historia ideológica del control social. (España–Argentina, siglos XIX y XX)*. Barcelona: PPU, 1989.

NASH, Mary. "Milicianas and Homefront Heroines: Images of Women in War and Revolution 1936–1939." *History of European Ideas* 11 (1989).

NASH, Mary. *Las mujeres en la Guerra Civil*. Madrid: Ministerio de Cultura, 1989.

NASH, Mary. "Dos Décadas de historia de las mujeres en España: una reconsideración." *Historia Social*, Num. 9 (Winter 1991).

NASH, Mary. "Social Eugenics and Nationalist Race Hygiene in Early Twentieth Century Spain." *History of European Ideas*, Vol. 15, Nums. 4–6 (1992).

NASH, Mary. "Women in War: Milicianas and Armed Combat in Revolutionary Spain, 1936–1939." *The International History Review*, Vol. XV, Num. 2 (May 1993).

NASH, Mary. "De "angel del hogar" a "madre militante" y "heroína de la retaguardia": Imágenes de mujeres y la redefinición de las relaciones sociales de género." In R. Radl Philipp and M. C. Garcia Negro (eds.). *A muller e a súa imaxe*. Santiago de Compostela: Universidad de Santiago de Compostela, 1993.

NASH, Mary. "Riforma sessuale e 'nuova morale' nell'anarchismo spagnolo." In G. Di Febo and C. Natoli (eds.). *Spagna anni Trenta. Società, cultura, istituzioni*. Milan: Franco Angeli, 1993.

NASH, Mary. "Identidad de género, discurso de la domesticidad y la definición del trabajo de las mujeres en la España del siglo XIX." In Georges Duby y Michelle Perrot. *Historia de las mujeres en Occidente*. Vol. 4. Madrid: Taurus, 1993.

NASH, Mary. "Maternidad, maternología y reforma eugénica en España." In Georges Duby y Michelle Perrot. *Historia de las mujeres en Occidente*. Vol. 5. Madrid: Taurus, 1993.

NASH, Mary. "Identidades, representación cultural y discurso de género en la España Contemporánea." In P. Chalmeta and F. Checa Cremades, et al. *Cultura y culturas en la Historia*. Salamanca: Universidad de Salamanca, 1995.

NASH, Mary. "Experiencia y aprendizaje: la formación histórica de los feminismos en España." *Historia Social*, num. 20 (Autumn 1994).

NASH, Mary, and TAVERA, Susana. *Experiencias desiguales. Conflictos sociales y respuestas colectivas (Siglo XIX)*. Madrid: Sintesis, 1994.

NATOLI, Claudio, and RAPONE, Leonardo, eds. *A Cinquant'anni dall Guerra di Spagna*. Milan: Franco Angeli, 1987.

NICOLÁS, M. E., and GARCÍA, Pedro, and LÓPEZ, Inmaculada, et al. "La Historiografía de la reconciliació': La Guerra d'Espanya de El País." *L'Avenç.*, num. 104 (April 1987).

Nuevas perspectivas sobre la mujer. Actas de las Primeras Jornadas de Investigación Interdisciplinaria. Madrid: Universidad Autónoma de Madrid, 1982.

NÚÑEZ PÉREZ, María Gloria. *Trabajadoras en la Segunda República. Un estudio sobre la actividad económica extradoméstica (1931–1936)*. Madrid: Ministerio de Trabajo, 1989.

NÚÑEZ PÉREZ, María Gloria. *Bibliografía comentada sobre la II República española (1931–1936). Obras publicadas entre 1940 y 1992*. Madrid: Fundación Universitaria Española, 1993.

O'CONNOR, Patricia W. *Gregorio and María Martínez Sierra*. Boston: Twayne Publishers, 1977.

Octubre 1934. Cincuenta años para la reflexión. Madrid: Siglo XXI, 1985.

OFFEN, Karen. "Defining Feminism. A Comparative Historical Approach." *Signs. Journal of Women in Culture and Society*, Vol. 14, num. 1 (1988).

OFFEN, K., ROACH PIERSON, R., and RENDALL, R. *Writing Women's History. International Perspectives*. London: Macmillan, 1991.

PAGÉS, Pelai. *Andreu Nin y su evolución política*. Madrid: Ed. Zero, 1975.

PAGÉS, Pelai. "Le mouvement trotskyste pendant la guerre civile d'Espagne." *Cahiers Léon Trotsky* 10 (June 1982).

PÀMIES, Teresa. *Una española llamada Dolores Ibarruri*. Barcelona: Martinez Roca, 1975.

PANIAGUA, Javier. *La sociedad libertaria. Agrarismo e industrialización en el anarquismo español, 1930–1939*. Barelona: Crítica, 1982.

PASTOR HOMS, M. I. *La educación femenina en la postguerra (1939– 1935): el caso de Mallorca*. Madrid: Ministerio de Cultura, 1984.

PAYNE, Stanley G. *The Spanish Revolution*. New York: W. W. Norton, 1970.

PAYNE, Stanley G. "Recent Historiography on the Spanish Republic and Civil War." *The Journal of Modern History*, vol. 60, num. 3 (September 1988).

PÉREZ–FUENTES HERNÁNDEZ, Pilar. "Mujer, Trabajo y Reproducción." In *El trabajo de las mujeres en la España de los siglos XIX y XX: Algunas consideraciones metodológicas*. III Congreso del ADEH. 22–24 de abril de 1993. Universidad do Minho, Braga. (forthcoming)

PÉREZ–FUENTES HERNÁNDEZ, Pilar. *Vivir y morir en las minas. Estrategias familiares y relaciones de género en la primera industrialización vizcaína: 1877–1913*. Bilbao: Editorial de la Universidad del Pais Vasco, 1993.

PÉREZ–VILLANUEVA TOVAR, I. *María de Maeztu. Una mujer en el reformismo educativo español*. Madrid: UNED, 1989.

PERROT, Michelle, ed. *Une histoire des femmes est–elles possible?* Paris: Rivages, 1984.

PESET, J. L., ed. *Ciencias y enseñanza en la revolución burguesa*. Madrid: Siglo XXI, 1978.

PHILLIPS, W. D., and PHILLIPS, C. *Marginated Groups in Spanish and Portuguese History*. Proceedings of the 17th Annual Meeting of the Society for Spanish and Portuguese Historical Studies. Minneapolis: University of Minnesota Press, 1989.

PONS, Félix. *Converses amb Frederica Montseny: Frederica Montseny, sindicalisme i Acràcia*. Barcelona: Laia, 1977.

POTTS, Malcolm, DIGGORY, Peter, and PEEL, John. *Abortion*. Cambridge: Cambridge University Press, 1977.

PRESTON. Paul. *The Coming of the Spanish Civil War. Reform, Reaction and Revolution in the Second Republic*. London: Routledge, 1994.

PRESTON. Paul. "Spain's October Revolution and the Rightist Grasp for Power." *Journal of Contemporary History* 10, Num. 4 (1975).

PRESTON. Paul. *Revolution and War in Spain, 1931–1939*. London: Methuen, 1984.

PUERTAS I NOVAU, Silvia. *Artesanes i obreres. Treballadores de l'agulla a la Barcelona contemporània*. Lerida: Diario La Mañana, 1994.

RAMOS, M. D. *Mujeres e Historia. Reflexiones sobre las experiencias vividas en los espacios públicos y privados*. Málaga: Universidad de Málaga, 1993.

RANZATO, Gabriel. "Dies Irae. La persecuzione religiosa nella zona repubblicana durante la Guerra Civile Spagnola (1936–1939)." *Movimiento Operario e Socialista*, Num. 2 (May–June 1988).

RAQUER, Hilari. "L'Església i la Guerra Civil (1936–1939). Bibliografía Recent (1975–1985)." *Revista Catalana de Teología* XI/1 (1986).

"Reassessments of 'First Wave Feminism.'" Special Issue. *Women's Studies International Forum* 5,6 (1982).

RENDALL, Jane. *Equal or Different. Women's Politics. 1800–1914*. Oxford: Basil Blackwell, 1987.

RIMBAU, Cristina. "Una aportació a la reflexió sobre l'organització dels serveis socials." *Revista de Treball Social*, vol. 107, num. 9 (1987).

RODRIGO, A. *María Lejárraga. Una mujer en la sombra*. Barcelona: Círculo de Lectores, 1992.

RODRIGO, A. *Mujeres de España. (Las silenciadas)*. Barcelona: Plaza y Janés, 1979.

ROLDÁN, S., DELGADO, J. L., and MUÑOZ, J. *La formación de la sociedad capitalista en España. 1914–1920*. 2 Vols. Madrid: Confederación Española de Cajas de Ahorros, 1973.

SAMANIEGO BONEU, Mercedes. *La política educativa de la 11 República*. Madrid: C.S.I.C., 1977.

SAMANIEGO BONEU, Mercedes. *Los seguros sociales en la España del siglo XX. La unificación de los seguros sociales a debate. La Segunda República*. Madrid: Ministerio de Trabajo y Seguridad Social, 1988.

SÁNCHEZ I FERRÉ, Pere. "Els orígens del feminisme a Catalunya. 1870–1920." *Revista de Catalunya*, Num. 45 (October 1990).

SÁNCHEZ LÓPEZ, Rosario. *Mujer española, una sombra de destino en lo universal: trayectoria histórica de Sección Femenina de Falange (1934–1977).* Murcia: Universidad de Murcia, 1990.

SANTACREU SOLER, J. M. *L'economia valenciana durant la guera civil. Protagonisme industrial i estancament agrari.* Valencia: Edicions Alfons el Magnànim, 1992.

SANTONJA, G. *La república de los libros. El nuevo libro popular de la II república.* Barcelona: Anthropos, 1986.

SCANLON, Geraldine. *La polémica feminista en la España Contemporánea,(1868–1974).* Madrid: Siglo XXI, 1976. (2nd. Ed. Madrid: Akal, 1986).

SCHNIEDER, William H. *Quality and Quantity. The Quest for Biological Regeneration in Twentieth–century France.* Cambridge: Cambridge University Press, 1990.

SCHUBERT, Adrian. *The Road to Revolution in Spain: the Coal Mines of Asturias, 1860–1934.* Champaign: University of Illinois, 1987.

SCOTT, Joan W. and TILLY, Louise A. *Women, Work and Family.* New York. Holt, Rinehart and Winston, 1978.

SEIDMAN, Michael. "The Unorwellian Barcelona." *European History Quarterly 20* (1990).

SEIDMAN, Michael. "Towards a History of Workers' Resistance to Work: Paris and Barcelona during the French Popular Front and the Spanish Revolution. 1936–1938." *Journal of Contemporary History* 23 (April 1988).

SHLAPENTOKH, Vladimir. "The Stakhanovite Movement: Changing Perceptions over Fifty Years." *Journal of Contemporary History* 23 (1988).

SLAUGHTER, Jane, and KERN, R., eds. *European Women on the Left. Socialism, Feminism and the Problems Faced by Political Women. 1880 to the Present.* Westport, CT: Greenwood Press, 1981.

SMYTH, M. T. *La CNT al País Valencià, 1936–1939.* Valencia: Edicions Alfons el Magànim, 1987.

SOLOWAY, Richard A. *Demography and Degeneration. Eugenics and the Declining Birthrate in Twentieth Century Britain.* London: North Carolina Press, 1990.

STARCEVIC, Elisabeth: *Carmen de Burgos, defensora de la mujer.* Almeria: Editorial Cajal, 1976.

TAVERA, Susana. "Soledad Gustavo, Frederica Montseny i el periodisme àcrata. ¿Ofici o militància?" *Annals del Periodisme Català.* Núm. 14 (March–June 1988).

THEBAUD, Françoise. *La femme au temps de la guerre de 14.* Paris: Stock, 1986.

THOMAS, Hugh. *The Spanish Civil War.* Middlesex: Penguin Books, 1965.

TILLY. L., and TILLY, C., eds. *Class Conflict and Collective Action.* London: Sage Publications, 1981.

TISA, John. *Recalling the Good Fight. An Autobiography of the Spanish Civil War.* MA: Bergin and Garvey Publishers, 1985.

TUÑÓN DE LARA, Manuel, ed. *Historia de España. Revolución burguesa, oligarquía y constitucionalismo (1834–1923).* Barcelona: Labor, 1981.

TUÑÓN DE LARA, Manuel, ed. *Historia de España. La crisis del Estado: Dictadura, República, Guerra (1923–1939).* Barcelona: Labor, 1981.

TUÑÓN DE LARA, Manuel, ed. *Comunicación, cultura y política durante la II República y la Guerra Civil.* Bilbao: Servicio de Publicaciones de la Universidad del País Vasco, 1990.

TUÑON DE LARA, Manuel, ARÓSTEGUI, Julio, VIÑAS, Angel, CARDONA, Gabriel, and BRICALL, Josep Maria. *La guerra civil española. 50 años después.* Barcelona: Ed. Labor, 1985.

TYLEE, Claire M. "'Maleness Run Riot' – the Great War and Woman's Resistance to Militarism." *Women's Studies International Forum* 11,3 (1988).

UCELAY DA CAL, Enric. *La Catalunya populista. Imatge, cultura i política en l'etapa republicana. (1931–1939).* Barcelona: La Magrana, 1982.

UCELAY DA CAL, Enric. "El concepte de 'vida quotidiana' i l'estudi de la Guerra Civil." *Acàcia.,* Num. 1 (1990); 67 (1988).

UCELAY DA CAL, Enric. "Gabriel Ranzato: 'Ira di Dio,' ma rabbia di chi?" *Movimiento Operario e Socialista.* Vol. XII. Nova serie. (January–August 1989).

UGALDE SOLANO, Mercedes. *Mujeres y nacionalismo vasco. Génesis y desarrollo de*

Emakume Abertzale Batza (1906–1936). Bilbao: Universidad del País Vasco, 1993.

Ugarte, Michael. "The Generational Fallacy and Spanish Women Writing in Madrid at the Turn of the Century." *SigloXX/Twentieth Century*, Núm. 12 (1994).

VARELA, Santiago. *Partidos y parlamento en la II República*. Barcelona: Ariel – Fundación Juan March, 1978.

VENZA, Claudio. "Convegni sulla guerra civile spagnola. Nuove problematiche." *Qualestoria* 1 (April 1987).

VINYES, Ricard. *La Catalunya Internacional. El Frontpopulisme en l'exemple català*. Barcelona: Curial, 1983.

WALL, Richard, and WINTER, Jay. *The Upheaval of War. Family, Work and Welfare in Europe, 1914–1918*. Cambridge: Cambridge University Press, 1988.

WARD, Margaret. *Unmanageable Revolutionaries. Women and Irish Nationalism*. London: Pluto Press, 1983.

WEINDLING, Paul. *Health, Race and German Politics between National Unification and Nazism. 1870-1945*. Cambridge: Cambridge University Press, 1991.

DISSERTATIONS AND UNPUBLISHED RESEARCH

CASTELLS, Antoni. "La colectivización y socialización de la industria y los servicios en Barcelona Ciudad y Provincia. Las agrupaciones o concentraciones de empresa." Juan García Durán Prize. University of Barcelona, 1986.

FREDERICKS, Shirley. "Social and Politial Thought of Federica Montseny, 1923–1937". Ph.D. diss, University of New Mexico, 1972.

FROIDEVAUX, Michelle. "Les Avatars de L'Anarchisme. La Révolution et la Guerre Civile en Catalogne (1936–1939) vues au travers de la presse anarchiste." Ph.D. diss.. Université de Lausanne, 1985.

MACIÀ I ENCARNACIÓN, Elisenda. "Ensenyament professional i orientació católica d'una nova professió femenina: la dona oficinista (1909–1936)." Master's diss., Barcelona University, 1986.

PEÑALVER, Carmen. "Les associacions populars a Barcelona. 1923–1930." Master's diss., University of Barcelona, 1985.

RIMBAU I ANDREU, Cristina. "L'Obra assistencial de la Generalitat de Catalunya. 1931–1936." Master's diss. University of Barcelona, 1985.

SANTACREU SOLER, J. M. "Cambio económico y conflicto bélico. Transformaciones económicas en la retaguardia republicana. (Alicante 1936–1939)." Ph.D. diss., University of Alicante, 1988.

SIERRA PERRÓN, María Carmen. "Lerrouxismo femenino. El papel de las Damas Rojas en la política del Partido Radical." Master's diss., Universidad Autónoma de Barcelona, 1984.

VILLALAÍN GARCÍA, P. "Mujer y política. La participación de la mujer en las eleciones generales celebradas en Madrid durante la II República (1931–1936)." Ph.D. diss., Universidad Autónoma de Madrid, 1993.

OTHER SOURCES

INTERVIEWS

Interviews with 56 women of diverse social backgrounds, mostly non–politicized or of rank and file. Mary Nash, Oral History Project: *The Family in Autonomous Catalonia. 1931–1939*. University of Barcelona, 1982–1984.

Interview with Teresa Pàmies, Barcelona, June 1974.

Interview with Suceso Portales. Montady, summer 1973 and 1974.

Interview with Sara Guillen. Montady, summer 1973 and 1974.
Interview with Lola Iturbe. Barcelona, November 1981.
Interview with Isabel Gonzalez Sugrañes. October 1981.
Interview with Mercedes Marquillas. Barcelona, 22 July 1981.
Interview with Conchita Pérez Collado. Barcelona, 16 June 1981.
Interview with Dr. Ramón Casañellas. Barcelona, 15 February 1982.
Interview with Antonia García. Barcelona, December 1983.
Interview with María Manonelles. Barcelona, September 1984.
Interview with Maria Teresa Andrade. Madrid, October 1984.
Interview with Rosario Sánchez. Barcelona, October 1987.
Interview with Carmen Rodriguez. Salamanca, October 1989.
Interview with L. A. by Elisabet Ibáñez, Lucia Liria, Mireiea Ribera, and Goretti Triquell. Granollers, June 1988.

VIDEO

BERGER, L., and MAZER, C. *De Toda la Vida.*

Index

255